BARRON'S

PSAT/NMSQT® 1520
AIMING FOR NATIONAL MERIT

SECOND EDITION

Brian W. Stewart, M.Ed.
President
BWS Education Consulting, Inc.

BARRON'S

DEDICATION

Dedicated to my wife Caitlin—who had the idea for this book—my son Andrew, and my daughter Eloise. Thank you to my mom, my dad, Andrew, Alaina, Michal, Katie, Hannah, Sarah, and Doug for their help with this undertaking. I would especially like to thank Peter Mavrikis and Jennifer Giammusso for their editorial help. And thanks to all of my students over the years—I have learned far more from you than you have learned from me.

ABOUT THE AUTHOR

Brian W. Stewart is the founder and President of BWS Education Consulting, Inc., a tutoring and test preparation company based in Columbus, Ohio. He has worked with thousands of students to help them improve their scores and earn admission into selective schools. Brian is a graduate of Princeton University (A.B.) and the Ohio State University (M.Ed.). You can connect with Brian at *www.bwseducationconsulting.com*.

Published by Kaplan, Inc., d/b/a Barron's Educational Series
750 Third Avenue
New York, NY 10017
www.barronseduc.com

ISBN: 978-1-4380-1191-2
Library of Congress Control Number: 2016935467

9 8 7 6 5 4 3 2 1

Kaplan, Inc., d/b/a Barron's Educational Series print books are available at special quantity discounts to use for sales promotions, employee premiums, or educational purposes. For more information or to purchase books, please call the Simon & Schuster special sales department at 866-506-1949.

Contents

PRACTICE TEST

Note: The link to the online practice test is *http://bit.ly/barrons-PSAT-1520*. The practice test can also be accessed on all mobile devices, including tablets and smartphones.

Introduction to Barron's *PSAT/NMSQT 1520— Aiming for National Merit*

1

WHO SHOULD USE THIS BOOK?

This book is the first major text expressly designed for students who want to earn a top score on the PSAT/NMSQT and want to earn a National Merit Scholarship. The practice exercises in this book are designed to be representations of the most challenging passages and questions you will face on test day. The thinking behind this is very simple—*if you practice with challenging material, the real test will seem much easier and you will perform your best.* Given that the PSAT is very much like the SAT, using this book will also help in your SAT preparation.

Instead of providing an extensive review of every basic strategy and basic concept, this book briefly reviews fundamental concepts while heavily focusing on the types of questions most likely to give stronger students difficulty. For an approachable introduction to the PSAT, please check out *Barron's Strategies and Practice for the PSAT/NMSQT*. For a comprehensive review of all PSAT material and several practice tests, use *Barron's PSAT/NMSQT*. If you are ready to push yourself in order to achieve top PSAT performance, this book is exactly what you need.

WHAT ARE SOME BASICS ABOUT THE PSAT?

- Two hours and 45 minutes in length
- Two major sections

    1. **EVIDENCE-BASED READING AND WRITING:** Half is a reading comprehension section. The other half, known as "Writing and Language," tests your grammar and editing skills.
    2. **MATH:** Half is without a calculator, and the second half is with a calculator.

- The two sections are each scored between 160 (minimum) and 760 (maximum), for a total possible score between 320 and 1520. *There is no penalty for guessing, so be sure to answer every question.*
- Administered in mid-October, typically during the school day.

TIP

The PSAT is very similar to the SAT. However, the SAT is slightly longer, has a bit more advanced math, and has an optional essay. This book will help you with both the PSAT and most of what you will find on the SAT.

The PSAT sections come in the following order:

1. **READING TEST:** 60 minutes, 47 questions, 5 passages. Questions occur in a random order of difficulty.
2. **WRITING AND LANGUAGE TEST:** 35 minutes, 44 questions, 4 passages. Questions occur in a random order of difficulty.
3. **MATH TEST—NO CALCULATOR:** 25 minutes, 17 questions (13 multiple choice, 4 grid-in). Questions generally become more difficult as you go.
4. **MATH TEST—CALCULATOR:** 45 minutes, 31 questions (27 multiple choice, 4 grid-in). Questions generally become more difficult as you go.

Be certain to bring the following on test day:

- Several number 2 pencils.
- A permitted calculator (see *https://www.collegeboard.org/psat-nmsqt/approved-calculators* for a complete list).
- A watch to monitor your pacing. (Be sure it doesn't make noise.)
- A photo ID.
- An e-mail address so colleges can contact you and you can access your scores online.
- Do NOT bring snacks, drinks, an electronic tablet, or a cell phone into the room. During the break, you can have a snack or drink, but you may not check your cell phone or tablet.

Make sure you get plenty of sleep before the test. No matter how much you prepare, if you are fatigued during the PSAT, you will not perform your best. Conserve your mental energy by knowing your strategic approach ahead of time—that way you can devote your full attention to solving problems instead of experimenting with strategies during the test.

WHAT IS THE NATIONAL MERIT SCHOLARSHIP PROGRAM?

The National Merit Scholarship Program gives scholarships to students principally based on high performance on the PSAT. In addition to the direct scholarships from the National Merit Program, many schools use National Merit status to award enormous academic scholarships, all the way up to full rides plus stipends, room, and board. To be a National Merit Scholar, you must typically perform in the top one-half of 1 percent of students. Find out the latest details about the National Merit program at *www.nationalmerit.org*. To achieve some sort of National Merit recognition, such as Semifinalist or Commended Scholar, you typically should score in the top 5% of test takers. There are also additional scholarship programs, such as the National Achievement Program for African-American Students, that are tied to top PSAT performance.

TIP

Remember that the strategy that works for one student may not work for another. This book is designed to help you customize your strategy and your practice.

What Are the Requirements to Participate in the National Merit Scholarship Program?

- Take the PSAT/NMSQT no later than the third year of high school.
- Be a high school student in the United States or its territories, or be a U.S. citizen or resident attending high school abroad.
- Be on track for high school graduation and college admission the fall after high school graduation.

HOW CAN YOU USE THIS TEXT TO PREPARE?

This book allows you to focus on your areas of weakness and customize your strategies and mindset depending on your particular situation. Not only can you spend your time practicing math, you can spend your time practicing the types of math questions that are most challenging for you, be they algebra or data analysis. The practice exercises are designed to give you comprehensive coverage of all of the most likely types of challenging questions you will face. There is an extensive vocabulary resource at the end of the book if questions about word meaning give you trouble. If you work through everything in this text, it is very unlikely that you will have surprises on test day. If you are unsure what areas of the test are most difficult for you, start with the full-length practice PSAT at the end of the book. Evaluate your performance to see what types of passages and questions give you the most difficulty. Then work through the corresponding types of material to sharpen your skills. When you are done, you can do further practice with the accompanying online practice PSAT to see how you have improved. Keep in mind that since the questions in this book are more challenging than normal, *you should not beat yourself up if you are missing more questions than you usually do.* Use missed questions as a learning opportunity so you can ultimately do your very best on the actual test.

If I Am Preparing for the PSAT 10, How Can This Book Help Me?

The PSAT 10 and the PSAT/NMSQT are identical tests. Therefore, if you would like to prepare for the PSAT 10, this book will help you just as it will for the PSAT/NMSQT. Although the tests themselves are the same, there are three significant differences between the PSAT/NMSQT and the PSAT 10:

- The PSAT 10 is given in the spring, while the PSAT/NMSQT is given in the fall.
- The PSAT 10 is for tenth-grade students, while the PSAT/NMSQT is for eleventh-grade students. (Many schools do encourage their freshmen and sophomores to take the PSAT/NMSQT for practice, however.)
- The PSAT 10 will not enter students in the National Merit scholarship competition, while juniors who take the PSAT/NMSQT can enter this competition. Students who take either exam will be considered for other scholarship programs through the Student Search Service®.

If your school does not offer the PSAT 10 and you would like to try the PSAT as a tenth grader, talk to your guidance counselor about taking the PSAT/NMSQT in the fall of your tenth-grade year.

> Don't forget that you have *two* full-length practice PSAT tests with this book— one at the end of the book and one online. The link to the online practice test is *http://bit.ly/barrons-PSAT-1520.*

WHAT IF YOU HAVE A LIMITED AMOUNT OF TIME TO PREPARE?

Here are some suggested plans depending on how long you have to prepare:

If you have one day, read through the strategies in the chapters for each test section: reading, writing and language, and math. Look through the full-length practice test at the end of the book to become familiar with the directions, time requirements, and structure of the PSAT. Try a few practice questions.

If you have one week, read through all the strategies in the chapters for the test sections. Target your areas of weakness by working through selected review drills. The drills are broken down by categories, so it will be easy to pick out where you should focus. Do the full-length practice test at the end of the book under timed conditions.

If you have one month, systematically work through everything in this book. The strategies, content review, drills, and practice tests will give you the best possible preparation to achieve a top score on the PSAT/NMSQT. You may want to start by taking the practice test at the end of the book as a diagnostic to determine your areas of weakness. Then, after studying the review chapters and practice drills, you can take the full-length online practice test that accompanies the book to see how much progress you have made.

If you have even more time available to prepare, you may want to take the SAT once before you take the PSAT—an SAT test is offered in October shortly before the PSAT administration. If you are a sophomore or freshman, you may want to take the PSAT when it is offered at your school even though it will not count toward National Merit consideration. The pressures of these actual tests will prepare you for when it is most important for you to do well on the PSAT—in October of your junior year. The better prepared you are, the less anxiety you will feel on test day.

Let's get to work!

Be sure to check out the appendix in this book—*After the PSAT*—once your scores come back, to help you understand what comes next.

Reading

2

HOW IS THE READING SECTION DESIGNED?

- First section of the test
- 60 minutes long
- 47 questions total

  - Approximately 9 questions on defining words in context
  - Approximately 4 questions on graph analysis
  - Approximately 10 questions related to finding evidence in the passage
  - Remaining 24 questions a mixture of sentence-level, paragraph-level, and whole-passage comprehension

- Five total passages

  - One fiction passage (a short story or an excerpt from a novel)
  - One social science passage (e.g., sociology, economics, psychology)
  - One great global conversation passage (typically a historical document related to the ideas of democracy)
  - Two science passages (could be an article or a book excerpt about biology, geology, astronomy, or another science field)
  - One passage made of two smaller selections that must be compared

- The questions are in a random order of difficulty.
- The questions generally follow the order in the passage.

HOW SHOULD I USE THIS CHAPTER?

- Start with the section "PSAT 1520 Reading Mindset" to develop a personalized strategy for this section.
- Review the section "How to Handle Tricky Questions" so you can avoid common pitfalls
- Use the "Troubleshooting" guide to help you work through strategic issues you have encountered in the past or are finding as you work through problems.
- Use what you have learned to practice as effectively as possible in the Reading Drills chapter that follows.

PSAT 1520 READING MINDSET

Personalize your strategy for top performance. Here are the most common reading strategy questions top students have, followed by ideas to help you decide what makes sense for your situation.

Should I Read the Passages First or the Questions First?

Most students find it helpful to read the passage first. Why? The PSAT Reading primarily has questions that require you to make inferences about the text, making a general understanding of the passage essential. Many questions ask about the purpose of the passage, the tone of the passage, the function of a paragraph, and what a phrase suggests. If you do not understand the overall meaning of the passage, you will not be able to figure out the answers to these types of questions. Some students like to take a quick look at what the questions ask before they start. If you do this, *be sure you don't focus too much on specifics when you go back and read the passage—be sure you focus on the big picture.* Look at the questions with the mindset that you are trying to get a quick preview of what the passage will likely be about. Students run into trouble when they use the question preview as a mental checklist as they read, because they focus too heavily on the details and not on the larger connections.

Should I Read All the Passages the Same Way?

Here are some approaches to the passages that typically work for all students.

- **TAKE YOUR TIME READING THE PASSAGE.** You can take about four to five minutes to read a single passage, which comes out to a pace of only around 120–150 words a minute. You have much more time on the PSAT reading passages than you do on other reading tests you will take later on, like the ACT.
- **READ THE PASSAGE TITLE AND BACKGROUND INFORMATION.** The little blurbs that come before each actual essay are very helpful in previewing what the passage will be about. You will be apprised of the topic and other information about when and where the passage was written.
- **PARAPHRASE AS YOU READ.** You do not need to memorize information—after all, this is an open-book test. Ask questions, and try to put the ideas from the passage into your own words as you read. This makes the questions much, much easier because the questions require you to paraphrase and analyze, not just to find words in the passage.

There are different types of passages. Most students find it helpful to harness their focus a bit differently depending on the passage type. Here is what generally works for different types of passages.

- **FICTION AND LITERATURE:** Read the first paragraph or two a bit more carefully, and then read the remainder of the passage normally. This can help you fully grasp the beginning of the plot, the setting, and the characters before you move into the rest of the story.
- **NONFICTION (SOCIAL STUDIES AND SCIENCE):** Read the first paragraph, first sentences of each paragraph, and last paragraph a bit more carefully. Read the rest normally. Nonfiction is typically more structured than fiction. So these passages will typically give you more critical information, such as the thesis of the essay and general topics about each paragraph.

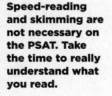

TIP

Speed-reading and skimming are not necessary on the PSAT. Take the time to really understand what you read.

- **PASSAGE 1 AND PASSAGE 2:** Read these with a focus on the general meaning, but pay close attention to the *overall relationship* between the two passages. Why? Several questions will ask you to compare the similarities and differences between the two reading selections.

If you have extraordinary reading comprehension and speed, do not worry about the above recommendations about how to focus your energy differently on different passages. Just read the passages the way you normally would. The PSAT Reading is fundamentally a test of your general reading skill. So if that skill is solid, keep doing what you're doing.

Should I Underline and Annotate?

You can underline and annotate if you find doing so helpful. You are absolutely permitted to write all over the test. So if making notes and underlining key words helps you stay focused while you read, go for it. You do not need to underline and annotate as you would when reading a school textbook. When reading a portion of a textbook, you need to take notes in such a way that you will be able to review them prior to the big exam. On the PSAT, you will immediately go from reading the passage to answering the questions. So you do not need to be as thorough as you would if there were a big break between the reading and the studying.

Should I Do Passages in Order or Out of Order?

Most students simply prefer to go in order. Doing the passages out of order can be helpful if either of the following applies to you.

- **YOU LIKE TO BUILD MOMENTUM.** The reading section comes first on the PSAT, so you may benefit from a little warm-up before you tackle the most challenging passages. Perhaps you know that a certain type of passage—such as social science—is always easiest for you. If so, locate this passage and start with it. Perhaps you can start with the passages that happen to have topics that are naturally much more interesting to you. If so, check out the introductory blurbs of the different passages. Start with the passage that intrigues you the most, and save the most difficult one for the end.
- **YOU LIKE TO GET THE TOUGHEST PASSAGE OUT OF THE WAY.** If you are likely to be fresh and energized at the beginning of the test, you may want to start with the passage that is typically most difficult for you. Why? You will be able to give it your maximum focus and energy before you feel depleted after doing other passages. You can decide which passage to start with either ahead of time if you know that a certain type of passage is consistently most challenging or on the morning of the test after you briefly survey the passage topics.

Should I Go Back to the Passage When I Answer the Questions?

Do not hesitate to go back to the passage. This is an open-book test, and you will likely have plenty of time to review adequate context. You will probably want to go back to the passage on about 75–80% of the questions. The ones that do not necessitate going back to review the passage are more general questions about the purpose or tone of the passage—you likely will be fine with these from your initial reading. The PSAT makes it easy for you to go back and review context, generally putting the questions in the order of where they are in the passage

TIP

The passages are there any time you need to refer to them. Take advantage of this!

and giving you plenty of line references. Go back and check out as much context as you need to answer the questions successfully.

How Carefully Should I Read the Questions?

The questions demand the closest possible reading of anything you do on the reading section. You can underline key words in the questions as you read them, and you can reread the questions if necessary. If you are not 100% clear about what is being asked, you will run into serious difficulty when you review the choices. Fortunately, the questions are not as long and tricky as they have been on previous PSATs, but they still demand a very careful reading.

Should I Answer the Questions in Order or Out of Order?

Most students prefer to do the questions in the order that they are written—this enables students to avoid expending energy trying to determine which questions to do first and which to do last. There are a few considerations when doing the questions out of order.

TIP

Sometimes it helps to start with the "trees" and gradually move toward the "forest." You might want to begin with questions that are straightforward with line references and move toward those that are big picture.

- **DO NOT HESITATE TO COME BACK TO A QUESTION IF YOU ARE STUCK AFTER GIVING IT A GOOD TRY.** Simply circle the question and move on to the next one. Doing so does not mean that you have given up on the question. On the contrary—you are allowing more time to read other parts of the passage that will help you arrive at the answer. You are also allowing more time for your subconscious mind to process the question further. When you come back to the question with fresh eyes, you will likely find that it is far easier than it appeared at first glance.
- **IF THE PASSAGE WASN'T CLEAR TO YOU, START WITH MORE SPECIFIC QUESTIONS AND BUILD TOWARD THE BIG-PICTURE QUESTIONS.** The first question on a reading passage is frequently a big-picture question. If you didn't quite understand the passage, wait on questions like these. Instead, answer the questions that ask about the meanings of words and what can be inferred from small parts of the passage. After doing these more specific questions, revisit the big-picture questions. The answers will come much more easily.

Should I Use the Process of Elimination with the Choices?

The choices on the math questions can really help you see where a question is headed. With the reading questions, though, the choices more often than not confuse you if you jump into them too quickly. As much as you possibly can, *come up with your own general idea of an answer before checking out the choices*. Once you have done this, the process of elimination can be very helpful. When you review the choices, however, be careful not to eliminate choices too quickly. Methodically review the choices, seeing which one captures the broad idea of what the question requires and eliminating those choices that have flaws, even a single word that is mistaken.

How Can I Avoid Being Indecisive When Answering?

The PSAT Reading is not a factual recall test—it demands thoughtful analysis and interpretation. To avoid being indecisive on the choices, here are some thoughts.

- **FOCUS ON THE *FRONT* OF THE QUESTION, NOT ON THE *BACK* OF THE QUESTION.** Spend the majority of your time on a question carefully reading what the question is asking and formulating your own answer. Doing this will allow you to be much more decisive when you evaluate the choices, just as you are more decisive when you go to a store if you have a list of what you want to purchase ahead of time. Strive to minimize or eliminate time that you spend after you have made a decision on your answer—double-checking and redoing questions is usually a recipe for trouble because you allow the wrong answers to get inside your head.

■ **REALIZE THAT THE CORRECT ANSWER IS 100% RIGHT.** On math questions, you feel confident that there is just one correct answer. On the PSAT Reading Test, it is the same—there is just one 100% correct answer. Most reading and literature tests you have taken likely have some vagueness or error, but don't let that influence your mindset on the PSAT. The quality of the questions is extremely high, so don't waste any time thinking that there are in fact two right answers. Sure, there are answers that come close to being correct. However, even a small flaw keeps them from being the right option.

■ **TRUST YOUR INTUITION.** If you understand the passage, understand the question, and feel confident in your choice, pick it and don't look back. Your job while taking the PSAT is not to come up with an elaborate justification for your answer—you must simply answer the questions correctly. If you have approached the question with patience and care, you have done all you can do and it is time to trust yourself.

TIP

Be careful to not be *too* decisive—take the time necessary to really think through the questions. Just don't overdo it.

What Should My Pace Be?

Since the passages all have nine to ten questions, you can pace yourself by taking about *12 minutes per passage.* This would involve taking about *5 minutes to read the passage* and about *7 minutes to do the accompanying questions.* Here is a table of how you might want to allocate your time for a typical reading section as a whole. Note that you can adjust this based on your personal situation, but the breakdown shown in the table will work for many students.

A Total of 5 Passages, 47 Questions, 60 Minutes		
Passage 1, Fiction, 9 questions	5 minutes reading	7 minutes answering questions
Passage 2, Social Science, 9–10 questions	5 minutes reading	7 minutes answering questions
Passage 3, Science, 9–10 questions	5 minutes reading	7 minutes answering questions
Passage 4, Social Studies (Great Document), 9–10 questions	5 minutes reading	7 minutes answering questions
Passage 5, Science, 9–10 questions	5 minutes reading	7 minutes answering questions

The major adjustment you can make is *to take more time on the passages that are tough for you and less time on the passages that are easier for you.* After you practice using the passages in this book, you will have a good sense of which passages demand more time and which demand less time. Some students even find it helpful to adopt the extreme tactic of rereading an entire passage. If you have the time to do so, this can absolutely be justified, especially if it helps you have a firm grasp of a passage before doing the questions.

 TIP

Remember that you are in control—allocate your time as works best for you.

HOW TO HANDLE TRICKY QUESTIONS

Read this social science passage, and work through the question types that often give top students difficulty.

A political economist and a political philosopher present their views on the state of interest rates as of the beginning of the year 2016.

Passage 1

The economy is a delicate creature. In its fragility, it must be coddled and swaddled; prune and trim it, water and bathe it in sunlight as needed and it shall bear forth all the fruits of a healthy capitalist market. Contrarily, abandon the economy
Line and she shall grow wild with thorns jutting out at the flanks—the rebellion of the
(5) shrubbery overshadowing the beauty of the roses within.

The economy now is that rose bush; she has been left alone too long. Graciously, amazingly, she has not collapsed in her solitude. In fact, modest growth has occurred, and, for this, we must be ecstatic at our good fortune. But, that growth has soured of late, and we have fallen into a state of inertia.

(10) Yes, I will readily admit that a recession most likely is not imminent, but the time is not now to count our blessings and bask in the complacent contentment of a tragedy averted. No, we must act with haste. Money has been too cheap for far too long now, and such low interest rates are not the remedy for economic stagnation. Currently, rates are next to nothing, which was a fine solution during the
(15) crisis of 2008 and 2009. But, the stock market no longer is in a state of crisis; in fact, both equities and bonds are criminally priced.

As a value investor, with the exception of a handful of companies, there simply is not a stock that I can pinpoint as a wise investment at this juncture. Historically, the price-to-earnings ratio of the S&P 500 stock index has hovered around 15 to 1.
(20) Now, however, that ratio has ballooned to nearly 21, and opportunities for investment are scarce. Simply put, everything is overpriced, and our rose bush must be reined back in.

These minuscule interest rates just are not sustainable. Economic growth is no longer occurring, but investors continue driving up prices as if it were. Overall, I
(25) fear we are reaching a bubble, and bubbles, as you might well know, are prone to not being bubbles for long.

Passage 2

The tragedy of asking the wrong question is that, no matter how poignant or precise the diction, one cannot possibly attain the right answer. For instance, if my goal were to locate a wrench, I could go to my local improvement store using my
(30) most ornate of vocabulary and ask, "Where doth thou maintain thy hammers?" Alas, the store clerk might find me educated and mysterious, but he would direct me toward the wrong tool.

When I sit at the diner for lunch, I hear voices at the table next to me debating whether the Federal Reserve should raise interest rates. "Of course they should,"

(35) one voice will opine. "Inflation sows the seeds of collapse." And, when I wait in line at the Bureau of Motor Vehicles to renew my license, I hear the same debate. "Why in the world should we raise interest rates?" asks another. "Do we really believe the economy is strong enough to withstand the crunch that will follow?"

See, the crisis is not to do with interest rates, but in our questioning. It is not
(40) a matter of raising or maintaining rates, but whether the federal government should be so heavily involved in monetary policy in the first place. We must look to Thomas Jefferson for our guidance on this matter: "That government is best which governs least, because its people discipline themselves."

We must return to our Laissez Faire roots, for the economy will take care of itself
(45) if given the opportunity. Interest rates are not the issue. And, like my example at the home improvement store, the situation calls for a wrench, but all we ever ask ourselves is which hammer to swing.

1. As used in line 16, "criminally" most closely means

(A) exorbitantly.
(B) unlawfully.
(C) illicitly.
(D) feloniously.

2. What is the primary purpose of the paragraph in lines 17–22?

(A) To provide evidence in support of a claim
(B) To define "price-to-earnings ratio"
(C) To showcase the popularity of value investing
(D) To recount the history of the stock market

3. It is reasonable to infer that the author of Passage 2 believes the primary issue with our current approach to economics is that we

(A) are unwilling to consider alternative viewpoints.
(B) fail to make relevant inquiries.
(C) do not engage in interpersonal debate.
(D) do not know biographical details of historical figures.

4. Which option gives the best evidence for the answer to the previous question?

(A) Lines 33–35 ("When . . . collapse")
(B) Lines 35–38 ("And . . . follow")
(C) Lines 39–41 ("See . . . place")
(D) Lines 41–43 ("We . . . themselves")

5. The general attitude of the author of Passage 1 toward the state of the stock market in 2016 can best be described as

(A) steadily optimistic.
(B) mostly apathetic.
(C) generally concerned.
(D) totally panicked.

Answer Explanations with Strategic Guidance

1. **What gives students trouble?**

   The passage uses a different definition of a commonly used word.

   Everyone is familiar with the common definition of *criminal* as "illegal." Choices (B), (C), and (D) all use a variation of this common definition. However, there is no evidence to support the idea that the author believes that the prices of the stocks are illegal. The paragraph provides evidence that follows that the author believes that stocks are priced too high. So the correct definition in this context is Choice (A)—*exorbitantly*; the prices are unjustifiably high in the opinion of the author. On questions like these, be careful that you go to the surrounding context to come to your conclusion. Do not rely on your recall of the definitions of words.

TIP

Remember that all the information you will need to figure out the answer will be right there in the passage.

2. **What gives students trouble?**

   Students get caught up in the small details instead of the big picture.

   The question asks what the *primary purpose* of the paragraph is; it does not ask for a mere summary of the paragraph or for small excerpts of it. Choices (B), (C), and (D) all focus on small parts of the paragraph but do not focus on its larger purpose. Only Choice (A) captures the broad purpose of this paragraph—to provide evidence (statistics and examples) in support of a claim (that stocks are overpriced). When working through questions that ask you to find the primary function or purpose, be sure you focus on the big picture. Don't get trapped by small details.

3. and 4. **What gives students trouble?**

   Students ignore the evidence in the passage as suggested by the follow-up "where is the evidence?" question.

   There will be approximately nine "where is the evidence?" questions on the PSAT Reading—use them to your advantage! Rather than getting stuck on a question because you are not sure where to find the information in the passage, use the line excerpt questions as a guide. When we look at lines 39–41, it becomes clear that the primary issue the author believes we have with our current approach to economics is that we fail to ask the right questions. In other words, we fail to make relevant inquiries, making Choice (B) correct for question 3 and Choice (C) correct for question 4. After looking at the other excerpts, we see that none gives a clear indication as to the author's sense of what the *primary issue with our current approach to economics is.*

5. **What gives students trouble?**

   Students pick an answer that generally fits instead of the precisely correct one.

TIP

On the PSAT, if an answer is only partially right, it is completely wrong.

   This is an issue usually faced by strong math and science students. Why? They are accustomed to problems where there are more black-and-white answers. As such, they often gravitate toward something that is more extreme or broad instead of something that is more nuanced. On this question, many students may formulate the answer as "the author thinks stocks are bad." Thinking along these imprecise lines could lead students to pick Choice (D) because it clearly represents a negative attitude. The correct answer, however, is Choice (C). Lines 10–12 indicate that the author does not think economic collapse is imminent. The essay's final paragraph, however, indicates that the author is generally concerned about a stock market bubble. On questions like these, pick the option that captures exactly what is intended, not the option that roughly captures it.

TROUBLESHOOTING

Here are some further pointers for common issues.

"I can't stay focused when I read."

- Be certain you get a good night's sleep before the PSAT. You will start the PSAT with the reading section. So if you are tired and groggy, it will go poorly. Staying focused is extremely difficult when you are exhausted. Don't stay up late the night before the test doing last-minute cramming; it is not worth the drowsiness.
- Don't try to remember too much when you read. You need to remember only the general meaning of the passage—you should go back when you need to find details. This is not a school-based test for which you need to memorize many details.
- Try doing the passages in an order you choose. The simple act of choosing what passages to try first empowers you to take more ownership of what you read, instead of feeling that you're stuck reading a boring passage out of necessity. Build momentum by starting with the passages that come easiest to you.

TIP

Do not underestimate how important it is to be well rested on test day.

"I finish too early."

- Consider what would be the best use of your extra time—surely it is not just to sit there and stare off into space for several minutes at the end of the test. Perhaps you can spend more time reading the passages, formulating your own answers to questions, or carefully dissecting the answer choices. Experiment with some practice passages to see where the extra time will be most helpful for you.
- Have a watch when you take the test so you can be mindful of how quickly you are working. Try to maintain about a five-minute pace when reading each passage and about a seven-minute pace when completing the set of accompanying questions for each passage.

"I go too slowly."

- Diagnose what is taking you the most time. Typically, students spend too much time either reading the passages or in evaluating each answer choice. If you are spending too much time reading the passage, remind yourself that this is an open-book test and that you only need to paraphrase the general idea of the passage. If you are spending too much time breaking down the choices, shift your energy to reading the questions more carefully and formulating your own answer; that way, you will be much more decisive when you choose answer choices.
- Let go of perfectionist tendencies. You will not have time to double-check every answer, and you may not even have time to do every question. The PSAT is heavily curved. You can still achieve National Merit recognition even if you miss some questions.

Practice under timed conditions so that proper pacing becomes second nature.

"I get it down to two choices, but I can't decide which one is correct."

- Even though this isn't the math section, know that there will be one answer that is definitely correct. If you are not seeing it, make sure you have understood the context of the passage and make sure you have a firm grasp of what the question is asking. Do not allow yourself to become frantic and panicked because you feel you have come across a trick question.

■ Look for "contamination" in the choices. Even one incorrect word can ruin an entire answer choice. Instead of looking for the best answer, look for the flawless answer— this mindset will help you more rigorously analyze the answer choices without being seduced by the incorrect options.

FURTHER PREPARATION

What else can I do beyond the drills and practice tests in this book to prepare for the PSAT Reading?

TIP

Use the "Vocabulary Resource" appendix at the end of this book if you have trouble with the words-in-context questions.

■ Practice with the other Barron's books for the PSAT: *Barron's Strategies and Practice for the PSAT/NMSQT* and *Barron's PSAT/NMSQT*.

■ Use the free practice tests and resources provided by the College Board on *KhanAcademy.org*.

■ Focus on your most difficult passage types—fiction, global documents, science, etc.— and turn them into strengths. Given that the PSAT in its current form is relatively new, seek out other sources of rigorous practice reading tests. You may want to try reading for the GRE, GMAT, and MCAT—the passages you find on these sorts of tests will surely be more challenging than what you will face on test day.

■ Read, read, read. At a minimum, read high-quality books for pleasure, such as ones that have won the Pulitzer or Booker Prize. You may want to seek out articles and books that you find extremely challenging and read those in your spare time. The more widely you read, the greater the likelihood that you will have some baseline familiarity with the topics you encounter on the PSAT.

Note: The link to the online practice test is *http://bit.ly/barrons-PSAT-1520*. The practice test can also be accessed on all mobile devices, including tablets and smartphones.

Reading Drills

3

This chapter consists of drills that represent the most challenging types of passages you will encounter on the PSAT. You can practice all of these or focus on the passage types that give you the most difficulty. The passages are arranged by genre.

18 SAMPLE PASSAGE PRACTICE DRILLS

- Fiction: *Almayer's Folly*
- Fiction: *Dubliners*
- Fiction: "The Fall of the House of Usher"
- Fiction: "Adventure"
- Fiction: *Oliver Twist*
- Great Global Conversation: Jefferson
- Great Global Conversation: Obama Inaugurals
- Great Global Conversation: Frederick Douglass
- Great Global Conversation: Emerson and Arnold
- Great Global Conversation: *The Souls of Black Folk*
- Social Studies: Russian Depopulation
- Social Studies: The Emu War
- Science: Caffeine
- Science: Genetics
- Science: Fungi
- Science: Methanogenesis
- Science: Wound Healing
- Science: Synthetic Intermediates

> To practice these passages under timed conditions, take about 12 minutes per drill.

> Comprehensive answer explanations to all of these drills come at the end of the chapter.

Fiction: *Almayer's Folly*

Almayer's Folly is Joseph Conrad's first novel, published in 1895. Almayer, a poor businessman, dreams of acquiring wealth.

"Kaspar! Makan!"

The well-known shrill voice startled Almayer from his dream of splendid future into the unpleasant realities of the present hour. An unpleasant voice too. He had

Line heard it for many years, and with every year he liked it less. No matter; there would
(5) be an end to all this soon.

He shuffled uneasily, but took no further notice of the call. Leaning with both his elbows on the balustrade of the verandah, he went on looking fixedly at the great river that flowed—indifferent and hurried—before his eyes. He liked to look at it about the time of sunset; perhaps because at that time the sinking sun
(10) would spread a glowing gold tinge on the waters of the Pantai, and Almayer's thoughts were often busy with gold; gold he had failed to secure; gold the others had secured—dishonestly, of course—or gold he meant to secure yet, through his own honest exertions, for himself and Nina. He absorbed himself in his dream of wealth and power away from this coast where he had dwelt for so many years, for-
(15) getting the bitterness of toil and strife in the vision of a great and splendid reward. They would live in Europe, he and his daughter. They would be rich and respected. Nobody would think of her mixed blood in the presence of her great beauty and of his immense wealth. Witnessing her triumphs he would grow young again, he would forget the twenty-five years of heart-breaking struggle on this coast where
(20) he felt like a prisoner. All this was nearly within his reach. Let only Dain return! And return soon he must—in his own interest, for his own share. He was now more than a week late! Perhaps he would return to-night. Such were Almayer's thoughts as, standing on the verandah of his new but already decaying house—that last fail-ure of his life—he looked on the broad river. There was no tinge of gold on it this
(25) evening, for it had been swollen by the rains, and rolled an angry and muddy flood under his inattentive eyes, carrying small driftwood and big dead logs, and whole uprooted trees with branches and foliage, amongst which the water swirled and roared angrily.

One of those drifting trees grounded on the shelving shore, just by the house,
(30) and Almayer, neglecting his dream, watched it with languid interest. The tree swung slowly round, amid the hiss and foam of the water, and soon getting free of the obstruction began to move down stream again, rolling slowly over, rais-ing upwards a long, denuded branch, like a hand lifted in mute appeal to heaven against the river's brutal and unnecessary violence. Almayer's interest in the fate
(35) of that tree increased rapidly. He leaned over to see if it would clear the low point below. It did; then he drew back, thinking that now its course was free down to the sea, and he envied the lot of that inanimate thing now growing small and indistinct in the deepening darkness. As he lost sight of it altogether he began to wonder how far out to sea it would drift. Would the current carry it north or south? South, prob-
(40) ably, till it drifted in sight of Celebes, as far as Macassar, perhaps!

Macassar! Almayer's quickened fancy distanced the tree on its imaginary voyage, but his memory lagging behind some twenty years or more in point of time saw a young and slim Almayer, clad all in white and modest-looking, landing from the Dutch mail-boat on the dusty jetty of Macassar, coming to woo fortune in the
(45) godowns of old Hudig. It was an important epoch in his life, the beginning of a new existence for him. His father, a subordinate official employed in the Botanical Gardens of Buitenzorg, was no doubt delighted to place his son in such a firm. The young man himself too was nothing loth to leave the poisonous shores of Java, and the meagre comforts of the parental bungalow, where the father grumbled all day
(50) at the stupidity of native gardeners, and the mother from the depths of her long easy-chair bewailed the lost glories of Amsterdam, where she had been brought up, and of her position as the daughter of a cigar dealer there.

Almayer had left his home with a light heart and a lighter pocket, speaking English well, and strong in arithmetic; ready to conquer the world, never doubting
(55) that he would.

1. How do the opening lines of the essay, lines 1–5 ("Kaspar . . . this soon"), serve to illustrate the overall internal conflict throughout the passage?

   (A) Almayer's dreams of wealth are interrupted by mundane reality.
   (B) Almayer's lack of cultural proficiency prevents him from achieving internal peace.
   (C) Almayer's relatively low personal assertiveness keeps him from having fulfilling relationships.
   (D) Almayer's struggles with hallucinations haunt his quest for rational thought.

2. How does Almayer contrast himself with those who have been more financially successful?

   (A) He argues that he is more intelligent.
   (B) He acknowledges that they are more motivated.
   (C) He asserts that he is more virtuous.
   (D) He grants that they are more clever.

3. Which option gives the best evidence for the answer to the previous question?

   (A) Lines 6–8 ("He shuffled . . . his eyes")
   (B) Lines 10–13 ("Almayer's . . . Nina")
   (C) Lines 16–20 ("They would . . . prisoner")
   (D) Lines 21–24 ("He was . . . river")

4. As used in line 21, "share" most closely means

   (A) part.
   (B) communication.
   (C) gift.
   (D) disclosure.

5. Almayer's attitude as expressed in lines 36–38 ("It did . . . darkness") compares in what way to his attitude when he first set out on his journey?

    (A) More optimistic
    (B) Less troubled
    (C) More hopeless
    (D) Less honest

6. Which option gives the best evidence for the answer to the previous question?

    (A) Lines 18–20 ("Witnessing . . . prisoner")
    (B) Lines 29–30 ("One of . . . interest")
    (C) Lines 50–52 ("the mother . . . there")
    (D) Lines 53–55 ("Almayer . . . would")

7. It is most reasonable to infer that Dain is someone who Almayer believes

    (A) is a skilled seafarer.
    (B) will help him become rich.
    (C) is a close relative.
    (D) will take him and his daughter to Europe.

8. As used in line 36, "free" most closely means

    (A) willful.
    (B) unhindered.
    (C) empowered.
    (D) inexpensive.

9. What personality characteristic does the author most strongly suggest that Almayer has taken from his parents?

    (A) A disappointment that he is continually unable to find adequate nourishment
    (B) A cosmopolitan open-mindedness to new cultures and experiences
    (C) A fear of venturing too far from one's native land
    (D) A disregard for what he believes his station in life should be and what it actually is

Fiction: *Dubliners*

"An Encounter" is part of James Joyce's 1914 short story collection, Dubliners. *A young, unnamed narrator searches for release from the constraints of daily routine.*

It was Joe Dillon who introduced the Wild West to us. He had a little library made up of old numbers of *The Union Jack, Pluck* and *The Halfpenny Marvel*. Every evening after school we met in his back garden and arranged Indian battles. He and
Line his fat young brother Leo, the idler, held the loft of the stable while we tried to carry
(5) it by storm; or we fought a pitched battle on the grass. But, however well we fought, we never won siege or battle and all our bouts ended with Joe Dillon's war dance of victory. His parents went to eight-o'clock mass every morning in Gardiner Street and the peaceful odour of Mrs. Dillon was prevalent in the hall of the house. But he played too fiercely for us who were younger and more timid. He looked like some
(10) kind of an Indian when he capered round the garden, an old tea-cosy on his head, beating a tin with his fist and yelling:

"Ya! yaka, yaka, yaka!"

Everyone was incredulous when it was reported that he had a vocation for the priesthood. Nevertheless it was true.
(15)   A spirit of unruliness diffused itself among us and, under its influence, differences of culture and constitution were waived. We banded ourselves together, some boldly, some in jest and some almost in fear: and of the number of these latter, the reluctant Indians who were afraid to seem studious or lacking in robustness, I was one. The adventures related in the literature of the Wild West were remote from
(20) my nature but, at least, they opened doors of escape. I liked better some American detective stories which were traversed from time to time by unkempt fierce and beautiful girls. Though there was nothing wrong in these stories and though their intention was sometimes literary they were circulated secretly at school. One day when Father Butler was hearing the four pages of Roman History clumsy Leo
(25) Dillon was discovered with a copy of *The Halfpenny Marvel*.

"This page or this page? This page Now, Dillon, up! *Hardly had the day...* Go on! What day? *Hardly had the day dawned...* Have you studied it? What have you there in your pocket?"

Everyone's heart palpitated as Leo Dillon handed up the paper and everyone
(30) assumed an innocent face. Father Butler turned over the pages, frowning.

"What is this rubbish?" he said. "*The Apache Chief!* Is this what you read instead of studying your Roman History? Let me not find any more of this wretched stuff in this college. The man who wrote it, I suppose, was some wretched fellow who writes these things for a drink. I'm surprised at boys like you, educated, reading
(35) such stuff. I could understand it if you were... National School boys. Now, Dillon, I advise you strongly, get at your work or..."

This rebuke during the sober hours of school paled much of the glory of the Wild West for me and the confused puffy face of Leo Dillon awakened one of my consciences. But when the restraining influence of the school was at a distance I
(40) began to hunger again for wild sensations, for the escape which those chronicles of disorder alone seemed to offer me. The mimic warfare of the evening became

at last as wearisome to me as the routine of school in the morning because I wanted real adventures to happen to myself. But real adventures, I reflected, do not happen to people who remain at home: they must be sought abroad.

1. A major underlying theme in the essay as a whole is best described as the conflict between

(A) order and chaos.
(B) peacefulness and warfare.
(C) racism and tolerance.
(D) energy and laziness.

2. According to the first paragraph, Joe Dillon's personality is mostly

(A) accommodating.
(B) forceful.
(C) compromising.
(D) dishonest.

3. As used in line 13, "incredulous" most closely means

(A) disappointed.
(B) skeptical.
(C) enamored.
(D) inspired.

4. Joyce uses lines 16–19, "We banded . . . was one," to most directly suggest that the narrator was motivated to play Wild West with his friends because of

(A) a quest to fight a common enemy.
(B) a need to satisfy a moral code.
(C) desire to meet his peers' expectations.
(D) a reluctance to stand up against prejudice.

5. The narrator's willingness to follow the intellectual requirements of his school can best be described as

(A) openly rebellious.
(B) peacefully obedient.
(C) studiously ignorant.
(D) half-hearted.

6. Which option gives the best evidence for the answer to the previous question?

   (A) Lines 2–3 ("Every evening . . . battles")
   (B) Lines 26–28 ("This page . . . pocket?")
   (C) Lines 34–36 ("I'm surprised . . . work or")
   (D) Lines 39–41 ("But when . . . offer me")

7. Father Butler uses what approach in lines 34–35 ("I'm surprised . . . School boys") to encourage obedience?

   (A) An appeal to pride
   (B) A fear of failure
   (C) A disgust with learning
   (D) A request for curiosity

8. The most significant role that the Wild West games played in the life of the narrator is best described as

   (A) an introduction to a love of literature.
   (B) a turning point in his choice of careers.
   (C) the way to achieve independence from his parents.
   (D) a gateway to new thinking.

9. Which option gives the best evidence for the answer to the previous question?

   (A) Lines 1–3 ("It was . . . battles")
   (B) Lines 8–11 ("But he . . . yelling")
   (C) Lines 22–25 ("Though there . . . *Marvel*")
   (D) Lines 41–44 ("The mimic . . . sought abroad")

Fiction: "The Fall of the House of Usher"

Below is the opening excerpt from Edgar Allan Poe's 1839 short story, "The Fall of the House of Usher," in which an unnamed narrator approaches the home of his childhood friend Roderick Usher after not having seen him for many years.

During the whole of a dull, dark, and soundless day in the autumn of the year, when the clouds hung oppressively low in the heavens, I had been passing alone, on horseback, through a singularly dreary tract of country, and at length found
Line myself, as the shades of the evening drew on, within view of the melancholy House
(5) of Usher. I know not how it was—but, with the first glimpse of the building, a sense of insufferable gloom pervaded my spirit. I say insufferable; for the feeling was unrelieved by any of that half-pleasurable, because poetic, sentiment, with which the mind usually receives even the sternest natural images of the desolate or ter-rible. I looked upon the scene before me—upon the mere house, and the simple
(10) landscape features of the domain—upon the bleak walls—upon the vacant eye-like windows—upon a few rank sedges—and upon a few white trunks of decayed trees—with an utter depression of soul which I can compare to no earthly sensa-tion more properly than to the after-dream of the reveller upon opium—the bit-ter lapse into every-day life—the hideous dropping off of the veil. There was an
(15) iciness, a sinking, a sickening of the heart—an unredeemed dreariness of thought which no goading of the imagination could torture into aught of the sublime. What was it—I paused to think—what was it that so unnerved me in the contemplation of the House of Usher? It was a mystery all insoluble; nor could I grapple with the shadowy fancies that crowded upon me as I pondered. I was forced to fall back
(20) upon the unsatisfactory conclusion, that while, beyond doubt, there *are* combina-tions of very simple natural objects which have the power of thus affecting us, still the analysis of this power lies among considerations beyond our depth. It was pos-sible, I reflected, that a mere different arrangement of the particulars of the scene, of the details of the picture, would be sufficient to modify, or perhaps to annihilate
(25) its capacity for sorrowful impression; and, acting upon this idea, I reined my horse to the precipitous brink of a black and lurid tarn that lay in unruffled lustre by the dwelling, and gazed down—but with a shudder even more thrilling than before—upon the remodelled and inverted images of the gray sedge, and the ghastly tree-stems, and the vacant and eye-like windows.

(30)   Nevertheless, in this mansion of gloom I now proposed to myself a sojourn of some weeks. Its proprietor, Roderick Usher, had been one of my boon companions in boyhood; but many years had elapsed since our last meeting. A letter, however, had lately reached me in a distant part of the country—a letter from him—which, in its wildly importunate nature, had admitted of no other than a personal reply.
(35) The MS. gave evidence of nervous agitation. The writer spoke of acute bodily illness—of a mental disorder which oppressed him—and of an earnest desire to see me, as his best and indeed his only personal friend, with a view of attempting, by the cheerfulness of my society, some alleviation of his malady. It was the manner in which all this, and much more, was said—it was the apparent *heart* that went
(40) with his request—which allowed me no room for hesitation; and I accordingly obeyed forthwith what I still considered a very singular summons.

Although, as boys, we had been even intimate associates, yet I really knew little of my friend. His reserve had been always excessive and habitual. I was aware, however, that his very ancient family had been noted, time out of mind, for a pecu-
(45) liar sensibility of temperament, displaying itself, through long ages, in many works of exalted art, and manifested, of late, in repeated deeds of munificent yet unobtrusive charity, as well as in a passionate devotion to the intricacies, perhaps even more than to the orthodox and easily recognizable beauties, of musical science. I had learned, too, the very remarkable fact, that the stem of the Usher race, all
(50) time-honored as it was, had put forth, at no period, any enduring branch; in other words, that the entire family lay in the direct line of descent, and had always, with very trifling and very temporary variation, so lain.

1. Which option best describes what happens in the passage?

   (A) A traveler contemplates the best solution to a problem.
   (B) A man attempts to reconnect with his childhood best friend.
   (C) A character recounts his impressions and analysis of a situation.
   (D) A narrator tells the story of a famous and idiosyncratic family.

2. The tone of the first paragraph is one of

   (A) destruction.
   (B) sorrow.
   (C) foreboding.
   (D) mindfulness.

3. What best captures the narrator's sentiments about his capacity to understand the mystery of the House of Usher?

   (A) He feels intellectually capable.
   (B) He feels professionally untrained.
   (C) He feels largely optimistic.
   (D) He feels generally inadequate.

4. Which option gives the best evidence for the answer to the previous question?

   (A) Lines 6–9 ("I say . . . terrible")
   (B) Lines 14–16 ("There was . . . sublime")
   (C) Lines 18–19 ("It was . . . pondered")
   (D) Lines 25–27 ("I reined . . . before")

5. As used in line 38, "society" most closely means

    (A) civilization.
    (B) culture.
    (C) association.
    (D) order.

6. It can most reasonably be inferred from the passage that the narrator responds as he did to the letter out of a sense of

    (A) obligation.
    (B) sorrow.
    (C) longing.
    (D) terror.

7. Which option gives the best evidence for the answer to the previous question?

    (A) Lines 5–6 ("I know . . . spirit")
    (B) Lines 14–18 ("There was . . . Usher")
    (C) Lines 38–41 ("It was . . . summons")
    (D) Lines 43–46 ("I was . . . exalted art")

8. As used in line 43, "reserve" most closely means

    (A) greed.
    (B) openhandedness.
    (C) preparedness.
    (D) detachment.

9. Lines 49–52 ("I had . . . so lain") suggest that at any point in its history, the Usher family would have had how many heirs at a given time?

    (A) None
    (B) One
    (C) Two or more
    (D) The family had no heirs.

Fiction: "Adventure"

The passage below is adapted from "Adventure," in Sherwood Anderson's 1919 short-story collection Winesburg, Ohio.

Alice Hindman, a woman of twenty-seven when George Willard was a mere boy, had lived in Winesburg all her life. She clerked in Winney's Dry Goods Store and lived with her mother, who had married a second husband.

Line
(5) At twenty-seven Alice was tall and somewhat slight. Her head was large and overshadowed her body. Her shoulders were a little stooped and her hair and eyes brown. She was very quiet but beneath a placid exterior a continual ferment went on.

When she was a girl of sixteen and before she began to work in the store, Alice had an affair with a young man. The young man, named Ned Currie, was older (10) than Alice. He, like George Willard, was employed on the Winesburg Eagle and for a long time he went to see Alice almost every evening. Together the two walked under the trees through the streets of the town and talked of what they would do with their lives. Alice was then a very pretty girl and Ned Currie took her into his arms and kissed her. He became excited and said things he did not intend to say (15) and Alice, betrayed by her desire to have something beautiful come into her rather narrow life, also grew excited. She also talked. The outer crust of her life, all of her natural diffidence and reserve, was torn away and she gave herself over to the emotions of love. When, late in the fall of her sixteenth year, Ned Currie went away to Cleveland where he hoped to get a place on a city newspaper and rise in the (20) world, she wanted to go with him. With a trembling voice she told him what was in her mind. "I will work and you can work," she said. "I do not want to harness you to a needless expense that will prevent your making progress. Don't marry me now. We will get along without that and we can be together. Even though we live in the same house no one will say anything. In the city we will be unknown and people (25) will pay no attention to us."

Ned Currie was puzzled by the determination and abandon of his sweetheart and was also deeply touched. He had wanted the girl to become his mistress but changed his mind. He wanted to protect and care for her. "You don't know what you're talking about," he said sharply; "you may be sure I'll let you do no such (30) thing. As soon as I get a good job I'll come back. For the present you'll have to stay here. It's the only thing we can do."

On the evening before he left Winesburg to take up his new life in the city, Ned Currie went to call on Alice. They walked about through the streets for an hour and then got a rig from Wesley Moyer's livery and went for a drive in the country. The (35) moon came up and they found themselves unable to talk. In his sadness the young man forgot the resolutions he had made regarding his conduct with the girl.

They got out of the buggy at a place where a long meadow ran down to the bank of Wine Creek and there in the dim light became lovers. When at midnight they returned to town they were both glad. It did not seem to them that anything that (40) could happen in the future could blot out the wonder and beauty of the thing that had happened. "Now we will have to stick to each other, whatever happens we will have to do that," Ned Currie said as he left the girl at her father's door.

The young newspaper man did not succeed in getting a place on a Cleveland paper and went west to Chicago. For a time he was lonely and wrote to Alice
(45) almost every day. Then he was caught up by the life of the city; he began to make friends and found new interests in life. In Chicago he boarded at a house where there were several women. One of them attracted his attention and he forgot Alice in Winesburg. At the end of a year he had stopped writing letters, and only once in a long time, when he was lonely or when he went into one of the city parks and saw
(50) the moon shining on the grass as it had shone that night on the meadow by Wine Creek, did he think of her at all.

1. The major thematic focus of the passage is on what characteristic of love?

   (A) Its impermanence
   (B) Its beauty
   (C) Its wholesomeness
   (D) Its potential for abuse

2. It is reasonable to infer that George Willard was approximately what age at the time that Alice initiated her affair with Ned Currie?

   (A) Unborn
   (B) Seven
   (C) Sixteen
   (D) Twenty-three

3. As an adult, the attitude that Alice has toward her past is best described as

   (A) fond.
   (B) forgetful.
   (C) unsettled.
   (D) sedate.

4. Which option gives the best evidence for the answer to the previous question?

   (A) Lines 4–6 ("At twenty-seven . . . brown")
   (B) Lines 6–7 ("She was . . . went on")
   (C) Lines 43–45 ("The young . . . every day")
   (D) Lines 48–51 ("At the end . . . her at all")

5. As used in line 27, "touched" most closely means

   (A) assaulted.
   (B) dashed.
   (C) matched.
   (D) moved.

6. Compared to Ned, Alice is much more

   (A) willing to make sacrifices for the benefit of their relationship.
   (B) determined to advanced her professional status.
   (C) motivated by physical attractiveness.
   (D) interested in moving away from their provincial small-town life.

7. Which option gives the best evidence for the answer to the previous question?

   (A) Lines 8–9 ("When she . . . man")
   (B) Lines 16–18 ("She also . . . love")
   (C) Lines 26–27 ("Ned . . . touched")
   (D) Lines 32–33 ("On the . . . Alice")

8. As used in line 36, "resolutions" most closely means

   (A) promises.
   (B) purposes.
   (C) solutions.
   (D) entreaties.

9. The surrounding context around Ned's statement in lines 41–42, "Now we . . . do that," suggests that this quote was

   (A) an outright deception.
   (B) somewhat disingenuous.
   (C) given under duress.
   (D) motivated by true love.

Fiction: *Oliver Twist*

In 1838, Charles Dickens published Oliver Twist, *the story of a young orphan who is apprenticed to an undertaker and later runs off to London. Below, Oliver's quick ascent under Mr. Sowerberry incites the jealousy of Noah, another apprentice.*

The month's trial over, Oliver was formally apprenticed. It was a nice sickly season just at this time. In commercial phrase, coffins were looking up; and, in the course of a few weeks, Oliver had acquired a great deal of experience. The suc-
Line cess of Mr. Sowerberry's ingenious speculation exceeded even his most sanguine
(5) hopes. The oldest inhabitants recollected no period at which measles had been so prevalent, or so fatal to infant existence; and many were the mournful processions which little Oliver headed in a hat-band reaching down to his knees, to the indescribable admiration and emotion of all the mothers in the town. As Oliver accompanied his master in most of his adult expeditions too, in order that he
(10) might acquire that unanimity of demeanour and full command of nerve which are so essential to a finished undertaker, he had many opportunities of observing the beautiful resignation and fortitude with which some strong-minded people bear their trials and losses.

For instance, when Sowerberry had an order for the burial of some rich old lady
(15) or gentleman, who was surrounded by a great number of nephews and nieces, who had been perfectly inconsolable during the previous illness, and whose grief had been wholly irrepressible even on the most public occasions, they would be as happy among themselves as need be—quite cheerful and contented, conversing together with as much freedom and gaiety as if nothing whatever had happened
(20) to disturb them. Husbands, too, bore the loss of their wives with the most heroic calmness; and wives, again, put on weeds for their husbands, as if, so far from grieving in the garb of sorrow, they had made up their minds to render it as becoming and attractive as possible. It was observable, too, that ladies and gentlemen who were in passions of anguish during the ceremony of interment, recovered
(25) almost as soon as they reached home, and became quite composed before the tea-drinking was over. All this was very pleasant and improving to see, and Oliver beheld it with great admiration.

That Oliver Twist was moved to resignation by the example of these good people, I cannot, although I am his biographer, undertake to affirm with any degree
(30) of confidence; but I can most distinctly say, that for many months he continued meekly to submit to the domination and ill-treatment of Noah Claypole, who used him far worse than ever, now that his jealousy was roused by seeing the new boy promoted to the black stick and hat-band, while he, the old one, remained stationary in the muffin-cap and leathers. Charlotte treated him badly because Noah
(35) did; and Mrs. Sowerberry was his decided enemy because Mr. Sowerberry was disposed to be his friend: so, between these three on one side, and a glut of funerals on the other, Oliver was not altogether as comfortable as the hungry pig was, when he was shut up by mistake in the grain department of a brewery.

And now I come to a very important passage in Oliver's history, for I have to
(40) record an act, slight and unimportant perhaps in appearance, but which indirectly produced a most material change in all his future prospects and proceedings.

One day Oliver and Noah had descended into the kitchen, at the usual dinner-hour, to banquet upon a small joint of mutton—a pound and a half of the worst end of the neck; when, Charlotte being called out of the way, there ensued a brief

(45) interval of time, which Noah Claypole, being hungry and vicious, considered he could not possibly devote to a worthier purpose than aggravating and tantalising young Oliver Twist.

Intent upon this innocent amusement, Noah put his feet on the table-cloth, and pulled Oliver's hair, and twitched his ears, and expressed his opinion that he

(50) was a "sneak," and furthermore announced his intention of coming to see him hung whenever that desirable event should take place, and entered upon various other topics of petty annoyance, like a malicious and ill-conditioned charity-boy as he was. But, none of these taunts producing the desired effect of making Oliver cry, Noah attempted to be more facetious still, and in this attempt did what many

(55) small wits, with far greater reputations than Noah, notwithstanding, do to this day when they want to be funny;—he got rather personal.

"Work'us," said Noah, "how's your mother?"

"She's dead," replied Oliver; "don't you say anything about her to me!"

1. The passage suggests that the financial interests of undertakers are

    (A) more subject to unpredictable social patterns than the interests of other professionals.
    (B) the subject of dinner table conversation in homes across the country.
    (C) surprisingly in accord with the political goals of the powers that be.
    (D) at odds with the overall interests of the population as a whole.

2. As used in line 4, "sanguine" most closely means

    (A) trivial.
    (B) worldly.
    (C) optimistic.
    (D) ancient.

3. It is reasonable to infer that what characteristic of Oliver may have made him a better undertaker apprentice than Noah?

    (A) His physical presence
    (B) His ability to forecast the future
    (C) His even-temperedness
    (D) His personal wealth

4. Which option gives the best evidence for the answer to the previous question?

    (A) Lines 2–3 ("In commercial . . . experience")
    (B) Lines 23–26 ("It was . . . over")
    (C) Lines 34–36 ("Charlotte . . . his friend")
    (D) Lines 53–54 ("But, none . . . Oliver cry")

5. What general attitude toward death does the narrator most strongly suggest that Oliver would respect?

   (A) A joyful one
   (B) A stoic one
   (C) An expressive one
   (D) A melancholy one

6. Which option gives the best evidence for the answer to the previous question?

   (A) Lines 5–8 ("The oldest . . . in the town")
   (B) Lines 14–16 ("For instance . . . illness")
   (C) Lines 23–27 ("It was . . . admiration")
   (D) Lines 30–34 ("but I can . . . leathers")

7. The purpose of the paragraph in lines 39–41 is most likely

   (A) to provide a transition to an important anecdote.
   (B) to introduce the primary characters of the narrative.
   (C) to describe a vital life event.
   (D) to address a likely objection by the reader.

8. As used in line 41, "material" most closely means

   (A) economic.
   (B) significant.
   (C) tactile.
   (D) pessimistic.

9. Noah's taunting of Oliver throughout the passage can best be described as

   (A) increasingly below the belt.
   (B) consistently lighthearted.
   (C) violently physical.
   (D) largely justifiable.

Great Global Conversation: Jefferson

Below are two letters sent by Thomas Jefferson of the United States of America, the first to Benjamin Franklin in 1777 and the second to George Washington in 1781.

Passage 1

Honorable Sir,

    I forbear to write you news, as the time of Mr. Shore's departure being uncertain, it might be old before you receive it, and he can, in person, possess you of all we have.
Line With respect to the State of Virginia in particular, the people seem to have laid aside the
(5) monarchical, and taken up the republican government, with as much ease as would have attended their throwing off an old and putting on a new suit of clothes. Not a single throe has attended this important transformation. A half dozen aristocratical gentlemen, agonizing under the loss of pre-eminence, have sometimes ventured their sarcasms on our political metamorphosis. They have been thought fitter objects of pity than of pun-
(10) ishment. We are at present in the complete and quiet exercise of well organized govern-ment, save only that our courts of justice do not open till the fall. I think nothing can bring the security of our continent and its cause into danger, if we can support the credit of our paper. To do that, I apprehend one of two steps must be taken. Either to procure free trade by alliance with some naval power able to protect it; or, if we find there is no
(15) prospect of that, to shut our ports totally to all the world, and turn our colonies into manufactories. The former would be most eligible, because most conformable to the habits and wishes of our people. Were the British Court to return to their senses in time to seize the little advantage which still remains within their reach from this quarter, I judge that, on acknowledging our absolute independence and sovereignty, a commer-
(20) cial treaty beneficial to them, and perhaps even a league of mutual offence and defence, might, not seeing the expense or consequences of such a measure, be approved by our people, if nothing in the mean time, done on your part, should prevent it. But they will continue to grasp at their desperate sovereignty, till every benefit short of that is for ever out of their reach. I wish my domestic situation had rendered it possible for me to join
(25) you in the very honorable charge confided to you. Residence in a polite Court, society of literati of the first order, a just cause and an approving God, will add length to a life for which all men pray, and none more than

Your most obedient
and humble servant,
(30) Th: Jefferson.

Passage 2

Sir,

    I have just received intelligence, which, though from a private hand, I believe is to be relied on, that a fleet of the enemy's ships have entered Cape Fear river, that eight of them had got over the bar, and many others were lying off; and that it was supposed

(35) to be a reinforcement to Lord Cornwallis, under the command of General Prevost. This account, which had come through another channel, is confirmed by a letter from General Parsons at Halifax, to the gentleman who forwards it to me. I thought it of sufficient importance to be communicated to your Excellency by the stationed expresses. The fatal want of arms puts it out of our power to bring a greater force into the field,

(40) than will barely suffice to restrain the adventures of the pitiful body of men they have at Portsmouth. Should any more be added to them, this country will be perfectly open to them, by land as well as water.

I have the honor to be, with all possible respect,
Your Excellency's most obedient
(45) and most humble servant,
Th: Jefferson.

1. In Passage 1, Jefferson describes the Virginia governmental transition as

   (A) peaceful and orderly.
   (B) challenging and violent.
   (C) vengeful and political.
   (D) easy and trivial.

2. In Passage 1, Jefferson suggests that the American people would be open to which of the following with the British?

   (A) Political dependence
   (B) Economic reconciliation
   (C) Religious integration
   (D) Intellectual exchange

3. Which option gives the best evidence for the answer to the previous question?

   (A) Lines 10–13 ("We are . . . our paper")
   (B) Lines 13–16 ("Either to . . . manufactories")
   (C) Lines 19–22 ("a commercial . . . prevent it")
   (D) Lines 24–27 ("I wish . . . more than")

4. As used in line 13, "apprehend" most closely means

   (A) believe.
   (B) capture.
   (C) cease.
   (D) invent.

5. Jefferson uses lines 16–17 ("The former . . . people") to imply most directly that

(A) Americans would prefer to continue to be able to purchase manufactured goods from abroad.
(B) Americans are eager to achieve economic independence by creating domestic factories.
(C) Americans are unwilling to engage in an entangling alliance with another country that would require the United States to enter foreign conflicts.
(D) Americans are weary of the revolutionary conflict and would like to see its swift end.

6. The implied meaning of Jefferson's message in Passage 2 is that at the time of the letter, the American defense against the invading British force was

(A) incapable of resistance.
(B) likely to collapse if there were British reinforcements.
(C) likely to defeat the insignificant force at Portsmouth.
(D) capable of meeting and defeating the British on an open battlefield.

7. As used in line 39, "want" most closely means

(A) desire.
(B) abundance.
(C) lack.
(D) danger.

8. Both Passage 1 and Passage 2 have a tone of

(A) obedience and inferiority.
(B) aggression and anxiety.
(C) practicality and avarice.
(D) formality and deference.

9. Which of Jefferson's statements from Passage 1 demonstrated the greatest foresight given the issues mentioned in Passage 2?

(A) Lines 7–9 ("A half dozen . . . metamorphosis")
(B) Lines 10–11 ("We are . . . the fall")
(C) Lines 13–14 ("Either to . . . protect it")
(D) Lines 24–25 ("I wish . . . to you")

10. The respective general themes of Passage 1 and Passage 2 are

(A) militaristic and economic.
(B) personal and reflective.
(C) strategic and tactical.
(D) pedestrian and urgent.

Great Global Conversation: Obama Inaugurals

Passage 1 is the opening to President Barack Obama's first Inaugural Presidential Address in 2009. His second Presidential Address in 2013 is adapted for Passage 2.

Passage 1

My fellow citizens:

I stand here today humbled by the task before us, grateful for the trust you have bestowed, mindful of the sacrifices borne by our ancestors. I thank President
Line Bush for his service to our nation, as well as the generosity and cooperation he has
(5) shown throughout this transition.

Forty-four Americans have now taken the presidential oath. The words have been spoken during rising tides of prosperity and the still waters of peace. Yet, every so often the oath is taken amidst gathering clouds and raging storms. At these moments, America has carried on not simply because of the skill or vision of
(10) those in high office, but because we the people have remained faithful to the ideals of our forebears, and true to our founding documents.

So it has been. So it must be with this generation of Americans.

That we are in the midst of crisis is now well understood. Our nation is at war, against a far-reaching network of violence and hatred. Our economy is badly
(15) weakened, a consequence of greed and irresponsibility on the part of some, but also our collective failure to make hard choices and prepare the nation for a new age. Homes have been lost; jobs shed; businesses shuttered. Our health care is too costly; our schools fail too many; and each day brings further evidence that the ways we use energy strengthen our adversaries and threaten our planet.

(20) These are the indicators of crisis, subject to data and statistics. Less measurable but no less profound is a sapping of confidence across our land—a nagging fear that America's decline is inevitable, and that the next generation must lower its sights.

Today I say to you that the challenges we face are real. They are serious and
(25) they are many. They will not be met easily or in a short span of time. But know this, America—they will be met.

On this day, we gather because we have chosen hope over fear, unity of purpose over conflict and discord.

Passage 2

Vice President Biden, Mr. Chief Justice, members of the United States Congress,
(30) distinguished guests, and fellow citizens:

Each time we gather to inaugurate a President we bear witness to the enduring strength of our Constitution. We affirm the promise of our democracy. We recall that what binds this nation together is not the colors of our skin or the tenets of our faith or the origins of our names. What makes us exceptional—what makes
(35) us American—is our allegiance to an idea articulated in a declaration made more

than two centuries ago: "We hold these truths to be self-evident, that all men are created equal; that they are endowed by their Creator with certain unalienable rights; that among these are life, liberty, and the pursuit of happiness."

(40) Today we continue a never-ending journey to bridge the meaning of those words with the realities of our time. For history tells us that while these truths may be self-evident, they've never been self-executing; that while freedom is a gift from God, it must be secured by His people here on Earth. The patriots of 1776 did not fight to replace the tyranny of a king with the privileges of a few or the rule of a mob. They gave to us a republic, a government of, and by, and for the people,
(45) entrusting each generation to keep safe our founding creed.

And for more than two hundred years, we have.

Through blood drawn by lash and blood drawn by sword, we learned that no union founded on the principles of liberty and equality could survive half-slave and half-free. We made ourselves anew, and vowed to move forward together.

(50) Through it all, we have never relinquished our skepticism of central authority, nor have we succumbed to the fiction that all society's ills can be cured through government alone. Our celebration of initiative and enterprise, our insistence on hard work and personal responsibility, these are constants in our character.

But we have always understood that when times change, so must we; that fidel-
(55) ity to our founding principles requires new responses to new challenges; that pre-serving our individual freedoms ultimately requires collective action.

My fellow Americans, we are made for this moment, and we will seize it—so long as we seize it together.

1. The tone struck by President Obama in the first passage is best described as

   (A) resolute.
   (B) discouraged.
   (C) timid
   (D) insatiable.

2. As used in line 7, "still" most closely means

   (A) static.
   (B) downcast.
   (C) calm.
   (D) contrast.

3. What is the purpose of the paragraph in lines 13–19?

   (A) To consider objections to the introductory sentence of the paragraph ("That we are . . . understood")
   (B) To give reasons in support of President Obama's pessimism
   (C) To cite statistics to prove a wider point
   (D) To provide specific examples in support of a claim

4. It is reasonable to infer from the first passage that President Obama is attempting to address what fear held by parents of young children?

(A) That they would not be able to attend school
(B) That they are likely to lead greedy and irresponsible lives
(C) That they would not have a strong background in mathematics
(D) That they would have lives worse than those of their parents

5. Which option gives the best evidence for the answer to the previous question?

(A) Lines 14–15 ("Our economy . . . some")
(B) Lines 17–19 ("Our health . . . planet")
(C) Line 20 ("These are . . . statistics")
(D) Lines 21–23 ("A nagging . . . sights")

6. What does President Obama suggest about the nature of our rights in Passage 2?

(A) Although they are self-evident, they can be implemented only through action.
(B) The Creator has fully blessed everyone with the results of freedom.
(C) Mankind did not have the capacity for rights until the overthrow of a tyrannical monarchy.
(D) It has not yet been proven that Americans should have the rights laid out in the founding documents.

7. Which option gives the best evidence for the answer to the previous question?

(A) Lines 36–38 ("We hold . . . happiness")
(B) Lines 40–42 ("For history . . . Earth")
(C) Lines 42–44 ("The patriots . . . mob")
(D) Lines 50–52 ("Through it . . . alone")

8. As used in line 51, "cured" most closely means

(A) solved.
(B) medicated.
(C) preserved.
(D) exacerbated.

9. An introductory strategy used in both passages is to

(A) cite specific language from foundational American documents.
(B) use religiously evocative language.
(C) place the inauguration in broader historical context.
(D) offer thanks to the distinguished guests in the audience.

10. President Obama's statements in lines 31–38 about the foundations of American unity are most closely aligned with which selection from Passage 1?

(A) Lines 2–3 ("I stand . . . ancestors")
(B) Lines 9–11 ("America . . . documents")
(C) Lines 20–23 ("These are . . . sights")
(D) Lines 24–26 ("Today . . . be met")

Great Global Conversation: Frederick Douglass

Below is the beginning of the autobiography Narrative of the Life of Frederick Douglass, *which was published in 1845 and became significant to the abolitionist movement.*

I was born in Tuckahoe, near Hillsborough, and about twelve miles from Easton, in Talbot County, Maryland. I have no accurate knowledge of my age, never having seen any authentic record containing it. By far the larger part of the slaves know
Line as little of their ages as horses know of theirs, and it is the wish of most masters
(5) within my knowledge to keep their slaves thus ignorant. I do not remember to have ever met a slave who could tell of his birthday. They seldom come nearer to it than planting-time, harvest-time, cherry-time, spring-time, or fall-time. A want of information concerning my own was a source of unhappiness to me even during childhood. The white children could tell their ages. I could not tell why I ought to
(10) be deprived of the same privilege. I was not allowed to make any inquiries of my master concerning it. He deemed all such inquiries on the part of a slave improper and impertinent, and evidence of a restless spirit. The nearest estimate I can give makes me now between twenty-seven and twenty-eight years of age. I come to this, from hearing my master say, some time during 1835, I was about seventeen
(15) years old.

My mother was named Harriet Bailey. She was the daughter of Isaac and Betsey Bailey, both colored, and quite dark. My mother was of a darker complexion than either my grandmother or grandfather.

My father was a white man. He was admitted to be such by all I ever heard speak
(20) of my parentage. The opinion was also whispered that my master was my father; but of the correctness of this opinion, I know nothing; the means of knowing was withheld from me. My mother and I were separated when I was but an infant— before I knew her as my mother. It is a common custom, in the part of Maryland from which I ran away, to part children from their mothers at a very early age.
(25) Frequently, before the child has reached its twelfth month, its mother is taken from it, and hired out on some farm a considerable distance off, and the child is placed under the care of an old woman, too old for field labor. For what this sepa- ration is done, I do not know, unless it be to hinder the development of the child's affection toward its mother, and to blunt and destroy the natural affection of the
(30) mother for the child. This is the inevitable result.

I never saw my mother, to know her as such, more than four or five times in my life; and each of these times was very short in duration, and at night. She was hired by a Mr. Stewart, who lived about twelve miles from my home. She made her jour- neys to see me in the night, travelling the whole distance on foot, after the perfor-
(35) mance of her day's work. She was a field hand, and a whipping is the penalty of not being in the field at sunrise, unless a slave has special permission from his or her master to the contrary—a permission which they seldom get, and one that gives to him that gives it the proud name of being a kind master. I do not recollect of ever seeing my mother by the light of day. She was with me in the night. She would lie
(40) down with me, and get me to sleep, but long before I waked she was gone. Very little communication ever took place between us. Death soon ended what little we

could have while she lived, and with it her hardships and suffering. She died when I was about seven years old, on one of my master's farms, near Lee's Mill. I was not allowed to be present during her illness, at her death, or burial.

(45)   She was gone long before I knew any thing about it. Never having enjoyed, to any considerable extent, her soothing presence, her tender and watchful care, I received the tidings of her death with much the same emotions I should have probably felt at the death of a stranger.

1. The general point Douglass conveys in the first paragraph (lines 1–15) about knowing one's age is that

    (A) slaves managed to celebrate birthdays through careful estimations of their actual ages.
    (B) slaves were not granted basic personal identifying characteristics taken for granted by others.
    (C) there were some kind masters who overcame societal prejudice to see slaves as people, not property.
    (D) slaves did not know the fundamentals of arithmetic, having been denied math education by their masters.

2. As used in line 7, "want" most closely means

    (A) desire.
    (B) obstacle.
    (C) lack.
    (D) command.

3. Douglass expresses that his primary vehicle for learning about his origins was

    (A) his mother's private conversations.
    (B) the anecdotes of others.
    (C) documentary evidence.
    (D) spiritual revelation.

4. Which option gives the best evidence for the answer to the previous question?

    (A) Lines 11–12 ("He deemed . . . spirit")
    (B) Lines 19–20 ("My father . . . my father")
    (C) Lines 36–38 ("unless . . . master")
    (D) Lines 39–40 ("She was . . . gone")

5. It can reasonably be inferred from lines 27–30 that Frederick Douglass

   (A) was disappointed in his mother's lack of affection toward him.
   (B) was conditioned to feel little emotion toward his mother.
   (C) understands the true reason for the separation from his mother.
   (D) feels that the lack of his mother in his life hindered his intellectual development.

6. Douglass suggests that he met his father at what point in time?

   (A) As an infant
   (B) As a young child
   (C) As an adult
   (D) At no point

7. Douglass implies that his mother visited him only during the night because

   (A) she would face a harsh reprisal if she visited during the day.
   (B) she had other economic priorities besides child rearing.
   (C) she lived at an insurmountable distance from her son.
   (D) she had an unusual biological clock that made daytime activity a challenge.

8. Which option gives the best evidence for the answer to the previous question?

   (A) Lines 31–33 ("I never . . . home")
   (B) Lines 35–38 ("She was . . . master")
   (C) Lines 39–40 ("She was . . . gone")
   (D) Lines 40–42 ("Very little . . . suffering")

9. As used in line 47, "tidings" most closely means

   (A) news.
   (B) offerings.
   (C) remnants.
   (D) causes.

Great Global Conversation: Emerson and Arnold

The first passage is adapted from Ralph Waldo Emerson's essay "Nature," a foundational text of transcendentalism. Matthew Arnold, inspired by Emerson, wrote Literature and Science, *which is adapted for the second passage.*

Passage 1

Our age is retrospective. It builds the sepulchres of the fathers. It writes biographies, histories, and criticism. The foregoing generations beheld God and nature face to face; we, through their eyes. Why should not we also enjoy an original rela-
Line tion to the universe? Why should not we have a poetry and philosophy of insight
(5) and not of tradition, and a religion by revelation to us, and not the history of theirs? Embosomed for a season in nature, whose floods of life stream around and through us, and invite us by the powers they supply, to action proportioned to nature, why should we grope among the dry bones of the past, or put the living generation into masquerade out of its faded wardrobe? The sun shines to-day also.
(10) There are new lands, new men, new thoughts. Let us demand our own works and laws and worship.

Undoubtedly we have no questions to ask which are unanswerable. We must trust the perfection of the creation so far, as to believe that whatever curiosity the order of things has awakened in our minds, the order of things can satisfy. Every
(15) man's condition is a solution in hieroglyphic to those inquiries he would put. He acts it as life, before he apprehends it as truth. In like manner, nature is already, in its forms and tendencies, describing its own design. Let us interrogate the great apparition, that shines so peacefully around us. Let us inquire, to what end is nature?
(20) All science has one aim, namely, to find a theory of nature. We have theories of races and of functions, but scarcely yet a remote approach to an idea of creation. We are now so far from the road to truth, that religious teachers dispute and hate each other, and speculative men are esteemed unsound and frivolous. But to a sound judgment, the most abstract truth is the most practical. Whenever a true
(25) theory appears, it will be its own evidence.

Passage 2

Practical people talk with a smile of Plato and of his absolute ideas; and it is impossible to deny that Plato's ideas do often seem unpractical and impracticable, and especially when one views them in connexion with the life of a great work-a-day world like the United States. The necessary staple of the life of such a world
(30) Plato regards with disdain; handicraft and trade and the working professions he regards with disdain; but what becomes of the life of an industrial modern community if you take handicraft and trade and the working professions out of it? The base mechanic arts and handicrafts, says Plato, bring about a natural weakness in the principle of excellence in a man, so that he cannot govern the ignoble growths
(35) in him, but nurses them, and cannot understand fostering any other. Those who

exercise such arts and trades, as they have their bodies, he says, marred by their vulgar businesses, so they have their souls, too, bowed and broken by them.

Nor do the working professions fare any better than trade at the hands of Plato. He draws for us an inimitable picture of the working lawyer, and of his life of bond-
(40) age; he shows how this bondage from his youth up has stunted and warped him, and made him small and crooked of soul, encompassing him with difficulties which he is not man enough to rely on justice and truth as means to encounter, but has recourse, for help out of them, to falsehood and wrong. And so, says Plato, this poor creature is bent and broken, and grows up from boy to man without a
(45) particle of soundness in him, although exceedingly smart and clever in his own esteem.

One cannot refuse to admire the artist who draws these pictures. But we say to ourselves that his ideas show the influence of a primitive and obsolete order of things, when the warrior caste and the priestly caste were alone in honour, and the
(50) humble work of the world was done by slaves. We have now changed all that; the modern majority consists in work, as Emerson declares; and in work, we may add, principally of such plain and dusty kind as the work of cultivators of the ground, handicraftsmen, men of trade and business, men of the working professions.

1. The fundamental question raised by the first paragraph of Passage 1 is

   (A) why is it that scientific inquiry is dismissed in favor of political dogma?
   (B) why are philosophers considered superior to more practical professionals?
   (C) why shouldn't archaeology take precedence over historical research?
   (D) why can't modern society directly have transcendental experiences?

2. As used in line 3, "original" most closely means

   (A) special.
   (B) creative.
   (C) inventive.
   (D) formal.

3. According to Passage 1, Emerson has what attitude toward the human capacity for understanding?

   (A) Optimism
   (B) Skepticism
   (C) Abstraction
   (D) Historicism

4. Which option gives the best evidence for the answer to the previous question?

   (A) Lines 3–6 ("Why should . . . theirs")
   (B) Lines 12–14 ("Undoubtedly . . . satisfy")
   (C) Lines 17–19 ("Let us . . . nature")
   (D) Line 20 ("All science . . . nature")

5. According to Passage 2, Matthew Arnold has what overall feelings about Plato's ideas?

    (A) That they are interesting yet overly practical
    (B) That they are comprehensive yet indecipherable
    (C) That they are admirable yet outdated
    (D) That they are melancholy yet applicable

6. Which option gives the best evidence for the answer to the previous question?

    (A) Lines 35–37 ("Those who . . . by them")
    (B) Lines 43–46 ("And so . . . his own esteem")
    (C) Lines 47–50 ("But we say . . . by slaves")
    (D) Lines 51–53 ("and in work . . . professions")

7. As used in line 45, "soundness" most closely means

    (A) safety.
    (B) strength.
    (C) intelligence.
    (D) eloquence.

8. In Passage 2, Arnold's description of Plato's philosophy toward work can be summarized as

    (A) true strength is evident only in those who put the needs of others before themselves.
    (B) those who cannot make themselves useful to society are little more than parasites.
    (C) the demands of one's profession will limit the loftiness of one's being.
    (D) true nobility of soul is more likely to be found among those who work by hand than in those who use machines.

9. According to Passage 1 and Passage 2, Emerson and Plato, respectively, place great value on what in their pursuits of wisdom?

    (A) Religious revelation and scientific inquiry
    (B) Practical observation and abstract ideas
    (C) Legal theory and mathematical reasoning
    (D) Professional experience and industrial engineering

10. Which statement from Passage 1 is it reasonable to infer that Plato would have found most offensive?

    (A) Lines 3–4 ("Why should . . universe")
    (B) Line 10 ("There are . . . thoughts")
    (C) Lines 17–18 ("Let us . . . around us")
    (D) Line 23 ("speculative . . . frivolous")

Great Global Conversation: *The Souls of Black Folk*

Below is an excerpt adapted from a section of W. E. B. Du Bois's The Souls of Black Folk *titled "Of Sorrow Songs."*

They that walked in darkness sang songs in the olden days—Sorrow Songs—for they were weary at heart. And so before each thought that I have written in this book I have set a phrase, a haunting echo of these weird old songs in which the soul of the black slave spoke to men. Ever since I was a child these songs have

(5) stirred me strangely. They came out of the South unknown to me, one by one, and yet at once I knew them as of me and of mine. Then in after years when I came to Nashville I saw the great temple builded of these songs towering over the pale city. To me Jubilee Hall seemed ever made of the songs themselves, and its bricks were red with the blood and dust of toil. Out of them rose for me morning, noon, and

(10) night, bursts of wonderful melody, full of the voices of my brothers and sisters, full of the voices of the past.

Little of beauty has America given the world save the rude grandeur God himself stamped on her bosom; the human spirit in this new world has expressed itself in vigor and ingenuity rather than in beauty. And so by fateful chance the Negro

(15) folk-song—the rhythmic cry of the slave—stands to-day not simply as the sole American music, but as the most beautiful expression of human experience born this side the seas. It has been neglected, it has been, and is, half despised, and above all it has been persistently mistaken and misunderstood; but notwithstanding, it still remains as the singular spiritual heritage of the nation and the greatest

(20) gift of the Negro people.

Away back in the thirties the melody of these slave songs stirred the nation, but the songs were soon half forgotten. Some, like "Near the lake where drooped the willow," passed into current airs and their source was forgotten; others were caricatured on the "minstrel" stage and their memory died away. Then in war-time came

(25) the singular Port Royal experiment after the capture of Hilton Head, and perhaps for the first time the North met the Southern slave face to face and heart to heart with no third witness. The Sea Islands of the Carolinas, where they met, were filled with a black folk of primitive type, touched and moulded less by the world about them than any others outside the Black Belt. Their appearance was uncouth, their

(30) language funny, but their hearts were human and their singing stirred men with a mighty power. Thomas Wentworth Higginson hastened to tell of these songs, and Miss McKim and others urged upon the world their rare beauty. But the world listened only half credulously until the Fisk Jubilee Singers sang the slave songs so deeply into the world's heart that it can never wholly forget them again.

(35) What are these songs, and what do they mean? I know little of music and can say nothing in technical phrase, but I know something of men, and knowing them, I know that these songs are the articulate message of the slave to the world. They tell us in these eager days that life was joyous to the black slave, careless and happy. I can easily believe this of some, of many. But not all the past South, though it rose

(40) from the dead, can gainsay the heart-touching witness of these songs. They are the music of an unhappy people, of the children of disappointment; they tell of death and suffering and unvoiced longing toward a truer world, of misty wanderings and hidden ways.

1. What is the point of the passage?

    (A) To introduce a topic
    (B) To analyze a disagreement
    (C) To examine an event
    (D) To provide a personal anecdote

2. Du Bois most strongly suggests that general American creativity is focused on

    (A) lyrical beauty.
    (B) musical innovation.
    (C) energetic inventiveness.
    (D) mystical contemplation.

3. Which option gives the best evidence for the answer to the previous question?

    (A) Lines 9–11 ("Out of . . . the past")
    (B) Lines 13–14 ("the human . . . beauty")
    (C) Lines 22–24 ("Some . . . died away")
    (D) Lines 40–43 ("They are . . . hidden ways")

4. As used in line 19, "singular" most closely means

    (A) lonely.
    (B) extraordinary.
    (C) odd.
    (D) remote.

5. Du Bois suggests that the meaning of the slave songs is both

    (A) technical and complex.
    (B) scholarly and esoteric.
    (C) consequential and eloquent.
    (D) eternal and incomprehensible.

6. Which option gives the best evidence for the answer to the previous question?

    (A) Lines 17–18 ("It has been neglected . . . misunderstood")
    (B) Lines 22–24 ("Some, like . . . died away")
    (C) Lines 35–37 ("I know . . . the world")
    (D) Lines 39–40 ("But not . . . these songs")

7. Du Bois implies in lines 24–34 ("Then in . . . them again") that the initial greater public reception to the songs of the slaves of the Sea Islands was

(A) patiently analytical and systematic.
(B) blatantly belligerent and argumentative.
(C) warmly receptive and tolerant.
(D) overly superficial and dismissive.

8. "They" in line 37 most likely refers to

(A) slaves.
(B) society.
(C) slave owners.
(D) musicians.

9. As used in line 42, "misty" most closely means

(A) vaporous.
(B) cloudy.
(C) steamy.
(D) dewy.

Social Studies: Russian Depopulation

Russia, the geographically largest country in the world, is facing the biggest long-term problem any country can: depopulation. This problem is difficult to solve, however, as no one factor caused it. Rather, the roots of the issue lie in low

Line life expectancy, low birth rates, and the gradual disintegration of the traditional
(5) Russian family.

The beginning of the demographic problem is in Russia's low life expectancy. The life expectancy at birth for Russian males is only 64.7 years, and while the life expectancy for women is much longer, having the male half of the population die so early, before many men in the United States even retire, causes great
(10) concern.[1] This low male life expectancy has been attributed to both an increase in alcoholism and to the breakup of the Soviet Union, which have led to high labor turnover and increased crime rates.[2] Compared to many less developed countries in the world, a life expectancy of 64.7 is fairly high. These less developed countries, however, are not experiencing the drastic drop in population with which Russia is
(15) currently struggling. This is due to the high birth rates that counteract the low life expectancy. Russia, unfortunately, has no such advantage.

Low birth rates are the most critical factor in the Russian population crisis. The average fertility rate for Russian women is at 1.61 children per women; this results in a population growth rate of –0.04 each year. Russian women have practically
(20) ceased having children altogether, putting extreme pressure on the population.

These demographic numbers show a society that desires family and children very little. Generally, in richer countries, the birth rate drops as the quality of life increases. Yet in Russia, the high quality of life that would justify the present low rates does not exist. The low birth rates must then point to some societal lack of
(25) value of family and children. Interestingly, this contention is not supported by a survey conducted in 2007 that found that sixty-seven percent of Russian people thought that the love of the parents was the most important aspect in raising any child, and around sixty percent of all age groups found family, home, and comfort to be "very important" in their lives.[3]

(30) Despite Russian people espousing these values of family life, reality says something different. Studies of the artwork of children who draw family life, as well as the children's game of "house" show that the average Russian father is often absent in daily life.[4] Thus, while Russians see parental love and care as being vital to the wellbeing of their children, in general, men in Russia do not act to give this
(35) love and care to their children. As rational humans, it can be concluded that the women of Russia, wanting their children to have good lives, are less likely to have kids since they know that it is very possible that their children will have absentee fathers. This may be a conscious or unconscious decision but it seems to have been imprinted upon the people of Russia, giving the entire society an attitude
(40) whereby they value children but they don't have any themselves. With each generation that passes, this mindset grows, the men drift further, and the birth rate drops. This low birth rate is the main factor in the population decline in Russia.

All of these problems—the low life expectancy, low birth rate, and dissolution of the traditional family—are contributing to population declines in Russia.
(45) Vladimir Putin, in his 2006 State of the Nation Address, showed that he fails to see

the underlying causes of the problem: the lack of family support and the deep societal lack of desire for children. He focused on the economic problems instead, encouraging social programs to help pay for children.[5] He understands there is a problem but doesn't know how to fix it, which lies in the mindset, not necessarily (50) the pocketbooks, of the Russian people. Without a change in mindset, the population of Russia is destined to grow ever smaller.

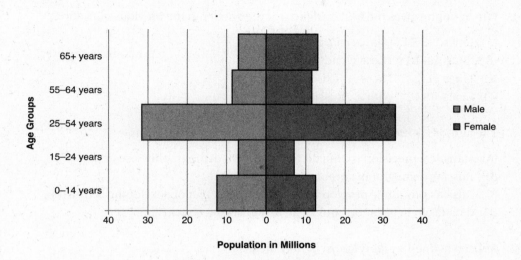

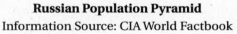

Russian Population Pyramid
Information Source: CIA World Factbook

---

[1]All demographic information sourced from the CIA World Factbook. https://www.cia.gov/library/publications/the-world-factbook/

[2]Julie DaVanzo and Clifford Grammich, *Dire Demographics: Population Trends in the Russian Federation* (Santa Monica: Rand, 2001), 40.

[3]E.I. Pakhomova, "Is it Reasonable to Speak of a Crisis of the Family?" *Russian Social Science Review* 48, no. 5(2007): 70, 79.

[4]Pakomova, 70, 79.

[5]Vladimir Putin, "State of the Nation Address 2006," *Population and Development Review* 32, no. 2 (2006), 386.

1. It is most reasonable to infer that the author considers the problem of Russian depopulation to be

    (A) complex yet manageable.
    (B) dire yet common.
    (C) serious and multifaceted.
    (D) unfortunate and nebulous.

2. Which option gives the best evidence for the answer to the previous question?

    (A) Lines 1–3 ("Russia . . . caused it")
    (B) Lines 13–16 ("These . . . advantage")
    (C) Lines 21–24 ("These . . . exist")
    (D) Lines 40–42 ("With . . . Russia")

3. The author's primary purpose in lines 12–16 is to demonstrate how

    (A) statistical precision is difficult to come by in demographic research.
    (B) Russia's demographic problems are not unique.
    (C) Russia's economic development is worse than that of developing countries.
    (D) data taken in isolation could lead to a mistaken conclusion.

4. As used in line 13, "fairly" most closely means

    (A) justly.
    (B) relatively.
    (C) equally.
    (D) exclusively.

5. As used in line 37, "absentee" most closely means

    (A) dead.
    (B) uninvolved.
    (C) far away.
    (D) incarcerated.

6. It can be reasonably inferred that Vladimir Putin's approach to depopulation as presented in lines 47–48 ("He focused . . . children") focuses on

    (A) the shifting mindset in the Russian population over the past century.
    (B) what is within the power of government to do.
    (C) the root causes of the issue.
    (D) centralized family planning.

7. Which of the following would be the most effective solution (unmentioned by the author) to the major problem that the author argues Russia faces?

   (A) More precise statistical study of demographic trends
   (B) Changing the Russian attitude toward fatherhood
   (C) Allowing increased immigration to Russia
   (D) Convincing Russians of the value of childhood

8. If Russia were able to follow the advice of the author, how would a reformed population distribution chart compare to the figure provided in the passage?

   (A) It would have a greater percentage of youth.
   (B) It would have a greater percentage of elderly.
   (C) It would have a greater percentage of people in their 40s and 50s.
   (D) It would have relatively more males than females.

9. Based on the figure provided and the passage, how does the distribution of ages within the 65+ group of women most likely compare to the distribution of ages within the 65+ group of men?

   (A) More divergent
   (B) Less divergent
   (C) Nearly identical
   (D) Differing values for the youngest ages

10. Which option gives the best evidence for the answer to the previous question?

   (A) Lines 6–10 ("The beginning . . . concern")
   (B) Lines 10–13 ("This low . . . high")
   (C) Lines 17–20 ("Low birth . . . population")
   (D) Lines 24–29 ("The low . . . their lives")

Social Studies: The Emu War

The best-laid plans often have unexpected consequences. Popular among chaos theorists, the butterfly effect refers to the interdependence of all events, and how even seemingly trivial changes in any of these can cause disproportional
Line differences in the non-linear space-time continuum. Chances are that following
(5) World War I, when British veterans were encouraged by the government to farm wheat in Western Australia, they had no idea they would be setting into motion another deadly conflict: The Great Emu War of 1932.

The end of World War I had many positive effects on the world: the end of world violence, the beginning of talks of worldwide peace organizations and treaties.
(10) However, there were also negative impacts. The end of the war also meant the end of many war-related jobs. Additionally, thousands of soldiers were returning home to economies already unable to provide enough employment opportunities to citizens. While different countries had different solutions to the problem, in Australia the government encouraged British veterans to take up farming. Subsidies were
(15) guaranteed but either failed to be provided, or weren't enough. As a result, by October 1932, wheat prices fell dangerously low.

Justifiably outraged, the farmers and government entered a time of rising tensions. Matters were made appreciably worse when over 20,000 emus entered the scene. Emus follow predictable migration patterns and when the farmers settled
(20) the land, the emus were residing in the coastal regions. In October, they started their migration toward the warmer, inland areas of Australia. Due to the extensive farming that had taken place, the land had been cleared—allowing easier migration—and there was a plentiful water supply from irrigation systems. In essence, the emus had found a perfect habitat. They destroyed much of the underpriced
(25) crop the farmers had painstakingly grown. This was the final straw for the farmers and they demanded the government provide them military aid.

The government assigned the emu mission to Major G.P.W. Meredith, along with two soldiers to assist him. Beginning in November, Major Meredith, the two soldiers, two Lewis guns, and 10,000 rounds of ammunition arrived to "take care
(30) of" the emu problem. Similar to a typical war involving humans on both sides, there were several "engagements" in this "war." A variety of borderline comical events took place from the soldiers underestimating the emus' military prowess (they broke into several guerilla like groups), to the Lewis guns jamming, to Major Meredith deciding to mount the guns on a military vehicle. In the end, the war was
(35) an overall failure and Major Meredith and his men returned home with only a fraction of the emu pelts they were supposed to have acquired.

The retreat of Major Meredith allowed the emus to return to the farmlands and once again ravage the crops. The farmers again called on the government for aid, and the Minister of Defense approved another military engagement with
(40) the emus. Despite his previous failure, Major Meredith was sent back to the field. Drawing on his previous experience, he was reportedly much more successful this time around.

Following the "war," word travelled and eventually reached Great Britain. Several newspapers had comical responses to the so-called "Great Emu War."
(45) While it undoubtedly had comedic threads, the emus did have a devastating effect

on an already tenuous situation. A bounty system was reinstated to avoid government involvement and potential future embarrassment should they lose another "war" to these large, flightless birds. Despite this, the farmers called again for government aid in 1934, 1943, and 1948. However, the bounty system ended up being
(50) much more effective as locals were more well equipped and knowledgeable about hunting the emus than was the military.

Significant Events in the Emu War

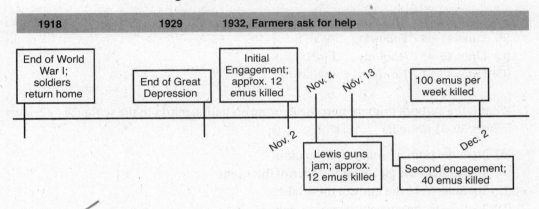

1. The author uses the introductory paragraph (lines 1–7) to

   (A) demonstrate how a military decision led to environmental catastrophe.
   (B) anticipate objections that the reader will have to the main argument.
   (C) provide a personal anecdote to draw the reader's attention.
   (D) place the topic of the passage in a greater context.

2. The author suggests that the military's initial mindset on their capacity to remove the emus was one of

   (A) overconfidence.
   (B) bravery.
   (C) humility.
   (D) fanaticism.

3. Which option gives the best evidence for the answer to the previous question?

   (A) Lines 4–7 ("Chances . . . 1932")
   (B) Lines 24–26 ("They . . . military aid")
   (C) Lines 31–33 ("A variety . . . groups")
   (D) Lines 37–40 ("The retreat . . . emus")

4. As used in line 14, the phrase "take up" most closely means

   (A) seize.
   (B) engage in.
   (C) study for.
   (D) invent.

5. Out of the following choices, which does the narrator suggest was of the greatest importance for people to fight the emus effectively?

(A) Military training from elite academies
(B) First-hand experience with the emus
(C) A scholarly understanding of emu anatomy
(D) A sophisticated relationship with the media

6. Which option gives the best evidence for the answer to the previous question?

(A) Lines 25–26 ("This was . . . aid")
(B) Lines 43–44 ("Following . . . War")
(C) Lines 46–48 ("A bounty . . . birds")
(D) Lines 49–51 ("However . . . military")

7. What is the author's primary purpose in using quotation marks in the sentence in lines 30–31 ("Similar . . . 'war'")?

(A) To quote primary source information
(B) To highlight the global importance of this event
(C) To underscore the irony of these labels
(D) To dispute the veracity of certain claims

8. As used in line 46, "tenuous" most closely means

(A) precarious.
(B) fatalistic.
(C) biological.
(D) cosmopolitan.

9. The figure is most useful in elaborating on which of the following selections from the passage?

(A) Lines 27–28 ("The government . . . him")
(B) Lines 28–30 ("Beginning . . . problem")
(C) Lines 30–31 ("Similar . . . 'war'")
(D) Lines 31–34 ("A variety . . . vehicle")

10. Based on the figure, the military's effectiveness in fighting the emus can best be described as

(A) gradually increasing over time.
(B) steadily decreasing over time.
(C) relatively constant over time.
(D) generally inconsistent.

Science: Caffeine

Passage 1

All told, there exist just over sixty species of plant known to produce caffeine, among the mostly widely cultivated of which are coffee from the berries of the *Coffea arabica* plant, tea from the leaves of *Camellia sinesis*, and chocolate from the seeds of the *Theobroma cacao* tree. Caffeine, curiously enough, is in its struc-
(5) ture quite closely related to adenine and guanine, the two purine nitrogenous bases that comprise about half of our DNA. Moreover, it is precisely this structural similarity between caffeine and nucleic acids that gives coffee, tea, and chocolate their uniquely stimulating properties. While amphetamine, ephedrine, nicotine, cocaine, and the vast majority of other common psychoactive stimulants work to
(10) modulate the dopaminergic circuits of the central nervous system, the stimulation we feel from ingesting caffeine arises from a completely distinct neural pathway.

Within every metabolically active cell of the human body, a molecule called adenosine triphosphate acts as a major reservoir of transferrable chemical energy. That is, in the thermodynamically favorable liberation of phosphate groups from
(15) adenosine, free energy is released that can be harnessed to drive forward a variety of the thermodynamically unfavorable chemical reactions required to sustain life. For our purposes, the main implications of this system are fairly intuitive: cells with significant energy reserves will be those with a large amount of adenosine triphosphate at their disposal, while those that have exhausted their reserves will
(20) contain merely adenosine, and inorganic phosphate.

Throughout our evolution, the neurons that make up our brain and spinal cord have adapted to detect the presence of adenosine, and to react to it by increasing the secretion of melatonin from the pineal gland, which in turn mediates feelings of "drowsiness" or somnolence. The purpose, one might reason, is simply to pro-
(25) mote sleep; a state that is minimally taxing to the metabolism of the central ner- vous system, and will allow its cells an opportunity to replenish their energy stores.

Adenosine itself is made up merely of an adenine nitrogenous base attached via a beta-glycosidic bond to a pentose sugar. Thus, it is simply the approximate structural correspondence between caffeine and adenosine that enables caffeine
(30) to interact with and antagonize adenosine-sensing receptors without chemi- cally activating them. The end result is a general blunting of the brain's ability to perceive how much energy it has expended; though the effect, it should be men- tioned, is self-limited. As the concentration of adenosine increases to critical lev- els, adenosine displaces caffeine from its inhibitory position on the receptor in a
(35) phenomenon known colloquially to some consumers of coffee and cola beverages as "the crash."

Passage 2

Caffeine, admittedly, seldom kills. A toxic dose to an adult is roughly equivalent to the amount contained in somewhere between eighty and one-hundred mid-sized cups of coffee. This is not to say, however, that caffeine is completely innocuous.
(40) By some estimates, more than 90% of the American adult population uses caffeine

on a daily basis, and it is far and away the most widely consumed psychostimulant worldwide. It is somewhat shocking, therefore, that its distribution remains wholly unregulated by the Food and Drug Administration.

While the recreational use of caffeine is infrequently fatal, abuse of caffein-
(45) ated supplements, medications, and beverages can precipitate a wide range of detrimental effects on the body, particularly among individuals with underly-ing vulnerabilities. For instance, in those already at risk for osteoporosis—such as post-menopausal women, and those suffering from hyperparathyroidism— caffeine has been shown to significantly accelerate the rate of bone loss, chiefly
(50) by increasing basal metabolic rate. Similarly, multiple studies have demonstrated a positive correlation between the agitating, stimulant-effects of caffeine use on the limbic system and acute exacerbations of panic disorder and anxiety disor-ders. Caffeine increases blood pressure. It promotes electrical dysrhythmias of the heart. It is anything but harmless, and yet contrary to popular belief, the most
(55) commonly heard health complaint concerning caffeine is something of a fallacy. That is to say, while chemical dependence, tolerance, and withdrawal from the stimulant are familiar entities to those who consume large quantities, genuine pathological addiction to caffeine has not been documented in humans, and as such is omitted from both the DSM-5, and the ICD-10 as well.

1. The respective purposes of Passage 1 and Passage 2 are best described as

   (A) analytical and narrative.
   (B) persuasive and descriptive.
   (C) expository and argumentative.
   (D) medical and economic.

2. Which of these gives the correct sequence of processes as described in the paragraphs in lines 12–26?

   (A) Adenosine triphosphate is formed in the pineal gland from the reaction between natural melatonin and artificial adenosine.
   (B) Adenosine and adenosine triphosphate stimulate the production of melatonin in the pineal gland.
   (C) Adenosine and melatonin from the pineal gland cause energy to be released in the creation of adenosine triphosphate.
   (D) Melatonin is released from the pineal gland as a result of detection of adenosine, which comes from the breakdown of adenosine triphosphate.

3. As used in line 14, the phrase "thermodynamically favorable" most closely refers to a reaction in which

   (A) the reactants are exclusively biological.
   (B) a subject consciously chooses to undergo the process because of its positive effects.
   (C) the reactants have more energy than the products.
   (D) the products have more energy than the reactants.

4. The process whereby caffeine works, according to Passage 1, is best paraphrased as

   (A) caffeine tricks the body into thinking it has not used as much energy as it in fact has.
   (B) caffeine causes the release of adenosine, stimulating the central nervous system.
   (C) caffeine strongly hinders the body's ability to produce adenosine, resulting in greater alertness.
   (D) caffeine helps the body generate more adenosine triphosphate storage, creating greater stores of energy.

5. Which option gives the best evidence for the answer to the previous question?

   (A) Lines 12–16 ("Within . . . life")
   (B) Lines 24–26 ("The purpose . . . stores")
   (C) Lines 28–33 ("Thus . . . self-limited")
   (D) Lines 33–36 ("As the . . . 'the crash'")

6. As used in lines 39–40, "innocuous" most closely means

   (A) harmless.
   (B) stimulating.
   (C) legal.
   (D) popular.

7. Which of the following does the author of Passage 2 suggest is a way that caffeine does NOT present a danger to humans?

   (A) Through exacerbation of panic disorders
   (B) Through pathological addiction
   (C) Through increasing blood pressure
   (D) By accelerating bone loss among at-risk populations

8. Which option gives the best evidence for the answer to the previous question?

   (A) Lines 47–50 ("For instance . . . rate")
   (B) Lines 50–53 ("Similarly . . . disorders")
   (C) Lines 53–54 ("Caffeine . . . heart")
   (D) Lines 56–59 ("That is . . . well")

9. When taken together, these two passages present a solid overview of caffeinated stimulation's

   (A) origins and history.
   (B) benefits and pitfalls.
   (C) causes and effects.
   (D) evolution and devolution.

Science: Genetics

Two scientists analyze the impact of advances in genetic research.

Passage 1

The completion of the Human Genome Project in February 2001 marked a new era for individualized patient medicine. With a complete genetic map of humans available to scientists and researchers all over the world, new diagnostic tools, pre-
Line vention methods, and treatments for diseases are created on a daily basis. While
(5) many new genetic technologies are decades away from being introduced to the general public, there are still many other genetic technologies in use today that are changing previously negative outcomes to positive ones for many patients.

The move from broad-spectrum interventions to individualized treatments based on a patient's genetic map is a sign that the future of medicine is here. For
(10) example, 20 years ago, if a patient were diagnosed with breast cancer, she would be offered the routine treatment of surgery, chemotherapy, and radiation. While this treatment plan was successful for many, there was still a very high percentage of disease relapse in patients. Treatment options for breast cancer patients today have radically changed with the discovery of genetic variation in cancers. While
(15) the previous medical professional theory was that breast cancer was the same in all patients, the finding of BRCA1 and BRCA2 genes revolutionized the way physicians prevent and treat breast cancer in women. With a focused treatment plan such as dietary changes, targeted chemotherapy, and general lifestyle changes, patients are experiencing better outcomes. Testing for BRCA1 and BRCA2 genes in
(20) family lines has also given women the opportunity to know if they are susceptible to the disease, which can significantly decrease the rate of occurrence.

Individualized patient medicine is not limited to the prevention and treatment of cancer. As genetic technologies continue to improve, parents can determine if they are a carrier of a recessive gene that may be passed to their child or adults can
(25) prepare to tackle a degenerative disease, such as Huntington's disease. For some, it is extremely helpful to know what medical trials they may face in the future so that they can make informed decisions about early intervention options. While many treatment options are still in the trial phase, patients receiving the treatment have not only seen an increase in life expectancy, but an increase in quality of life
(30) during those years. This is a triumphant achievement in medicine, as just a few years ago some patients, upon receiving a diagnosis, would be told that there were no treatment options even available. However, now physicians are able to provide targeted treatment options based on a patient's genetic make-up. As genetic technologies continue to develop, additional treatments will become available that
(35) will hopefully eradicate many prominent diseases.

Passage 2

Where do we draw the line with the advancement of genetic research? This is an important question to answer as new genetic research is performed on a daily basis and only some regulations are in place to monitor the research on an international level. While many argue that genetic research, thus far, has been posi-

(40) tive, others have expressed concern that the continued development of genetic research could lead to severe consequences for society.

The completion of the human genome sequence has helped researchers identify key components of what makes a human. While the identification of certain genes in the genome has led to the advancement of treatment for prominent dis-
(45) eases, like cancer, other identified genes have started the discussion of "designer babies." Since we now know what genes contribute to our hair, eye, and skin color, it is possible to create a baby that displays many desired physical attributes. To some, this genetic alteration is harmless, but others believe it could cause irrevocable harm to nature. Medical professionals have expressed additional concern
(50) with the unknown, long-term effects of deleting and inserting gene sequences as this technology is only in the beginning stages. Due to many unknowns of this technology, the United States government has placed a ban on germline manipulation until research can confirm that the benefits outweigh the risks.

Others worry about the possibility of genetic discrimination. As the genetic
(55) research community continues to explore the human genome, there will be an increase in the identification of different genes that contribute to diseases such as diabetes and mental illness. Some fear that identification of such genes could lead to discrimination against individuals seeking health insurance coverage or even a job. Finding a balance with genetic research will be vitally important as research-
(60) ers navigate new discoveries, so that advancements will help society, not harm it.

1. The author of Passage 1 suggests that a current advantage of genetically based medical treatments over more conventional treatments is their

   (A) greater future potential.
   (B) greater precision.
   (C) ethical objectivity.
   (D) increased popularity.

2. Which option gives the best evidence for the answer to the previous question?

   (A) Lines 1–2 ("The completion . . . medicine")
   (B) Lines 4–6 ("While many . . . public")
   (C) Lines 17–19 ("With a . . . outcomes")
   (D) Lines 33–35 ("As genetic . . . diseases")

3. The sentence in lines 4–7 ("While many . . . patients") primarily serves to

   (A) consider objections to the author's views.
   (B) describe details of newfound medical processes.
   (C) suggest that science is slow to advance.
   (D) state the thesis of the passage.

4. As used in line 11, "routine" most closely means

   (A) typical.
   (B) repetitive.
   (C) personalized.
   (D) simple.

5. What is the point of Passage 2?

    (A) To consider the possible implications of an issue
    (B) To forecast the results of a scientific advance
    (C) To survey scholarly opinion on the foundations of genetics
    (D) To argue against scientific progress

6. As used in line 58, "discrimination" most closely means

    (A) racism.
    (B) bias.
    (C) hatred.
    (D) prosecution.

7. The author of Passage 2 would most likely categorize the author of Passage 1 under which of the following labels?

    (A) "Many," line 39
    (B) "Others," line 40
    (C) "Researchers," line 42
    (D) "Professionals," line 49

8. The author of Passage 2 would most likely raise which of the following concerns about the situation mentioned in lines 23–25 of Passage 1 ("As genetic . . . disease")?

    (A) That the child who has a chance of receiving the gene may be discriminated against by insurance companies
    (B) That the parents would not be able to predict the likelihood of their child developing the disease
    (C) That the child would have his or her facial features artificially manipulated in his or her childhood
    (D) That the resources spent on the child's care could be better spent on other scientific research

9. Which option gives the best evidence for the answer to the previous question?

    (A) Lines 36–39 ("This is . . . level")
    (B) Lines 46–47 ("Since we . . . attributes")
    (C) Lines 49–51 ("Medical . . . stages")
    (D) Lines 57–59 ("Some . . . job")

10. The authors of Passage 1 and Passage 2 have respective attitudes toward genetic research that are best described as

    (A) positive, negative
    (B) scientific, historical
    (C) optimistic, cautious
    (D) hopeful, apocalyptic

Science: Fungi

With good reason, biologists have frequently described fungi as the "forgotten kingdom." Despite demonstrating a diversity and evolutionary resilience to rival plants and animals alike, for many of us, our day-to-day familiarity with fungi
Line reaches little further than to a handful of domesticated mushrooms, and perhaps
(5) the *Penicillium* molds that imbue blue cheese with their distinctive color and smell. In reality, fungi are all around us, and contribute biochemically to a remarkable variety of both natural and artificial processes: from the vital decomposition of organic matter commonly described as "rotting" to the yeast-mediated fermentation of polysaccharides into ethanol and gaseous carbon dioxide which allows
(10) a baker's bread to rise. Even so, perhaps due to their obscure, soil-dwelling lifestyles, the manifold functions that fungi execute in our lives are more often than not inconspicuous, and all too easily overlooked.

The health sciences especially are rife with novel applications for mycology (that is, the branch of biology emphasizing fungi). Famously, the first commercially
(15) available antibiotics capable of curing streptococcal and staphylococcal infections were discovered quite by accident when Scottish scientist Alexander Fleming noticed how the growth of a staphylococcus culture had been drastically inhibited following its contamination with a *Penicillium chrysogenum* mold. Notably, the unique mechanism by which this inhibitory effect is accomplished has since led
(20) to the development of not one but three distinct classes of antimicrobial medications—penicillins, cephalosporins, and beta-lactamase inhibitors—and accelerated a set of fascinating genetic mutations which confer antibiotic resistance among strains of bacteria.

In penicillins and cephalosporins, the so-called "beta-lactam ring" is known to
(25) be the principle structure responsible for their antimicrobial properties. This ring binds avidly to specialized cross-linking proteins found within the peptidoglycan layer of bacterial cell walls, subsequently blocking a bacterium's attempts at reproduction, as well as the replication of its intracellular organelles. As it is not found naturally within the cells of animals, plants, or fungi, peptidoglycan polymers are
(30) highly peculiar to bacteria, and antimicrobial agents targeting peptidoglycan possess a very low potential for toxic cross-reactivity with other types of cells.

Even into the 21st century, beta-lactam compounds still comprise more than half of all antibiotics prescribed worldwide, and it is widely believed that their pervasive usage has helped to promote the novel synthesis of beta-lactamases among
(35) a wide array of common pathogenic bacterial species. To clarify, beta-lactamases are a class of enzymes capable of hydrolyzing the beta-lactam ring, and are often secreted in the presence of antibiotics. While these enzymes are nigh ubiquitous among bacteria today, prior to the commercial availability of penicillin, their endogenous synthesis was limited to a fairly small number of gram-negative
(40) organisms. The startling rapidity with which bacteria have developed resistance against beta-lactams may have far reaching implications for the health of human populations in the future.

Although penicillin is perhaps the most memorable example, it is hardly the only contribution fungi have made to improving human health. In recent years,
(45) a number of medicinally significant fungal isolates have emerged to treat not just

infection, but metabolic, immunologic, and neoplastic diseases as well. Of particular note, 3-hydroxy-3-methylglutaryl-CoA reductase inhibitors—more commonly called "statins"—are considered the first-line pharmacological therapy for hypercholesterolemia, and are the only cholesterol-lowering class of medications
(50) that have been proven in peer-reviewed longitudinal studies to lower an individual's risk of major cardiovascular disease. Mechanistically, rather than blocking the absorption of dietary cholesterol or enhancing its excretion, statins work to reduce the *de novo* biosynthesis of cholesterol molecules in the body by inhibiting the rate-limiting enzyme in its anabolic pathway.

(55)   It would not be overstating the matter to say that statins have transformed the treatment of both acquired and congenital cholesterol-related diseases. But what's more, the first generation of statins was discovered, oddly enough, by Japanese scientist Akira Endo during his research into the antimicrobial properties of the mold *Penicillium citrinum*. Not unlike Alexander Fleming one-half century ear-
(60) lier, Endo serendipitously discovered yet another compound from this curious genus of fungi destined to do no less than revolutionize the medical maintenance of human health. One must wonder, therefore, what more we stand to learn from fungi, and what still-greater mysteries they may yet be concealing in the soil.

1. As described in the passage, the gradual process of changes in bacterial resistance to antibiotics is most similar to which of the following situations?

   (A) An artificial intelligence program analyzes multiple instances of computer viruses, increasing its antiviral effectiveness as it gathers more applicable data.
   (B) A television show is extremely popular in its first season but becomes less popular as its novelty wears off.
   (C) A school initiates antiplagiarism software that is highly useful in stopping cheating at the outset but becomes less useful as more students catch on.
   (D) A car's tires become worn thin after thousands of miles of wear and tear.

2. The author primarily uses the introductory paragraph, lines 1–12, to

   (A) demonstrate the applications of fungi in cooking.
   (B) refute widespread misinformation about fungi.
   (C) establish the relevance of the essay's topic.
   (D) point out the easy visibility of fungal influence.

3. As used in line 11, "execute" most closely means

   (A) destroy.
   (B) camouflage.
   (C) entice.
   (D) perform.

4. The author suggests that some of the most important fungi-related medical innovations came about primarily as a result of

   (A) luck.
   (B) evolution.
   (C) economic investment.
   (D) genetic engineering.

5. Which option gives the best evidence for the answer to the previous question?

   (A) Lines 18–23 ("Notably . . . bacteria")
   (B) Lines 32–35 ("Even into . . . species")
   (C) Lines 46–51 ("Of particular . . . disease")
   (D) Lines 59–62 ("Not unlike . . . health")

6. As used in line 30, "peculiar" most closely means

   (A) strange.
   (B) unique.
   (C) diseased.
   (D) helpful.

7. The author implies that a property of antibiotics that makes them particularly helpful to diseased animals is that they

   (A) are not widely recognized and can therefore be inconspicuous.
   (B) cause the diseased tissue to mutate into healthy tissue.
   (C) help the organism develop long-term immunity against infection.
   (D) attack the bacteria without attacking the host organism.

8. Which option gives the best evidence for the answer to the previous question?

   (A) Lines 10–12 ("Even so . . . overlooked")
   (B) Lines 18–23 ("Notably . . . bacteria")
   (C) Lines 28–31 ("As it is . . . cells")
   (D) Lines 40–42 ("The startling . . . future")

9. The author most likely uses the final sentence of the passage (lines 62–63, "One must . . . soil") to suggest

   (A) that geological exploration deserves funding.
   (B) that further study of fungi is warranted.
   (C) skepticism about the prospects for scientific research.
   (D) a more balanced approach to the analysis of fungi.

Science: Methanogenesis

Methanosphaera stadtmanae, the first single-celled (archaeal) commensal (i.e., two organisms have a relationship wherein one benefits, and the other has no harm nor benefit) organism to have its genome sequenced, is an anaerobic, *Line* non-moving, sphere-shaped organism that inhabits the human gastrointesti-
(5) nal tract. Of all methanogenic (methane-producing) Archaea, *Methanosphaera stadtmanae* has been found to have the most restrictive energy metabolism as it can generate methane only by reduction of methanol with H_2 and is dependent on acetate as a carbon source. These unique energy conservation traits are what make *Methanosphaera stadtmanae* beneficial to its human host and not an oppor-
(10) tunistic pathogen.

Methanosphaera stadtmanae's genome lacks 37 protein-coding sequences present in the genomes of all other methanogens. Among these are the pro-tein coding sequences for synthesis of molybdopterin, which is required for the enzyme catalyzing the first step of methanogenesis from CO_2 and H_2, as well as
(15) for the synthesis of the CO dehydrogenase/acetyl-coenzyme A synthase complex. This explains why *Methanosphaera stadtmanae* cannot reduce CO_2 to methane nor oxidize methanol to CO_2. While this is the typical path of methanogenesis for many archaeal methanogens, it is not the path for *Methanosphaera stadtmanae*.

Methanogenic Archaea are naturally occurring components of the human
(20) gut microbiota. The two original methanogenic species belonging to the order Methanobacteriales, *Methanobrevibacter smithii* and *Methanosphaera stadtma-nae*, were identified over 30 years ago by the detection of methane in the breath, and eventually isolated from fecal samples. *Methanosphaera stadtmanae*, one of the major archaeal inhabitants of the gut, is able to thrive in the human digestive
(25) system because methanol is a product of pectin degradation in the intestine by *Bacterioides* species and other anaerobic bacteria. *Methanosphaera stadtmanae* reduces methanol produced by the anaerobic bacteria with H_2 present to produce methane. Production of methane in this manner is beneficial to the human host because of energy conservation. Methanogens, like *Methanosphaera stadtmanae*,
(30) also play an important role in digestion by improving efficiency of polysaccharide fermentation by helping to prevent accumulation of acids, reaction end products, and gaseous hydrogen. It is thought that *Methanosphaera stadtmanae*'s energy conserving methanogenesis process is one of the ways it helps in maintaining homeostasis (biological equilibrium) within the human gut microbiota.

(35) Homeostasis of the human gut microbiota is a delicate balance, and if disrupted can cause serious issues for humans. One of these issues is the growing number of cases of IBD (Inflammatory Bowel Disease). IBD is a term used in the medical field to describe conditions of the gastrointestinal tract that have chronic or recurring immune responses and inflammation. *Methanosphaera stadtmanae*'s commensal
(40) role with the human can be disrupted when other bacteria in the highly immuno-logically active intestinal tract stop performing their normal processes. While the details of all of the processes that bacteria perform are not completely known, it is understood that *Methanosphaera stadtmanae* reacts to the adverse effects by inducing the release of proinflammatory cytokine TNF in peripheral blood cells.
(45) By releasing this, *Methanosphaera stadtmanae* produces a four-times stronger

response than any other methanogen of the gut microbiota. This response causes increased inflammation in the gastrointestinal tract, and can only stop when balance within the gut microbiota is restored.

(50) One method physicians have found to help restore the homeostasis of the gut microbiota is the administration of archaebiotics. Archaebiotics colonize in the gastrointestinal tract to help restore balance by eliminating and controlling bacteria or archaea that disrupted the balance in the first place. Archaebiotics also help by keeping commensal methanogens, like *Methanosphaera stadtmanae*, so that they can continue to perform their necessary role of methanogenesis. It is impera-

(55) tive to maintain methanogenesis so that proper digestion and energy conservation can happen for the human.

Understanding the role *Methanosphaera stadtmanae* plays in the human gastrointestinal tract has been extremely important in the advancement of understanding IBD, as well as the development of treatments. Identification of

(60) additional archaeal and bacterial species will continue to help develop the field so that scientists and physicians can better understand how different organisms work with each other or against each other.

Pathway	Complete/Incomplete/ Absent	Intermediates
Glycolysis (Embden-Meyerhof)	Incomplete	Missing glucose and D-glucose 6-phosphate
Entner-Doudoroff (Semi-phosphorylative Form)	Both Absent	Missing all intermediates
Pentose Phosphate	Incomplete	Missing all intermediates except D-ribulose-5-phosphate and D-ribose-5-phosphate
Pyruvate Oxidation	Complete	All intermediates present
Citrate Cycle (Glyoxylate Cycle)	Both Incomplete	Missing citrate and isocitrate as intermediates. Pyruvate feeds into the Citrate Cycle via oxaloacetate. Glyoxylate Cycle only contains oxaloacetate and malate.
Reductive Citrate Cycle	Incomplete	Missing all intermediates except oxaloacetate and malate
Calvin Cycle	Incomplete	Missing Erythrose-4P, Sedoheptulose 1,7P, Sedoheptulose 7P, and Ribulose 1,5P
Methanogenesis	Complete	All intermediates present (can only use methanol and H_2 to produce methane)
Reductive Acetyl-CoA	Incomplete	Missing all intermediates except 5,10-Methylene-THF and THF (come in from a different pathway)

Figure 1: The above chart lists the known mechanisms that bacterial and archaeal organisms use for energy purposes. The chart lists if *M. stadtmanae* has the necessary intermediates present in the human digestive system to have a functional energy pathway given a particular mechanism.

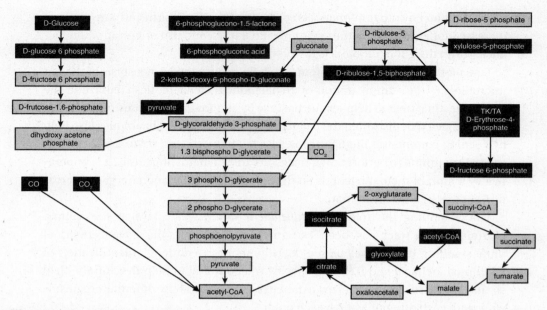

Figure 2: The intermediates in the black boxes are ones that *M. stadtmanae* cannot use or does not have. The intermediates in the gray boxes are ones that *M. stadtmanae* does use or has.

1. It is most reasonable to infer that the author of the passage believes that scientific understanding of how archaeal and bacterial species interact with the human digestive system is

   (A) largely settled.
   (B) making progress.
   (C) generally mystified.
   (D) static.

2. According to the third paragraph (lines 19–34), the presence of methanogenic species in the human digestive system was first detected from

   (A) observation of a product of a chemical reaction.
   (B) isolation from human bowel movements.
   (C) the decoding of the DNA of methanogens.
   (D) the discovery of its essential role in human homeostasis.

3. As used in line 27, "reduces" most closely means

   (A) subtracts.
   (B) diminishes.
   (C) transforms.
   (D) persecutes.

4. What is the primary purpose of lines 42–44 ("it is . . . cells")?

   (A) To address an objection
   (B) To provide speculation
   (C) To explain a process
   (D) To cite an authority

5. As used in line 44, "inducing" most closely means

   (A) causing.
   (B) suggesting.
   (C) releasing.
   (D) persuading.

6. According to the passage as a whole, the overall role of *Methanosphaera stadtmanae* with respect to human health is

   (A) uniformly positive.
   (B) primarily beneficial.
   (C) somewhat harmful.
   (D) mostly parasitic.

7. The processing or lack thereof of which chemical intermediate shown in Figure 2 does the author argue is particularly distinctive for *Methanosphaera stadtmanae* relative to other methanogens?

   (A) H_2
   (B) oxaloacetate
   (C) CO_2
   (D) succinate

8. Which option gives the best evidence for the answer to the previous question?

   (A) Lines 11–12 ("*Methanosphaera* . . . methanogens")
   (B) Lines 16–18 ("This explains . . . *stadtmanae*")
   (C) Lines 23–26 ("*Methanosphaera* . . . bacteria")
   (D) Lines 29–32 ("Methanogens . . . hydrogen")

9. How does the information in Figures 1 and 2 help make the author's case that *Methanosphaera stadtmanae* is helpful to humans, relative to many other similar bacteria and archaeal organisms?

   (A) The figures show that pentose phosphate does not have the needed intermediates to carry out the development of methanol.
   (B) The figures demonstrate that *M. stadtmanae* is genetically similar to the more common *Methanobrevibacter smithii*.
   (C) The figures detail the chemical process whereby inflammatory bowel disease can be avoided.
   (D) The figures show that *M. stadtmanae* lacks the necessary intermediates for most of the common energy pathways.

10. Which option gives the best evidence for the answer to the previous question?

    (A) Lines 5–10 ("Of all . . . pathogen")
    (B) Lines 20–23 ("The two . . . samples")
    (C) Lines 35–41 ("Homeostasis . . . processes")
    (D) Lines 49–54 ("One method . . . methanogenesis")

Science: Wound Healing

An Occupational Therapist Describes the Process of Wound Healing

Even when a laceration as small as a paper cut happens to a person, complex reactions begin within the body almost instantaneously. Were these processes to be disrupted for any number of reasons, even the most insignificant of scrapes could prove fatal for the victim. Thus, it is of the utmost importance to know the typical progression for how a wound heals so that the afflicted can seek medical attention should the wound prove aggravated.

Immediately after the initial laceration transpires, the body responds and initiates action. Known as the "inflammatory phase" of wound healing, this is when the body first begins to repair the damage it encountered. In order to prevent excessive blood loss, the first step is vasoconstriction in which the blood vessels near the affected area are constricted. Nearly concurrently, phagocytosis begins as white blood cells are sent to the wound. Phagocytes are cells that consume the debris in the wound, which aids in the cleansing of damaged tissue as well as foreign matter.

Phagocytosis is completed quite quickly—a mere 30 minutes for culmination and inception of the next stage. Following the cleaning, mast cells arrive and release histamine which causes vasodilation; this opening of the blood vessels vastly increases the flow of fluid into the affected area and results in the inflammation for which this stage is named. This inflammation decreases the available capacity of the area and leads to increased amounts of pain and discoloration in and around the wound site. From vasoconstriction to dilation, the inflammatory phase may last between two days and two weeks (depending on the severity of the wound).

Following this somewhat preparatory stage, the proliferative phase marks the beginning of the actual healing process. Within this second stage, there are four mini steps that are crucial for the wound to close properly. Granulation is the first of these four steps. It is indicated by the body beginning to lay down different connective tissues like collagen; these tissues help fill the empty space or hole created by the affliction. The body, however, is not only constructed of connective tissue. Angiogenesis, the second of the four steps, is when the body embarks on the arduous process of growing new blood vessels. Intertwining networks of vessels are laid down, oft called capillary beds. These growing, weaving vessels give a new wound its distinctive pink coloration. The third stage, wound contraction, is the first stage in which the raw edges of the wound begin to adjoin to each other. The wound does not experience complete closure until the final stage of the four stages of proliferation—epithelization. Epithelial cells—or skin cells—move over the granulated tissue from the first step. The four stages of the proliferative phase can last anywhere from 3–21 days. The timeline is, once again, dependent on how poignant the wound is.

It is critical to be protective of a newly healed wound at the beginning of the third stage: maturation. The new skin is quite fragile and can easily reopen if too much stress is placed on it. The maturation stage can last up to two years as the scar forms and hardens. In some cases the scar will disappear with time, but in

others it's a permanent addendum to a person's body. Even once the scar has fully
(45) matured, scar tissue is only 80% as strong as skin, meaning it is prone to re-injury.

Several factors can influence the quality and timeliness of wound healing, many of which—circulation, chemical stress, temperature of the wound bed, amount of moisture in and around the wound, and age—are outside the control of the individual. The individual can control other factors, like nutrition, medication, and
(50) infection. Maintaining a well-balanced diet, consulting a doctor about medications, and keeping the wound site clean can all have a positive effect on wound closure and healing.

The Wound Healing Process

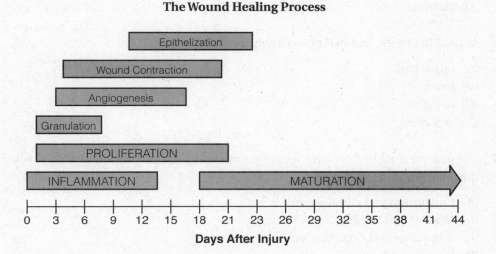

Days After Injury

1. What is the overall structure of the passage?

   (A) Chronological
   (B) Pro and con
   (C) Spatial
   (D) Persuasive

2. What is the primary purpose of the passage?

   (A) To highlight medical abnormalities
   (B) To argue in favor of a theory
   (C) To detail helpful information
   (D) To confront conventional wisdom

3. Which option gives the best evidence for the answer to the previous question?

   (A) Lines 1–2 ("Even . . . instantaneously")
   (B) Lines 4–6 ("Thus . . . aggravated")
   (C) Lines 46–49 ("many . . . individual")
   (D) Lines 50–52 ("Maintaining . . . healing")

4. What is the primary function of the sentence in lines 12–14 ("Phagocytes . . . matter")?

(A) To clarify a specialized term
(B) To explain the derivation of a word
(C) To highlight an irony
(D) To offer a solution to a health care predicament

5. As used in line 34, "raw" most closely means

(A) unprocessed.
(B) primal.
(C) uncooked.
(D) inflamed.

6. As used in line 40, "critical" most closely means

(A) important.
(B) harsh.
(C) negative.
(D) analytical.

7. The passage and the figure, respectively, portray the steps of wound healing in which of the following different ways?

(A) Concurrent and chronological
(B) Gradual and sudden
(C) Sequential and simultaneous
(D) Internal and external

8. If the author wished to extend the *x*-axis of the figure to portray the point at which a wound would nearly certainly be healed without extending the graph unnecessarily, which of the following would serve as the most logical final value for days?

(A) 10
(B) 100
(C) 1,000
(D) 10,000

9. Which option gives the best evidence for the answer to the previous question?

(A) Lines 15–17 ("Phagocytosis . . . vasodilation")
(B) Lines 24–27 ("Following . . . steps")
(C) Lines 36–39 ("Epithelial . . . wound is")
(D) Lines 41–43 ("The new . . . hardens")

Science: Synthetic Intermediates

It's fair to say that the world in which we live is made up of chemicals, though the cultural emphasis in recent years on natural or "organic" products has somewhat demonized this notion. "Chemophobia," in fact, is a term that has emerged
Line to describe the irrational fear of chemistry and chemical nomenclature. In gen-
(5) eral, individuals affected by chemophobia tend to view the precisely planned manipulation of molecular compounds with suspicion, and perceive products rendered by these means as both "unnatural" and inherently inferior to those derived through cruder avenues. In reality, nothing could be more natural than the intricate, multi-step reactions of organic chemistry. Life itself could not exist
(10) without a constant, dynamic stream of these complicated interactions, and very often the role of industrial chemists has not been to confound the processes we observe in nature, but merely to simplify and refine them.

Retrosynthetic analysis is a quintessential example of this task. Frequently, after isolating and identifying the structure of a valuable biochemical compound,
(15) a chemist is confronted with the problem of how to efficiently and effectively reproduce the compound by artificial means. More often than not, the biosynthetic pathways found *in vivo* employ a staggering number of highly specialized enzymes and enzymatic cofactors, and are utterly impractical for a laboratory setting. The task of the chemist, then, is to conceptually deconstruct the compound
(20) into successively simpler constituent pieces in such a way as will facilitate its synthesis through the smallest number of individual reactions, and yield an end product with the highest achievable degree of chemical purity.

It is necessary to remember that harvesting biochemical compounds directly from their natural sources is often not only costly, but more wasteful than artificial
(25) synthetic alternatives. Through careful retrosynthetic analysis, chemists can help us to meet the public demand for a product, and in certain cases spare the unnecessary destruction of scarce environmental resources. For instance, paclitaxel is a critically important component of the chemotherapy regimen for breast, ovarian, lung, and pancreatic cancers. Prior to the successful retrosynthesis of paclitaxel—
(30) a landmark achievement that took a team of chemists more than twenty years to complete—the only known source of this compound was from the bark of the Pacific Yew tree. Had not artificially synthesized paclitaxel become available when it did, many ecological biologists have projected that the tree would have soon been harvested to extinction.

(35) Still, some will contend that the true problem of retrosynthesis lies not in the end-products, but rather in the byproducts and novel synthetic intermediates required to artificially reproduce biochemical compounds. It must be acknowledged that this is indeed a valid concern. The design of stable synthetic intermediates not found in nature has at times led to unforeseen consequences.
(40) Methyldioxymethamphetamine, for example, is a dangerous and highly concerning drug of abuse among youth. It was first designed in 1912 by the Merck Corporation as a synthetic intermediate in the production of the hemostatic agent hydrastine, a compound traditionally extracted from a then-endangered perennial herb.

(45)   Even so, there have also been occasions in which the chemical ingenuity required to design new synthetic intermediates has unexpectedly yielded a useful product in and of itself. Aspartame, notably, was among the first non-disaccharide sweeteners to become available as a food additive. Aspartame itself is a derivative of two conjoined amino acids—specifically, aspartic acid, and phenylalanine—but
(50) it was originally created as synthetic intermediate in an attempt to make gastrin, a hormone produced by the parietal cells of the stomach that stimulates secretion of hydrochloric acid. Due perhaps to the chemophobic public perception of aspartame as an "unnatural" compound, for nearly half a century the sweetener has been a subject of ongoing controversy, and despite reliable evidence to the con-
(55) trary, it has been incorrectly associated with both cancer and Alzheimer's disease. Most likely, a segment of the population will never accept the safety of aspartame. It is perhaps worth reflecting, however, that sucrose and fructose—two sweeteners harvested naturally from plant sources—through their exacerbation of diabetes mellitus are known to contribute directly to the leading cause of blindness in the
(60) United States, to more than half of all non-traumatic amputations, and to our seventh leading cause of death.

1. What is the author's overall point about synthetic intermediates?

    (A) The dangers of their overuse need to be widely publicized.
    (B) It is time that industries begin using them.
    (C) Further study is needed before they should be used.
    (D) The pros of using them outweigh the cons.

2. Which of the following does the author acknowledge as a negative consequence of synthetic intermediates?

    (A) The production of addictive substances
    (B) Justifiable skepticism about industrial technology
    (C) Decreased professional opportunities for scientists
    (D) Overreliance on large corporations for economic growth

3. Which option gives the best evidence for the answer to the previous question?

    (A) Lines 4–8 ("In general . . . avenues")
    (B) Lines 19–22 ("The task . . . purity")
    (C) Lines 38–41 ("The design . . . youth")
    (D) Lines 41–44 ("It was . . . herb")

4. As used in line 15, "confronted" most closely means

    (A) defied.
    (B) presented.
    (C) tackled.
    (D) rebelled.

5. The second paragraph, lines 13–22, suggests that retrosynthetic analysis is most similar to which of these situations?

(A) A teacher oversimplifying the explanation of a difficult concept
(B) A car repair shop using nonbrand name parts to craft an inferior product
(C) Traveling to the same destination but by a less circuitous route
(D) A political scientist analyzing the pros and cons of a current controversy

6. As used in line 23, "harvesting" most closely means

(A) farming.
(B) deriving.
(C) building.
(D) deconstructing.

7. What is the author's view on natural substances relative to synthetic ones?

(A) Natural substances are inherently superior.
(B) Natural substances can sometimes be more harmful.
(C) Natural substances are more environmentally friendly.
(D) Natural substances are less scientifically linked to disease.

8. Which option gives the best evidence for the answer to the previous question?

(A) Lines 23–27 ("It is . . . resources")
(B) Lines 29–34 ("Prior . . . extinction")
(C) Lines 52–55 ("Due perhaps . . . disease")
(D) Lines 57–61 ("It is . . . death")

9. The author primarily uses lines 45–56 ("Even so . . . aspartame") to argue that

(A) accidental discoveries are typically more fruitful than sustained scientific research.
(B) food additives should be avoided so that healthier, more natural flavorings can be used.
(C) the culinary benefits of aspartame outweigh the negative health consequences from its use.
(D) fear about synthetic compounds simply due to their artificiality is unwarranted.

ANSWERS EXPLAINED

Fiction: *Almayer's Folly*

1. **(A)** The passage begins with an "unpleasant voice" interrupting Almayer's dreams of a "splendid future." This pattern is characteristic of the passage as a whole. Almayer imagines a life of wealth but is constantly reminded of his dull, wretched reality, making Choice (A) correct. Choices (B) and (C) are not evidenced by the passage; actually, Almayer demonstrates both cultural proficiency and assertiveness. Choice (D) wrongfully assumes that Almayer wishes to be grounded in the rational when actually he prefers his wishful fantasies.

2. **(C)** Almayer justifies his failure to secure gold by asserting that those successful few have secured it dishonestly. He, instead, hopes to gain wealth and power "through his own honest exertions." Therefore, his contrast is one of virtue and morality. Choice (A) is not evidenced, although he might, too, believe this. Choices (B) and (D) are not only without evidence but contrary to Almayer's character.

3. **(B)** Lines 10–13 tell us that Almayer contrasts himself to the dishonest procurers of gold, providing evidence for the previous question. Choice (A) provides detail of Almayer's response to the call but does not talk about financial circumstances. Choice (C) creates images of Almayer's fantasy of wealth and power but does not address his opinion toward those more financially successful. Choice (D) reports Almayer's thoughts about Dain and his belated return but, again, doesn't address the previous question.

4. **(A)** Here, Almayer reassures himself that his fantasies are within reach if only Dain returns. Likewise, Dain must return for "his own share." Since Dain is obviously connected to Almayer's desire for wealth, we can substitute "share" with "part of the money," making Choice (A) the correct option. It is nonsensical to think that Dain must return for his own "communication" or "disclosure." Although Choice (C) may be tempting, we cannot assume that Almayer is gifting something to Dain but, instead, that Dain has a stake in the gold per previous agreement.

5. **(C)** Throughout the passage, we can see that Almayer still wishes for wealth but is constantly in despair because of his grim, impoverished circumstances. In comparison to the hopeful Almayer who "left his home with a light heart . . . ready to conquer the world," we can infer that he is now more hopeless than earlier in life when he never doubted his success. Now, he hopes for wealth but certainly has doubts and dark thoughts, making Choices (A) and (B) incorrect. We have no evidence for Choice (D), particularly because Almayer still considers himself to be very honest.

6. **(D)** Lines 53–55 reference the beginning of Almayer's journey when he embarked optimistically and "ready to conquer the world." This is in stark contrast to his current internal turmoil that reveals his feelings of hopelessness and disempowerment. Choice (A) actually refers to how he imagines he will feel when he obtains wealth. Choice (B) might be tempting because it is close to the lines referenced in the above question and deals with Almayer's interest in the tree; however, it reveals nothing about his attitude earlier in life. Choice (C) does, in fact, deal with Almayer's early life but with the attitude of his mother rather than of himself.

7. **(B)** To approach this question, ask yourself what we know about Dain. We know that Almayer impatiently awaits Dain's return because his arrival is somehow tied to a prosperous future—a future "nearly within his reach." Therefore, we can reasonably conclude that Dain is somehow aiding Almayer in his financial goals. Although Choices (A), (C), and (D) could all be true, they are not evidenced and so could equally be false.

8. **(B)** Here, the powerless and formerly stuck tree is now "free" to drift into the sea. So we could substitute *unimpeded* or *no longer restrained*, which makes Choice (B) correct. Choice (A) conveys the idea that the tree has a feeling or an attitude of its own. Choice (C) is tempting but again evokes the idea that the tree has gained power rather than merely escaped to freedom. Choice (D) refers to free as a financial concept, as in *without cost*, which does not fit here.

9. **(D)** Look for evidence about what Almayer's parents believed. His father, a "subordinate," is delighted at his son's prospects for a better future. His mother is nostalgic for Amsterdam and her former "position." Thus, both parents are concerned with social mobility. Since this pattern coincides with Almayer's own refusal to accept a low social position, Choice (D) is the correct choice. Choices (A) and (C) are not evidenced in the passage. Choice (B) can be ruled out by Almayer's father's intolerant reaction to the natives.

Fiction: *Dubliners*

1. **(A)** The protagonist struggles to find adventure in routine. The appeal of the Wild West tales is that they allow escape from the order and monotony of everyday living, making Choice (A) the correct option. Our protagonist, although he reenacts battles between American Indians and cowboys with his friends, is not actually involved in warfare or racial intolerance. Choice (D) is incorrect because although excitement and idleness are details within the essay, they are not the focus.

2. **(B)** Joe Dillon is the character who introduces the narrator to the Wild West stories. He is described as fiercer than the other children, making Choice (B) correct. He doesn't ever allow the enemy side to win, so Choices (A) and (C) can be ruled out. No evidence is provided to support Choice (D).

3. **(B)** Here, everyone shows surprise and doubt when the boisterous and adventurous Joe Dillon pursues a career within the church. The text suggests that this "boring" choice is contrary to Joe's "excitable" nature. Hence, "skeptical" is a near synonym for "incredulous" in this instance. "Incredulous" means unwilling or unable to believe something. Even if you don't know the word's definition, no evidence is provided to suggest that people were disappointed or inspired by Joe's priestly ambitions; instead, they are merely doubtful or confused. "Enamored" means in love with or showing great admiration for and, likewise, does not fit.

4. **(C)** In lines 16–19, the narrator situates himself among those reluctant few who play "in fear" because they are "afraid to seem studious." "Studious" might be substituted with *bookish* or *overly academic*. So these lines specifically reference the narrator's desire to fit in, making Choice (C) the best answer. These lines never specifically mention a common enemy or prejudice among the children playing. Choice (B) seems tempting

but fails to capture the narrator's fear of seeming too scholarly among his more popular peers; he is not overly concerned with morality but, instead, desires inclusion.

5. **(D)** Approach this question by asking what we know about our narrator's attitude toward school. He calls his hours spent at school "sober" and begins to "hunger again for wild sensations" because the routine of school is "wearisome." So Choice (D) best describes his apathy toward schoolwork. Although other students might, the narrator doesn't express open rebellion. Choice (B) is too passive; we know the narrator longs to escape and participates in activities deemed inappropriate. Don't fall for Choice (C) just because "studious" is included in the answer. Instead, the narrator's concern over seeming too studious, or academically motivated, discourages any claim that he is ignorant of the school's expectations.

6. **(D)** In these lines, our narrator voices his discontent with the requirements of school and his attention toward other "wild sensations," supporting the idea that his interest toward his studies is only half-hearted. Choices (A), (B), and (C) are incorrect because they do not provide evidence of our character's willingness to follow and participate in school requirements.

7. **(A)** Here, Father Butler calls the American-Indian story "rubbish" and expresses disappointment that boys of high education would show interest in it. He insinuates that the students should take themselves more seriously and read loftier, canonical texts; hence, he appeals to their pride. He is not disgusted by learning but, instead, by what he believes is pointless learning. Likewise, he is not trying to inspire curiosity in the story but quell it. Choice (B) is a tempting answer because he hints that reading this sort of nonsense would make the students less worthy, but he doesn't actively try to convince them that they'll fail.

8. **(D)** If we look at the last paragraph, we see that the Wild West eventually became dull for the narrator as well. However, the stories did succeed in stirring within him a desire for "real adventures," which he concludes "must be sought abroad." So our narrator develops and ultimately seeks out something he didn't previously want, making Choice (D) the correct option. Because he doesn't particularly enjoy the Wild West stories, Choice (A) is not correct. His career choice is not mentioned at all, making Choice (B) incorrect. Although the character's adventures probably do lead to independence, he is concerned less with demanding parents and more with boring day-to-day studies.

9. **(D)** For proof of the narrator's character development, refer to lines 41–44 where we see how the Wild West stories eventually influence him. Choice (A) merely introduces how he became acquainted with the Wild West; Choice (B) describes Joe Dillon; Choice (C) discusses how Father Butler came to find a specific story among the boys.

Fiction: "The Fall of the House of Usher"

1. **(C)** This is a big-picture question. First, the narrator tells us about a time when he approached a particularly gloomy looking house, explains the events that led to his arrival, and then delivers a general sense of his relationship to the home's occupant. Choice (C) is the only option that fits this pattern, an impression of the house and then an analysis of how the narrator came to be there. The narrator does not suggest that he is solving a problem as in Choice (A). Although he may attempt to reconnect with an old

friend, the events of the passage take place before that. Choice (D) serves as a detail of the passage but not an overall description.

2. **(C)** Words like "dull," "dark," "dreary," "gloom," and "desolate" provide evidence to support Choice (C). Although the narrator is certainly aware, as in Choice (D), of how the home is in a destructive state, as mentioned in Choice (A), and that he feels both despair and melancholy, found in Choice (B), none of these describes the tone, or the general attitude of the paragraph. Since "foreboding" means a feeling that something bad will happen, it is the correct answer.

3. **(D)** Throughout the passage, the narrator is generally aware of the gloomy, ominous feeling the house gives off, but he cannot explain it. Even after trying to change his attitude and his view of the house, he cannot express why or how it has such power over him. So Choice (D) is correct. Choices (A) and (C) describe feelings opposite of uncertainty. Since it doesn't have to do with professional training, you can rule out Choice (B) as well.

4. **(C)** Lines 18–19 explicitly state the narrator's feeling that "[i]t was a mystery" and thus back up the answer for the previous question. Choices (A), (B), and (D) depict scenes in which the narrator feels unnerved but cannot shake his apprehension. As such, they evidence how the house makes the narrator feel but not how he understands his ability to assess that reaction.

5. **(C)** A good approach to this question is to replace "society" with a simple synonym like *company*, which is closest to Choice (C). The other choices all refer to the alternate meaning of society that refers to an aggregate of people living together under a system of order.

6. **(A)** From the passage, we know the narrator and his friend haven't seen each other for a long time. However, they were friends "in boyhood" and Roderick is ill, hoping to feel better in the presence of "his only personal friend." Thus, we can infer the narrator feels obligated, as in Choice (A), to submit to the request. His feelings of "sorrow" and "terror" are brought on by the house, not by his friend's letter. Choice (C) is too extreme since it implies that the narrator held a strong desire or yearning to visit his old friend.

7. **(C)** Here, the narrator states that "it was the apparent *heart*" of the letter, despite the odd request, that made him say yes. This provides sufficient evidence that the narrator feels a certain responsibility to his friend and yields the answer for the previous question. Choices (A) and (B) merely discuss his uneasiness upon approaching the house. Choice (D) gives the narrator's limited knowledge concerning Roderick's family history.

8. **(D)** Use context clues. Despite their intimacy, the narrator doesn't know much about his friend. So "reserve" must mean something like shyness or reticence, making Choice (D) the correct answer. Choice (B) is an antonym. On the other hand, neither greed nor preparedness means that Roderick is detached or unwilling to share much about himself.

9. **(B)** This is tough reading, but don't be intimidated; break it down. The family is peculiar, or odd; has a great interest in art, charity, and musical science; but is not enduring. In fact, the line of descent is direct and has always been so. Thus, there is only one descendant. We know that the family has a long history and that Roderick is the cur-

rent heir, ruling out Choices (A) and (D). The word "direct" implies that the inheritance has always been passed down from one to the next without any extra heirs, eliminating Choice (C).

Fiction: "Adventure"

1. **(A)** The question asks for the thematic focus, which can be summarized as two lovers whose circumstances bring together and then gradually apart. Thus, love is fleeting, transient, or temporary, making Choice (A) the correct answer. Although love may be beautiful or wholesome more generally speaking, this passage focuses on its impermanence. Choice (D) is misleading because the two characters do not wish to abuse love but, instead, drift apart despite their good intentions.

2. **(A)** We know from lines 1–2 that George is only a boy when Alice is twenty-seven. Since her affair with Ned began when she was sixteen, eleven years have passed. If George is a small boy now, we can reasonably assume that eleven years ago, he was unborn. Choices (C) and (D) would make him much older than he is. Although Choice (B) might be tempting, that would make George eighteen at the time of this passage, not a boy.

3. **(C)** The imagery in lines 4–7 reveals a lot about Alice as an adult. She is "stooped" and "quiet," despite the "ferment" brewing under her surface. Synonyms of *ferment* include tumult, turmoil, and disquiet, so "unsettled" is the correct answer. Although she may be fond of Ned, their unresolved love affair has taken its toll on her—she still lives with her mother and there is no evidence to suggest she has since moved on to another lover. Choice (B) is characteristic of Ned, not Alice. The word "sedate," which means calm and peaceful, describes Alice's exterior but remains in contrast to her restless interior.

4. **(B)** As stated above, the description of the adult Alice occurs in the first two paragraphs, eliminating Choices (C) and (D), which describe instances of Alice's teenage years. When deciding between Choices (A) and (B), you should focus on the words "beneath a placid exterior a continual ferment went on." Even if you don't know what "ferment" means, you can assume that it is in contrast to her placid, quiet exterior. Choice (A), in contrast, deals more with her physical appearance and not her attitude.

5. **(D)** Here, Ned is "puzzled" but "touched." He had desired Alice only physically, but here "changed his mind" and became more emotionally attached to her. So if you substitute a word or words for "touched," you might use *stirred emotionally* or "moved" as in Choice (D). Choice (A) refers to touching someone physically in a violent manner. Choice (B) can be used as a verb meaning to hurry or as a feeling of disappointment as in *dashed hopes*; neither fits here. Choice (C) is irrelevant since it might mean to correspond or resemble another, or to be equal to something in quality or strength.

6. **(A)** The evidence for this question is scattered throughout the essay. Alice is both willing to move to a new city and to live unmarried with Ned. For her, their being together is most important. Ned is "puzzled," or confused, by her devotion. Despite his intention to "protect and care" for Alice, he is unwilling to take her with him, becomes interested in other women, and very nearly forgets her altogether. Choices (B), (C), and (D) better describe Ned than Alice.

7. **(C)** Lines 26–27 reveal much about both Alice's and Ned's feelings. He is confused but pleased by Alice's devotion. A good approach to this question is to eliminate the other answer choices. Choice (A) gives us only facts about Alice, not anything about their attitudes toward the affair itself. Choice (B) gives us information about Alice's infatuation but nothing about Ned's feelings. Choice (D), like Choice (A), reports facts but reveals little about the couple's inward emotions. Choose Choice (C) because it's the only choice that provides evidence of how both lovers feel toward one another.

8. **(A)** Ned, sad about leaving his home and his sweetheart, forgets his "resolutions" concerning Alice. Before this, he has refused to live with her unmarried and, instead, resolves to return to care for her in more traditionally appropriate ways. Instead, he forgets that plan. The couple, ignited by emotions, becomes lovers and makes further promises that are likewise disregarded. Thus, Choice (A) is the correct option. It is not appropriate to say he forgot his "purposes" or "solutions." Choice (D) means requests rather than pledges.

9. **(B)** Lines 41–42 consist of Ned's promise to always be with Alice. Since he later glosses over this commitment to Alice, it is appropriate to infer that he was disingenuous, misleading, or insincere. Choice (A) is an extreme that is ultimately unfair to Ned, who attempts, somewhat halfheartedly, to keep the love alive through his letters. Choice (C) indicates that he committed himself to Alice under great pressure or force, which is untrue. Choice (D) is another extreme that lacks evidence; later, he casually neglects Alice for present, temporary amusements.

Fiction: *Oliver Twist*

1. **(D)** This question asks about the financial interests of the funeral business, which in this passage becomes quite prosperous when the measles breaks out and claims a multitude of lives. Hence, the undertaker makes money when people die, making his financial situation very much at odds with the general wishes of people (which of course do not include burying their loved ones). Choice (B) incorrectly links the profits of undertakers with how often people talk about them at dinner. Choice (C) assumes political powers want people dead, which is not evidenced in the passage. Choice (A), albeit tempting, is incorrect because many professions are subject to "social patterns," such as social class and welfare.

2. **(C)** Use context clues here. The "sickly season" increases "commercial" business so that even the undertaker's hopeful expectations are exceeded. "Sanguine" means optimistic in bad situations. "Trivial" means unimportant, and "ancient" means old or belonging to the distant past. Choice (B) implies that the undertaker's hopes were concerned with material gains rather than spiritual existence, which is certainly true. However, it is more accurate to say his hopes were high or "optimistic" than to suggest the author means the undertaker's hopes were in contrast to spiritual endeavors.

3. **(C)** Reword this question. "What qualities does Oliver seem to have that Noah does not?" We know Oliver is dedicated and attentive to his work; his efforts are rewarded in quick advancement and favor. We also know he usually submits willingly to Noah's ill-treatment. Of Noah, we know only that he acts jealously and spitefully, often trying to upset Oliver's cool indifference with insults and personal taunts. Thus, we can infer

Oliver is normally even-tempered in comparison to Noah's impetuous cruelty. We have no evidence to support Choices (A), (B), or (D).

4. **(D)** In lines 53–54, Oliver ignores Noah's incessant taunts and provocations, providing support for the distinction in their respective characters. Choice (A) provides proof of the undertaker's booming business. Choice (B) discusses the differences between the reactions of people when at their loved ones' funerals and when at home. Choice (C) gives us an idea of how people other than Noah treat Oliver.

5. **(B)** Oliver reacts to death quite apathetically; he doesn't seem to show any emotion or feeling either way except in the instance of his own mother. Similarly, he admires those who remain "composed." So look for the answer that sounds dispassionate or indifferent. Choices (A), (C), and (D) all suggest a strong showing of emotion. Choice (B) is the only answer that implies that Oliver respects those who endure death without extended or unnecessary emotional reaction.

6. **(C)** Here we are looking for lines that prove that Oliver respects stoicism, or an endurance without emotion. Choice (C) gives evidence of Oliver's "great admiration" for those who "recovered almost as soon as they reached home." Choice (A) tells us why the undertaker's business is doing so well financially, namely the spread of the measles. Choice (B) ends at line 16 and so discusses an emotional reaction to death but never gets to the part that Oliver respects, the "content" that comes soon after. Finally, Choice (D) merely depicts Oliver's reaction, or lack thereof, to Noah's cruelty.

7. **(A)** Ask yourself not what this paragraph says but what it does. Before this, we have been hearing about Oliver's experience under Mr. Sowerberry. After this, we move into the particular incident where Noah finally elicits a reaction out of Oliver. This paragraph, then, moves from the broad description of experience to a particular event that proves significant for Oliver, making Choice (A) correct. The characters are already introduced, ruling out Choice (B). Be careful to avoid Choice (C): the actual description of the event comes later. This paragraph just tells us we are now moving to that event. Choice (D) wrongfully assumes the reader would oppose or take issue with something that was just said.

8. **(B)** Here, the important act despite its trivial appearance "produced a most material change." We could substitute *significant* or *substantial* for "material," making Choice (B) the correct answer. Choices (A) and (C) refer to other definitions of "material." Choice (D) wrongly implies that the change itself has feeling and thinks the worst will happen.

9. **(A)** Noah tries everything to upset Oliver and finally succeeds by getting very personal—by mentioning Oliver's dead mother. Hence, Noah's insults get more and more vindictive until Oliver finally reacts. Choicees (B) and (D) both imply that Noah is not unnecessarily cruel to Oliver, which we know to be untrue. Choice (C) is incorrect because the passage doesn't evidence "physical" abuse, only verbal.

Great Global Conversation: Jefferson

1. **(A)** Jefferson explains the transition from monarchy to republic as one as natural and easy as "throwing off an old and putting on a new suit of clothes." Hence, Choice (A)

is correct. Choices (B) and (C) describe situations contradictory to the one Jefferson presents. Choice (D) is incorrect because of the word "trivial," which means insignificant or inconsequential.

2. **(B)** Jefferson prefers the first of his two proposals, "Free trade by alliance with some naval power." He argues that if the British Court were willing, an alliance "might . . . be approved by our people." Hence, Jefferson suggests that the people would see the benefits of economic trade with the British, as in Choice (B). Choices (A) and (D) don't express the idea of free trade. Choice (C) does not work because the passage does not focus on the desire of the American people as a whole for religious integration with the British.

3. **(C)** Lines 19–22 supply Jefferson's direct proposal that a free trade alliance with Britain will benefit both countries and be generally supported by the American people. Choice (A) discusses Virginia's smooth transition into a republic. Choice (B) is Jefferson's proposal but fails to address how the American people might react. Choice (D) expresses Jefferson's desire to be serving with Benjamin Franklin, for whom he obviously has great respect.

4. **(A)** Read the sentence before looking at the answer choices. You might substitute "apprehend" with *anticipate* or *think* since Jefferson is proposing his ideas. Thus, Choice (A) is correct. Choices (B) and (C) refer to the other meaning of "apprehend," as in arresting someone for an offense or crime. Choice (D) implies creation rather than opinion.

5. **(A)** Check the sentence before this one. Jefferson says free trade with an alliance is preferable because it aligns with the American people's "habits and wishes." Here, he implies that Americans would like to have access to imports from abroad rather than making everything themselves. This coincides with Choice (A) but contradicts Choices (B) and (C). Choice (D) brings up the American Revolution. Although it seems plausible that Americans do not desire further conflict, that is not the subject of these lines.

6. **(B)** The meaning of his second letter concerns "a fleet of the enemy's ships" that will easily have access to America's shores "[s]hould any more be added to them." Hence, Jefferson worries that American defenses will fail if more British ships arrive, as in Choice (B). Choice (C) says the opposite. Choice (D) is wrongly concerned with the "open battlefield." Although Choice (A) is tempting, it is too extreme. Certainly, Jefferson believes American defenses can resist. However, he also believes that they will be quickly overcome if the situation gets any worse.

7. **(C)** Here, the "want of arms" inhibits America from bringing the amount of forces necessary to defeat the British fleet. So Jefferson means that there is a continual need or demand for limited military power. It is the "lack" of arms that prevents appropriate defense operations. If America had an abundance of military powers, as in Choice (B), this would not be an issue. Since this is dealing with the availability of military forces, "danger" is not an appropriate choice. Choice (A) is appealing because Jefferson does desire more forces. However, read the sentence with "desire" in place before you choose it. It is not the desire for arms itself that prevents adequate defense but, instead, that the desire cannot be fulfilled.

8. **(D)** The tone, or overall feel/attitude, of the passages can be described as serious, official, and respectful. Choice (D) best describes these feelings since "formality" refers to a stateliness and "deference" implies a respectfulness. Jefferson offers ideas of his own,

rather than submitting himself as subservient like in Choice (A). Although Jefferson may be anxious because of the severity of his letters, he is far from aggressive. Practical could readily describe Jefferson's tone, but avarice, or greed, does not.

9. **(C)** First, think about what the question is asking. "Foresight" means that Jefferson was able to predict what might happen. So we are looking in the first passage for a prediction that comes true or could come true according to the second passage. Choice (C) is the only choice in which Jefferson anticipates America's vulnerability at its coasts, which is the topic of the second passage.

10. **(C)** Notice the word "respective" in the question, meaning that these answers have to go in order: the first word has to describe the first passage and the second should apply to Passage 2. In the first passage, Jefferson proposes ideas about how to move forward economically. In the second, he plans for military engagement. Choice (A) has these switched, so eliminate it. Jefferson never shows evidence of being overly concerned with his personal issues, as in Choice (B). The first passage is far from "pedestrian," or dull and unconcerned.

Great Global Conversation: Obama Inaugurals

1. **(A)** For questions about tone, think of the overall attitude of the passage. President Obama's tone can be described as determined, which is a synonym of "resolute." He demonstrates purpose, hope, and optimism despite difficult circumstances, eliminating Choices (B) and (C). Choice (D) means impossible to satisfy or uncontrollable, so it is inaccurate.

2. **(C)** Here, Obama contrasts "prosperity and the still waters of peace" with "gathering clouds and raging storms." So he juxtaposes calm with turmoil, making Choice (C) correct. It is not accurate to describe waters of peace as "contrast"; instead, they are merely being contrasted to the present disorder. Choice (A) refers more to a state of inaction. Choice (B) suggests a negative connotation, which would be illogical since it is associated with a lack of war.

3. **(D)** This is a purpose question, so look for the main idea—*what it does* rather than the details of the paragraph. Generally, Obama outlines the current crisis of the nation in its many forms from war to economics to education. Hence, Choice (D) is correct. Choice (A) is incorrect because that is the claim he is supporting, not refuting. Choice (B) is too extreme since Obama is optimistic despite his practical outlook on the current crisis. The flaw in Choice (C) is "statistics," which implies data, numbers, and other empirical evidence. Perhaps these claims can be validated by statistics, but they are not the statistics themselves.

4. **(D)** This question asks what fear parents have that was addressed or quelled by Obama's first inauguration speech. We know that Obama believes the nation's circumstance has resulted in expensive health care and failing schools—both of which certainly affect children. However, the fear is referenced in lines 20–23: the overall decline of America. Although Choices (A) and (C) are possible implications of this larger worry, Choice (D) best summarizes the general fear that America is going downhill. Choice (B) is a minor detail mentioned earlier as a contributor to the current situation.

5. **(D)** In these lines, Obama specifically addresses the broad fear of the nation's decline, which supports the answer to the previous question. Choice (A) provides an economic example of the crisis. Choice (B) gives health care, education, and environmental examples. Choice (C) is a general statement transitioning from the hard evidence to the more general fear. However, Choices (A), (B), and (C) all fail to provide direct evidence of the fear itself.

6. **(A)** President Obama insists on basic human rights but shows that they have always had to be worked for, making Choice (A) correct. Choice (B) wrongly assumes everyone experiences freedom. Choice (C) argues that those rights are not natural, a direct contradiction of Obama's assertion. Choice (D) is counterintuitive, making the claim that somehow Americans are unworthy of basic human rights.

7. **(B)** Beginning in line 40, President Obama specifically states that those unalienable rights laid out in America's founding documents are obvious but not given without intervention or action. This provides direct evidence for the answer to the previous question. Choice (A) quotes the Declaration of Independence but does not include Obama's insight. Choice (C) merely states the intentions of the founding fathers. Choice (D) discusses broad ideals embodied by American government and way of life.

8. **(A)** Here, the president addresses broad beliefs, stating that we do not believe "all society's ills can be cured through government." So we could substitute *fixed* quite easily. Choice (A) closely resembles this substitution and is the correct answer. Choice (D) means to make worse, an antonym of what we want. Choices (B) and (C) refer to other meanings of cure, as in to relieve symptoms and to preserve meat.

9. **(C)** The question asks about the introductions, so look closely at the beginning of each passage. In both instances, Obama discusses inauguration in broader terms by referring to the presidents who served before him. Hence, Choice (C) makes the most sense here. Choices (A) and (B) are perhaps strategies used within the speeches but not specifically in the introduction. Choice (D) is utilized only in Passage 2; Passage 1 addresses all citizens broadly.

10. **(B)** Break up this question and paraphrase it. First, we need to look at lines 31–38. Then we need to find similar lines in the first passage. Here, Obama discusses the historical context of the Presidential Address and what it means to Americans, their values, and their founding documents. That strategy closely resembles the second paragraph of the first passage, making Choice (B) correct. Choice (A) includes President Obama's expressions of thanks. Choice (C) discloses what Obama sees as the general fear of Americans. Choice (D) transitions into the hope that the problems America faces will be addressed.

Great Global Conversation: Frederick Douglass

1. **(B)** Notice the question asks for a general point, or main idea, from the first paragraph. In these lines, Douglass discusses his broad autobiographical information, his birthplace and age, emphasizing the obscurity about his age. The rest of the paragraph expresses that this ignorance is commonplace among slaves. Choice (A) wrongly assumes celebration, which is not mentioned here. Choice (C) is not evidenced; "kind" masters are referenced as those who give their slaves permission to visit another plantation—an

allowance that is far from overcoming prejudice. Math education, although conceivable as a detail, is not the main point of the first paragraph, eliminating Choice (D).

2. **(C)** In lines 7–9, Douglass validates his distress at not having access to his own basic personal information. If you replace "want" with *absence*, you can see that Choice (C) is appropriate. Although Choice (A) might be tempting, read the sentence with *obstacle* substituted for "want." You'll quickly see that the desire for information is not what produced unhappiness but that the need was denied. It isn't appropriate to say the "obstacle" or "command" of information produced unhappiness.

3. **(B)** What the author does know about himself comes from others' conversations or stories, making Choice (B) correct. We know Douglass didn't speak much with his mother, and she died while he was very young. Choice (C) is incorrect because this evidence was purposefully denied him. Choice (D) is not discussed in the passage.

4. **(B)** To approach this question, look for lines in which Douglass receives information about his past through others, as in Choice (B). Choice (A) evidences the master's tendency to refuse to answer questions concerning a slave's past. Choice (C) explains why it was especially tough for Douglass's mother to visit him. Choice (D) gives the only example of Douglass's history that he seems to remember for himself.

5. **(B)** In these lines, Douglass describes the effects of taking mothers from their children under institutionalized slavery. He concludes that this tendency impeded the child's affection and curtailed the mother's nurturing. Hence, Choice (B) is correct. Although Douglass may have wished for a better relationship with his mother, he seems quite fond of, rather than disappointed by, her commitment to seeing him whenever possible. Choice (C) is appealing, but Douglass says himself that he can't be sure why. He doesn't discuss his intellectual development, eliminating Choice (D).

6. **(D)** Douglass is unsure of who his father is, so Choice (D) is correct. Although Douglass admits that a rumor spread that his master was his father, the rumor was never confirmed. So Douglass does not suggest that he actually met his father. Since this information is completely withheld from him, we cannot assume Choices (A), (B), or (C).

7. **(A)** Douglass's mother sneaks out at night, walks 12 miles to visit him, and then has to make the journey again before morning so she can work in the fields all day. Her priorities are not economic as in Choice (B). Although 12 miles is quite a bit to walk, her presence proves that it is not insurmountable, making Choice (C) incorrect. Choice (D) is never mentioned.

8. **(B)** Beginning in line 35, we learn about the circumstances under which Douglass's mother visits him, risking "a whipping" if not back "in the field at sunrise." Hence, these lines provide direct evidence for the previous question. Choices (A), (C), and (D) tell us briefly about Douglass's relationship with his mother but not why she was forced to visit only at night.

9. **(A)** Here, Douglass describes his numbness at the news of his mother's death. "Tidings" means news or information, making Choice (A) correct. Although Choices (B) and (C) don't describe this same idea of hearing about her death, Choice (D) might tempt you. Just remember that it's inaccurate to say Douglass would receive the "causes" of her death.

Great Global Conversation: Emerson and Arnold

1. **(D)** In the first passage, Emerson is concerned with why the current age is retrospective, or always looking back into the past. He advocates, instead, for "a poetry and philosophy of insight" rather than relying on traditional discourses. Similarly, he says we should "demand our own works" and interrogate what is natural. Hence, he raises the question of why we rely on what others have said instead of having our own experiences and creating our own theories, making Choice (D) correct. He is not concerned with feuds or inconsistencies between separate fields as in Choices (A), (B), and (C).

2. **(A)** Here, Emerson argues that past generations "beheld God and nature face to face" while the current generation experiences them only through the words and records of those who have come before. So "original" means unique or special, making Choice (A) correct. We can rule out Choices (B) and (C) because they mean the same thing, both suggesting that the new ways be somehow groundbreaking. Choice (D) is wrong because Emerson does not suggest that the relationship be ceremonial in any way.

3. **(A)** Emerson believes in "the perfection of the creation so far," arguing that man can "satisfy" all "curiosity." So Emerson's attitude is optimistic that as long as we pose questions, we can intelligently and coherently discover answers. Choice (B) is the opposite. Although Emerson's argument is abstract, or existing through ideas and theoretical concepts, this doesn't describe his attitude toward human understanding. Similarly, historicism is the theory that culture is determined by history. This is what Emerson desires to change. Again, it is not accurate in describing his attitude toward human understanding.

4. **(B)** These lines summarize Emerson's belief that all questions can be answered, all curiosities can be satisfied, and thus provide evidence that he is optimistic that the current generation can come to their own understanding of the human experience. Choice (A) is merely where Emerson's question is posed. Choice (C) suggests that the current generation must look for its own answers but does not explicitly reveal his attitude toward the possibility of accomplishing this task. Choice (D) simply states what Emerson believes is the objective of science.

5. **(C)** Of Plato, Arnold says that "[o]ne cannot refuse to admire the artist," yet his notions are "primitive," making Choice (C) correct. Plato, who held disdain for the man who worked rather than spent all his time thinking and speculating, is viewed as neither practical nor applicable, ruling out Choices (A) and (D). Since Arnold summarizes Plato's beliefs, it is not accurate to call them "indecipherable" as in Choice (B).

6. **(C)** Here, Plato's ideas are called "primitive" based on a time when society was categorized into warriors, priests, and slaves. Further, his ideas are "admirable" because the first sentence of the selection states that one "cannot refuse to admire the artist who draws these pictures." Choices (A) and (B) both explain Plato's argument. Choice (D) does not focus on what Arnold thinks of Plato's ideas.

7. **(B)** This word is used in Plato's description of the "working lawyer" who is bonded, "bent and broken . . . without a particle of soundness in him." A good approach to this question is to substitute a word like *health*. The example paints the picture of a man "smart and clever" who has not been able to meet his potential because of the strains of life, ruling out Choice (C). It is inaccurate to say somebody doesn't have "safety" in them. The word "eloquence" means being articulate or expressive. Plato does not think

the lawyer cannot be persuasive but, instead, that the lawyer doesn't have the time or strength to devote to his own refinement.

8. **(C)** Simply put, Plato is scornful of all working professions. So look for an answer that says something to the effect of labor detracting from one's self-worth. That is Choice (C). Choices (A) and (D) favor those who work or service others and so contradict Plato's belief. Choice (B) is too extreme since Plato seems to pity the "bent and broken" victims of the labor force.

9. **(B)** To approach this question, think of what we know Emerson and Plato value. Emerson values independent thinking, observing, and asking of questions in the first passage. Emerson is briefly mentioned in the second paragraph as advocating for working professionals since they are "the modern majority." Plato, on the other hand, believes any kind of organized work or profession detracts from one's strength and intellectual potential. Hence, Choice (B) is correct. Plato never advocates for mathematical reasoning or industrial engineering, eliminating Choices (C) and (D). Although Choice (A) is tempting, recall that religious revelation is only one detail of Emerson's argument and that Plato is not focused on the sciences but on the pursuit of knowledge apart from the burden of a job.

10. **(D)** Know what you are looking for by paraphrasing this question. We want to find what Emerson said that would explicitly offend Plato. Choice (D) is correct because here Emerson voices a common belief that "speculative men," or men like Plato who spend their time thinking, are "unsound and frivolous." Choices (A), (B), and (C) consist of Emerson's argument that the current generation should seek its own knowledge, an idea with which Plato would most likely agree.

Great Global Conversation: *The Souls of Black Folk*

1. **(A)** This passage introduces sorrow songs and their impact on the writer, making Choice (A) the correct answer. The passage in its entirety does reference disagreement, specific events, and personal stories but only as details rather than as the main purpose.

2. **(C)** To approach this question, look for what Du Bois says about American creativity. Specifically, he states America has given little beauty to the world (aside from the slave songs, which are the exception to him), instead expressing itself in "vigor and ingenuity." So general American creativity aligns with Choice (C). Choices (A), (B), and (D) might describe aspects of the slave songs, but again, these are the exception to "general American creativity."

3. **(B)** Lines 13–14 remark on America's general contribution to the world and thus evidence what Du Bois sees as its attention to "vigor" (strength and determination) and "ingenuity" (inventiveness and insight) over beauty. Choice (A) illustrates the impact the sorrow songs had on Du Bois. Choice (C) discusses how some songs were lost or forgotten. Choice (D) concludes Du Bois's ideas on the lasting effect and significance of the songs.

4. **(B)** Here Du Bois claims that the slave songs are "the sole American music," remaining "the singular spiritual heritage of the nation." Try to substitute a synonym for "singular." You might pick *unique* or *remarkable*. Surely, Du Bois isn't saying they are the only heri-

tage out there but, instead, that they are truly definitive of the nation and exceptional in their expression of the national history. Choices (A) and (D) imply isolation and distance. Choice (C) evokes a negative connotation meaning strange or peculiar.

5. **(C)** A good approach to this question is process of elimination. Du Bois says he is not concerned with technical aspects of the songs, so get rid of Choice (A). Although he undeniably believes they are worthy of study, the songs themselves are not scholarly in meaning, making Choice (B) incorrect. You can eliminate Choice (D) because although some meaning is lost through the distance of time and language, Du Bois does understand the songs and believes they can tell us a lot. He believes they impact us (consequential) and give an articulate message (eloquent), making Choice (C) correct.

6. **(C)** These lines specifically reference Du Bois's claim that the songs prove particularly important because they "are the articulate message of the slave to the world." Thus, they provide evidence that the sorrow songs are both consequential and eloquent, the correct answer to the previous question. Choices (A) and (B) do not indicate the meaning of the songs but merely how the songs have been forgotten and misunderstood. Choice (D) doesn't specifically reference what Du Bois sees as the meaning of the songs (that comes in the following lines); instead, these lines evidence the limits to society's message that slavery was mostly carefree for the enslaved.

7. **(D)** We are looking for the initial reaction to the slave songs of the Sea Islands. Despite people like Higginson and McKim, "the world listened only half credulously" at first. So look for an answer that says the songs were largely ignored initially. Choices (A) and (C) suggest that the songs were given much more attention than is evidenced in the passage. Choice (B) is too extreme since the songs weren't treated seriously.

8. **(B)** The question asks who might have declared "that life was joyous to the black slave" despite proof in the sorrow songs that it was not. Since the passage talks about slavery as something of the past, Choices (A) and (C) can be ruled out—also consider that the slaves told a very different story in their songs. The only musicians referenced in the passage are the Jubilee Singers who repeated and ingrained the sorrow songs into the public imagination, ruling out Choice (D). Hence, it is most likely that "they" refers broadly to society or the general public.

9. **(B)** Use the other adjectives to make sense of this use of "misty." The music tells of "unvoiced" longing and "hidden" ways. So think *unclear* or *indistinct*, which are closest to "cloudy." Choices (A), (C), and (D) evoke images nearer to evaporation or sticky humidity.

Social Studies: Russian Depopulation

1. **(C)** The author presents several contributing factors to the population problem and ends on a less than hopeful note that the population will continue to decline if great changes are not made. Thus Choice (C) makes the most sense here. Choice (A) might tempt you, but "manageable" implies that the problem could be taken care of without difficulty, which is not the author's opinion. Since Russia seems to be an aberration rather than the norm, we can rule out Choice (B). "Nebulous" means unclear, but the author seems to believe he knows the factors behind the decline in population, which eliminates Choice (D).

2. **(A)** In the very first paragraph, the author states that Russia faces "the biggest long-term problem" and lists the many factors influencing the problem. This provides direct evidence for the previous question, making Choice (A) correct. Choice (B) supports the idea that Russia is an anomaly. Choices (C) and (D) discuss the author's opinions regarding Russian family values. Only Choice (A) gives evidence of the author's overall attitude toward the issue.

3. **(D)** This is a purpose question. Ask yourself what the author is doing in these lines. These lines compare Russia to less-developed countries, illustrating how life expectancy alone cannot explain Russia's decline in population. Instead, Russia is combatting a more complex problem where life expectancy and birth rates are simultaneously low. These lines show how we need more than one number to evaluate Russia's situation effectively, making Choice (D) correct. We are given precise data, so Choice (A) doesn't work. These lines actually contradict Choice (B). Be careful with Choice (C); we are examining demographics, not economics.

4. **(B)** "Fairly" can be substituted with *comparably* here. So Choice (B) is the correct choice. The idea is that the expectancy can be considered high in relation to less-developed countries. Choice (A) wrongly assumes we are using morals as judgment measures. Choice (C) inaccurately equates the expectancy rates. Choice (D) would mean that we are looking at a sole figure rather than comparing multiple figures.

5. **(B)** This line refers to fathers who are often absent, or "uninvolved," in the raising of their children. We cannot assume the fathers are in jail, deceased, or geographically distant.

6. **(B)** The author sees Putin's solution as limited because it "fails to see the underlying causes" and instead focuses on "economic programs." Choices (A) and (C) contradict this view. Choice (D) assumes too much; although the article references social programs, it does not include details.

7. **(C)** We are looking for two things here. First, we want a solution that would increase Russia's population. Second, we want something that was not considered in the passage. Hence, Choice (C) is correct. Choices (B) and (D) were both mentioned by the author. Choice (A) wouldn't actually change the population at all.

8. **(A)** This question has two parts. First, decide what the author offered as advice. The author argues that the mindset of Russians has to change. She identifies the causes as lack of family support and lack of desire for children. So if those two things changed to increase the population, Russians would have more children. Hence, the new figure would show an increase in the youth population. Choice (A) accurately describes that change. Choice (B) wrongly implies that the author suggests a solution that extends life expectancy. Choices (C) and (D), by emphasizing other subsections of the population, both fail to account for the rise in births that the author ultimately advocates for.

9. **(A)** The question asks for the difference in Russia's male and female elderly populations. We know from the passage that women live much longer than men in Russia. Hence, their ages will diverge more. Choice (D) is nonsensical, claiming different values for the same numbers. Choices (B) and (C) don't account for the tendency for elderly women to live longer than elderly men.

10. **(A)** Look for the lines that indicate the gap in life expectancy between males and females in Russia. Since that occurs around lines 6–10, Choice (A) is correct. Choice (B) explains some causes of the low male life expectancy. Choice (C) transitions into birth rates. Choice (D) examines the inconsistencies between demographic data and supposed family values.

Social Studies: The Emu War

1. **(D)** The question is asking what the first paragraph *does*. That paragraph discusses the butterfly effect generally before closing in on a particular instance between British veterans and emus in Western Australia. So Choice (D) is correct. This paragraph is concerned with introducing the topic in a creative way, not in demonstrating a decision (which comes much later in the passage) or countering objections. Choice (C) is incorrect because the first paragraph does not utilize a personal story.

2. **(A)** We know that the military initially thought they could easily handle the emus, but they failed miserably, making Choice (A) correct. The author does not suggest that it requires extraordinary bravery to face flightless birds, ruling out Choice (B). Choice (C) is actually the lesson learned from the military's overconfidence: because it was particularly presumptuous, the military learned a lesson in modesty. Choice (D) means excessively enthusiastic or extreme, which is not accurate here.

3. **(C)** These lines specifically state that the troops underestimated the emus and failed to accomplish their mission. Hence, they give direct support for the previous question. Choice (A) introduces the event but doesn't reveal the military mindset toward the emus. Choice (B) explains the damage inflicted by the emus. Choice (D) affirms the major's failure but, again, doesn't give evidence of his initial attitude.

4. **(B)** Here, the veterans are encouraged to participate in farming. Choice (B) sounds most like that. Choice (A) inaccurately implies that the veterans should *grab* farming. Choice (C) is wrong because no evidence is given that the veterans had to study farming first; instead, they are involved in actual farming. Of course, the veterans were not inventing or creating farming for the first time, making Choice (D) incorrect.

5. **(B)** It might be helpful to paraphrase this question. *What changed between the ineffective and the effective raids on the emus?* The passage attributes Major Meredith's minimal success his second time around to "his previous experience." Later, the locals succeed because they are "well equipped and knowledgeable." So Choice (B) is the correct answer. No evidence indicates that the major or the locals receive further training, academic or military. Choice (D) inappropriately implies that the media was somehow responsible for the more successful onslaughts.

6. **(D)** These lines state that the bounty system—a measure that prevented government involvement—worked well because the locals were better able to hunt the emus. Thus, we can infer that their first-hand experience gave them an advantage. Choice (A) states only that government aid was requested. Choice (B) references the media's involvement but, of course, does not connect the media with the successful fight against the emu population. Choice (C) includes the lines where the bounty system is explained, but fails to explain why it was successful. So Choice (D) is the only answer that gives evidence as to what attributed to the effective attacks on the emus.

7. **(C)** Why might the author choose to use quotation marks here? You might be thinking for dramatic effect. The usage of "war" in this context is comical because a military force is being called in to fight birds, and the birds are ironically winning. So these terms usually mean something very different in warfare. Hence, Choice (C) is correct. The author is not citing quotations or research. This event is actually quite trivial in the global context of war. Choice (D) is tempting but implies that the author is disputing facts, whereas he/ she is actually calling attention to the absurdity of equating a fowl hunt to true warfare.

8. **(A)** To approach this question, use context clues and substitute your own synonym. The successful resistance of the emus, though humorous, was actually harmful to the veterans' already dangerously uncertain situation. Choice (A) sounds most like *uncertain* or *unpredictable*. Choice (B) is too extreme because it implies a submission to fate, but the veterans/farmers are not merely resigned to fail. Choice (C) just means that the situation is related to living organisms. Choice (D) means cultivated in the sense of being well-traveled.

9. **(C)** This question focuses on what the figure can help explain. So first ask what the figure does. It gives a general timeline of the war very similar to the ones constructed to outline the battles of extended warfare. Then ask which of these choices discusses the varied events of the so-called war. Choice (C) specifically mentions the engagements of the war, and so it is correct. Choice (A) just tells who was assigned to the task. Choice (B) describes what the forces took for the first engagement. Choice (D) again describes one event but doesn't reference several like (C) does.

10. **(A)** From the figure, we can see that the forces were generally ineffective at first, improved with time, and then became particularly efficient by December. Choice (A) accurately accounts for this gradual increase in efficiency. Choices (B) and (C) do not reflect this improvement, and Choice (D) inaccurately implies that we cannot find a general pattern.

Science: Caffeine

1. **(C)** Passage 1 examines how caffeine works in the body by inhibiting the body's ability to sense how much adenosine is in the body. It is neutral and informative. Passage 2 seems to serve as a warning to the reader that although caffeine isn't typically deadly, it does have many negative health consequences. Passage 2 is primarily persuasive. Therefore, Choice (C) is correct. Choice (A) is wrong because although Passage 1 is analytical, Passage 2 is not narrative, or telling a story. Choice (B) is wrong because it flips the two passages. Choice (D) is incorrect because although Passage 1 is somewhat medical, Passage 2 doesn't focus on economics.

2. **(D)** The first of these two paragraphs says that in a thermodynamically favorable reaction, adenosine triphosphate releases its phosphates and free energy, leaving just adenosine and inorganic phosphate. The next paragraph talks about how we have neurons that have evolved to detect the presence of adenosine and then to direct the pineal gland to secrete melatonin. This sequence is described by answer Choice (D). Choice (A) is wrong because the pineal gland secretes melatonin, rather than forms adenosine triphosphate. Choice (B) is wrong because the detection of just adenosine triggers the melatonin response; the presence of adenosine triphosphate does not have this effect.

Choice (C) doesn't work because the energy is released when adenosine triphosphate decomposes to adenosine and inorganic phosphate.

3. **(C)** This paragraph describes the process by which adenosine triphosphate undergoes a thermodynamically favorable process to form adenosine and inorganic phosphate and to release free energy. If energy is released in the reaction, it means that energy was being stored in the reactants, so the reactants have more energy than the products, Choice (C). Choices (A) and (B) are incorrect because this term refers to an energy differential. Choice (D) is backward.

4. **(A)** In paragraph 3, the author talks about how the body knows to sleep when a large amount of adenosine is sensed by receptors in the neurons. In the last paragraph, the author says that caffeine (because it has a very similar structure to adenine) can interact with these receptors, tricking the body into thinking less adenosine is present than really is. This corresponds to Choice (A), because energy consumption in the body corresponds to conversion of adenosine triphosphate into adenosine. Choices (B), (C), and (D) aren't supported anywhere in the passage.

5. **(C)** The correct answer is Choice (C) because this is the part of the passage that discusses how caffeine works. These lines talk about caffeine interacting with adenosine receptors that are intended to sense how much energy the body has expended. Choice (A) is wrong because it introduces the concept of adenosine triphosphate as a source of energy. Choice (B) merely suggests a purpose for sleep. Choice (D) is wrong because it talks about a time when caffeine doesn't work—when the body has simply expended too much energy and the body's adenosine levels have become too high.

6. **(A)** This line is used to contrast the beginning of the paragraph, which states that caffeine isn't typically deadly. The "however" in this line tips us off to the fact that the author wants to make a contrast. What he's saying is that although caffeine isn't deadly, it's also not ____. It makes sense to say that although caffeine isn't deadly, it's also not "harmless," which is Choice (A). Choices (B), (C), and (D) are incorrect because caffeine is all of these things.

7. **(B)** The author states in the final paragraph that pathological addiction to caffeine has never been documented in humans, so the correct answer is Choice (B). The rest of the answer choices are mentioned as detriments of caffeine (Choice (A): lines 52–55; Choice (C): line 55; Choice (D): lines 49–52).

8. **(D)** Choice (D) is correct because these lines state that pathological addiction to caffeine has never been documented. The other choices all mention negative effects of caffeine: bone loss, anxiety, and heart dysrhythmias.

9. **(C)** Passage 1 primarily examines how caffeine stimulation works in the body. Passage 2 argues that although caffeine isn't deadly, it can have many negative side effects in certain groups of people. Therefore, the correct answer is Choice (C). Choice (A) is wrong because although Passage 1 does touch on the origins of caffeine, it doesn't discuss the history. Choice (B) is wrong because Passage 1 talks about how caffeine works rather than its benefits. Choice (D) is incorrect because neither passage discusses the evolution of caffeine stimulation.

Science: Genetics

1. **(B)** The author states in line 17 that individualized ("genetically based") treatments are more focused than broad-spectrum ("traditional") treatments. Therefore, individualized treatments are more precise, as in Choice (B). Furthermore, the author also states in lines 9–13 that although traditional methods do work for many patients, many patients also relapse. This shows that precision is lacking in the traditional methods. Choice (A) is incorrect because the question asks for a current advantage rather than a future one. Choice (C) is incorrect because the ethics of treatment are not discussed in the passage. Choice (D) is wrong because the author states in lines 4–6 that many of these new methods are far from being available to the general public.

2. **(C)** The correct answer is Choice (C) because these lines champion individualized medicine as more "focused" than traditional methods; in other words, they are more precise. Even without knowing the correct answer to the previous question, you could have used the process of elimination to realize that only Choice (C) discusses a current advantage of utilizing genetic advances in medicine. Choice (A) is incorrect because it merely says that the Human Genome Project revolutionized individualized medicine but doesn't give any advantages. Choice (B) is wrong because it states that much of individualized medicine is not yet readily available to the public, which clearly is not a current advantage. Choice (D) discusses the potential future directions of individualized medicine but not the current advantages.

3. **(D)** It's best to approach these questions by summing up the lines in your own words. The gist of these lines is that the field of genetic medicine still has a long way to go but is already making a positive difference in the lives of patients. Because this also sums up the passage, it's a good thesis statement, Choice (D). It supports the author's view rather than considering objections, making Choice (A) incorrect. Choice (B) is incorrect because it certainly doesn't describe any medical processes in detail. Choice (C) may be tempting because these lines say that much of this technology isn't readily available to the public. However, the author is simply stating this rather than passing judgment about the pace of development.

4. **(A)** For this question, you can come up with your own synonym for the word given the context and then match it to an answer choice. In this case, "routine treatment" may be replaced with something like *standard treatment*. The closest choice to *standard* is Choice (A), "typical." This makes sense given the context because the author is referring to this treatment in contrast with the cutting-edge genetic treatment. Choice (B) doesn't make sense because we don't know how repetitive the standard treatment is. Choice (C) would be correct in referring to the genetic treatment but not to the broad-spectrum treatment referenced here. Choice (D) is wrong because it's unlikely that the combination of surgery, chemotherapy, and radiation is simple.

5. **(A)** Passage 2 raises the question of how far people are willing to go with genetic research and then considers possible implications such as negative effects from altering genes and discrimination against those with certain genes. Therefore, this could be described as considering the implications of an issue, as in answer Choice (A). Choice (B) doesn't work because the author is just considering what might happen, not predicting or forecasting it. Choice (C) is wrong because no scholarly opinions are considered.

Choice (D) is incorrect because the author admits that genetic research can be very helpful in treating certain diseases.

6. **(B)** This line is about the discrimination of people with certain genes; another way to say this is that these people may experience a bias, Choice (B). Racism, as in Choice (A), is another type of discrimination. However in this case, the discrimination is against people with certain genes rather than of certain races. Choice (C) is too extreme. Choice (D) is wrong because legal action isn't going to be taken against these people.

7. **(A)** Choice (A) refers to "many" people who argue that genetic research has been positive. The author of Passage 1 could certainly fall into this group of people, because Passage 1 is about how genetic research is leading to more effective, individualized medical treatment. Choice (B) is wrong because Passage 1 doesn't consider any severe consequences of genetic research. Choices (C) and (D) don't work because we have no reason to believe that the author of Passage 1 is either a researcher or a medical professional.

8. **(A)** The author of Passage 2 would most likely be concerned that this sort of information could actually be harmful because of the potential for genetic discrimination. The excerpt from lines 57–59 supports this notion. Passage 2 does not indicate that any of the other instances would present major concerns.

9. **(D)** These lines provide direct support to the notion that parents may have trouble finding health insurance for a child who had a condition that was expensive to cover. The other options do not provide direct support for this claim.

10. **(C)** Passage 1's author primarily considers the benefits of genetic research, so his viewpoint could be expressed as positive, optimistic, or hopeful. Passage 2's author concedes that genetic research can be very helpful in treating some diseases but is not without risks. Therefore, this author can best be described as cautious or balanced. Choice (C) has correct adjectives for both authors. Choice (A) is incorrect because Passage 2's author is more balanced than negative. Choice (B) is incorrect because neither passage is overly scientific or historical. Choice (D) is incorrect because "apocalyptic" is far too negative for Passage 2.

Science: Fungi

1. **(C)** First, summarize what happened with antibiotics and antibiotic resistance: certain classes of antibiotics were wildly effective in eradicating bacteria, but some were resistant. As these classes of antibiotics were used more rampantly, much larger numbers of the bacteria became resistant. Thus, the situation described is one in which initial efficiency decreases as something becomes better at beating the system. This matches Choice (C): the software is initially effective. However, as more students learn to beat the system, the software loses its effectiveness. Choice (A) isn't the same, because its efficiency increases over time. Choices (B) and (D) are tempting, but nothing is learning to beat the system in either case.

2. **(C)** This paragraph gives a general introduction of fungi, emphasizing that many people don't realize how prevalent they are in our lives. The essay then goes on to discuss several examples of the applications of fungi. Therefore, the answer is Choice (C): the author relates fungi to our lives. Choice (A) is wrong because the author mentions fungi only as

food here, but the essay doesn't focus on it. Chocie (B) doesn't work because the author simply says that many people don't realize how important fungi are—not that they're wrong about fungi. Choice (D) is incorrect because the author says that the importance of fungi is easily overlooked rather than easily visible.

3. **(D)** This line says that fungi execute many functions in our lives. In other words, they *perform* many functions, which is Choice (D). Choice (A) is another definition of "execute." However, the fungi aren't destroying functions, they're carrying out functions. They're also not hiding functions, as in Choice (B), or enticing functions, as in Choice (C).

4. **(A)** The author talks about Alexander Fleming somewhat accidentally discovering the antibiotic properties of penicillin (lines 14–18) and Akiro Endo discovering the benefits of statins while attempting to study *Penicillium citrinum*'s antimicrobial properties. What these major discoveries have in common is that they were somewhat accidental. Thus, the answer is Choice (A). These discoveries weren't a product of evolution or genetic engineering as in Choices (B) or (D). Although they may have required economic investment, as in Choice (C), the author doesn't mention this.

5. **(D)** The correct answer is Choice (D) because these lines state that both Alexander Fleming and Akira Endo made their discoveries serendipitously, meaning with a bit of chance or luck. Choice (A) talks about how Fleming's discovery contributed to science, but none of the answer choices from the previous question apply. Choice (B) talks about how widespread use of antibiotics contributed to antibiotic resistance—not exactly a medical innovation. Choice (C) simply defines statins.

6. **(B)** Consider the context. These lines state that peptidoglycan polymers are highly peculiar to bacteria and that the antimicrobial agents that target peptidoglycan don't harm other cells. In other words, only bacteria are affected by these agents because only bacteria have peptidoglycan polymers. Therefore, the polymers are *unique* to bacteria, Choice (B). Choice (A) is another common use of the word "peculiar." In this case, though, it is somewhat opposite of what the author means since peptidoglycans are common to bacteria. Choice (C) is wrong because these polymers are normal, not diseased. Choice (D) is wrong because although peptidoglycans certainly are helpful, this doesn't fit the contrast in the latter part of the sentence.

7. **(D)** The answer can be found in the third paragraph, where the author details the mechanism by which antibiotics work. He says that antibiotics target peptidoglycan polymers, which are present only in bacteria. Therefore, antibiotics harm the bacteria without harming the host's cells, Choice (D). Choice (A) is incorrect as evidenced by the fact that many bacteria have developed antibiotic resistance. Neither Choice (B) nor Choice (C) is supported anywhere in the passage.

8. **(C)** The correct answer is Choice (C) These lines state that antibiotics work by targeting something present strictly in bacteria. Choice (A) doesn't discuss antibiotics. Choice (B) merely mentions that a fungus led to the development of three classes of antibiotics. Choice (D) references antibiotic resistance but not what makes antibiotics effective.

9. **(B)** This sentence beckons the reader to ask what is left to be discovered if some of our biggest findings in medicine have been the accidental results of studying fungi. The author is hinting that it's almost certain that fungi have more benefits to provide but that we must look for them. Thus, Choice (B) is correct. Choice (A) is wrong because the

author mentions neither geology nor funding. Choice (C) is wrong because the author thinks there's much research left to be done, and Choice (D) is wrong because nowhere in the passage does the author criticize mycology.

Science: Methanogenesis

1. **(B)** The answer to this question can be found in the last paragraph. The author states that understanding *Methanosphaera stadtmanae* has been immensely helpful in understanding and treating IBD. He also acknowledges that further understanding of archaeal and bacterial species will lead to a better understanding of how all of these things interact. Therefore, progress is being made on the subject, Choice (B). It isn't Choice (A), "largely settled," because he admits that it can be better understood. It isn't Choice (C) because he talks about how scientists have come to better understand the relationships. It isn't Choice (D) because scientists are still working to understand how archaeal and bacterial species interact with the human anatomy.

2. **(A)** According to lines 20–26, methanogenic bacteria were first identified in the gut microbiota after methane was detected in the breath. Methanogens are defined throughout the passage as species that produce methane, so this presence of methane in the breath eventually led to the identification of methanogenic species in the human digestive system. Thus, the answer is Choice (A). Choice (B) is incorrect because it says that the methanogens were eventually identified in fecal samples, but this wasn't how they were originally discovered. Choices (C) and (D) are details of the passage mentioned in other paragraphs but not in the third paragraph and not about how methanogens were discovered.

3. **(C)** In these lines, the author is referring to methanol being reduced to methane. Since these are two different chemical compounds, you can infer that methanol is being converted or *transformed* into methane, choice (C). The other choices are all different meanings of the word that don't apply here, as methanol cannot be subtracted, diminished, or persecuted into methane.

4. **(C)** Consider the context. Prior to these lines, the author stated that *Methanosphaera stadtmanae* is somehow connected to the occurrence of IBD. These lines serve to explain to the reader the role that *M. stadtmanae* plays in this process—it triggers the proinflammatory cytokines. Thus, he is explaining a process, Choice (C). The answer isn't Choice (A) because the author hasn't introduced any objections that he's trying to disprove. The answer isn't Choice (B) because he's talking about a partially known scientific fact rather than a speculation. Choice (D) is incorrect because the author doesn't attribute this fact to anyone.

5. **(A)** This line says that *Methanosphaera stadtmanae* induces the release of proinflammatory cytokine TNF. This seems to be a cause-and-effect relationship: *M. stadtmanae* senses something and makes something else happen. Another way to describe this might be that *M. stadtmanae* triggers the release, or *causes* the release, Choice (A). Choices (B) and (D) are too personified—it's more automated than something that is suggested or persuaded. Choice (C) doesn't work because the organisms can't release a release.

6. **(B)** The author states that *Methanosphaera stadtmanae* is helpful to humans because it conserves energy and aids in digestion (lines 52–56). He also says that it likely con-

tributes to IBD in some individuals. Therefore, *M. stadtmanae* plays an important and helpful role in the body. However, if homeostasis is not maintained, it can also have negative effects in the body. Therefore, it is primarily beneficial, Choice (B). It isn't uniformly positive, Choice (A), because of its role in IBD. It isn't somewhat harmful, as in Choice (D), because the author explicitly states in the first paragraph that *M. stadtmanae* is beneficial to humans. It's necessary for energy conservation and digestion.

7. **(C)** In the second paragraph, the author explains how *Methanosphaera stadtmanae* is different from other methanogens. These other methanogens can reduce CO_2 to methane, but *M. stadtmanae* lacks the enzyme to initiate this pathway. Thus, *M. stadtmanae* can reduce methanol only to methane. Therefore, the inability to process CO_2 sets the species apart from other methanogens. Choice (A) is incorrect because all of the methanogens the author references use H_2 in reduction. Choices (B) and (D) aren't mentioned in the passage.

8. **(B)** Choice (B) is the correct answer because these lines explicitly state that the inability of *Methanosphaera stadtmanae* to reduce carbon dioxide to methane is what sets it apart from other methanogens. Lines 11–12 and 23–26 also give examples of differences among *M. stadtmanae* and other methanogens, but these lines don't mention any of the answers to the previous question. Choice (D) provides a similarity between *M. stadtmanae* and the other methanogens.

9. **(D)** First, consider why the author says that *Methanosphaera stadtmanae* is beneficial to the host. In the first paragraph, he talks about how this species has a particularly restrictive energy metabolism, stating that "these unique energy conservation traits are what make *Methanosphaera stadtmanae* beneficial to its human host and not an opportunistic pathogen." Thus, we're looking for an answer choice from the figures that shows that this species conserves energy. Notice that for most of the pathways, Figure 1 says that at least some sort of intermediate is missing. In Figure 2, many of the boxes are black, meaning intermediates are missing. Thus, the answer is Choice (D). Choices (A) and (B) aren't mentioned in the passage, and Choice (C) isn't supported by the figures.

10. **(A)** The correct answer is Choice (A). These lines suggest that this species is helpful to humans rather than harmful because it has a very restrictive metabolism, meaning it's limited in its pathways. This is what's being shown by the two figures. Choice (B) is about the history of the discovery of methanogens in the gut. Choice (C) is a negative side effect of what can happen if the balance of methanogens isn't maintained, so it's about how they can be harmful to humans, rather than helpful. Choice (D) is about how homeostasis of the gut microbiota may be restored when it's disturbed. However, Choice (D) is unrelated to the figures, as well as to how *M. stadtmanae* is beneficial to humans.

Science: Wound Healing

1. **(A)** The passage starts with what happens immediately after a laceration occurs and continues through the stages of wound healing; thus, it is chronological as in Choice (A). Choices (B) and (D) are incorrect because the passage is merely informative and does not consider pros and cons or attempt to be persuasive. Choice (C) is incorrect because these steps all occur in the same space.

2. **(C)** The main purpose of the passage is to inform the reader of what happens after a person sustains a wound so that he or she may know to seek medical attention if a wound isn't properly healing. This makes Choice (C) the correct answer. Choice (A) is wrong because the author details the normal healing process rather than any abnormalities. Choices (B) and (D) are incorrect because the author is simply stating the current understanding of wound healing rather than arguing anything.

3. **(B)** Lines 4–6 give the author's purpose: to detail the typical wound progression so that a reader may know what to expect and when to be concerned. So Choice (B) is correct. Furthermore, either the beginning or the end of the first paragraph is often where the author will clearly state his or her thesis, so it is unsurprising to find the answer in these lines. Choice (A) only introduces the reader to the topic of wound healing without stating why it is important that a reader understands the subject. Choice (C) lists aspects of wound healing that a reader can't control. Choice (D) gives the reader some advice. However, both Choices (C) and (D) miss the big picture by merely providing details.

4. **(A)** Consider the context here. The previous sentence introduces the term *phagocytosis*. Because this is a scientific term that not all readers will know, the author then clarifies what phagocytes do in the process of phagocytosis. Therefore, the author is clarifying a specialized term, making Choice (A) correct. Choice (B) is incorrect because the author doesn't tell where the word comes from. Choices (C) and (D) are incorrect because the sentence does neither of these things.

5. **(D)** In this case, "raw" is referring to the edges of the wound. The author means raw as in damaged or inflamed, as is expected after the inflammatory stage, Choice (D). Choice (A) is incorrect because although it is a definition of the word "raw," it refers to materials rather than a wound. Choice (B) doesn't work because the skin isn't primitive. Choice (C) is a common definition of raw, but it refers more to uncooked food rather than to a wound.

6. **(A)** The author is emphasizing here that it is important to protect a wound in this stage, Choice (A). Neither Choice (B) nor Choice (C) works because each has a negative connotation. The author is just emphasizing something, not passing judgment. Choice (D) is wrong because one wouldn't say that protecting something is analytical.

7. **(C)** The passage lists the steps in terms of one occurring then the body moving on to the next. Therefore, the passage lists the steps in a sequential or chronological order. However, the figure shows great overlap among the steps; for instance, angiogenesis and wound contraction occur almost entirely at the same time. Therefore, the figure shows them as being concurrent or simultaneous. Thus, the correct answer is Choice (C) as it classifies the passage's description as sequential and the figure's description as simultaneous. Choice (A) has the passage and the figure backward. Choice (B) is incorrect because both show that the processes are gradual. Choice (D) is wrong because the figure simply shows a time depiction of when the steps occur but states nothing of where they occur.

8. **(C)** Lines 42–43 state that the last step of healing, the maturation stage, may last up to two years. The inflammatory phase lasts between 2 and 14 days, and the proliferative phase lasts between 3 and 21 days. Therefore, the whole healing phase may last 14 + 21 + 365 + 365 = 765 days. Thus, the closest answer is 1,000. In 1,000 days, the wound will almost certainly be healed, Choice (C).

9. **(D)** Lines 41–43 give the timeline for the longest-lasting stage—up to two years. Therefore, we know that even the worst wounds should be healed in just over two years, making 1,000 days a reasonable estimate. Choices (A) and (C) give the timeline for much faster steps, but they don't give a reasonable estimate of the whole timeline. Choice (B) doesn't discuss time.

Science: Synthetic Intermediates

1. **(D)** Throughout the passage, the author argues that chemophobia is unwarranted. He concedes that creating novel byproducts and intermediates can be harmful, as in the case of methyldioxymethamphetamine, but the vast majority of the passage is about the pros of synthesizing chemicals. This makes Choice (D) correct. Choice (A) is wrong because the author focuses on the benefits rather than the dangers. Choice (B) is wrong because many industries are already using synthetic intermediates, as evidenced by the passage. Choice (C) is wrong because he thinks that they have their place in society now.

2. **(A)** The author says that certain synthetic intermediates can have unforeseen consequences and then goes on to discuss the case of the addictive methyldioxymethamphetamine, making Choice (A) correct. Choice (B) is wrong because although he admits that skepticism is justifiable in this industry, this isn't a negative consequence. Choice (C) is wrong because there are plenty of opportunities for scientists in the field of industrial chemistry, as shown in the first paragraph. Choice (D) is wrong because the author doesn't discuss this.

3. **(C)** Choice (C) is correct because these lines consider a time when a synthetic intermediate had negative consequences. Choice (A) simply discusses chemophobia. Choice (B) talks about the opportunities for scientists: a pro rather than a con. Choice (D) gives the circumstances surrounding the creation of methyldioxymethamphetamine, but it's more in the context of a pro—that scientists were trying to create a more sustainable source of hydrastine.

4. **(B)** The sentence states that "a chemist is *confronted* with the problem of how to efficiently and effectively reproduce the compound by artificial means." The word "confronted" most nearly means "presented" because the process of scientific inquiry as described in the passage does not have confrontation or violence associated with it. The other choices all suggest too much negativity and hostility.

5. **(C)** This paragraph describes retrosynthetic analysis as finding the most efficient way of constructing a compound. This is best described by Choice (C), which is also maximizing efficiency. Choice (A) is wrong because it's making something overly simple rather than improving efficiency. Choice (B) comes at the cost of quality. Choice (D) is incorrect because it has nothing to do with finding the most efficient way of doing something.

6. **(B)** This line talks about getting biochemical compounds from nature. In terms of chemistry, "deriving" means exactly this, so Choice (B) is the correct answer. Choices (A) and (C) don't work because these are more like creating than harvesting. Choice (D) is wrong because it's talking about obtaining the compounds rather than breaking them down.

7. **(B)** The author thinks that synthetic substances have a largely unsubstantiated bad reputation. He also talks about two natural substances—sucrose and fructose—that have negative impacts on health. Thus, he believes that natural substances can sometimes be more harmful than synthetic substances, Choice (B). Choices (A) and (D) express viewpoints that the author explicitly disagrees with. Choice (C) is wrong because he talks about several instances in which harvesting natural substances from plants can have devastating effects on the environment.

8. **(D)** The correct answer is Choice (D) because it gives a concrete example of when natural substances can be more harmful than synthetic—this is something about which the author is trying to persuade the reader. Choices (A) and (B) talk about when harvesting natural resources is harmful to the environment. Choice (C) discusses the bad reputation that synthetic compounds get but only to disagree.

9. **(D)** The author's main purpose in these lines is to argue that the chemophobic public's unease over synthetic substances—in this case, aspartame—sometimes persists even when science says that the fear is unsubstantiated. This matches the sentiment in Choice (D). Choice (A) is wrong because the author simply says that accidental discoveries can be helpful but not that they're more helpful than more intentional findings. Choice (B) expresses the chemophobic view that the author disagrees with; Choice (C) says that aspartame is unhealthy, something the author explicitly disagrees with.

Writing and Language

4

HOW IS THE WRITING AND LANGUAGE SECTION DESIGNED?

- Second section of the test
- 35 minutes long
- 44 questions total

  - Approximately 20 questions on Standard English Conventions
  - Approximately 24 questions on Expression of Ideas; approximately 3 of these questions will relate to analysis of graphs

- Four total passages

  - One with a career theme
  - One from humanities
  - One from science
  - One from social studies

- The questions are in random order of difficulty

HOW SHOULD I USE THIS CHAPTER?

- Start with the section "Instructional Exercises: Review PSAT Grammar Essentials" to review the key grammar knowledge you need for the test.
- Carefully read the section "PSAT 1520 Writing and Language Mindset" to develop a personalized strategy for this section.
- Review the section "How to Handle Tricky Questions" so you can avoid common pitfalls.
- Use the "Troubleshooting" guide to help you work through strategic issues you have encountered in the past or are finding as you work through problems.
- Use what you have learned to help you practice as effectively as possible in the Writing and Language Drills chapter that follows.

INSTRUCTIONAL EXERCISES—REVIEW PSAT GRAMMAR ESSENTIALS

Grammar Basics Review Quiz—Is (A) or (B) Correct?

1. (A) Talking on her phone while driving the car. (B) My friend was talking on the phone while driving the car.

2. (A) I swim in the pool to cool off in the summer. (B) I swim in the pool I like to cool off in the summer.

3. A long time ago, the queen (A) rescued or (B) rescues the king.

4. He had (A) eating or (B) eaten the spoiled food before he had indigestion.

5. The people who left a big mess on the table need to mind (A) their or (B) its manners.

6. Jill and Jane forgot to pick up (A) her or (B) Jane's deliveries.

7. The man who owns three cars (A) have or (B) has quite a garage.

8. Because (A) it is or (B) they are quite interesting, the art museum and the natural history museum are worth a visit.

TIP

A great way to master the rules of English grammar is to study another language. When you have to identify how another language treats subject-verb agreement, verb tense, and idioms, you will be more attuned to how these are treated in English.

Answer	General Tip
1. (B) My friend was talking on the phone while driving the car. *(A) is a sentence fragment.*	A **sentence** expresses a complete thought with both a subject and predicate, i.e., a subject and a verb. A **sentence fragment** expresses an incomplete thought with only a subject or a predicate. A **run-on sentence** consists of two or more complete sentences that are joined together without appropriate punctuation or transitions.
2. (A) I swim in the pool to cool off in the summer. *(B) is a run-on sentence.*	
3. A long time ago, the queen (A) rescued the king. *This takes place in the past since it says "a long time ago." So we need the past tense verb.*	Watch for verb tense consistency. Consider the entirety of at least the sentence, and often more context elsewhere in the passage, in order to determine when the action takes place.
4. He had (B) eaten the spoiled food before he had indigestion. *"Had eaten" is the correct past perfect form of "to eat."*	
5. The people who left a big mess on the table need to mind (A) their manners. *The word "their" refers to "people" and is correct because both the noun (people) and the pronoun (their) are plural.*	Be certain that pronouns are correct in their number agreement. Singular pronouns like "he," "she," "one," and "it" must stand in the place of singular words. Plural pronouns like "they" and "we" must stand in the place of plural words. If a pronoun is vague, pick the answer that clarifies the pronoun—you will never have to worry about whether the replacement is true, just if it is grammatically correct.
6. Jill and Jane forgot to pick up (B) Jane's deliveries. *Two females are mentioned. If the owner of the deliveries is not clarified, the sentence will be vague.*	

Answer	General Tip
7. The man who owns three cars (B) <u>has</u> quite a garage. *The subject is "man," which is singular.*	Watch for subject-verb agreement, especially when the subject and the verb are not close to one another.
8. Because (B) <u>they are</u> quite interesting, the art museum and the natural history museum are worth a visit. *The word "they" refers to both of the museums.*	

Frequently Confused Words Questions—Is (A) or (B) Correct?

1. Who is going to (A) <u>accept</u> *or* (B) <u>except</u> the award at the ceremony this evening?

2. The politician had a profound (A) <u>affect</u> *or* (B) <u>effect</u> on her country.

3. Criminals typically try to (A) <u>allude</u> *or* (B) <u>elude</u> arrest.

4. I have a great (A) <u>amount</u> *or* (B) <u>number</u> of respect for my teacher.

5. (A) <u>Beside</u> *or* (B) <u>Besides</u> being a nice guy, he is extremely intelligent.

6. (A) <u>Between</u> *or* (B) <u>Among</u> all the people in the world, she won the Nobel Peace Prize this year.

7. Make sure you (A) <u>choose</u> *or* (B) <u>chose</u> the best candidate when you vote today.

8. It is nice to pay your instructor a (A) <u>complement</u> *or* (B) <u>compliment</u> when he or she explains things really well.

9. Sometimes it is difficult to (A) <u>elicit</u> *or* (B) <u>illicit</u> responses from surveys.

10. If I could (A) <u>have</u> *or* (B) <u>of</u> performed better on the test, my grade would have been much better for the semester.

11. Please respond to (A) <u>I</u> *or* (B) <u>me</u> when you receive the voice mail.

12. There are (A) <u>fewer</u> *or* (B) <u>less</u> pieces of gum in my pocket than in my drawer.

13. When the teacher extended the deadline for the project, there was (A) <u>many</u> *or* (B) <u>much</u> happiness in the classroom.

14. Don't forget to (A) <u>lay</u> *or* (B) <u>lie</u> your assignment on the teacher's desk.

15. It doesn't matter whether you win or (A) <u>loose</u> *or* (B) <u>lose</u>—it's how you play the game.

16. Civil rights advocates have very strong (A) <u>principals</u> *or* (B) <u>principles</u> for which they fight.

17. This clock is better at keeping time (A) <u>than</u> *or* (B) <u>then</u> that clock.

18. If you stay up (A) <u>to</u> *or* (B) <u>too</u> late before the test, you may not perform well.

19. My new pickup truck, (A) <u>which</u> *or* (B) <u>that</u> cost $20,000, has plenty of storage space.

20. From (A) <u>who</u> *or* (B) <u>whom</u> did you receive that lovely bouquet of flowers?

TIP

The proper usage of these words may be different from how you use them in casual conversation. When taking the PSAT, be sure you are using the word forms you would use in a formal essay.

Correct Answer	Confused Words	General Rules
1. Who is going to (A) <u>accept</u> the award at the ceremony this evening?	**Accept vs. Except**	*accept*: receive *except*: excluding
2. The politician had a profound (B) <u>effect</u> on her country.	**Affect vs. Effect**	*affect*: typically a verb, "to influence" *effect*: typically a noun, "a result or change"
3. Criminals typically try to (B) <u>elude</u> arrest.	**Allude vs. Elude**	*allude*: indirectly refer to *elude*: escape from
4. I have a great (A) <u>amount</u> of respect for my teacher.	**Amount vs. Number**	*amount*: usually not countable *number*: usually countable
5. (B) <u>Besides</u> being a nice guy, he is extremely intelligent.	**Beside vs. Besides**	*beside*: next to *besides*: in addition to
6. (B) <u>Among</u> all the people in the world, she won the Nobel Peace Prize this year.	**Between vs. Among**	*between*: comparing one thing at a time, typically just two objects *among*: comparing nondistinct items or three or more objects
7. Make sure you (A) <u>choose</u> the best candidate when you vote today.	**Choose vs. Chose**	*choose*: present tense *chose*: past tense
8. It is nice to pay your instructor a (B) <u>compliment</u> when he or she explains things really well.	**Complement vs. Compliment**	*complement*: complete something *compliment*: flattery
9. Sometimes it is difficult to (A) <u>elicit</u> responses from surveys.	**Elicit vs. Illicit**	*elicit*: evoke or obtain *illicit*: illegal
10. If I could (A) <u>have</u> performed better on the test, my grade would have been much better for the semester.	**Have vs. Of**	*have*: verb (action word) *of*: preposition (connecting word)
11. Please respond to (B) <u>me</u> when you have received the voice mail.	**I vs. Me**	*I*: subject *me*: object
12. There are (A) <u>fewer</u> pieces of gum in my pocket than in my drawer.	**Fewer/many vs. Less/much**	*fewer/many*: usually countable *less/much*: usually not countable
13. When the teacher extended the deadline for the project, there was (B) <u>much</u> happiness in the classroom.		

Correct Answer	Confused Words	General Rules
14. Don't forget to (A) <u>lay</u> your assignment on the teacher's desk.	**Lie vs. Lay**	*lie*: recline *lay*: place
15. It doesn't matter whether you win or (B) <u>lose</u>—it's how you play the game.	**Lose vs. Loose**	*lose*: suffer a loss *loose*: not tight fitting
16. Civil rights advocates have very strong (B) <u>principles</u> for which they fight.	**Principal vs. Principle**	*principal*: high-ranking person, or primary *principle*: rule or belief
17. This clock is better at keeping time (A) <u>than</u> that clock.	**Than vs. Then**	*than*: for comparisons *then*: for time
18. If you stay up (B) <u>too</u> late before the test, you may not perform well.	**To vs. Too**	*to*: connecting preposition *too*: comparisons or in addition
19. My new pickup truck, (A) <u>which</u> cost $20,000, has plenty of storage space.	**Which vs. That**	*which*: nonrestrictive (extra information), takes a comma *that*: restrictive (essential information), does not take a comma
20. From (B) <u>whom</u> did you receive that lovely bouquet of flowers?	**Who vs. Whom**	*who*: subject *whom*: object. (use "who" when you would use "he" or "she," and use "whom" when you would use "him" or "her")

Punctuation and Possession—Is (A) or (B) Correct?

1. If you want to finish your (A) <u>homework, you should</u> *or* (B) <u>homework you, should</u> probably stop watching television.

2. The weather forecast was (A) <u>promising but</u> *or* (B) <u>promising, but</u> the gloomy sky told a different story.

3. This computer (A) <u>virus, I am sorry to report, does</u> *or* (B) <u>virus I am sorry to report, does</u> not have an easy fix.

4. My favorite pizza toppings are (A) <u>mushrooms green peppers cheese,</u> *or* (B) <u>mushrooms, green peppers, cheese,</u> and onions.

5. The car (A) <u>, that just crashed,</u> *or* (B) <u>that just crashed</u> is being retrieved by the fire department.

6. The harsh winds and pounding (A) <u>hail made</u> *or* (B) <u>hail, made</u> the long walk home quite challenging.

7. Sam (A) <u>Walton, the founder of Walmart, still</u> *or* (B) <u>Walton, the founder of Walmart</u> <u>still</u> drove a pickup truck even after becoming wealthy.

8. Pumpkins were not in (A) <u>season; we</u> *or* (B) <u>season, we</u> decided to make a cherry pie instead.

9. Our high school class went on a grand tour of the European capitals of <u>Paris, France,</u> <u>Berlin, Germany, and Bern, Switzerland</u> *or* (B) <u>Paris, France; Berlin, Germany; and</u> <u>Bern, Switzerland</u>.

10. When you go to the store, please pick up these (A) <u>items milk</u> *or* (B) <u>items: milk</u>, bread, and eggs.

11. Before you bring out the birthday cake, don't forget the most important (A) <u>thing: to</u> *or* (B) <u>thing; to</u> light the candles.

12. The gas station offers a variety of (A) <u>products the station</u> *or* (B) <u>products—the station</u> is more of a convenience store than a mere fuel depot.

13. My friend's (A) <u>house much to my surprise was</u> *or* (B) <u>house—much to my surprise—</u> <u>was</u> up for sale.

14. When my pizza (A) <u>came—nearly an hour after I ordered it—I</u> *or* (B) <u>came—nearly an</u> <u>hour after I ordered it, I</u> was quite ravenous.

15. (A) <u>One person's joy can be another's sorrow.</u> *or* (B) <u>One persons joy can be anothers</u> <u>sorrow.</u>

16. (A) <u>Two car's</u> *or* (B) <u>Two cars'</u> parking spaces are equivalent to one truck's parking space.

17. The 2015 (A) <u>Women's</u> *or* (B) <u>Womens'</u> World Cup was hosted in Canada.

18. (A) <u>It's</u> *or* (B) <u>Its</u> a nice day to go for a hike.

19. When you take a message, be sure that (A) <u>your</u> *or* (B) <u>you're</u> handwriting is legible.

20. (A) <u>Who's</u> *or* (B) <u>Whose</u> book is on top of the shelf?

TIP

Do not worry about the possibility of two answers being right on PSAT punctuation questions. Although many forms of punctuation are interchangeable, there will only be one correct answer out of the given options.

Answer	General Rule
1. If you want to finish your (A) <u>homework,</u> <u>you should</u> probably stop watching television.	Use a comma to separate an introductory phrase (dependent clause) from what could be a complete sentence (independent clause).
2. The weather forecast was (B) <u>promising,</u> <u>but</u> the gloomy sky told a different story.	Use a comma to join two complete sentences when there is a transitional word, like the "FANBOYS": *for, and, nor, but, or, yet,* and *so.*
3. This computer (A) <u>virus, I am sorry to</u> <u>report, does</u> not have an easy fix.	Separate extra thoughts (parenthetical phrases) from the rest of the sentence.

Answer	General Rule
4. My favorite pizza toppings are (B) <u>mushrooms, green peppers, cheese,</u> and onions.	Separate items in a list with commas. Don't worry about the serial or Oxford comma (i.e., the one that is between "cheese" and "and"). There is no consensus on the use of this comma, so the PSAT will not test it.
5. The car (B) <u>that just crashed</u> is being retrieved by the fire department.	Don't use commas to separate parts of a sentence if everything in the sentence is needed to make the sentence clear and logical. (In this case, the sentence must clarify that the car is the one that just crashed.)
6. The harsh winds and pounding (A) <u>hail made</u> the long walk home quite challenging.	Just because a sentence is long doesn't mean that it needs a comma. Look more closely at the structure of the sentence than at its length. In this case, there is a compound subject of "winds" and "hail." So no break is needed before the verb.
7. Sam (A) <u>Walton, the founder of Walmart, still</u> drove a pickup truck even after becoming wealthy.	A clarifying phrase (appositive) needs to be separated with commas. The name is enough to know who the person is in this case, so commas are needed to separate the description. If the description is too vague to narrow down the item precisely, then no commas should separate descriptive phrases. For example, "President Sam Walton" would not require a comma after "President" because that title is too vague to know which person we are talking about.
8. Pumpkins were not in (A) <u>season; we</u> decided to make a cherry pie instead.	You can use a semicolon to separate two complete, related sentences. Although a period could also work, the semicolon can add variety to your writing. A comma cannot separate two complete sentences by itself unless it is accompanied by a transitional word like "and" or "but."
9. Our high school class went on a grand tour of the European capitals of (B) <u>Paris, France; Berlin, Germany; and Bern, Switzerland.</u>	Use a semicolon to separate items in a list when even one listed item (other than the last one) has a comma or commas within it. If we used commas instead, the sentence would literally say that France, Germany, and Switzerland were capital cities as well.
10. When you go to the store, please pick up these (B) <u>items: milk,</u> bread, and eggs.	Use a colon after a complete sentence to set off a list.

Answer	General Rule
11. Before you bring out the birthday cake, don't forget the most important (A) <u>thing:</u> <u>to</u> light the candles.	Use a colon after a complete sentence to set off a clarification. A semicolon must have a complete sentence before and after it to work, while a colon requires only a complete sentence beforehand.
12. The gas station offers a variety of (B) <u>products—the station</u> is more of a convenience store than a mere fuel depot.	Although other punctuation can often work (in this case, a colon or semicolon could work instead of the dash), the dash can provide variety when you need to indicate an interruption or change of thought. Don't worry—the PSAT will not have two right answers on any question. Out of the possible choices, only one will work.
13. My friend's (B) <u>house—much to my</u> <u>surprise—was</u> up for sale.	A dash can be used to interrupt a sentence and provide a change of voice. In this sentence, the parenthetical phrase "much to my surprise" indicates an interruption in thought.
14. When my pizza (A) <u>came—nearly</u> <u>an hour after I ordered it—</u>I was quite ravenous.	Dashes can set off a parenthetical phrase. If you start with a dash on one end of the phrase, you need to use a dash on the other end of it for consistency. This goes the same for commas and parentheses—start and end a parenthetical phrase with the same sort of punctuation.
15. (A) <u>One person's joy can be another's</u> <u>sorrow.</u>	Use an apostrophe before the *s* to indicate that a singular entity possesses something.
16. (B) <u>Two cars'</u> parking spaces are equivalent to one truck's parking space.	Use an apostrophe after the *s* to indicate that a plural entity possesses something.
17. The 2015 (A) <u>Women's</u> World Cup was hosted in Canada.	Use an apostrophe before the *s* to indicate possession after a noun that is already plural, like "men" or "children."
18. (A) <u>It's</u> a nice day to go for a hike. *This is the same as "it is a nice day."*	*its*: possession *it's*: "it is" (*its'* is always incorrect)
19. When you take a message, be sure that (A) <u>your</u> handwriting is legible. *The handwriting belongs to "you."*	*your*: possession *you're*: "you are"
20. (B) <u>Whose</u> book is on top of the shelf? *Showing possession of the book.*	*whose*: possession *who's*: "who is"

Advanced Odds and Ends—Is (A) or (B) Correct?

1. He was unsure of his future career (A) <u>path, so</u> *or* (B) <u>path, but</u> he entered college with an "undecided" major.

2. (A) <u>Because</u> *or* (B) <u>Even though</u> the store was "officially" out of the new book, the manager somehow found a copy for me.

3. On the morning of the PSAT, try to relax, (A) <u>to breathe</u> *or* (B) <u>breathe</u> deeply, and to remember your pencils.

4. Reading the questions carefully and (A) <u>taking</u> *or* (B) <u>to take</u> your time are strategies that are often helpful on standardized tests.

5. (A) <u>Texting while driving, the car swerved off the road.</u> *or* (B) <u>While the driver was texting, his car swerved off the road.</u>

6. (A) <u>The athlete loved his new shoes, running on the track.</u> *or* (B) <u>The athlete, running on the track, loved his new shoes.</u>

7. His project was better than (A) <u>anyone else's</u> *or* (B) <u>anyone's</u> in his class.

8. The treasurer of the Spanish club is more qualified than (A) <u>the French club's.</u> *or* (B) <u>the French club.</u>

9. (A) <u>Supposably,</u> *or* (B) <u>Supposedly,</u> the game tomorrow will be quite exciting.

10. People from all walks (A) <u>of</u> *or* (B) <u>in</u> life find your advice helpful.

Answer	General Concept
1. He was unsure of his future career (A) <u>path, so</u> he entered college with an "undecided" major. *The two parts of the sentence need to have a cause-and-effect relationship.*	**Transitional Words** Make sure the meaning conveyed by a connecting word, like "but," "also," and "because," fits logically within the context. You should consider at least the entire sentence that the transitional word is in, and you should sometimes consider even more context. Transitions are such a major part of the PSAT that there is an in-depth transition review exercise later in this chapter.
2. (B) <u>Even though</u> the store was "officially" out of the new book, the manager somehow found a copy for me. *The two parts of the sentence show a contrast.*	
3. On the morning of the PSAT, try to relax, (A) <u>to breathe</u> deeply, and to remember your pencils. *Each phrase in the list has the word "to." For consistency, put the word "to" in front of "breathe."*	**Parallelism** Phrasing and style should be consistent. Parallelism questions often concern parallel structure within a sentence, although sometimes the parallelism can extend to a paragraph.
4. Reading the questions carefully and (A) <u>taking</u> your time are strategies that are often helpful on standardized tests. *The sentence starts with "Reading." To be consistent in the phrasing, say "taking."*	

Answer	General Concept
5. (B) <u>While the driver was texting, his car swerved off the road.</u> *The other option literally means that the car was texting.*	**Modifier Placement** Watch for misplaced modifiers. Modifying words, like adjectives, and the words they modify, like nouns, should be clearly stated and in a proper sequence.
6. (B) <u>The athlete, running on the track, loved his new shoes.</u> *The other option literally means that the shoes were running.*	
7. His project was better than (A) <u>anyone else's</u> in his class. *"His project" needs to be compared to the projects of other students in the class, not to his own project. If the sentence said "anyone's," then his own project would be included in the comparison.*	**Logical Comparison** Compare a part to a part, and compare a whole to a whole. Don't compare a part to a whole or vice versa. Be sure that the literal comparison is logical.
8. The treasurer of the Spanish club is more qualified than (A) <u>the French club's.</u> *Compare the treasurer of one club to the treasurer of another—don't compare the treasurer of one club to the other entire club.*	
9. (B) <u>Supposedly,</u> the game tomorrow will be quite exciting.	**Conventional Expressions** Watch for idiomatic usage of phrases and words. On questions like these, trust your instincts as far as what common use dictates.
10. People from all walks (A) <u>of</u> life find your advice helpful.	

PSAT 1520 WRITING AND LANGUAGE MINDSET

Personalize your strategy for top performance. Here are the most common Writing and Language strategy questions top students have, followed by ideas to help you decide what makes sense for your situation.

What Should Be My Overall Approach to the Writing and Language Test?

The Writing and Language section is quite a bit different from many other standardized tests you have taken. You are being assessed on your skill in finding and fixing errors in essays. Because of this, your overall mindset should be this: *How would a good editor approach this?* After all, editing is exactly what you are doing. Remember the following:

- **GOOD EDITING TAKES TIME.** This is no time for speed-reading or skimming. Pick up on all the inconspicuous and subtle issues by using all of the allotted 35 minutes.
- **GOOD EDITING ASSESSES CONTEXT.** Whether you need to find subject-verb agreement within a sentence or choose an appropriate transition between paragraphs, context is essential. Be sure you check out enough of the surrounding sentences to make a well-founded choice.

- **GOOD EDITORS "LISTEN" TO HOW THE WORDING SOUNDS.** While you work through the Writing and Language section, you may find it extremely helpful to mouth things silently as you evaluate the passage. This way, you can allow your intuition to guide you to the correct answer. Be mindful that listening can take you only so far since spoken English is sometimes less formal than written English—you need to have a solid understanding of the grammar rules tested to do your very best.
- **GOOD EDITORS MAKE SURE THINGS MAKE SENSE.** In order for an essay to be well written, it must go beyond merely following basic grammar rules—it must be logical and consistent. While you work through the Writing and Language section, don't lose sight of the big picture because you are so focused on small-picture details.

Should I Read the Passage First or Look at the Questions First?

Most students prefer to go right to the questions, evaluating relevant context along the way. The Writing and Language test is not a reading comprehension assessment—it is an assessment of editing skills. However, some students find it useful to read the entire passage before trying the questions. For whom would this alternative be helpful? Students who routinely finish the Writing and Language section with eight or more minutes to spare may want to read the passage before trying the questions. Doing so would allow them time to develop a better sense of the overall flow of the passage, in turn, helping them with questions about transitions, sentence order, and the addition or deletion of sentences.

How Can I Avoid Being Indecisive?

- **REALIZE THAT THE WRITING AND LANGUAGE SECTION TESTS AGREED-UPON GRAMMAR RULES, NOT "PET PEEVES."** There will not be questions about concepts that are up for debate, such as the serial or Oxford comma, whether you must use the third person in formal essays, or whether it is acceptable to start a sentence with "but" or "because." There will be questions on subject-verb agreement rules, how to use a semicolon or colon, and what verb tense is consistent with the essay.
- **TRUST YOUR INSTINCTS.** Ideally, you will review all of the grammar rules in this chapter. On test day, however, you may forget the exact rule that applies in a given situation. If this happens, do not overthink the question. Trust your feel for the English language that you have developed through speaking and reading.
- **CONSIDER COVERING UP THE ANSWER CHOICES.** If you find that you jump to the choices before you have carefully considered the surrounding context, cover up the answers. This will force you to slow down your thinking so that you will be much more thorough in your thought process.

How Should I Pace Myself?

Most students find that they have *plenty* of time on the PSAT Writing and Language section. You will have 35 minutes to work through 44 questions, which are equally divided into four passages. Since some questions will take quite a bit more time than others (such as those that ask you to put sentences into the appropriate order), it is generally preferable to pace yourself *by passage* instead of *by question*. You can take approximately nine minutes per passage (technically eight minutes and 45 seconds) to finish right on time. Make sure you are taking the full amount of time available to do the questions one time well.

HOW TO HANDLE TRICKY QUESTIONS

Work through samples of question types that often give top students difficulty.

The Field of Nursing

Hoping to secure the position of nurse as a true profession, Florence Nightingale established the first nursing school in 1860. ❶ Nursing was practiced throughout the world from the Middle Ages all the way until the present day. While acceptance of nurses has been slow for many decades, recent surveys show that the public currently views nursing as one of the most trusted and respected professions.

The nursing profession has significantly grown and developed since the ❷ opening of the first school over 150 years ago. The first schools were known as certificate programs where hospital site training typically lasted around two years. Certificate schools still exist today, but the majority of schools have transitioned to associate 2-year or bachelor 4-year degree programs. This shift has occurred because, as the population increases and life expectancy is greater, there is a crucial need for health care professionals who are well trained to handle the growing rate of people in hospitals and long-term care facilities.

❸ Medical facilities have truly been experiencing explosive growth in recent years. After receiving their registered nurse (RN) licensure, nurses can continue their schooling to specialize in certain areas, such as cardiology, critical care, and hospital administration. Advanced-practice nursing has also seen a rise in the last decade as more training programs have opened and state governments have decreased strict regulations on what nurses can and cannot do. This includes prescribing medications, administering anesthesia, and performing advanced procedures. It is important for nurses to enter advanced-practice nursing as a growing population means an increasing demand for services.

1. Suppose the author wants a sentence at this point in the paragraph that supports the idea that nursing had not been a widely respected profession prior to the 1860s. Which choice would best accomplish the author's goal?

   (A) NO CHANGE
   (B) The profession of nursing involves rigorous training in medical science and patient interaction.
   (C) Nurses had consistently been held in the same esteem as other professionals even though many nurses were underpaid.
   (D) Until this point, nurses lacked recognition from doctors and the general public as real health care providers.

2. (A) NO CHANGE
   (B) inaugural activity
   (C) foundational ceremonial commencement
   (D) germinal occurrence

3. Which option provides the best transition from the previous paragraph and the most logical introduction to the paragraph?

   (A) NO CHANGE
   (B) The field of nursing also continues to grow because of the professional opportunities available to nurses.
   (C) Many professions have licensure requirements, ensuring that practitioners maintain the highest professional standards.
   (D) With an increasing number of people who wish to age in place, medicine needs to adjust its approach to elder care.

While the demand for health care services is increasing, the supply of nurses is predicted to hit a shortage level over the next ten years. The reason for the shortage is because the current population of nurses consists of approximately 43% of people between the ages of 50 to 70. This means that a large portion of nurses ❹ have about to apply for retirement. As there is a large exit of nurses from the field, there are not enough nurses graduating from programs to fill the vacant spots. One of the contributing factors for this is not having enough qualified faculty to teach classes. To help solve this problem, the federal government is investing in nursing schools to help increase faculty and ultimately increase the number of seats available to students. The nursing field also faces a critical shortage of male nurses. While some believe this shortage is not ❺ detrimenting for the overall field of nursing, others believe it can be harmful to providing quality health care since we have an equal population of males and females. It is important to consider all facets of the nursing field so that the best care is available to patients.

4. (A) NO CHANGE
   (B) are
   (C) is
   (D) were

5. (A) NO CHANGE
   (B) detrimenting to
   (C) detrimental for
   (D) detrimental to

Answer Explanations with Strategic Guidance

1. **What gives students trouble?**

   Students do not fully understand what the question requires them to do.

   On a question like this, it is easy to miss a word or two. Underlining and circling key words while reading the questions can be extremely helpful, allowing you to digest the entirety of the information in the text. According to the question, the author wants a sentence to support the idea that nursing was not very respected prior to the 1860s. Choice **(D)** is the only option that accomplishes this complete goal since it states that nurses had not been considered "real health care providers." Choices (A) and (B) relate to nursing but not to the stated goal of the author. Choice (C) expresses the opposite of the intended meaning. You will have enough time on the PSAT Writing and Language section to read questions like this carefully and avoid making careless mistakes.

2. What gives students trouble?

Students mistakenly believe that "fancy" wording is always preferable.

Unfortunately, many students believe that good writing involves using extremely difficult vocabulary. On the contrary—sophisticated vocabulary has its place but only when it helps communicate ideas more precisely. When sophisticated vocabulary merely confuses and distracts the reader, it is not useful. In this case, Choice **(A)** is correct. The word "opening" fully expresses the intended meaning. The other options all are too wordy and use overly complex vocabulary.

3. What gives students trouble?

Students do not consider enough context on a large scale.

When asked about providing a good transition between two paragraphs, be sure to read the entirety of both paragraphs to ensure you are making the proper connection. The previous paragraph makes the case that the nursing profession has grown quite a bit. The current paragraph elaborates on the training that nurses can do and how certain nursing fields are increasing as demand for their services increases. Choice **(B)** gives the best connection between these two larger themes, since it mentions the growth of the nursing field and connects the growth to increasing professional opportunities. Choice (A) is only loosely related to the previous paragraph. Choice (C) only somewhat connects to the current paragraph. Choice (D) is only vaguely connected to the subject of the essay as a whole.

4. What gives students trouble?

Students do not consider enough context within a sentence.

It is easy to jump to a conclusion on a question like this by assuming that the verb must agree with the noun that comes immediately beforehand—in this case, "nurses." In fact, the verb needs to agree with the early word "portion." The phrase "of nurses" does not act as a subject. Instead, it acts as a description of "portion." The correct answer is **(C)** because it is the only singular verb. Avoid issues with questions like these by considering the entirety of the context of the sentence.

5. What gives students trouble?

Students fail to trust their instincts when it comes to prepositions and idioms.

Students who look for "mathematical-style" rules with grammar will find questions involving prepositions and idiomatic expressions frustrating. They will seek out some general rule about preposition usage for a variety of words, only to be disappointed to find that there are many exceptions in the English language. On a problem like this, trust your background knowledge and your instincts. The correct answer is **(D)** because "detrimental," which means harmful, is the more widely used word and is coupled with the preposition "to" in a context like this. In fact, "detrimenting" is not a widely accepted word. It would therefore be inappropriate in this context. Sometimes the only justification you will need is that something violates common usage.

TIP

It is easy to mistake overly wordy and complex writing for good writing. Do not fall into this trap.

Punctuation Exercise

Recovering History

The title of Erna **❶** Brodber's third novel, _Louisiana,_ has a triple meaning: it refers to a state in the United States, a place of the same name in Jamaica, and the name taken by Ella **❷** Townsend the novel's protagonist. Ultimately, the word's fluidity emphasizes the connection between African Americans and African Caribbeans, as well as between the living and dead. The eponymous **❸** protagonist: a Colombian anthropology student ventures to St. Mary, Louisiana, to study Black folk life and, instead, finds herself taken over by the spirit of Mammy. Mammy, formally civil rights activist Sue Ann Grant King and more generally called Anna, is Ella's research target. A matriarch of obscure but certain significance, Mammy gradually reveals her own history (as well as Ella's) via a psychic, spiritual **❹** connection that changes the young academic's trajectory in unexpected ways.

Ella Townsend earned a fellowship in 1936 to collect and record the history of Blacks of Southwest Louisiana using one of the university's first tape recorders but never returned. The text opens with a confusing transcript of multiple voices that are all but nonsense to the **❺** reader, Ella, later called Louisiana, endeavors for most of the novel to make sense of the data collected on the tape recorder, confronting her own

1. (A) NO CHANGE
   (B) Brodber's third novel _Louisiana,_ has
   (C) Brodbers' third novel, _Louisiana_ has
   (D) Brodber's third novel, _Louisiana_—has

2. (A) NO CHANGE
   (B) Townsend; the novel's protagonist.
   (C) Townsend, the novel's protagonist.
   (D) Townsend: the novels protagonist.

3. (A) NO CHANGE
   (B) protagonist, a Colombian anthropology student, ventures
   (C) protagonist, a Colombian anthropology student ventures
   (D) protagonist a Colombian anthropology student ventures

4. (A) NO CHANGE
   (B) connection, that changes the young academic's trajectory in unexpected ways.
   (C) connection that changes, the young academic's trajectory, in unexpected ways.
   (D) connection that changes the young academics' trajectory, in unexpected ways.

5. (A) NO CHANGE
   (B) reader; Ella later called Louisiana, endeavors
   (C) reader: Ella—later called Louisiana, endeavors
   (D) reader; Ella, later called Louisiana, endeavors

preconceptions of voodoo and acknowledging her supernatural connection with two dead women, Anna (Mammy) and Louise. **❻** <u>Ella embraces this spiritual connection only after listening through the tape recorder's reel and witnessing her own out-of-body experiences.</u> Although she has no recollection of her interactions on the tape, she hears her voice speaking unintelligibly, a phenomenon that she must either investigate or accept as proof of her insanity.

After Mammy's funeral, Ella begins to understand the recorded transcript as a tri-party **❼** <u>dialogue an interaction among her, Anna, and</u> Anna's long-dead friend, Louise. Louisiana then gets her name by combining those of her spiritual sisters. When Caribbean sailors visit Ella and sing folk songs to her, Ella's past is revealed to her in a trance-like vision and formally initiates her into the art of prophecy. **❽** <u>From then on: her journey is one of guiding</u> other diaspora in reliving their pasts and speaking with Louise and Anna to recover a communal history of resistance.

❾ <u>Louisianas supernatural powers however, are</u> not universally commended. She faces isolation from academia, her parents, and the larger Western social sphere. When she finally completes her project and sketches out Mammy's family history, Louisiana nears death. The reader accompanies Louisiana on her revelation and expansion of the original transcription, engaging with oral folk traditions to rewrite history. Brodber's novel testifies to African **❿** <u>survivals; folk traditions that</u> have made it through the Middle Passage.

6. (A) NO CHANGE
   (B) Ella embraces this spiritual connection, only after listening through, the tape recorder's reel and witnessing her own out-of-body experiences.
   (C) Ella embraces this spiritual connection only after listening through the tape recorder's reel; and witnessing her own out-of-body experiences.
   (D) Ella embraces this spiritual connection only after listening, through the tape recorder's reel and witnessing her own out-of-body experiences.

7. (A) NO CHANGE
   (B) dialogue—an interaction among her, Anna, and
   (C) dialogue, an interaction among her Anna and
   (D) dialogue; an interaction among her, Anna and

8. (A) NO CHANGE
   (B) From then on, her journey is one of guiding
   (C) From then on; her journey is one of guiding
   (D) From then on her journey, is one of guiding

9. (A) NO CHANGE
   (B) Louisianas' supernatural powers, however are
   (C) Louisiana's supernatural powers, however are
   (D) Louisiana's supernatural powers, however, are

10. (A) NO CHANGE
    (B) survivals; folk traditions, that
    (C) survivals: folk traditions that
    (D) survivals: folk traditions, that

Answers Explained

1. **(A)** "Erna Brodber" is a singular person. To show that she possesses the novel, the apostrophe must be placed like this: *Brodber's*. The name of the novel can also be set off/separated from the rest of the sentence by commas because the description that precedes it—Brodber's third novel—is sufficient to narrow down the information to exactly which novel it is. The answer is not Choice (B) because there is not a comma after "novel." It is not Choice (C) because of improper apostrophe and comma use. It is not Choice (D) because the punctuation that starts and ends a parenthetical description must be consistent. Parenthetical information cannot start with a comma and end with a dash.

2. **(C)** This choice properly places a comma before the clarifying description; it also correctly uses the apostrophe and *s* after "novel" to indicate singular possession. Choice (A) is incorrect because there is no break before the clarifying phrase. The answer is not Choice (B) because a semicolon must have a complete sentence both before and after it. Choice (D) is wrong because this option does not properly show possession.

3. **(B)** This is the only option that properly sets off the appositive phrase with commas. Choice (C) does so only at the beginning of the phrase. Choice (D) has no commas. Choice (A) does not correctly use the colon since a colon must have a complete sentence before it.

4. **(A)** There is no need to insert commas into this phrase since the phrase is describing an essential characteristic of the spiritual connection. All of the other options insert unnecessary punctuation.

5. **(D)** This choice separates the two independent clauses with a semicolon. Moreover, it surrounds the parenthetical phrase with commas. Choice (A) is wrong because this option results in a run-on sentence. Choice (B) is incorrect because there is not a comma at the beginning of the parenthetical phrase. The answer is not Choice (C) because there is inconsistent punctuation around the parenthetical phrase.

6. **(A)** No additional punctuation is needed in this complete and logical sentence. Choices (B) and (D) insert unnecessary commas, which interrupt the sentence. Choice (C) does not have a complete sentence after the semicolon.

7. **(B)** A dash can provide the heavy pause needed to come before a clarification like this. The answer is not Choice (A) because there is no pause between "dialogue" and the clarification that follows. It is not Choice (C) because this option lacks needed commas to differentiate the items in the list. The answer is not Choice (D) because there is not a complete sentence after the semicolon.

8. **(B)** This choice provides a break between the introductory phrase and the complete sentence that follows. The answer is not Choice (A) because there is not a complete sentence before the colon. Choice (C) is incorrect because there is not a complete sentence before the semicolon. Choice (D) is wrong because the comma provides an interruption too late in the sentence.

9. **(D)** This is the only option that places needed commas around the word "however." In addition, this option properly uses the apostrophe to indicate singular ownership.

10. **(C)** This option provides a clear break before the clarification. The answer is not Choices (A) or (B) because there is not a complete sentence after the semicolon. It is not Choice (D) because there is an unnecessary comma after "traditions."

Transitions Exercise

The Benefits of Earthquakes

An earthquake results from tectonic plate activity, which starts from forces within the Earth that eventually break blocks of rock in the outer layers of the Earth. The rocks then move along a fault, or crack, ❶ and most of the energy that is released travels away from the fault in different types of seismic waves.

❷ Because earthquakes are often called natural disasters, in and of themselves, they are part of the forces of nature that actually help to sustain life on Earth. ❸ On the other hand, the carbon cycle is made possible by plate tectonics, which, together with the water cycle, keep nutrients, water, and land available for life. This process also regulates the global temperature. Tectonic activity builds mountains and forms lakes and waterfalls as well, providing an environment in which plant and animal life can flourish. ❹ In addition to their contributions to Earth's habitability, earthquakes also help scientists to make discoveries. By using seismographs around the Earth to measure seismic waves, geophysicists can determine the structure of Earth's interior.

Despite these benefits, it is still common to think of the damage that earthquakes cause. ❺ Unfortunately, most earthquakes have not been disastrous. There are as many as a million earthquakes per year, ❻ because most occur below the oceans sometimes as deep as about 435 miles below the Earth's surface. There was also more tectonic plate activity earlier in Earth's history, which released trapped nutrients, methane, and hydrogen that provided sufficient energy for some life-forms. Providing for a greater diversity and amount of life ❼ although prepared an environment that could support advanced life. Today, the amount of earthquakes is not so great as to prevent humans from living in cities.

❽ Furthermore, some earthquakes are destructive. Such destruction, however, could be avoided. About ninety-five percent of earthquakes

1. (A) NO CHANGE
    (B) but
    (C) since
    (D) while

2. (A) NO CHANGE
    (B) For
    (C) Although
    (D) Therefore

3. (A) NO CHANGE
    (B) For example,
    (C) As a result,
    (D) Nevertheless,

4. (A) NO CHANGE
    (B) Of
    (C) In consideration with
    (D) As a result of

5. (A) NO CHANGE
    (B) Also,
    (C) And,
    (D) However,

6. (A) NO CHANGE
    (B) but
    (C) with
    (D) moreover

7. (A) NO CHANGE
    (B) shall
    (C) in turn
    (D) as

8. (A) NO CHANGE
    (B) To illustrate,
    (C) Subsequently,
    (D) Nevertheless,

happen in the Pacific Belt and the Mediterranean Belt. Even though it is known where earthquakes are likely to happen with a strong degree of confidence, there are still large cities in these areas that people have chosen to develop. Building cities **9** to soft ground in earthquake-prone areas leads to more damage and a greater loss of life. Structures can be built that are able to withstand even the most intense earthquakes, but this has often not been done. While tectonic plate activity provides a number of benefits, moving to locations **10** when earthquakes occur without the proper structures sometimes results in disasters.

9. (A) NO CHANGE
    (B) on
    (C) through
    (D) with

10. (A) NO CHANGE
    (B) which
    (C) where
    (D) that

Answers Explained

1. **(A)** "And" correctly expresses that the author is simply continuing the line of thought from the first part of the sentence into the second part of the sentence.

2. **(C)** "Although" gives a contrast between the ideas that earthquakes are both natural disasters and life-sustaining events.

3. **(B)** "For example" connects the previous statement that earthquakes are life sustaining and the example of the carbon cycle that follows.

4. **(A)** "In addition to" connects the previous sentence, which focuses on some of the ways in which earthquakes make Earth more habitable, to the current sentence, which makes the additional statement that earthquakes help scientific research.

5. **(D)** The previous sentence acknowledges that there is a widespread belief that earthquakes are associated with damage. The current sentence states that this is not as widespread as is commonly thought, so the contrast that "however" provides is appropriate.

6. **(B)** "But" provides a contrast between the statement that there are so many earthquakes and the statement that many earthquakes happen deep within the planet.

7. **(C)** "In turn" is the only option that uses proper wording to express the cause-and-effect relationship within the sentence.

8. **(D)** The previous paragraph asserts that earthquakes are not all that harmful, while the current paragraph starts with the assertion that some earthquakes are destructive. Therefore, a contrasting word like "nevertheless" is appropriate.

9. **(B)** Although "building" can be paired with any of these options, in this context, "building on" is logical since one would build a city *on* the ground.

10. **(C)** Since the sentence is referring to physical locations, "where" is appropriate.

Sentence and Paragraph Ordering Exercise

Art Theft by Government—The Issues with the British Museum

{1}

[1] The spoils of war have always gone to the winning side. [2] That has long been the general consensus among warring nations. [3] It seems quite obvious that those who win should take what they want. [4] However, in recent years, this practice has become more and more common and not just within wars. [5] They took control of vast swaths of land and the people and items on them. [6] During this colonial time, the British government removed much artwork they deemed valuable and shipped it back to the British Museum. ❶

{2}

[1] Indeed, it isn't difficult to understand why the British people don't want to give up parts of one of the most amazing historical art collections in the world. [2] The British Museum has carefully cultivated the collection to reflect worldwide cultures. [3] However, many of these pieces were not purchased but were taken as spoils of war and colonization. [4] Egyptian, Iraqi, and Greek peoples, along with people from many other cultures, must travel around the world and pay an entry fee to see pieces of their own history. ❷

{3}

[1] For this reason, if you visit the British Museum today, you can see artifacts from everywhere from ancient Egypt to ancient Greece, from India to China. [2] For a long time the British government has justified the exhibits simply by pointing out that the artifacts have been safer in Great Britain than in their native countries. [3] However, this argument can no longer be generally accepted. [4] Governments like the one in Greece are very well equipped to keep their cultural

1. The author would like to insert the following sentence into the previous paragraph:

   "The British government at one point in time had colonies around the world."

   Where would it most logically be placed?

   (A) Before sentence 2
   (B) Before sentence 3
   (C) Before sentence 4
   (D) Before sentence 5

2. To make the preceding paragraph most logical, sentence 4 should be placed

   (A) where it is now.
   (B) before sentence 1.
   (C) before sentence 2.
   (D) before sentence 3.

artifacts safe. [5] However, now that the time has come to return some of these artifacts to their rightful owners, the British government is dragging its feet.

{4}

Although it is true that the British Museum has kept these pieces safe for decades, that doesn't mean the pieces belong to it. Even in cases where the pieces would be undiscovered if not for British archaeology, they should still belong to the people who created them, not to those who discovered them. The British Museum and museums around the world should accumulate foreign collections only through purchase, not by claiming "finders keepers." The time has come for people around the world to say a polite "thank you" to Britain for keeping their treasures safe and for Britain to send those treasures home. ❹

3. The author would like to insert the following sentence into the preceding paragraph:

"Look at the recent ransacking of the National Museum of Iraq, for example."

Where would it most logically be placed?

(A) Before sentence 2
(B) Before sentence 3
(C) Before sentence 4
(D) Before sentence 5

4. Which ordering of the paragraphs is most logical?

(A) As they currently are
(B) 1, 4, 2, 3
(C) 1, 3, 2, 4
(D) 4, 1, 2, 3

Answers Explained

1. **(D)** Placing this sentence before sentence 5 is the most logical choice. Unless this is done, the "they" that starts sentence 5 would be completely vague.

2. **(A)** If this sentence were moved from its current placement, it would interrupt the narrative flow of paragraph 2. In its current location, the sentence concludes the paragraph by demonstrating the modern-day impact of the British collection of artwork from other countries.

3. **(B)** This sentence provides evidence in support of the claim made in sentence 2 that artifacts may be safer if they are taken away from their native countries. Therefore, this sentence logically follows sentence 2.

4. **(C)** Paragraphs 1 and 4 are appropriate where they are as they provide a logical introduction and conclusion, respectively. Paragraph 3 should be moved to follow paragraph 1 since the last sentence of paragraph 1 provides the "reason" mentioned at the beginning of paragraph 3. Also, paragraph 2 should come after paragraph 3. Paragraph 2 elaborates on why moving the artifacts back to their native countries would be sensible.

TIP

Perhaps more than any other type of question on the Writing and Language section, questions about paragraph and sentence order demand patience.

Writing Concisely Exercise

A Name That Says It All

As a high school student, I always appreciated the frankness of the War of 1812—it declared ❶ its milieu in its very name, making it the subject of the most painless question on the semester exam. You guessed it: the war took place in 1812. This two-and-a-half-year conflict, however, was far more complex ❷ than this. At best, it can be said to have been a war of mixed results.

James Madison ❸ , known as the "Father of the Constitution," put the fledgling founding document to its earliest test as the first president to ask Congress to declare war. At the top of the commander in chief's list of reasons for going to war were Great Britain's restrictions on U.S. trade, disregard and violation of maritime rights, and encouragement of Native-American attacks on U.S. colonies. ❹ Ultimately, he was afraid of what might happen if there were a reconquest of the colonies by Great Britain's powerful naval forces.

According to the Federalists, particularly those of New England who depended on trade with Great Britain, the rationale for going to war wasn't as sincere as Madison would have liked everyone to believe. ❺ They argued, instead, that the justifications for war were barely camouflaged

1. (A) NO CHANGE
   (B) the very naming of its
   (C) that its nomenclature of this
   (D) the precise background of

2. (A) NO CHANGE
   (B) than what people have called it for some time.
   (C) than its name.
   (D) OMIT the underlined portion.

3. The author is considering removing the underlined phrase from the sentence. Should it be kept or removed?

   (A) Kept, because it provides a relevant and helpful detail
   (B) Kept, because it explains the origins of the United States
   (C) Removed, because it distracts from the essay's theme
   (D) Removed, because it unnecessarily changes the subject

4. (A) NO CHANGE
   (B) Ultimately, he feared the reconquest
   (C) Ultimately, a reconquest
   (D) In conclusion, he was mostly afraid of the ultimate reconquest and dismantling

5. The author is considering inserting the following sentence at this point in the essay:

   "Trade with Great Britain was instrumental to the jobs and fortunes of some American citizens."

   Should this sentence be inserted?

   (A) Yes, because it underscores the importance of an international relationship.
   (B) Yes, because it explains how economic policy influenced political thinking.
   (C) No, because it essentially repeats ideas already expressed in the essay.
   (D) No, because it shifts the topic of the paragraph.

excuses to expand the colonies without further **⑥** meddling and intrusion by Great Britain. At the time, British support of Tecumseh and the Shawnee Indians impeded westward expansion. Regardless of its ambiguous roots, in June of 1812, a divided Congress voted in favor of war.

By the time the Treaty of Ghent was signed in February 1815, Americans felt victory **⑦** but had achieved very little. Despite the War of 1812 being celebrated as a second war of independence, the original motivations for war were all but forgotten by its close. The U.S. had surrendered Detroit but found success in the Battle of Lake Erie, defended Baltimore and New Orleans just to have Washington, D.C. captured and burned. When Britain moved for an armistice, American patriotism soared, casually ignoring the **⑧** severely serious losses on its own end.

The war proved particularly useful for the military and political careers of famous American men like Andrew Jackson, John Quincy Adams, James Monroe, and William Henry Harrison, who in most cases entered the war as relatively anonymous but came out as eminent patriots. **⑨** Most of these men were recognized by few people before the war but afterward were widely known and respected by their countrymen. The real loss, on the other hand, befell the Native Americans. An armistice between the colonies and Great Britain not only marked a major failure in the Native-American end goal of self-government but also catalyzed a century of imperial expansion into Native-American territories **⑩** , which were areas of land.

6. (A) NO CHANGE
   (B) prying and interloping
   (C) interference
   (D) and additional involvement

7. (A) NO CHANGE
   (B) yet did not feel that they had achieved many of their aims.
   (C) but less too.
   (D) OMIT the underlined portion and end the sentence with a period.

8. (A) NO CHANGE
   (B) momentously dispiriting
   (C) grave
   (D) vitally important due to their infamy

9. The author is considering removing the underlined sentence from the essay. Should it be kept or removed?

   (A) Kept, because it clarifies the previous sentence
   (B) Kept, because it elaborates on personal motivations
   (C) Removed, because it repeats assertions made earlier in the paragraph
   (D) Removed, because it contradicts information found elsewhere in the essay

10. (A) NO CHANGE
    (B) , which consisted of land areas found in parts of North America
    (C) , which are relevant to geographic concepts
    (D) OMIT the underlined portion.

Answers Explained

1. **(A)** The last noun to which this could refer is "War of 1812." "Its" is sufficient because there is no other noun to which "its" could refer. The other choices are too wordy and repetitive.

2. **(C)** Choices (A) and (D) would leave this too vague. Choice (B) is far too wordy. Choice (C) provides the needed wording to make this a logical contrast.

3. **(A)** This phrase is relevant because it connects James Madison to the discussion of the "founding document" that immediately follows.

4. **(B)** This is the most concise option that will keep this as a complete sentence. Choice (C) would turn this into a fragment, and Choices (A) and (D) are too wordy.

5. **(C)** The beginning of the paragraph already mentions "those of New England who depended on trade with Great Britain." So inserting this sentence is unnecessary since it repeats an idea that has already been expressed.

6. **(C)** "Interference" means the same as all of the other choices yet expresses in a single word what the other choices express in multiple words.

7. **(A)** This choice expresses the idea fully and concisely. Choice (B) is too wordy and somewhat contradictory to the beginning of the sentence. Choices (C) and (D) are too vague.

8. **(C)** "Grave" when used as an adjective means "very serious." So it concisely expresses the same idea that the other choices express using multiple words.

9. **(C)** Immediately before the underlined portion, the passage states that many famous men entered the war as little-known figures and emerged from the war as respected patriots. Therefore, the underlined sentence repeats an assertion made earlier in the paragraph. So the underlined sentence should be removed.

10. **(D)** A reader can reasonably conclude that a "territory" is an area of land, both from the context of the passage and from the common understanding of the definition of "territory." Therefore, the wording should simply be removed as it is unnecessarily repetitive. If a sophisticated word that few readers would understand were used, including a definition of that word would be sensible.

TROUBLESHOOTING

Here are some further pointers for common issues.

"I never learned grammar rules."

- Review the concepts presented earlier in the chapter—the rules are presented in an extremely concise, easy-to-grasp way. If you need further review, take a look at *Barron's PSAT/NMSQT* for a more in-depth review of every grammar concept.
- Realize that you don't need to know the precise grammatical terminology for a concept being tested. As long as you have a good sense of what is correct, you do not need to give an elaborate justification for your answer—simply get it right.
- Actually read the editing marks and comments teachers make on your papers. Instead of just looking at your grade, look at what grammar mistakes you made and be sure you understand *why* they were mistakes. That way, you will gradually remedy gaps in your grammar knowledge.

"I finish too quickly."

- Try reading the passage before you look at the questions. Having a sense of the broad flow of the passage can be useful to you in answering many of the big-picture questions. This will be a more effective use of your time than doing nothing for several minutes at the end of the Writing and Language section.
- Pace yourself to take the full amount of time per passage. If you do not check your time as you go, you will likely rush to the end. Try to take the full nine minutes for each passage.

"I finish too slowly."

- Do not spend time overanalyzing your choice after you have made it. If you have read enough context and fully understand the requirements of the question, you have done all you can do; it is time to pick an answer choice and move on.
- Practice with timing so that on test day you do not fall prey to "paralysis by analysis." Any tendencies you have to go too slowly will only be exacerbated by the stresses of the actual PSAT.
- Try to spend no more than 90 seconds on a difficult question. If you have spent this much time and are not getting anywhere, you should cut your losses and take a guess. After all, there is no guessing penalty on the PSAT. You will not need to answer every question correctly to achieve National Merit recognition.

FURTHER PREPARATION

What else can I do beyond the drills and practice tests in this book to prepare for the PSAT Writing and Language?

- Practice with the other Barron's books for the PSAT: *Barron's Strategies and Practice for the PSAT/NMSQT* and *Barron's PSAT/NMSQT*.
- Use the free practice tests and resources provided by the College Board on *KhanAcademy.org*.
- Practice with ACT English tests—the grammar concepts and editing skills tested on the ACT are virtually identical to those tested on the PSAT Writing and Language section.
- Edit your friends' papers, and have them edit yours. Since the Writing and Language test is fundamentally an editing test, the more practice you have with editing, the better you will do.
- Read a variety of high-quality texts so that you develop a great feel for excellent writing.

> **Note:** The link to the online practice test is *http://bit.ly/barrons-PSAT-1520*. The practice test can also be accessed on all mobile devices, including tablets and smartphones.

Writing and Language Drills

5

This chapter consists of drills that represent the most challenging types of writing and language passages and questions you will encounter on the PSAT. The complete set of drills in this chapter comprehensively covers the most difficult question types you might find. Here are the titles of the passages should you wish to mark them off as you complete them.

12 SAMPLE PASSAGE PRACTICE DRILLS

- Female Resistance in Michelle Cliff's *Abeng*
- Beauty and Peril
- What Am I?
- Court Reporter
- Family Feud
- Bruce Hornsby
- I'll Take the Job
- Risk
- A Tricky Feline
- To Test or Not to Test
- Truman and MacArthur
- The Y-Bridge

> To practice these passages under timed conditions, take about nine minutes per drill.

> Comprehensive answer explanations to all of these drills come at the end of the chapter.

Female Resistance in Michelle Cliff's *Abeng*

[1] In contemporary critical work examining female subjectivities in ❶ <u>womens'</u> fiction, there is a tendency to privilege the overt insurgent over more ❷ <u>direct instances of insubordination.</u> [2] For most, it seems that the better story lies with psychically fragmented protagonists deviating from the world in which they live. [3] Michelle Cliff's 1984 *Abeng* tells the story of Clare Savage, a light-skinned Jamaican girl whose mixed racial heritage—in a world of strict oppositional binaries—incapacitates her chances for wholeness. [4] While Clare's complex subjectivity under the constraints of colonialist White supremacy certainly ❸ <u>calls for</u> examination as well as acclaim, other female characters' counter hegemonic personalities and actions, often less conspicuous, go predominantly ❹ <u>unseen and unnoticed.</u> [5] Thus, there is a presumption that these female characters are less courageous, less risky, less intellectual, less *something*. ❺

The novel, in some ways, magnifies the difference between insurgent and pacifist women in its juxtaposition of Nanny and Sekesu—the former a legendary leader of the Windward Maroons, and ❻ <u>the later</u> her sister who remained a slave. Accordingly, the islanders descend from either one or the other—rebel or conformist—implying a congenital difference in the people of Jamaica. A closer reading of several of the characters, however, suggests an identity more complex than mere compliance with White

1. (A) NO CHANGE
   (B) women's
   (C) womans'
   (D) womens

2. Which of the following provides the most logical ending to this sentence?

   (A) NO CHANGE
   (B) conspicuous happenings of belligerence.
   (C) indirect depictions of inconsistency.
   (D) subtle representations of resistance.

3. (A) NO CHANGE
   (B) call for
   (C) calls of
   (D) call of

4. (A) NO CHANGE
   (B) without anyone actually seeing them.
   (C) mostly without being viewed.
   (D) unnoticed.

5. The author wishes to place the following sentence into the previous paragraph.

   "In Caribbean women's fiction specifically, this commonality likely coincides with the tradition's inclination to be inherently subversive."

   Where would it most logically be placed?

   (A) Before sentence 1
   (B) Before sentence 2
   (C) Before sentence 3
   (D) Before sentence 4

6. (A) NO CHANGE
   (B) the opposition
   (C) the latter
   (D) the other one

patriarchal ideologies, a subjectivity amid the mire of institutionalized oppression that resists and survives in more nuanced ways. **❼ Rather than relying on colonialist binaries,** the female characters in *Abeng* demarcate a complex gradation of resistance from varying marginal spaces that ultimately works to dismantle the conceptual order of Western metaphysics. By interrogating the subjectivities of characters like Kitty, Mad Hannah, and Miss Winifred, readers can begin to understand various degrees of female resistance. **❽ Moreover, they will understand the roots of the motivations that empowered them to stand up for themselves.**

Cliff's novel is within the tradition of Jamaica Kincaid's *Annie John* **❾ (1985) Merle Hodge's *Crick Crack Monkey* (1981),** Oonya Kempadoo's *Buxton Spice* (1999), and Edwidge Danticat's *Clare of the Sea Light* (2013), in which young Caribbean girls' gender awakenings coincide with their political awakenings while they struggle to construct a Black female self without coherent mother-daughter relationships and without a clear sense of history. Clare typifies the **❿ double consciousness, her White external self attempts to reconcile internal feelings of Blackness.** In essence, the quest for Black female subjectivity coexists with the struggle against patriarchy, concurring with the feminist perspective that loving Blackness is itself political resistance. **⓫ Hence,** actions taken by women like Kitty, Mad Hannah, and Miss Winifred that may seem inconsequential actually serve socially and politically to challenge notions of patriarchal discourse by creating spaces of agency that refute, undermine, or opt out of systemic oppression.

7. Which of the following would provide the most effective and logical introduction to this sentence?

(A) NO CHANGE
(B) Instead of acting in a relativist fashion,
(C) In contrast with some documentary evidence,
(D) As opposed to seeing things along a spectrum,

8. The author is considering deleting the underlined sentence. Should it be kept or removed?

(A) Kept, because it provides a needed clarification
(B) Kept, because it justifies the author's line of thinking
(C) Removed, because it is unrelated to the previous sentence
(D) Removed, because it repeats an idea already expressed

9. (A) NO CHANGE
(B) (1985), Merle Hodge's *Crick Crack Monkey* (1981) Oonya
(C) (1985) Merle Hodge's, *Crick Crack Monkey* (1981) Oonya
(D) (1985), Merle Hodge's *Crick Crack Monkey* (1981), Oonya

10. (A) NO CHANGE
(B) double consciousness: her White external self attempts to reconcile internal feelings of Blackness.
(C) double consciousness her White external self, attempts to reconcile internal feelings of Blackness.
(D) double consciousness—her White external self—attempts to reconcile internal feelings of Blackness.

11. (A) NO CHANGE
(B) Additionally,
(C) Moreover,
(D) However,

Beauty and Peril

One would be hard-pressed to find more gorgeous scenery ❶ than that in California and the Pacific Northwest. From the Santa Monica Mountains to the Malibu lagoons, from the gorgeous Cascades and Mount Rainier to Puget Sound, the entirety of the coast from California to Washington is breathtaking. Tucked beneath that striking veneer, sinister and lurking, however, ❷ is secrets of a magnitude of which we are suspicious but uncertain. The reality, though, is as follows: ❸ a conspiracy is afoot.

For one, the region is threatened by the San Andreas fault line. Popularized by countless Hollywood films in the previous decades, San Andreas is perhaps the most recognizable (though, unfortunately, perhaps not even the most potentially destructive) of Pacific geological hazards. ❹ Extending for 810 miles in length through the bulk of California, the San Andreas fault line had its largest recorded earthquake in 1906, the infamous San Francisco earthquake with a magnitude of 7.8 on the Richter scale. The death count was 3,000, ❺ and that must be accompanied by the disclaimer that the population was significantly less then than it is today.

❻ In addition to the previously mentioned things, there is also the Juan de Fuca tectonic plate. This plate comprises part of the Cascadia subduction zone. Cascadia stretches all the way from Northern California to Canada's

1. (A) NO CHANGE
   (B) than
   (C) then those in
   (D) then

2. (A) NO CHANGE
   (B) was
   (C) are
   (D) has

3. Which of the following would provide wording that focuses on the overall message of the essay?

   (A) NO CHANGE
   (B) people need to get their priorities straight.
   (C) leadership depends on deeds, not words.
   (D) something cataclysmic is coming this way.

4. (A) NO CHANGE
   (B) Extending through
   (C) Extending for 810 miles through
   (D) Passing by

5. (A) NO CHANGE
   (B) moreover
   (C) but
   (D) also

6. Which of the following provides the best combination of the underlined sentences?

   (A) Additionally to the Juan de Fuca plate is the following, a plate that comprises part of the Cascadia subduction zone.
   (B) What is more, the Juan de Fuca tectonic plate is comprised with the Cascadia subduction zone.
   (C) Furthermore, the Juan de Fuca tectonic plate is the major component which partially comprises the zone, known as the "Cascadia subduction" zone.
   (D) Then there is the Juan de Fuca tectonic plate, which comprises part of the Cascadia subduction zone.

British Columbia, and this is the place where seismologists predict is the most likely spot for the "Big One." **7** For centuries North Americas continental shelf has ground against Juan de Fuca, and the shelf has been compressed upward all the while—every moment, every day, every century, a little bit more all the time. Predictions are that this sort of unrelenting stress **8** is approaching its breaking point of both literal and figurative nature. When that finally occurs (and advanced computer models put the likelihood of that catastrophe at greater than one in three in the next fifty years), it's difficult to affix an accurate estimation of the impending damages. Tens of thousands of deaths, hundreds of thousands of casualties, and billions of dollars in damaged property are not outside the scope of possibility. **9** Moreover, as both San Andreas and Juan de Fuca are coastal, subsequent tidal waves would accompany the earthquakes. And, at this point in our **10** wild goose chase, perhaps it is best not to venture any further down our path of apocalyptic prediction.

11 Despite all of these frightening possibilities, by no means am I advocating avoiding the Pacific coastal states. We must refuse to allow fear to dictate the courses of our lives—refuse to be deterred in our pursuit of happiness by the fragile futility of, "*Well, what if . . . ?*"

7. (A) NO CHANGE
   (B) For centuries, North Americas' continental
   (C) For centuries, North America's continental
   (D) For centuries North Americas' continental

8. (A) NO CHANGE
   (B) is approaching their
   (C) are approaching its
   (D) are approaching their

9. (A) NO CHANGE
   (B) Moreover as both San Andreas, and Juan de Fuca are coastal subsequent
   (C) Moreover as both San Andreas and Juan de Fuca are coastal subsequent
   (D) Moreover—as both San Andreas and Juan de Fuca are coastal subsequent

10. Which of the following would be most consistent with the tone and meaning of the passage?

   (A) NO CHANGE
   (B) conjecture
   (C) guesstimate
   (D) wisdom

11. Which of these options provides the most effective introduction to this sentence and paragraph as a whole?

   (A) NO CHANGE
   (B) Given the imminent catastrophe,
   (C) With the utter pointlessness of rampant speculation,
   (D) Granted that this is all hypothetical,

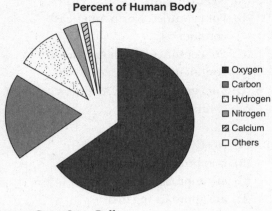

Percent of Human Body

- Oxygen
- Carbon
- Hydrogen
- Nitrogen
- Calcium
- Others

Source: OpenStax College

What Am I?

You can burn me for energy or find me in plastics. When I am soft, pliable, and dark, I am used to write with. When I am diamond shaped and clear, I go on your left hand. I might be in your stocking or your gas tank, and I always show up to the family barbecues. I make up **1** 2% of the human body, forming the basis of your very DNA. I am life when mixed with oxygen but death without enough of it. **2** It takes a lot to melt me, my nature is quite unreactive. With an atomic number of 6 and a weight of 12.011, I am the fourth most common element in the entire universe. I'm all about the bonds, attaching to up to four atoms at one time. **3** Chemists, casually refer to me as the basis of all plant and animal life, so you could say I have some big footprints to fill. **4**

If you guessed iron, you're wrong. If you guessed nitrogen, you are equally incorrect. **5** Sulfur, lacking in many of the characteristics of other atomic elements, is not suitable for this purpose. Carbon is the name; living organisms are the game. And it just so happens that I form more compounds than any other element, making me a building block of life on Earth. You might **6** have heard of my most common isotope, carbon-12, because it occurs naturally and makes up 99% of the carbon on your planet. If you happen to be more versed in the wonders of the chemical world, you might

1. Which of the following is supported by the information in the accompanying graph?

   (A) NO CHANGE
   (B) 10%
   (C) 19%
   (D) 65%

2. (A) NO CHANGE
   (B) It takes a lot to melt me my nature is quite unreactive.
   (C) It takes a lot to melt me: while my nature is quite unreactive.
   (D) It takes a lot to melt me; my nature is quite unreactive.

3. (A) NO CHANGE
   (B) Chemists casually refer to me, as the basis of all plant and animal life,
   (C) Chemists casually refer to me as the basis of all plant and animal life,
   (D) Chemists casually refer to me as the basis of all plant and animal life

4. Which option, if inserted here, would provide the most logical conclusion to the paragraph and the most effective transition to the next?

   (A) What am I?
   (B) Where am I?
   (C) What are these?
   (D) Who is this?

5. Which of the following is most consistent with the tone and style of the passage as a whole?

   (A) NO CHANGE
   (B) Nope, sulfur isn't cutting it either.
   (C) If you considered picking sulfur, that too would be a deleterious inclination.
   (D) Sulfur ain't right, too.

6. (A) NO CHANGE
   (B) of heard of
   (C) have heard have
   (D) of heard have

recognize me as the basis of graphene, a material stronger than steel but more flexible than rubber.

[1] My versatility is both gift and curse. [2] When I can find two oxygen atoms, I make carbon dioxide, which is found in Earth's atmosphere and used in photosynthesis. [3] Carbon footprint refers to the amount of greenhouse gas emissions generated by a particular country, organization, etc., and damages to Earth's ozone layer. [4] Hence, carbon dioxide—essential to life—can be detrimental in excess quantities. [5] **7** Accordingly, when I join with only one oxygen atom, I form a toxic gas known as carbon monoxide and **8** are responsible for fatal poisonings. **9**

For millions of years, I operated **10** between a balanced cycle. Plant life extracts me from the atmosphere in large quantities for food and energy, and I return to the atmosphere through respiration, **11** decomposing, and combustion. But humans disrupted my cycle by burning fossil fuels at rapid rates and destroying forests and plant life. Since I'm so critical to life, you may want to be more careful in the future.

7. (A) NO CHANGE
    (B) Furthermore,
    (C) Nevertheless,
    (D) Consequently,

8. (A) NO CHANGE
    (B) is
    (C) were
    (D) am

9. The author would like to insert the following sentence into the preceding paragraph.

    "However, too much of a good thing can be bad, really bad."

    Where would it most logically be placed?

    (A) After sentence 1
    (B) After sentence 2
    (C) After sentence 3
    (D) After sentence 4

10. (A) NO CHANGE
    (B) among
    (C) within
    (D) for

11. (A) NO CHANGE
    (B) decompose,
    (C) decomposed,
    (D) decomposition,

Court Reporter

In the court of law, a judge is the public official who presides over the hearing and is ultimately responsible for the administration of justice. An attorney or a lawyer advises and represents individuals, businesses, or agencies in legal disputes. Defense attorneys and prosecutors are the specific names given to lawyers ❶ <u>whom represent the accused or whom</u> represent local, state, or federal agencies as they accuse others of crimes, respectively. The jury consists of a body of people appointed to listen, consider evidence, and give a verdict on a ❷ <u>specific trial—essentially, jurors represent a panel of judges.</u> Responsible for maintaining order in the court is an officer, much like a police officer. And a court clerk maintains records of the court proceedings. Other than interested parties like the defendant and the witnesses, this list ❸ <u>composes</u> those occupants found in a normal legal proceeding. ❹ *Or will they?*

❺ <u>Court reporting an often-overlooked occupation of legal services—is essential to trials, depositions, committee</u> meetings, and basically any legal proceeding you can think of. A court reporter provides a verbatim record of court proceedings using recording equipment, stenographs, and stenomasks. ❻ <u>For this reason,</u> a court reporter transcribes any spoken dialogue, recorded speech, gestures, actions, etc. that occur in a legal environment where exact record of occurrences is mandatory. Hence, the oversight does not reflect the significance of the occupation itself. Court reporters are very important to the judicial system.

1. (A) NO CHANGE
   (B) who represent the accused or who
   (C) whom represent the accused or who
   (D) who represent the accused or whom

2. (A) NO CHANGE
   (B) specific trial, essentially jurors represent a panel of judges.
   (C) specific trial: essentially jurors represent, a panel of judges.
   (D) specific trial; essentially jurors, represent a panel of judges.

3. (A) NO CHANGE
   (B) compromises
   (C) comprises
   (D) comprising

4. Which of the following would provide the most logical and effective conclusion to this paragraph and transition to the next paragraph?

   (A) NO CHANGE
   (B) *Or does it?*
   (C) *Or can you?*
   (D) *Or did it?*

5. (A) NO CHANGE
   (B) Court reporting—an often-overlooked occupation of legal services, is essential to trials, depositions, committee
   (C) Court reporting, an often-overlooked occupation of legal services is essential to trials, depositions committee
   (D) Court reporting, an often-overlooked occupation of legal services, is essential to trials, depositions, committee

6. (A) NO CHANGE
   (B) In other words,
   (C) In contrast,
   (D) Because of this,

Stenographs are machines like keyboards that use key combinations rather than single characters **7** for effective communication. A court reporter using a stenomask, on the other hand, actually speaks into a covered microphone recording dialogue and reporting actions that a computer then transcribes. Recording equipment might consist of anything from a traditional tape recorder to more advanced digital audio recording with voice recognition technology. Whatever a court reporter chooses to use, **8** they are charged with generating exact records of what was said inside the courtroom and then providing accurate copies to courts, counsels, and other involved parties.

As you might guess, the occupational skills valued in a court reporter encompass clerical, listening, and writing skills; selective hearing; attention to detail; and knowledge of legal codes, jargon, and court procedures. That being said, it might surprise **9** you to learn that most entry-level positions require only an associate's degree or certificate program, and completion of licensing exams. **10** You are on your way to a six-figure salary and a front-row seat at local, state, or federal court proceedings in as little as two years. In addition, **11** a given court reporter's salary is more likely to be within a consistent range than the salaries of other major legal fields, making it a job you can count on to give you a solid paycheck.

Average Salaries for Legal Occupations, 2014

Annual, In Thousands of $

■ Highest 10% ▥ Median ■ Lowest 10%

Source: Onetonline.org

7. Which of the following provides the most logical and effective ending to this sentence?

(A) NO CHANGE
(B) for technological advantage.
(C) for speedy typing.
(D) to discourage sickness.

8. (A) NO CHANGE
(B) you are
(C) one are
(D) he or she is

9. (A) NO CHANGE
(B) him or her
(C) one
(D) them

10. Which of the following is both the most logical introduction to the sentence and supported by the information in the accompanying graph?

(A) NO CHANGE
(B) You will earn more than the typical American worker
(C) You will pay off your student loans in no time
(D) You could be on your way to a $60,000 salary

11. Which of the following properly uses information from the graph to build upon the author's argument in this paragraph?

(A) NO CHANGE
(B) court reporters earn an average salary that exceeds the median legal professional salary,
(C) court reporters are more likely to be hired for entry-level positions,
(D) a given court reporter's compensation is likely to be as much as the salaries of the attorneys who appear before them,

Family Feud

Like many of history's most legendary battles, the lawless family feud between the Hatfields and McCoys ❶ boiling down to the differences between two men. William Anderson Hatfield, known widely as "Devil Anse," was a mountain dweller and successful timber merchant. Randolph McCoy, or "Ole Ran'l," ❷ owned some land, and livestock in the same region; the borderlands dividing Kentucky and West Virginia. The clash between the two families brands the American memory—in the Midwest, the vendetta rivals that of the Capulets and Montagues but with a uniquely "hillbilly" twist.

Legend has it that the feud began somewhere near 1865 with the murder of Randolph's brother, Asa, who was accused of treason for fighting for the Union during the Civil War. ❸ As a result, the Hatfield family ran the Logan Wildcats, the local militia group responsible for Asa's murder. Years of deep dislike, bitter resentment, and minor confrontations passed before Randolph McCoy accused Floyd Hatfield of stealing a hog in 1878. Devil Anse's influence over the courts resulted in a quick clearing of Floyd's name but not before a McCoy relative testified on the Hatfield's behalf. ❹ The disloyalty sealed the witness's fate—he was violently killed by other McCoys.

It wasn't until the 1880s, though, that things spiraled out of control. Johnse Hatfield, son of Devil Anse, began dating Randolph's daughter, Roseanna. They devoted themselves to each other despite their ❺ family's disapproval. However, Johnse later left a pregnant Roseanna and married her cousin Nancy, stirring intra- and inter-familial conflicts. Things were unstable to say the least in August 1882, when three of Randolph's sons confronted two Hatfield brothers. ❻ The face-off turned to violence with quickness and rapidity, and Ellison Hatfield was stabbed and shot. To ❼ venge the family name, a group of Hatfields

1. (A) NO CHANGE
   (B) boils
   (C) boil
   (D) OMIT the underlined portion.

2. (A) NO CHANGE
   (B) owned some land, and livestock in the same region, the borderlands dividing Kentucky and West Virginia.
   (C) owned some land and livestock in the same region, the borderlands dividing Kentucky and West Virginia.
   (D) owned some land and livestock in the same region the borderlands dividing Kentucky and West Virginia.

3. (A) NO CHANGE
   (B) Nonetheless, the
   (C) Contradictorily, the
   (D) The

4. Which of the following would provide the most logical and effective introduction to this sentence?

   (A) NO CHANGE
   (B) He managed to keep his word
   (C) The judge and jury were unimpressed
   (D) The historical record did him no favors

5. (A) NO CHANGE
   (B) families
   (C) familys
   (D) families'

6. (A) NO CHANGE
   (B) The face-off turned violent,
   (C) Violent to the face-off turned,
   (D) Turning to a situation of violent confrontation,

7. (A) NO CHANGE
   (B) revenging
   (C) vengeance
   (D) avenge

found the three sons, bound them, and fired more than 50 bullets into them. Again, the prominent family ❽ eluded arrest.

[1] The media caught on, and the Hatfield/McCoy clash reached commercial popularity. [2] Suddenly newspapers produced article after article, painting the Hatfield family as particularly vicious and violent. [3] By 1887, the Hatfields spent most of their time dodging increasingly large bounties. [4] To put an end to the family rivalry, the Hatfields sought to end the McCoys once and for all. [5] In 1888, they ambushed the McCoy household, killing ❾ Old Ran'l's son and daughter, and brutally beating his wife. [6] Nine were arrested in connection to the atrocious crime. ❿

Eventually, the case made its way to the U.S. Supreme Court where eight of the nine received life in prison. ⓫ The ninth, a mentally handicapped Ellison Mounts, was hanged in February 1890. Today, both families hold celebrity status in the American consciousness.

8. (A) NO CHANGE
    (B) alluded
    (C) illuded
    (D) illuminated

9. The author is considering changing this phrase to "Mr. McCoy's." Is this change necessary?

    (A) Yes, because it provides a needed clarification.
    (B) Yes, because it uses more formal language.
    (C) No, because this logically refers to Mr. Hatfield.
    (D) No, because this nickname was already established in the essay.

10. The author would like to insert the following sentence into the previous paragraph:

    "With the journalistic sensationalism, the feud was revived."

    Where would it most logically be placed?

    (A) Before sentence 1
    (B) Before sentence 3
    (C) Before sentence 5
    (D) After sentence 6

11. Should the underlined sentence be kept or deleted?

    (A) Kept, because it provides a relevant clarification
    (B) Kept, because it gives a needed justification
    (C) Removed, because it is off topic
    (D) Removed, because it shifts the analysis too quickly

Bruce Hornsby

I struggle with the phenomenon of fame. ❶ Perhaps, as Andy Warhol once quipped, we are all destined to occupy the spotlight for fifteen minutes. But what, I ask, of those whose notoriety is longer sustained? How can a Hollywood family of dullards and never-do-wells mesmerize the whole of a nation with a smash-hit reality TV series, while someone of actual import and accomplishment—say, a heroic police officer or selfless organ donor— ❷ passes the entirety of his or her life in the thankless shadows? I don't wish to waste your time disputing the nature or purpose of celebrity, but pardon my tangential musing as I approach ❸ my true question, where is the love, for Bruce Hornsby?

❹ Powerfully, I now must tell you who Bruce Hornsby is, which further illustrates the criminality of his anonymity. A man so talented should require no introduction whatsoever. Alas, Hornsby is a singer, songwriter, and—in my esteemed opinion—as fine a piano player as Billy Joel (a man who requires no introduction, ❺ my point about the arbitrary nature of fame having been thus solidified). When Bruce plays the piano, the sound is so wonderfully rich that your brain can't help but be puzzled at the thought of human hands moving

1. The author is considering deleting the underlined sentence. Should this sentence be kept or removed?

   (A) Kept, because it provides a relevant elaboration
   (B) Kept, because it introduces the main person to be analyzed
   (C) Deleted, because it is inconsistent with the essay's tone
   (D) Deleted, because it distracts from the essay's principal argument

2. (A) NO CHANGE
   (B) pass
   (C) passing
   (D) past

3. (A) NO CHANGE
   (B) my true, question; where is the love for Bruce Hornsby?
   (C) my true question—where is the love for Bruce Hornsby.
   (D) my true question: where is the love for Bruce Hornsby?

4. Which word provides the most logical transition at this point in the essay?

   (A) NO CHANGE
   (B) Imaginatively,
   (C) Inevitably,
   (D) Obliquely,

5. (A) NO CHANGE
   (B) giving the solidity of a case to my point about the arbitrary nature of fame.
   (C) further solidifying my point about fame's arbitrary nature
   (D) making my point about the solidifying of the arbitration of fame

so deftly over the keys. And when he sings, there is a molasses-sweet timbre that communicates volumes about the human condition. **6**

Even more puzzling about Hornsby's lack of name recognition is that he has had a moderate amount of success throughout his career. Hornsby has won three Grammy awards (most notably in 1987 for best new artist), and his album *The Way It Is* attained multiplatinum status by selling more than two million units. His songs continue to receive radio airplay on **7** variety various stations, and he has toured and collaborated with such dynamos as The Grateful Dead, Don Henley, Bob Dylan, Stevie Nicks, Bonnie Raitt, and Crosby Stills and Nash **8** (all of whom have succeeded him greatly in notoriety and recognition). Moreover, Bruce Hornsby's music has transcended genre; it is a little-known fact that hip-hop legend Tupac Shakur's mega-hit "Changes" was actually an adaptation of Hornsby's "The Way It Is."

6. The author wishes to insert an aside to underscore his self-deprecating self-awareness that readers likely will not share his views about Hornsby. Which of the following would best be inserted at this point to accomplish the author's goal?

(A) There are those who can appreciate Hornsby, and there are those who not only cannot appreciate his work, but have no artistic sensibility whatsoever.

(B) Forgive my hyperbole, but so profound is my love for his music that I cannot help but get carried away with my adulation.

(C) As someone with extensive musical training, I can assure you that if you miss out on Hornsby, you are truly missing out.

(D) To listen to him play is like watching Michelangelo painting the Sistine Chapel—it is to see a master at work.

7. (A) NO CHANGE
(B) various variety
(C) variety, various
(D) various, variety

8. The author is considering deleting the underlined portion of the sentence. Should this portion be removed?

(A) Yes, because it does not focus on the essay's primary topic.

(B) Yes, because it unfairly disparages the protagonist of the passage.

(C) No, because it underscores the author's thoughts about Hornsby's lack of recognition.

(D) No, because it provides specific details in support of the following sentence.

⑨ Perhaps, like van Gogh's or F. Scott Fitzgerald's, Bruce Hornsby's legacy will grow with time. Perhaps society just isn't quite ready to award him his deserved credentials. **⑩** Consequently, I fear the opposite: now more than ever, we are a Justin Bieber and Eminem crowd. Bruce's time is past, and his just deserts will forever elude him as we continue to turn our attention to increasingly **⑪** lessening worthy recipients.

9. (A) NO CHANGE
   (B) Perhaps like van Gogh or F. Scott Fitzgerald Bruce Hornsby's legacy
   (C) Perhaps, like van Gogh or F. Scott Fitzgerald Bruce Hornsby's, legacy
   (D) Perhaps, like van Gogh or F. Scott Fitzgerald Bruce Hornsby's legacy

10. (A) NO CHANGE
    (B) But,
    (C) Therefore,
    (D) Accordingly,

11. (A) NO CHANGE
    (B) less worthy
    (C) fewer worthy
    (D) fewer worth of the

I'll Take the Job

{1}

The first three articles of a 1789 document—formally known as the United States Constitution—delineate the separation of powers ❶ in the core of American democracy. Divided into three branches, the federal government assigns law making to the legislative, law enforcing to the executive, and law interpreting to the judicial system. ❷ The separation of powers doctrine largely originated with the ideas of the French political philosopher, Baron de Montesquieu. The President of the United States is the nucleus of the Executive Branch, serving as both Head of State and Commander in Chief, and is the most prominent figure of American government. ❸ Thus, if one's career goals involve establishing oneself as one of the most important and well-known people in the world, then running for the national presidency makes a great deal of sense.

{2}

[1] The requirements are pretty straightforward: one must be a natural-born citizen who ❹ is at least the age of 35 years and for at least the duration of 14 years resided in the United States. [2] What it actually takes, however, is labyrinthine. [3] At the forefront of a successful campaign for presidency ❺ lie charisma. [4] One's public image must be maintained with a skeleton-free closet and consistent political views—nothing sabotages a presidential campaign like scandal or irregularity. [5] Even then, a likely candidate should endeavor to appeal to average Americans, appearing in churches and small businesses often and visiting frequently with veterans,

1. (A) NO CHANGE
   (B) with
   (C) at
   (D) on

2. The author is considering deleting the underlined sentence. Should it be removed?

   (A) Yes, because it interrupts the flow of the paragraph.
   (B) Yes, because it is unrelated to the facts of the paragraph.
   (C) No, because it defines a key term in the passage.
   (D) No, because it provides a relevant historical anecdote.

3. (A) NO CHANGE
   (B) Thus, if ones career goals involve establishing oneself
   (C) Thus if your career goals involve establishing yourself
   (D) Thus, if your career goals involve establishing oneself

4. (A) NO CHANGE
   (B) is at least 35 years old and has resided in the United States for 14 years or more.
   (C) is 35 and has lived in the U.S. for a long time.
   (D) meets the requirements as laid out in the Constitution.

5. (A) NO CHANGE
   (B) lay
   (C) lays
   (D) lies

blue-collar workers, and farmers. [6] Personal military experience never hurt anyone either. ❻

{3}

❼ Past presidents' age ranges from 44 (John F. Kennedy) to 76 (Ronald Reagan) but average at about 55 years old. U.S. presidents tend to be married with children and hold advanced degrees in law or business from elite universities. Most candidates possess resumes boasting of years in public service and political positions; the fast track to presidential candidacy comprises elected posts like mayor, governor, and senator. ❽ Still allure, a spotless background, and years in diplomatic service are a dime a dozen in presidential races. One needs money, and plenty of it, to run for the presidency.

{4}

Even after an exploratory committee predicts success and a potential candidate registers with the Federal Election Commission, one has to win support in a caucus, triumph in a primary, ❾ following an earning nationally in a convention, and raise millions of dollars in funds before the general election. ❿ Surprisingly, the *Washington Post* reported that both presidential candidates in 2012, Barack Obama and Mitt Romney, raised over $1 billion each to run their campaigns. Thinking of the White House as a future residence? Work on that billion-dollar smile. ⓫

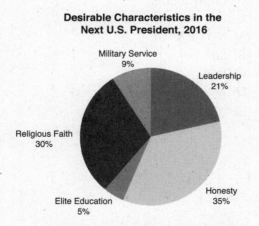

Desirable Characteristics in the Next U.S. President, 2016

Military Service 9%
Leadership 21%
Religious Faith 30%
Elite Education 5%
Honesty 35%

Survey of 1,000 randomly selected likely voters

6. The author would like to insert the following sentence into the previous paragraph:

"But mastering the charm, attractiveness, and likability to please the cameras—arguably one of the more mystifying qualifications of presidency—by itself falls short of an election."

Where would it most logically be inserted?

(A) After sentence 1
(B) After sentence 2
(C) After sentence 3
(D) After sentence 5

7. (A) NO CHANGE
(B) Past president's ages range
(C) Past president's age range
(D) Past presidents' ages range

8. (A) NO CHANGE
(B) Still, allure, a spotless background, and
(C) Still, allure a spotless background and
(D) Still, allure a spotless background, and

9. (A) NO CHANGE
(B) earn a following in a national convention,
(C) follow an earning nationally in a convention,
(D) follow a national earning in a convention

10. (A) NO CHANGE
(B) As a result,
(C) For instance,
(D) However,

11. The author would like to use the data from the accompanying chart to create a relevant sentence to insert in the essay. To which paragraph should such a sentence be added?

(A) Paragraph 1
(B) Paragraph 2
(C) Paragraph 3
(D) Paragraph 4

Risk

I remember the class well. ❶ We seniors understood academic principles and knew the roles that we would play when we moved into management jobs after graduation ❷ since we felt well-prepared for the profession we were about to enter. Most programs had a capstone course that pulled all of our coursework together, and this was no different. Our guide for this course was an experienced executive and not the normal academic ❸ who walked these halls. "What is the basic job of a general manager?" he asked. Hands shot up. "Maximize shareholder equity!" "Maximize profit." "Develop a strategic vision!" "Increase market share." To these responses and others, he said a simple "no." Finally, he told us what we would be doing as managers ❹ for the field. "Your job is to take risk. When analysis will not provide an answer, you have to make a decision and move the ball forward. ❺ Your decision-making performance will determine your worth to the enterprise."

1. (A) NO CHANGE
    (B) Us
    (C) That
    (D) This

2. The author is considering deleting the underlined portion. Should this selection be removed?

    (A) Yes, because it digresses from the main idea of the sentence
    (B) Yes, because it repeats ideas already implied in the sentence
    (C) No, because it provides relevant details in support of a claim
    (D) No, because it provides a needed contrast

3. (A) NO CHANGE
    (B) whom walked
    (C) who walking
    (D) whom walking

4. (A) NO CHANGE
    (B) fielding.
    (C) out in the field.
    (D) with a field.

5. Which of the following provides the most logical and relevant conclusion to the paragraph?

    (A) NO CHANGE
    (B) Significant wealth will inevitably follow.
    (C) Be sure you incorporate thorough analysis before you decide on your course of action.
    (D) Remember these words of advice when you go back to school.

Taking risk involves the understanding that various outcomes can arise when you make a choice. ❻ Some outcomes may spell disaster for your company, others may create exceptional financial returns for the shareholders. But hiding behind every one of these possible futures is the uncertainty of which one or some hybrid of several will actually occur. An ❼ affective manager has the confidence to face these outcomes and the inherent unknowns.

[1] Let's take a simple example. [2] How much inventory of a certain item should you hold so that you can provide exceptional customer service and not run out of product? [3] What affects the success of a chosen number of items to put on the shelf? [4] The other is the lead time that it takes to replenish the inventory when it begins to run low. [5] The tricky part is that both the demand for the product and the lead time to replenish are typically not known with certainty. [6] ❽ Books are going the way of the record player—technology has made mobile electronics far more preferable. [7] The publisher may tell you that the standard lead time is 8 weeks, but this can change due to other business it may be running in the printing factory. [8] And if you are at Amazon.com, there are millions of these decisions that are made, and ❾ the success of the business will be driven by how well you manage these variations.

6. (A) NO CHANGE
   (B) Some outcomes, may spell disaster for your company: others may create exceptional financial returns for the shareholders.
   (C) Some outcomes—may spell disaster for your company—others may create exceptional financial returns for the shareholders.
   (D) Some outcomes may spell disaster for your company; others may create exceptional financial returns for the shareholders.

7. (A) NO CHANGE
   (B) affecting
   (C) effective
   (D) effecting

8. Which of the following would provide the most specific example in support of the claim made in the previous sentence?

   (A) NO CHANGE
   (B) If Oprah selects a given book for her monthly review, copies will run off of the shelves and backorders will occur.
   (C) The definition of "lead time" varies a great deal depending on the business professor to whom you speak.
   (D) Publishers try to increase demand for profitable books, using methods like online advertising and public relations firms.

9. (A) NO CHANGE
   (B) the success of the business, will be driven by how well you manage these variations.
   (C) the success, of the business will be driven, by how well you manage these variations.
   (D) the success of the business will be driven by how well, you manage these variations.

[9] If you don't have the item, the customer will simply click on a competitor's website and make the purchase. [10] If you put too much on the shelf, the investment cost of this **⑩** <u>moving slowly inventory</u> can consume the working capital of the business. **⑪**

10. (A) NO CHANGE
    (B) slow inventory with respect to moving
    (C) slowly moving inventory
    (D) inventory, which is slowly moving at times,

11. The author wishes to place the following sentence into the previous paragraph:

    "One factor is the demand that you expect over a given time period, such as a month or quarter."

    Where would it most logically be placed?

    (A) Before sentence 2
    (B) Before sentence 4
    (C) Before sentence 9
    (D) Before sentence 10

A Tricky Feline

Isaac Newton and Albert Einstein are probably the only theoretical physicists to ever become household names, **①** because of the fictional character of physicist Sheldon Cooper. The layperson merely associates Newton with gravity and laws of motion, and Einstein with relativity and mass-energy equivalence, failing to understand the magnitude of **②** either scientist's contribution. In fact, "Einstein" is used more often as a synonym for "genius" than actually to reference his work. **③** Erwin Schrödinger a lesser recognized name, however, sought to tackle many of the same issues in physics as Einstein himself.

Schrödinger won the Nobel Prize in Physics in 1933 for his work in quantum mechanics, **④** since he is most remembered for a theoretical experiment he proposed two years later. In this thought experiment, Schrödinger hoped to illustrate the absurdity of the Copenhagen interpretation, a widely accepted notion of quantum physics that Einstein had an equally difficult time **⑤** smelling. Schrödinger offered a paradox that came to be known as Schrödinger's Cat. In this paradox, a cat is placed into a steel box with a vial of poison and a radioactive substance. When the radioactive substance decays, an internal monitor releases the poison and subsequently kills the cat.

[1] The trick here **⑥** lies in the unpredictability of radioactive material. [2] Called "superposition" by scientists, the decay is completely random, existing simultaneously in a state of decay and not. [3] The subatomic event simply may or may not occur. [4] Since the cat's fate is tied to the atom's, the cat would then exist in this same superposition, simultaneously dead and alive. [5] Yet, we know that the cat is not both dead *and* alive. [6] Schrödinger, then, posited

1. (A) NO CHANGE
   (B) notwithstanding
   (C) aside with
   (D) stemming in

2. (A) NO CHANGE
   (B) either scientists'
   (C) each scientists
   (D) each scientists'

3. (A) NO CHANGE
   (B) Erwin Schrödinger, a lesser recognized name, however sought
   (C) Erwin Schrödinger, a lesser recognized name however sought
   (D) Erwin Schrödinger, a lesser recognized name, however, sought

4. (A) NO CHANGE
   (B) for
   (C) but
   (D) and

5. Which ending to the sentence is most consistent with the sentence's meaning?

   (A) NO CHANGE
   (B) chewing.
   (C) tasting.
   (D) swallowing.

6. (A) NO CHANGE
   (B) lies to
   (C) lays in
   (D) lays on

the issue of when superposition collapses into reality—when multiple occupying states simultaneously ❼ becomes one or the other. ❽

❾ Quantum theory is carried about by specialists known as theoretical physicists. Since physicists know that particles as small as electrons do not follow the rules of Newton's laws, they account for all possible states that particles could be in at one time with the wave function. You cannot say, without direct observation, what subatomic particles are doing; instead, you say there is a combination of the multiple states in which the particle could possibly be. Schrödinger, a father of quantum mechanics himself, surely understood the uses of quantum superposition but also sought to bring attention to ❿ its shortcomings.

Although Schrödinger will never be as widely referenced as Einstein; he too was dissatisfied with quantum randomness. ⓫ It is truly a shame that Schrödinger's accomplishments are unknown to other scientists.

7. (A) NO CHANGE
   (B) become
   (C) have becoming
   (D) had becoming

8. The author wishes to insert the following sentence into the previous paragraph:

   "Hence, the flaw in this line of thinking."

   Where would it most logically be placed?

   (A) Before sentence 2
   (B) Before sentence 3
   (C) Before sentence 5
   (D) Before sentence 6

9. Which of the following provides the most logical introduction to the paragraph?

   (A) NO CHANGE
   (B) Quantum theory is concerned with the study of subatomic behaviors.
   (C) Quantum theory confirms the findings of those physicists who were apostles to Newton's theories.
   (D) Quantum theory focuses on the behavior of large physical entities, such as galaxies.

10. (A) NO CHANGE
    (B) it's
    (C) their
    (D) there

11. Which of the following would provide the most logical ending to this paragraph and to the essay as a whole?

    (A) NO CHANGE
    (B) The cat, after all, is either dead or alive—never both.
    (C) Both men were instrumental in confirming the Newtonian theoretical construct.
    (D) While Schrödinger was not recognized in his lifetime, that has finally begun to change.

To Test or Not to Test

❶ I find myself in a catch-22, an advocate of critical pedagogies who desperately, wishes to see my students succeed in high-stakes testing. Training to become a teacher is being assigned the texts of John Dewey, Paulo Freire, and Ira Shor, and then being handed a thirty-page mandated curriculum to be followed to the letter. The clash ❷ among pedagogy and practice is not a new one, nor is the contradiction between teaching stance and accountability measurements. By this, I mean that many scholars have addressed the underlying issues between what they believe the classroom should look like and what the institution says it must look like. As teachers, we empower our students, open their minds, and encourage social justice—a job not done well when teaching-to-the-test. Yet, assessment signifies what we value in the classroom and how we assign that value. ❸ In other words, to stop testing a subject is to see it all but disappear from the curriculum.

[1] Many argue that high-stakes testing is antithetical to the critical classroom. [2] An increase in required courses and standardized tests, for them, ❹ equating to the disempowerment of students. [3] Today's student, under this line of thinking, is told what is important and what is not, who is in authority and who will never be, and whose perspective is heard and whose is silenced. [4] Ira Shor, literacy and composition scholar, suggests that all education is, and has always been, political. [5] Whereas a traditional English teacher might assign canonical texts and then assess a ❺ classes understanding of plot, setting, and character analyses, a critical English teacher assigns literature with a goal in mind of what the class will get from that particular text, and then encourages the class to talk about how the social issues reflect their own lives, whose voices weren't heard, and how the story might be told differently from another perspective. ❻

1. (A) NO CHANGE
   (B) I find myself in a catch-22: an advocate of critical pedagogies who desperately wishes to see my students succeed in high-stakes testing.
   (C) I find myself in a catch-22—an advocate of critical pedagogies—who desperately wishes to see my students succeed in high-stakes testing.
   (D) I find myself in a catch-22; an advocate of critical pedagogies, who desperately wishes to see my students succeed in high-stakes testing.

2. (A) NO CHANGE
   (B) between
   (C) through
   (D) in

3. (A) NO CHANGE
   (B) For these reasons,
   (C) Due to this,
   (D) Henceforth,

4. (A) NO CHANGE
   (B) equation
   (C) equate
   (D) equates

5. (A) NO CHANGE
   (B) class'es
   (C) class's
   (D) classes'

6. The author would like to insert the following sentence into the previous paragraph:

   "Critical pedagogies, therefore, are committed to democracy and the questioning of power structures."

   Where would it most logically be placed?

   (A) After sentence 2
   (B) After sentence 3
   (C) After sentence 4
   (D) After sentence 5

❼ Yet, testing is not without its benefits. Educators agree that assessments encourage better instruction, improve motivation, and help teachers identify students' needs. Inside the classroom, students, their parents, and administrators all want high test scores. Effective schools are continually aligned with those **❽** that adequately prepare students for testing. And, when done correctly, tests should operate as an assessment of what is practiced on a daily basis inside the classroom. Classrooms that teach to well-written standards **❾** assure that students are prepared for the next grade level. Imagine the student who moves from grade to grade (or worse, school to school) without standards. While testing might not be perfect, it is necessary. **❿** Testing is critical to assessing what people are capable of doing. **⓫**

Gender Percentages of PSAT Test Takers

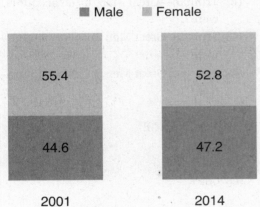

Source: The College Board

7. Which of the following would provide the most logical introduction to this paragraph?

(A) NO CHANGE
(B) The problems with widespread testing are clear.
(C) Scholars are in agreement when it comes to the shortcomings of testing.
(D) In fact, the time has come for educators to take a stand.

8. (A) NO CHANGE
(B) for which
(C) whom
(D) OMIT the underlined portion.

9. (A) NO CHANGE
(B) insure
(C) ensure
(D) reassure

10. Which of the following sentences most effectively and specifically builds off of the statement made in the previous sentence?

(A) NO CHANGE
(B) I cannot think of one career path that doesn't require a series of tests.
(C) Can someone think of a reasonable alternative to the tried and true avenue of testing?
(D) Students are far more than just a number based on a random assessment.

11. The author is considering incorporating information from the accompanying graph into her essay. Should she utilize this information?

(A) Yes, because it provides relevant facts on standardized testing.
(B) Yes, because it demonstrates cultural shifts over time.
(C) No, because it is only loosely related to the major theme of the passage.
(D) No, because it contradicts the author's principal claim.

Truman and MacArthur

Many of the greatest battles in history can be simplified to microcosmic struggles ❶ among two Great Men. Take Grant and Lee, for instance. Or consider David and Goliath if you prefer an older story. But not often ❷ do such a struggle occur when both Great Men are on the same side. And in those instances, you see, are when the fireworks really commence to combust. The old saying is that it's best to avoid having ❸ "a chicken in every pot"; it is best to have only one person making executive decisions and delegating orders to inferiors. General Douglas MacArthur and President Harry ❹ Truman—Great Men, by all accounts—were both American leaders in the late 1940s and early 1950s in the aftermath of the Allied victory during World War II. Naturally, only one of them could emerge victorious from the rubble of ❺ there power struggle.

MacArthur, so distinguished a war hero that he was awarded the illustrious and unparalleled Congressional Medal of Honor for his heroism during WWII, was the Army's most powerful and decorated general. He had been a Republican presidential candidate during the elections of 1944 and 1948, and was currently serving as the Supreme Commander of the Allied Powers ❻ —an office created specifically for General MacArthur in which he would oversee the Allied occupation of Japan after the war victory.

1. (A) NO CHANGE
   (B) between
   (C) within
   (D) throughout

2. (A) NO CHANGE
   (B) doing
   (C) does
   (D) OMIT the underlined portion.

3. What colloquial expression would be most appropriate, given the content of the sentence as a whole?

   (A) NO CHANGE
   (B) "a chip on your shoulder";
   (C) "too many cooks in the kitchen";
   (D) "a wild goose chase";

4. (A) NO CHANGE
   (B) Truman—Great Men, by all accounts, were
   (C) Truman: Great Men, by all accounts—were
   (D) Truman; Great Men, by all accounts—were

5. (A) NO CHANGE
   (B) their
   (C) his
   (D) one's

6. The author is considering deleting the underlined portion. Should it be kept or removed?

   (A) Kept, because it clarifies a key title
   (B) Kept, because it states the author's point of view
   (C) Removed, because it provides an unnecessary detail
   (D) Removed, because it distracts from the primary message of the sentence

7 Truman, a man now generally viewed by political scholars and historians as one of the finest commanders in chief of the 20th century had a military foundation of his own: he had served in the First World War and later held a reserve commission as colonel. **8** As a result, Truman distrusted the current crop of military executives at his disposal. He once remarked on his confusion that the U.S. Army could "produce men such as Lee, Pershing, Eisenhower and Bradley, and at the same time produce Custer, Patton, and MacArthur."

[1] The start of the Korean War in 1950 **9** made happen the cataclysm. [2] General MacArthur, often superseding orders by Truman, had instituted deft military strategic policy that prevented South Korea (a U.S. ally) from being overrun by North Korea **10** (which was being supported both militarily and financially by Communist China). [3] Momentum in the war began to shift, however, and soon South Korea was in a position to attack. [4] MacArthur assured Truman that a U.S.-led offensive into North Korea to eradicate Communism there would be met with little resistance from China. [5] China lashed back. [6] MacArthur proceeded to disobey numerous Truman orders and even began to publicly criticize Truman to the media. [7] Alas, the president had no choice, and MacArthur was relieved of his command on April 11, 1951. **11**

7. (A) NO CHANGE
    (B) Truman, a man now generally viewed by political scholars, and historians as one of the finest commanders in chief of the 20th century, had
    (C) Truman, a man now generally viewed by political scholars and historians as one of the finest commanders in chief of the 20th century, had
    (D) Truman a man now generally viewed by political scholars and historians as one of the finest commanders in chief of the 20th century had

8. (A) NO CHANGE
    (B) An observation:
    (C) Chronologically,
    (D) Nonetheless,

9. (A) NO CHANGE
    (B) precipitated
    (C) impeded
    (D) destroyed

10. The author is considering deleting the underlined portion. Should this selection be kept or deleted?

    (A) Kept, because it explains the Chinese motivations for supporting North Korea
    (B) Kept, because it makes a chain of events analyzed later in the paragraph more clear
    (C) Deleted, because it provides an irrelevant aside
    (D) Deleted, because it overuses the already utilized parenthetical phrase

11. The author would like to insert the following sentence into the previous paragraph:

    "This, unfortunately, was a grave miscalculation."

    Where would it most logically be placed?

    (A) Before sentence 4
    (B) Before sentence 5
    (C) Before sentence 6
    (D) After sentence 7

The Y-Bridge

States can best be characterized by their natural intricacies. Florida has its powdered sugar beaches; Nebraska, its butterscotch ❶ cornfields; and Arizona it's Grand Canyon. Cities, on the other hand, are known better by their man-made marvels. Everybody knows San Francisco as the Golden Gate City, just as Seattle is synonymous with the Space Needle and Saint Louis is famous for the Golden Gate Arch. Zanesville, Ohio may not be as large or as recognizable as those three municipal behemoths, but its quirky Y-Bridge serves as its focal point, ❷ once upon a time.

Zanesville natives often joke about the ❸ looks of incredulity they receive when visitors to the town ask for directions. "Go to the middle of the bridge and turn left," is a command to which most are unaccustomed, but it is commonplace in Zanesville. The Y-Bridge (named for its distinctive Y-shape) was designed to span the confluence of the Muskingum and Licking rivers. ❹ For it crosses both rivers, Ripley's Believe It Or Not once claimed that the Y-Bridge was the only bridge in the world where it was possible to cross and still end up on the same side of the river, and Amelia Earhart once called Zanesville ❺ "the most recognizable city on the country" because of the bridge.

Construction on the Y-Bridge began in 1812, and it opened officially in 1814. However, the first edition was riddled with issues: it required ceaseless ❻ repairs; and due, to its frailness, was destroyed by a flood in 1818. Construction on the second bridge began soon after, and it then

1. (A) NO CHANGE
   (B) cornfields: Arizona its Grand Canyon.
   (C) cornfields; and Arizona, its Grand Canyon.
   (D) cornfields, and Arizona, it's Grand Canyon.

2. Which of the following would be the most logical conclusion to this sentence?

   (A) NO CHANGE
   (B) for better or for worse.
   (C) just the same.
   (D) much to one's surprise.

3. Which of the following would be the most reasonable phrase to have at this point in the sentence?

   (A) NO CHANGE
   (B) casting of aspersions
   (C) dearth of piety
   (D) outright hostility

4. (A) NO CHANGE
   (B) Because
   (C) While
   (D) When

5. (A) NO CHANGE
   (B) "the most recognizing city for the country"
   (C) "the most recognizing city of the country"
   (D) "the most recognizable city in the country"

6. (A) NO CHANGE
   (B) repairs and—due to its frailness, was
   (C) repairs and—due to its frailness—was
   (D) repairs, and due to its frailness; was

officially opened in 1819 before being declared unsafe just 12 short years after. The third edition of the Y-Bridge ❼ enjoyed much greater longevity, spanning from 1832–1900. This third bridge, unlike the previous two, was a covered structure.

What doomed the third bridge, interestingly enough, was not ❽ public panic so much as hysteria; rumors began circulating that the bridge was unsafe, and locals voted to erect a new structure. This fourth Y-Bridge was completed in 1902, and was the first version to be constructed of concrete rather than wood. It stood until 1983 but was torn down and replaced by the fifth version, ❾ that still stands today. The fifth version, formed from steel and concrete, was designed to look like the fourth bridge.

While the greater part of this lengthy history is unknown by most Zanesvillians, all who ❿ reside there are proud of the bridge's legacy nonetheless. ⓫ So, if you ever find yourself passing through Central Ohio, be sure and make a quick stop in Zanesville. Just be sure to keep your poise when a local tells you to drive to the center of the Y-bridge and turn left!

7. Which of the following options provides the most fitting ending to the introductory phrase in the sentence?

(A) NO CHANGE
(B) failed to accomplish its goals,
(C) was much like its predecessor,
(D) captured the imaginations of passersby,

8. What word would be most appropriate given the context of the essay?

(A) NO CHANGE
(B) fear-mongering
(C) obsolescence
(D) decomposition

9. (A) NO CHANGE
(B) where it
(C) which
(D) when it

10. (A) NO CHANGE
(B) resides there is
(C) reside there is
(D) residing there are

11. (A) NO CHANGE
(B) However,
(C) Inevitably,
(D) Paradoxically,

ANSWERS EXPLAINED

Female Resistance in Michelle Cliff's *Abeng*

1. **(B)** A choice is needed that encompasses *fiction of women*. A possessive is required, and possession is demonstrated using *s*. Choice (D) can be eliminated, as it has no apostrophe. Choice (C) can be eliminated, as it reads as *fiction of womans*. Choice (A) can be eliminated as it reads as *fiction of womens*. Choice (B) is the only logical option.

2. **(D)** This question is largely about the vocabulary. A choice is needed that contrasts with "overt insurgent," which essentially means clear instance of rebellion. Choice (D), particularly with its usage of "subtle . . . resistance," forms a perfect contrast since *subtle* is an antonym for *overt*. Choices (A) and (B) are flawed in that they mean the same thing as "overt insurgent." Choice (C) is not logical in context. Instead, it is irrelevant to the topic.

3. **(A)** The subject is "subjectivity," which requires the singular verb form "calls." Eliminate Choices (B) and (D) accordingly. One "calls for" rather than "calls of." Eliminate Choice (C).

4. **(D)** All four choices represent the exact same sentiment. To be concise and avoid wordiness, Choice (D) is the best option.

5. **(C)** The proposed insertion mentions "Caribbean women's fiction." Sentence 3 references a story in Jamaica, which would be an example of "Caribbean women's fiction." The new sentence should therefore be inserted before sentence 3. In that position, the new sentence can act as an introductory sentence to the discussion of *Abeng*.

6. **(C)** A common verbal pattern involves the usage of *former* and *latter* in conjunction. This sentence is a perfect example of that pattern, and "the latter" is the correct answer. Choice (A), "the later," is used as an adjective or adverb, not as a noun. Choices (B) and (D) break with the pattern completely.

7. **(A)** Immediately before this sentence, the author writes about resisting oppression in more "nuanced" ways. The author then states that the characters act along a more "complex gradation of resistance." In other words, the characters act in such a way that their behavior should be considered to be along a spectrum. Therefore, Choice (A) is the most logical, because "relying on colonialist binaries" is a simplified way of interpreting their actions, as a "binary" provides only two extreme options. Choices (B) and (D) are incorrect because they express the opposite of what is intended. Choice (C) is incorrect because the author is suggesting how the interpretation of literature should be done—there is no question about the quality of the documentary sources themselves.

8. **(D)** In the sentence immediately before the underlined portion, the author states that "by interrogating the subjectivities of characters like Kitty, Mad Hannah, and Miss Winifred, readers can begin to understand various degrees of female resistance." Subjectivity refers to one's personal point of view, which gives insight into the person's motivations. The female resistance refers to actions one would take to stand up for oneself. Therefore, this sentence provides a subtle repetition of the idea expressed in the previous sentence. Choices (A) and (B) are incorrect because they would leave in an unneeded sentence. The answer is not Choice (C) because the underlined sentence is, in fact, related to the previous sentence.

9. **(D)** Notice the pattern here: there is an author, a title, a year, and then a comma. Eliminate Choices (A) and (C) for neglecting the comma after "(1985)." Eliminate Choice (B) since it does not include a comma after "(1981)."

10. **(B)** This sentence first mentions "double consciousness" and then proceeds to define that phrase. There must be adequate punctuation to separate the term from the definition. With Choice (A), a comma isn't a strong enough pause. A colon or dash would be ideal, and a semicolon could arguably work. However, a comma is not appropriate since it leaves a comma splice. Choice (C) neglects punctuation altogether. Choice (D)'s initial dash is acceptable, but the second dash is unnecessary. This isn't a parenthetical phrase and should not be treated as such. After eliminating those three choices, analyze Choice (B). Notice that it is properly punctuated, with the colon serving as a lead-in between the term and the definition.

11. **(A)** When working with transitions, analyze both the current sentence and the previous sentence to determine how they interrelate. In this case, there is a *cause-and-effect* relationship. "Hence" may not have been familiar to you, but it is a close approximation for *as a result, therefore,* or *accordingly.* Since "hence" can be used to transition between a cause and its effect, it is the best option. Notice that Choices (B) and (C) mean the same thing. So they can be eliminated for that reason. The word "however," in Choice (D) is a *contrasting* transition, but the sentences do not contrast.

Beauty and Peril

1. **(A)** Maintain a logical comparison in this sentence. "Then" is not used for comparisons, so eliminate Choices (C) and (D). Keep in mind that this is comparing the *scenery* of California to the *scenery* of other places, as opposed to comparing *California* itself to other places. Choice (B) attempts to compare apples to oranges, so it must be eliminated. Choice (A) is the only option that logically compares one place's scenery to another place's scenery.

2. **(C)** The subject comes after the verb, which can be confusing. Nonetheless, the subject is "secrets," a plural noun that requires a plural verb for agreement. Choices (A), (B), and (D) are all *singular* verbs and therefore must be eliminated. "Are" is the only acceptable option.

3. **(D)** This is a question that perhaps requires reading a little bit further into the passage to diagnose the theme, which is the possibility of "cataclysmic" natural disasters on the Pacific Coast. The passage has nothing to do with a "conspiracy," with people who "need to get their priorities straight," or with the concept of "leadership." Choice (D), with its speculation on the possibility of impending, devastating natural disasters, is the only logical solution.

4. **(C)** Eliminate Choice (D) immediately, as "passing by" California is incorrect; the San Andreas fault goes *through* California. From there, find the choice that has the perfect balance between concision and content. In Choice (A), it is unnecessary to say "810 miles *in length.*" *Length* is already implied. Choice (B) eliminates too much, as "810 miles" is still relevant and provides new, productive information. Choice (C), then, is the perfect balance.

5. **(C)** This question illustrates the principle of coordination and subordination. Essentially, to paraphrase this sentence: *the death toll then was only 3,000, **but** keep in mind that the death toll from a similar earthquake would probably be much higher today.* Choice (C) is the only option that expresses that disclaimer effectively. Choices (A), (B), and (D) really all communicate the same message of *additionally*, which is not logical in this sentence; the clauses do not build on each other. Also keep in mind that there can be only one correct answer, so any choices that are essentially identical must be eliminated.

6. **(D)** Choices (A), (B), and (C) all have some major flaw, and sometimes they have multiple flaws. There are grammatical issues with Choice (A), too, but its largest flaw is that it treats Juan de Fuca and Cascadia as two separate things, whereas the former is actually part of the latter. In Choice (B), the proper phrase is *comprised of,* not "comprised with." Choice (C) uses "which" where it should use "that"; it also places an unnecessary comma after "zone." Choice (D) is without flaw, and its use of "which" rather than *that* is perfect.

7. **(C)** The idea that should be expressed as a possessive is *the continental shelf of North America.* Choice (A), by omitting an apostrophe, fails to illustrate possession. Choices (B) and (D) read as if the continent were *North Americas,* as opposed to the correct *North America.*

8. **(A)** It can be argued that the item "approaching its breaking point" is either "stress" or *the plate.* Nonetheless, both are singular nouns that require singular verbs for concordance. Eliminate Choices (C) and (D) for using plural verbs. Next, the possessive pronoun form of one thing is "its." "Their" is used for multiple items (Choice B). Choice (A) is therefore the correct answer.

9. **(A)** The principal matter that separates the correct answer from all three incorrect choices is the issue of comma placement between "coastal" and "subsequent." The independent, main clause of the sentence is "subsequent tidal waves would accompany the earthquakes." The clause "as both San Andreas and Juan de Fuca are coastal," is separate and *dependent.* (It depends on the second clause to constitute a full sentence.) Since the two are separate clauses, the comma must be placed between them for separation.

10. **(B)** "Conjecture" most clearly means speculation, theory, or hypothesis. Since the author is speculating about the future throughout the passage, Choice (B) is the correct answer. A "wild goose chase" is a hectic, often-futile undertaking. This doesn't fit in context. "Wisdom" doesn't fit in context since the author actually *knows* nothing of the future but is merely speculating. "Guesstimate" is a *portmanteau* (combination of two words) that is too casual for the purposes of this passage.

11. **(A)** Choice (B) can be quickly eliminated since the author has made clear that the catastrophe is not "imminent" but, rather, *probable given a long enough period of time.* The paragraph goes on to address fear and to warn that we must not allow it to dictate our lives. Choices (C) and (D) address the futility of speculation, which does capture part of the paragraph's theme. However, they ultimately fail to make any mention of "fear." Choice (A) is the only option that addresses the concept that fear based on speculation is unproductive.

What Am I?

1. **(C)** Analyze the graph for this question. It's impossible to say *exactly* how much carbon is in the human body as there are no numbers provided. However, the carbon slice makes up just under one-fourth or one-fifth of the pie. The only answer that is even close to the 20% to 25% of the actual slice is 19%.

2. **(D)** The underlined section contains two *independent clauses:* they could be full sentences by themselves. Accordingly, we need to separate the two clauses. Choice (D) uses a semicolon to do this. Choice (A) is a comma splice. Choice (B) is a run-on sentence. Choice (C) would be acceptable if we had used a colon and maintained the two initial clauses. However, the use of "while" changes the second clause from independent to dependent, which doesn't function.

3. **(C)** There are two independent clauses here, with "so" used as a conjunction to unite them. Choice (A), by placing a comma after "chemists," breaks the first independent clause. Choice (B) incorrectly treats the phrase as an appositive. Choice (D) is a run-on sentence. Choice (C) is correct; it adds no unnecessary commas while still managing to insert the required one after "life."

4. **(A)** Analyze the first sentence of the next paragraph, "If you guessed iron, you're wrong." Iron is not a place, so eliminate Choice (B). It is not plural, so eliminate Choice (C). It is not a person, so eliminate Choice (D). It is a singular thing, which makes Choice (A) the correct answer.

5. **(B)** First, recognize tone: it is very casual, almost like an informal conversation. Choices (A) and (C) are far too formal. Choice (D) is incorrect, as one would say "sulfur ain't right, *either*" as opposed to "sulfur ain't right, *too.*" Choice (B) is both informal and without enormous grammatical flaws.

6. **(A)** Eliminate Choices (B) and (D) since the verb tense is "have heard." "Might of" is never a correct construction. Choice (C)'s error is in having an extra "have." One hears *of* something as opposed to hears *have* something.

7. **(B)** Analyze the relationship between this sentence and the previous sentence to diagnose the relationship between the two. In this case, each sentence independently builds on the statement in the first sentence of the paragraph that says that carbon can be a "curse." "Furthermore" is the best way to list an additional aspect to an argument. "Accordingly" and "consequently" express cause and effect, which is not what we want. "Nevertheless" is contrasting, which is equally incorrect.

8. **(D)** The subject is difficult to isolate, but it is "I." One would say, "I am," not *I are/is/were.*

9. **(B)** This sentence is most logically placed after sentence 2. A good thing, life-giving photosynthesis, is mentioned at the end of sentence 2. Then sentence 3 transitions to a contrasting bad thing, namely, the carbon footprint. Any of the other placements would make this logical transition unclear.

10. **(C)** When paraphrased, the clause becomes "I operated *inside* a balanced cycle," or "I operated *as part of* a balanced cycle." Choice (A), "between," requires operating *between two things.* Choice (B), "among," requires operating *among three or more things.* However, carbon is part of only *one thing*: as the cycle. Choice (D) implies a causal relationship that is not logical.

11. **(D)** Pay attention to context in order to maintain parallelism. The other words in the list are "respiration" and "combustion"—both nouns that end in *-tion*. "Decomposition" is one of two noun options, but it is the *-tion* ending that maintains parallelism better than the gerund "decomposing." Choices (B) and (C) are not nouns. Rather, they are verbs that do not maintain parallelism in the list.

Court Reporter

1. **(B)** When deciding on *who* versus *whom*, remember to rewrite the sentence using *he* or *him*. In this case, one would say *he represents* rather than *him represents*. Recall that he = who and him = whom, so one must use *who* here. Choices (A), (C), and (D) all have at least one instance of misusing *whom*, so Choice (B) is the only possible answer.

2. **(A)** The clause up to the word "trial" is independent, as is the clause after "trial." Accordingly, sufficient punctuation is needed to separate the two. Eliminate Choice (B) because it is a comma splice. In the second clause, "jurors represent a panel of judges," we want no punctuation separating the subject and predicate. Choices (C) and (D) both add unnecessary commas.

3. **(C)** This question is more a matter of vocabulary than anything else. After eliminating Choice (D)—a gerund that leaves a fragment in its wake—one must simply select the most apt vocabulary. *To comprise* means to consist of, so this is the most logical option. *To compromise* is to come to an agreement, which isn't logical. *To compose* is to create, which is equally illogical.

4. **(B)** First, maintain verb parallelism. The rest of the passage is in present tense, so eliminate Choice (D) for being past tense. Our proposed question refers to the previous sentence that refers to a list that "comprises those occupants found in a normal legal proceeding." The most logical follow-up is "Or does it?" This phrase means *does this list really comprise the occupants in the legal proceeding*? Choices (A) and (C) use pronouns that aren't logical in context.

5. **(D)** The phrase "an often-overlooked occupation of legal services" is a parenthetical phrase. If you remove it from the sentence, the clause still functions perfectly well. The rule for parenthetical phrases is that they can be separated from the main clause using either two commas or two dashes. Choices (A) and (C) bungle the parenthetical phrase completely. Choice (B) is close, but it uses one dash and one comma, whereas one needs to use two of the same punctuation marks.

6. **(B)** Notice that Choices (A) and (D) convey *the exact same meaning*. As there can be only one correct answer, eliminate those two (the relationship is not causal). Choice (C) declares a contrast, but this sentence does not contrast with the previous one. What actually happens is that the second sentence restates the first sentence in a more explanatory fashion. "In other words" is the correct answer.

7. **(C)** Consider what the sentence is implying: by using key combinations, it would be much quicker to type than if one had to punch each letter key individually. Choice (C) is most logical and effective. Choices (A) and (B) are logical, but they aren't terribly descriptive and thus not very effective. Choice (D) is completely irrelevant.

8. **(D)** The pronoun in the underlined portion must refer back to the singular "court reporter," which only Choice (D) successfully does. Choice (A) uses the plural "they." Choice (B) changes this from third person to second person. Choice (C) uses an incorrect verb.

9. **(A)** Notice the context of this paragraph: it is written in second person, consistently referring to *you*. Maintain that parallelism by staying in second person instead of switching to third person as the other choices do.

10. **(D)** Analyze the graph for this question, particularly the data about court reporter salaries. Notice that the top 10% make roughly $60,000 dollars per year, thus making Choice (D) the most logical and specific option. Choice (A) is incorrect, as this is a five-figure salary. Choice (B) is true but is not directly supported by the information in the graph since there are no statistics about the average American worker's salary, just statistics about those in legal professions. In this context, Choice (C) and "student loans" are wholly irrelevant.

11. **(A)** Analyze the graph for this question. Choice (B) is simply not supported by the data. Choice (C) is equally unsupported as there is no data on entry-level hiring. Choice (D) is entirely false; attorneys earn much more. After eliminating the three illogical choices, all that remains is the correct answer. Analyze Choice (A) just to make certain, and it is true.

Family Feud

1. **(B)** The subject here is "feud," which is a singular noun that requires a singular verb. Eliminate Choice (C) accordingly. Choice (A) would result in a sentence fragment. Delete Choice (D) for producing a fragment. "Boils" is the correct answer.

2. **(C)** The first issue is not to include an unnecessary comma between "land and livestock." No comma is required in a list of just two items. Eliminate Choices (A) and (B) for that reason. Choice (D) neglects necessary punctuation after "region," rendering it a run-on sentence.

3. **(D)** Choose the correct transitional word by analyzing the relationship between the current sentence and the previous sentence. There is no cause-and-effect relationship, so eliminate Choice (A). There is no contrasting relationship, so eliminate Choices (B) and (C). Ultimately, a transition wasn't necessary at all, and sometimes that is perfectly fine. Choice (D) is the correct answer.

4. **(A)** The concept here is that the McCoy witness's betrayal of his own family led to his death. The betrayal thus *sealed his fate*, and he was subsequently murdered by his family members. Choices (B), (C), and (D) provide no relevant, logical connection to the man being killed.

5. **(D)** In essence, we must select a possessive form of *disapproval of families*. Since there are plural *families*, eliminate Choice (A). Choices (B) and (C) neglect the necessary apostrophe that demonstrates possession.

6. **(B)** This choice uses concise wording that is in a logical order. Choice (A) is too wordy. Choice (C) uses awkward word order along with an unneeded "to." Choice (D) is also too wordy.

7. **(D)** We must work with the "to" already provided at the beginning of the sentence. This demonstrates that we need an infinitive verb. "Venge" is an archaic verb that was abandoned centuries ago. "Vengeance" is a noun, not a verb. "Revenging" would not work with the preceding "to" to create an infinitive.

8. **(A)** To "illude" means to create an illusion, so this is not logical in context. To "allude" is to refer to something, which is equally illogical. To "illuminate" is to shine light upon, which still does not make sense. To "elude," however, means to escape or avoid, which is perfect in this sentence.

9. **(D)** In the first paragraph, Randolph McCoy is referred to as "Old Ran'l." Continuing to refer to him as "Old Ran'l" avoids the ambiguity that would be caused by referring to him as "Mr. McCoy." In effect, everyone in the passage is either a Hatfield or a McCoy. So writing *Mr. McCoy* leaves the reader uncertain as to which McCoy is intended. Eliminate Choice (A), as this actually is *less* a clarification than a cause of confusion. Eliminate Choice (B), as "Old Ran'l" has already been established as acceptable and therefore formalities have already been abandoned. Choice (C)'s statement is simply incorrect.

10. **(B)** Sentence 2 refers to the publishing of inflammatory articles by newspapers, which matches the "journalistic sensationalism" mentioned in the proposed insertion. The insertion, then, must come either *before* or *after* sentence 2 in order to maintain coherence. As *before sentence 2* is not an option, "before sentence 3" (or *after sentence 2*) is the most logical selection.

11. **(A)** If the underlined sentence were deleted, most readers would wonder what was exceptional about the ninth person that permitted him to avoid life in prison. Thankfully, our underlined sentence answers this question for us: *the ninth wasn't so lucky; in fact, he was probably the least lucky of all*. Thus, the sentence must be kept as it "provides a relevant clarification" that removes confusion that might arise otherwise.

Bruce Hornsby

1. **(A)** If the author were to delete the sentence, it would then be unclear *why* he struggles with the phenomenon of fame. It "provides a relevant elaboration," as in Choice (A). Choice (B) is incorrect as Bruce Hornsby, not Andy Warhol, is "the main person to be analyzed."

2. **(A)** The subject here is "someone of actual import," and *someone* is a singular noun that requires a singular verb. Eliminate Choice (B) for being a plural verb, and eliminate Choice (D) for not being a verb at all. Choice (C), *a gerund*, does not provide a complete sentence. "Passes," however, is a singular verb.

3. **(D)** Choice (A) places an unnecessary comma after "love." Choice (B) places an unnecessary comma after "true." Choice (C) neglects to end with a question mark. Choice (D) is correct; the colon acts as a nice lead-in to the question.

4. **(C)** "Obliquely" means indirectly, and there is nothing indirect about the statement, just as there is nothing *imaginative* or *powerful* about it, as described by Choices (A) and (B). "Inevitably" means unavoidably. The author's point is that he *unavoidably* has to tell you who Hornsby is, and the fact that this is necessary is unfortunate.

5. **(C)** This question is difficult in that the choices are all fairly similar. Choice (A) transitions to passive voice, which is best to avoid if possible. In Choice (B), saying both "case" and "point" is wordy and unnecessary. ("Case in point" is a common phrase, but using "case" and "point" separately in this instance does not use the common idiom.) In Choice (D), "arbitration" is a process through which two parties resolve differences and is not connected with the adjective *arbitrary*.

6. **(B)** Choice (A) is not "self-deprecating" but, rather, deprecates *others*. Choice (C) is not self-deprecating in any way; rather it reads almost as more of a boast. Again, Choice (D) features nothing of self-deprecation. Choice (B), however, fits the question. Its use of "forgive my hyperbole" is an acknowledgment that the author is aware that he is *going overboard* in his praise, so to speak.

7. **(B)** This sentence reads awkwardly at first, particularly with the use of both "various" and "variety." But if you look closer, you will see that a "variety station" is a genre of radio channel and the "various" refers to the prevalence of those stations. Eliminate Choices (A) and (C) for not recognizing "variety stations." Just as one wouldn't say, "There are two, cars," one can't say, "various, variety stations." The quantifier must not be separate from what it is describing. Eliminate Choice (D) because of that unnecessary comma.

8. **(C)** Without the underlined portion, many high school readers would not recognize the fame of the musicians mentioned; thus, it provides an important distinction that again "underscores the author's thoughts about Hornsby's lack of recognition." In effect, *why are Hornsby's peers so much more famous than he is*?

9. **(A)** "Like van Gogh's or F. Scott Fitzgerald's" is an *appositive*. If you remove this portion, the sentence still functions perfectly acceptably. A correctly used appositive must be set off from the surrounding sentence with two commas or two dashes. Choice (B) forgets the punctuation completely. Choice (C) incorrectly diagnoses what the appositive actually is by misplacing the second comma. Choice (D) neglects the second comma. In addition, Choice (A) is the only option that makes a logical comparison, using the possessive "Gogh's" and "Fitzgerald's" to make these implicitly comparable to "Hornsby's legacy."

10. **(B)** The relationship between this sentence and the previous one is *contrasting*. When paraphrased, the sentences are *Maybe Hornsby will be famous later.* However, *I doubt it.* "But" is the only option that executes the contrast. Choices (A), (C), and (D) all are *cause-and-effect* transitions.

11. **(B)** To quantify adjectives, it is appropriate to use "less." For example, one would never say *he is fewer fast.* Rather, one would say *he is less fast.* Eliminate Choices (C) and (D) accordingly. "Lessening" cannot be used as a determiner, which is what this sentence requires.

I'll Take the Job

1. **(C)** Certain expressions are used frequently in the English language, and it is important to use the common preposition when using these expressions. The phrase "at the core" is an example of one of those expressions. Using "at" is far preferable to the other choices if only because that is the way this expression is typically written.

2. **(A)** The problem with this sentence is that it needed to be placed earlier if it was going to be used at all. The passage has drifted away from discussion of the separation of powers. To return to the topic would be flighty at this point, breaking with the flow of the passage. Choice (A) is the correct answer.

3. **(A)** Choice (B) is flawed because it omits an apostrophe on "one's." Choice (C) forgets a necessary comma after "thus." Choice (D) changes from second person to third person during the course of the sentence. Choice (A) is without blemish, and it is the correct answer.

4. **(B)** Choice (A) is very wordy. For instance, "for the duration of 14 years" can be much more effective if it is shortened to "for 14 years." Choice (C) reads as if the president must be exactly 35. Choice (D) is terribly general, providing us with no relevant, specific information. Choice (B) is the best combination of concision and specificity.

5. **(D)** "Charisma," a singular noun, is the subject. It requires a singular verb to maintain concordance. Eliminate Choices (A) and (B) accordingly. At this point, the decision is about "lies" versus "lays," which are two commonly confused verbs. To *lay* is the act of physically taking something and placing it elsewhere. To *lie* is the act of an object remaining at rest. "Lies" is far more appropriate in this context.

6. **(C)** Sentence 3 mentions "charisma." The proposed insertion practically gives us the complete definition of charisma by using the words "charm, attractiveness, and likability." The insertion, then, is best placed after sentence 3, which is Choice (C).

7. **(D)** The first part of the question regards proper use of the possessive for *the ages of presidents.* As there are multiple presidents, the apostrophe must go *after* the s. Eliminate Choices (B) and (C) accordingly. Now, as there were multiple presidents, there were multiple ages. Choice (A) reads as if the presidents all had one age—the same age. Choice (D), then, is the correct answer.

8. **(B)** "Still" is separate from the main clause. (In effect, if we remove "still," the clause is still perfect.) So we must place a comma after "still" to denote that required separation. Eliminate Choice (A) accordingly. From there is a list of three things: "allure, a spotless background, and years in diplomatic service." Eliminate Choices (C) and (D) for neglecting the comma after "allure."

9. **(B)** Take note of parallelism in this sentence: "one has *to win*" (*to win* is an infinitive verb) and "triumph" (*one has to* is implied, which makes this an infinitive verb). Therefore, eliminate Choice (A) since "following" is not an infinitive verb. We can eliminate Choice (D) for omitting the listing comma after "convention." From there, we can analyze the context to see what is most *logical*. To "earn a following" means to gain supporters, while to "follow an earning" is nonsensical. Choice (B) is the best answer.

10. **(C)** For transitions, analyze both the current sentence and the previous sentence to determine how they interrelate. The second sentence here gives a supporting example to bolster the claim made in the first sentence. "For instance" is the best option to illustrate an example. The second sentence isn't surprising but, rather, is to be expected based on sentence 1. Eliminate Choice (A) for that reason. Choice (B) implies a cause-and-effect relationship that is not apparent, while Choice (D) implies a contrast that is equally absent.

11. **(B)** Analyze the chart for this question. Notice that the chart refers to personal characteristics that voters have stated would be important to them in a presidential candidate. Paragraph 2 refers to personal characteristics, which makes that paragraph the most suitable place to insert a relevant sentence based on the data in our chart. Paragraph 1 is introductory, and there isn't any mention of personal characteristics there. Paragraph 4 refers to financial matters. Paragraph 3 is close, but it refers to more *concrete* qualifications, like education, seniority, and political credentials. Choice (B) is the correct answer.

Risk

1. **(A)** For one, notice that "we" is used throughout the sentence. That's indicative of the need to remain in first person plural, so eliminate Choices (C) and (D). Now ask, *Is it better to say "we understood" or "us understood"?* "We," of course, is the proper pronoun. Choice (A) is correct.

2. **(B)** When deciding to delete a portion, ask yourself, *Is this information relevant?* Then ask, *Does it repeat information or feature information that can be readily inferred?* Since the passage already states that the narrator knew the roles he or she would fulfill upon graduation, "we felt well-prepared for the profession we were about to enter" is a restatement of what is already known. Choice (B) is the correct answer. This portion must be deleted because it does not provide meaningful, new information.

3. **(A)** When deciding between *who* and *whom*, remember to rewrite the clause using *he* or *him*. We would say *he walked* rather than *him walked*, so we must use *who*. Eliminate Choices (B) and (D) accordingly. "Who walking" would leave a fragment—and a rough one at that—so Choice (A), "who walked," is the correct answer.

4. **(C)** There are certain phrases that the test writers assume are widely known. "Out in the field" is one of those. The meaning isn't that one is *literally* in a body of grass but, rather, that one is in a professional environment—i.e., the *field of business management* in this case. Choices (A), (B), and (D) simply do not suit the required purpose as Choice (C) does.

5. **(A)** Choice (D) can be immediately deleted as the professor is referring to *after* leaving school rather than returning to it. Choice (B) is somewhat relevant but is not a logical, effective conclusion to the argument. Choice (C) is relevant, but it *isn't effective;* it lacks the attention-getting quality of Choice (A), which essentially says, *You've taken all these courses to be a better manager. But the true value comes down to one simple question: can you take calculated risk?* Choice (A), then, is by far the best answer.

6. **(D)** There are two independent clauses, with the first ending at "company" and the second beginning at "others." Choice (A) is a comma splice. Choice (B) is flawed in multiple ways, but the first mistake is with the inclusion of an unnecessary comma after "outcomes." Choice (C) incorrectly attempts to employ a parenthetical phrase. Choice (D), however, correctly links the two independent clauses with a semicolon.

7. **(C)** "Affective" is a psychological term relating to moods and feelings, and it isn't logical here. Eliminate "affecting" for the same reason. "Effecting" is a word that isn't traditionally an adjective and isn't particularly logical in this case. This leaves only "effective," which is the correct answer.

8. **(B)** The question requires "the most specific example," with *specific* being the operative word. Choices (A) and (D) aren't relevant to the concept of trying to determine lead time. Choice (C) regards attempts to *define* lead time rather than calculate it for an actual business. Choice (B) provides a very *specific* example of how lead time can fluctuate in a *specific* industry after a *specific* event occurs.

9. **(A)** This is an example of an independent clause. The subject is "the success of the business," and the predicate is "will be driven by how well you manage these variations." There is no reason to insert any punctuation to separate the subject and predicate, so eliminate Choices (B), (C), and (D) accordingly.

10. **(C)** Choices (B) and (D) lack concision; eliminate them because they are wordy. The adverb "slowly" functions much more effectively when placed before "moving" as opposed to after. Choice (C), then, is the correct answer.

11. **(B)** Notice how sentence 4 says "the other" but is ambiguous in context. *What is the other?* The proposed insertion clarifies this, beginning with "one factor." "The other," then, refers to *the other factor*, which is much more logical when the insertion is placed before sentence 4.

A Tricky Feline

1. **(B)** "Notwithstanding" means in spite of or despite, which fits the meaning of this sentence perfectly. Choice (A) attempts to draw a causal relationship that is absent. "Aside with" should read *aside from*, and "stemming in" should read *stemming from*, which would still be incorrect in context. *Aside from* would be acceptable, but it is not an option.

2. **(A)** This needs a possessive to match the idea: *the contribution of either scientist*. As possession and an apostrophe are required, eliminate Choice (C). Eliminate Choices (B) and (D) for using the plural word "scientists" since the initial idea was *the contribution of either scientist*, not *the contribution of both scientists*.

3. **(D)** This sentence is a rare instance in which there are *two* uses of extra wording. Both "a lesser recognized name" and "however" can be removed from the sentence and still have the sentence function perfectly well. Accordingly, we must surround each phrase with a set of dashes or commas to isolate them from the rest of the sentence. Choice (A) omits the comma after "Schrödinger," which ruins the first phrase. Choice (B) ruins the second instance by forgetting the comma after "however." Choice (C) botches both instances. Choice (D), however, perfectly surrounds both instances with the required punctuation.

4. **(C)** To determine the correct conjunction to use, analyze the relationship between the two clauses. Here, the second clause contrasts with the first. Essentially, *although* Schrödinger won the Nobel Prize, he is more famous for something else. *Although*, like "but," is a contrasting term. Choice (C) is the correct answer. Choices (A) and (B) emphasize a causal relationship. Choice (D) is not contrasting but, rather, conjoining.

5. **(D)** *To swallow* has an alternative meaning outside of simple ingestion that most closely aligns with the verb *to accept*. In the context of the question, Einstein had a difficult time *accepting* the Copenhagen interpretation. "Swallowing" is the correct answer. None of the other choices has either a denotation or a connotation that matches the context of the sentence.

6. **(A)** At the core of this question is *lie* vs. *lay*. In context, the sentence most clearly means *"the trick here rests upon the unpredictability of radioactivity."* *Rests upon* corresponds to "lies," so we can eliminate Choices (C) and (D). The correct idiom is *lies in* rather than *lies on*, so the correct answer is Choice (A). Choice (B) improperly uses a "to."

7. **(B)** The verb refers to the plural "states" and so requires a plural verb—"become." Choice (A) is singular, and Choices (C) and (D) use incorrect verb tense.

8. **(D)** Sentence 5 mentions the mutually exclusive states of being dead and alive, which obviously *can't* occur simultaneously. "Hence the flaw in this line of thinking" follows that sentence perfectly as its presumption is certainly flawed. Choice (D) is the correct answer.

9. **(B)** The main theme of the paragraph is subatomic particles. Choice (B), particularly with its mention of "subatomic behaviors," is the best introduction to this paragraph. The paragraph mentions nothing of "theoretical physicists" or "large physical entities." Choice (C) is flawed in that subatomic particles go *against* Newton's theories.

10. **(A)** We need a possessive to serve as a stand-in for "quantum superposition," which is a singular noun. "Its" is the best substitute for *quantum superposition's*. Choices (B) and (D) are not possessive, and Choice (C) refers to *multiple* people or things. Quantum superposition is one thing.

11. **(B)** Although the passage briefly touches on Schrödinger's fame (or lack thereof), it is not the main idea. Eliminate Choices (A) and (D) because they focus on the wrong theme and thus provide ineffective conclusions. Similarly, the "Newtonian theoretical construct" is not the main idea, so eliminate Choice (C). Choice (B), however, is ideal. It mentions Schrodinger (the main character in the passage). It also refers to the cat, which is a key component of the article and its focus on quantum theory. Moreover, the very title of the article is "A Tricky Feline," further illustrating the significance of the cat.

To Test or Not to Test

1. **(B)** Choice (A) inserts an unnecessary comma after "desperately," separating verb and adverb. Choice (C) incorrectly treats an appositive. Choice (D)'s semicolon is incorrect since a semicolon requires an independent clause on both sides of the semicolon. The second clause is not complete. Choice (B) is perfect, inserting neither excessive commas nor improper punctuation.

2. **(B)** When a conflict occurs with two things/parties, "between" must be used. When it occurs with three or more parties, "among" must be used. As "pedagogy" and "practice" are two things, "between" is the correct answer. "Through" and "in" are not valid options.

3. **(A)** Analyze the relationship between this sentence and the previous statement. Essentially, the second sentence is a restatement of the previous sentence. "In other words" serves to introduce a restatement. Choices (B) and (C) create a cause-and-effect relationship that is not apparent here. "Henceforth" is often used chronologically to signify *from this point forward*.

4. **(D)** The subject is "increase," which is a singular noun that requires a singular verb. Eliminate Choice (C) because it uses a plural verb. Choice (A) is a fragment. Choice (B) does away entirely with the required predicate.

5. **(C)** The difficult part here is that the correct answer simply looks odd, despite being flawless. A possessive form of *understanding of the class* is needed: "class's" understanding is the proper way to illustrate this. Choice (A) is both plural and lacking an apostrophe. Choice (B) is an improper way to indicate possession. Choice (D) indicates multiple "classes," whereas there is actually only one class.

6. **(C)** Sentence 4, particularly with its mention of the "political," is the perfect sentence to precede the insertion. The insertion refers to politics, which is most apparent with its discussion of "democracy." Thus, sentence 4 acts as an introduction to the insertion, making Choice (C) the correct answer.

7. **(A)** Analyze the content of the entire paragraph to answer this question. Notice that this paragraph acts as a shift away from the detriments of testing; the passage is now presenting *good things* about testing. "Benefits" are *good things,* and Choice (A) is the correct answer. Choices (B), (C), and (D) fail to act as acceptable transitions from criticism to praise of testing.

8. **(A)** Choice (D) does away with the connector, ultimately leading to a broken clause. Choice (C), "whom," can be used only with people, whereas the author is discussing schools, not people. Choice (B) uses awkward wording, interjecting an unnecessary "for." This is a restrictive clause, so "that" makes sense.

9. **(C)** This question is all about vocabulary. To "assure" is to remove doubt, and it is generally done to another person. *I assured my father that I would be home by curfew.* To "ensure" means to make sure a thing will or won't happen. *I studied last night to ensure that I wouldn't fail the test.* To "insure" refers to car insurance, life insurance, health insurance, etc. To "reassure" is simply to "assure" someone multiple times. In this sentence, the classrooms are *ensuring* that something will happen: students will be prepared for the next grade. Choice (C) is the correct answer.

10. **(B)** The previous sentence says that testing, despite its flaws, is necessary. We need to find an option that "specifically" and "effectively" builds on that previous sentence. Choice (D) is most flawed in that it *refutes* entirely the previous sentence. Choices (A), (B), and (C) are all valid options at first glance. Look more closely, though, and see that Choice (B) is both more *specific* and more *effective.* Choices (A) and (C) are more general and somewhat blasé. Choice (B)'s connection between education and life after education is the most attention grabbing.

11. **(C)** The graph refers to testing by gender. As the passage itself has nothing to do with gender, the graph data isn't relevant to the passage and should not be included. Eliminate Choices (A) and (B) because they incorrectly state that the graph should be included. Eliminate Choice (D), as gender data contradicts nothing in the passage but, rather, is mostly irrelevant to the passage's main claim. Choice (C) is the correct answer.

Truman and MacArthur

1. **(B)** If a struggle occurs with three or more parties, that would be a *struggle among them.* We only have "two men," though. Something occurring with two parties happens *between them.* Choice (B), "between," is the correct answer. Choices (C) and (D) are not acceptable usage.

2. **(C)** The subject here is "a struggle," which is a singular noun. We will need a singular verb to match. "Does" is the correct answer. "Do" is a plural verb in this context, "doing" leads to gibberish, and Choice (D) eliminates a principal part of the predicate.

3. **(C)** This questions requires knowledge of colloquialisms. Choice (A) is used to symbolize prosperity for everybody. Choice (B) signifies a feeling of being slighted in some way, and motivated by that slight. Choice (C) refers to a situation in which there are too many people giving orders and not enough people *taking* orders. Choice (D) refers to undertaking a frenetic—and often futile—task. Since the second part of the sentence refers to giving and taking orders, Choice (C) is the correct answer.

4. **(A)** "Great Men, by all accounts" is a parenthetical statement. If you remove it from the sentence, the clause still functions perfectly well. The general rule with parenthetical statements is that there can be either two commas or two dashes separating the statement from the rest of the sentence. Choice (B) is close, but it starts with a dash and concludes with a comma, which breaks with parallelism.

5. **(B)** We need a possessive word to serve as a stand-in for *Truman and MacArthur.* Eliminate Choices (C) and (D) for being singular possessives. Eliminate Choice (A) for not being a possessive at all. "Their" is the correct answer.

6. **(A)** If we were to delete the underlined portion, the reader would be left wondering, *What does that title mean? It sounds illustrious, but what* is *it?* Choice (A), therefore, is correct as it "clarifies a key title." Choices (B), (C), and (D) all make erroneous statements.

7. **(C)** "A man now generally viewed by political scholars and historians as one of the finest commanders in chief of the 20th century" is an *appositive*: the phrase can be removed, and the sentence still functions perfectly well. So we must separate the appositive from the rest of the sentence using either two dashes or two commas. Eliminate Choice (A) for neglecting the second comma, and eliminate Choice (D) for neglecting both commas. Choice (B) executes the appositive correctly, but it inserts an unnecessary comma after "scholars" since there is no need to place a comma between two things in a list.

8. **(D)** Analyze the relationship between this sentence and the preceding sentence. When paraphrased, the sentences are *Truman was a military man,* but *he still was distrustful of military leadership. But* is a contrasting term, and "nonetheless" is also a contrasting term. Choice (A) implies a cause and effect that does not exist. Choice (B) is out of place. *Who is observing and why are you telling me you're observing?* Choice (C) deals with the progression of time and is illogical.

9. **(B)** *Precipitate* is a synonym for *cause, trigger,* or *spark.* The start of the Korean War *triggered* the cataclysm, so "precipitated" is the best answer. Choice (C) means prevented or blocked, which is the opposite of what occurred. Choice (D) is illogical since the meltdown wasn't destroyed. Choice (A) is a wordy and unacceptably informal way of saying *caused.*

10. **(B)** If we were to delete this portion, the conflict with China would be unexplained. The role of the Chinese government in the proceedings would be unclear. Choice (B) is the correct answer because "it makes a chain of events analyzed more clear." Choice (A) is flawed in that it mentions the Chinese support but *doesn't explain why they were supporting North Korea.* Choices (C) and (D) make wholly false claims.

11. **(B)** The "grave miscalculation" mentioned in the question refers to sentence 4, which mentions MacArthur's certainty that China would not interfere in an invasion of North Korea. Sentence 5 mentions the consequences of that "grave miscalculation." Thus, it is sensible to insert this sentence between sentences 4 and 5, as described in Choice (B).

The Y-Bridge

1. **(C)** Notice the parallelism of listing: as each item in the list has a comma inside the item, it is proper to separate the items using semicolons. Choices (B) and (D) do not have the proper structure. Now notice the comma after each state in the previous items. Choice (A) omits that comma after "Arizona." Additionally, Choice (A) makes use of "it's," meaning it is, where the correct answer should use the possessive form "its."

2. **(C)** It is probably easiest to determine the correct answer simply by eliminating all of the wrong answers. Choice (A) is a phrase used to refer to the past, whereas the verbs in this sentence are present tense. Choice (B) implies an ambivalence that does not match the author's tone; he is wholly enthusiastic about the bridge. Choice (D) is flawed in that there is nothing inherently *surprising* about this fact. We examine the remaining choice, "just the same," and realize that the author was making a comparison between the bridge and the collection of other notable landmarks of larger cities.

3. **(A)** To *cast aspersions* is to make rude or insulting remarks. Eliminate Choice (B) primarily because it is too similar to the "outright hostility" of Choice (D). There can only be one correct answer, so these two interchangeable choices are incorrect by default. Choice (C) means a lack of religious devotion, which is entirely irrelevant. "Looks of incredulity" is most appropriate here: the visitors, upon being told to go to the middle of the bridge and turn left, look at the locals in utter disbelief.

4. **(B)** This transition refers to the relationship between the first and second clauses in this sentence, where the first clause is the *cause* and the second clause is the *effect*. In essence, "because" of clause one, then clause two. Choice (A) leaves the sentence disjointed and lacking fluidity. Choice (C) is used to introduce simultaneous (but often contradictory) clauses, while Choice (D) is also generally a lead-in for two actions occurring at the same time.

5. **(D)** First, "recognizable," essentially *able to be recognized*, is superior to "recognizing." "Recognizing" means that the city would be recognizing others as opposed to *being* recognized by others. Eliminate Choices (B) and (C). Now, it is far superior to say "in the country" than "on the country." Unfortunately, there is no true rule behind this; preposition recognition in certain phrases often requires familiarity with the phrase, without substitute. Because Choice (A) is not something commonly said and Choice (D) is, the correct answer is Choice (D).

6. **(C)** "Due to its frailness" is a parenthetical phrase. If you remove it, the sentence still functions perfectly well. In order to denote our parenthetical phrase, we can surround it with two commas or two dashes. Choices (A) and (D) improperly use semicolons without having independent clauses on both sides of the semicolon. Choice (B) begins the parenthetical phrase with a dash but then breaks with parallelism by switching to a comma on the back end.

7. **(A)** It is important to analyze not only the entire sentence but also the qualities of this bridge relative to those of other bridges. The largest exception is that this bridge lasted much longer than the previous bridges. "Enjoyed much greater longevity" simply means lasted longer, so Choice (A) is the best option. Choices (B) and (C) make incorrect statements. Choice (D), though possibly correct in its statement, is illogical and out of context in conjunction with the rest of the sentence.

8. **(C)** Knowledge of vocabulary is critical here, particularly with Choice (C); obsolescence means the state of no longer being useful. In context, this is our best choice: the bridge was still perfectly usable, but the public felt a safer bridge was needed, ultimately dooming the bridge. Choices (A) and (B) are synonyms for the "hysteria" mentioned next and thus do not function in context. "Decomposition" is a term traditionally used to mean the breakdown of organic matter.

9. **(C)** This is a *nonrestrictive* clause (i.e., describing a nonessential characteristic) rather than a *restrictive* clause (i.e., describing an essential characteristic), so "which" is preferable to "that." Choice (B) can be used only after mentioning a place, while Choice (D) must be preceded by a chronological term (e.g., *In 1982,* or *On Tuesday*).

10. **(A)** "Zanesvillians" is a plural noun referring to citizens of Zanesville, so a plural verb must be used to maintain subject-verb agreement. Eliminate Choices (B) and (C) because they use "resides" and/or "is," which are singular verbs that do not agree with "Zanesvillians." "Residing," a *gerund*, does not provide an acceptable, complete sentence. Choice (A) is the only remaining option, and it ultimately matches the aforementioned criteria.

11. **(A)** "However" implies a contrast that is not apparent. "Inevitably" makes it sound as if the reader will *certainly* find herself/himself in Zanesville at some point. With Choice (D), there is no *paradox.* In common usage, a paradox refers to things that, in combination with each other, are ironic, unexpected, or sometimes seemingly self-contradictory while still maintaining validity. "So" is the best choice. It serves as a tidy way to conclude an argument, followed by another claim that is logical based on that argument. Such is the case with this sentence.

Math

6

HOW ARE THE MATH SECTIONS DESIGNED?

- Third and fourth sections of the test; first part no calculator, second part with calculator
- No-calculator Section:
  - 25 minutes
  - 17 questions
    - 13 multiple choice, 4 grid-in
- Calculator Section:
  - 45 minutes
  - 31 questions
    - 27 multiple choice, 4 grid-in
- Typical breakdown of all the test questions from both sections combined:
  - Heart of Algebra (primarily linear equations and systems): 16 questions
  - Problem Solving and Data Analysis (primarily demonstrating literacy with data and real-world applications): 16 questions
  - Passport to Advanced Math (primarily more complicated equations): 14 questions
  - Additional Topics in Math (geometry, trigonometry, and other advanced math): 2 questions
- The questions generally become more difficult as you go. The typical organization of difficulty is as follows:
  - No-calculator Section—Multiple-choice questions 1–13 progress from easy to hard. Grid-in questions 14–17 progress from easy to hard.
  - Calculator Section—Multiple-choice questions 1–27 progress from easy to hard. Grid-in questions 28–31 progress from easy to hard.

HOW SHOULD I USE THIS CHAPTER?

- Brush up on your content knowledge with the sections "Math Essentials Review Quiz" and "Advanced Math Review."
- Use the section "PSAT 1520 Math Mindset" to develop a personalized strategy for this section.
- Review the section "Frequent Mistakes and How to Avoid Them" so you can avoid common pitfalls.

- Use the "Troubleshooting" guide to help you work through strategic issues you have encountered in the past or are finding as you work through problems.
- Use what you have learned to practice effectively in the Math Drills chapter that follows.

MATH ESSENTIALS REVIEW QUIZ

This section contains concepts you probably already know but for which you may need a quick refresher. Complete this quiz to determine which concepts you still need to memorize.

1. To find the perimeter P of a rectangle with length L and width W, what is the correct formula?

   (A) $P = L \times W$ OR   (B) $P = 2L + 2W$

2. Which of these statements is true?

   (A) An isosceles triangle is always equilateral.   OR   (B) An equilateral triangle is always isosceles.

3. What is the value of the sine of angle C in the triangle below?

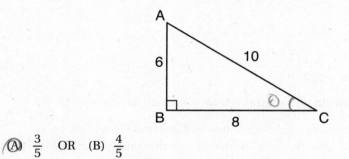

   (A) $\frac{3}{5}$ OR   (B) $\frac{4}{5}$

4. What is the y-intercept and slope of the line with the equation $y = 4x + 3$?

   (A) y-intercept: 4 and slope: 3   OR   (B) y-intercept: 3 and slope: 4

5. What is an expression to calculate the slope between the points (A, B) and (C, D)?

   (A) $\frac{B-D}{A-C}$ OR   (B) $\frac{A-C}{B-D}$

6. A line that is parallel to the line $y = 5x - 3$ would have what slope?

   (A) 5   OR   (B) −3

7. What is the slope of a line perpendicular to the line with the equation $y = -\frac{1}{5}x - 7$?

   (A) −5   OR   (B) 5

8. What is another way of writing $(a + b)(a - b)$?

   (A) $a^2 - b^2$ OR   (B) $a^2 + b^2$

9. What does $(4x - 3)^2$ equal?

(A) $16x^2 - 24x + 9$ OR   (B) $16x^2 + 9$

10. Which of these expresses an equivalent relationship?

(A) $|-3| = -|3|$ OR   (B) $|3| = |-3|$

11. Which of these expresses that x is 40% of y?

(A) $x = 0.4y$ OR   (B) $y = 0.4x$

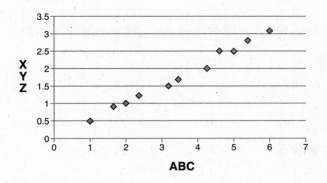

12. What is the best approximation of the slope of a best-fit line for the above graph?

(A) $\dfrac{1}{2}$ OR   (B) 2

13. How should you calculate the arithmetic mean of this set of numbers?

$$\{2, 3, 5, 7, 11\}$$

(A) Simply choose the middle value: 5   OR   (B) $\dfrac{2+3+5+7+11}{5}$

14. Which is larger for this set of numbers, mode or range?

$$\{1, 1, 4, 5, 12, 71\}$$

(A) Mode   OR   (B) Range

15. What is the probability that a two-sided coin will turn up heads when flipped?

(A) 0.5   OR   (B) 2

16. Which of these expressions states that x is less than or equal to 3?

(A) $x < 3$ OR   (B) $x \leq 3$

17. If $f(x) = 2x$ and $g(x) = x + 3$, what is the value of $f(g(2))$?

(A) 10   OR   (B) 13

18. Which of these is the correct quadratic formula for equations of the form $ax^2 + bx + c = 0$?

    (A) $\dfrac{-b \pm \sqrt{b^2 - 4ac}}{2a}$ OR (B) $\dfrac{b \pm \sqrt{b^2 + 4ac}}{a}$

19. Which of these systems of equations has infinitely many solutions?

    (A) $\begin{aligned} y &= 2x \\ y &= x+5 \end{aligned}$ OR (B) $\begin{aligned} y &= 2x+1 \\ 3y &= 6x+3 \end{aligned}$

20. The function $f(x) = \dfrac{x^2 + 5}{x - 3}$ is undefined when x equals what number?

    (A) $x = 3$ OR (B) $x = \sqrt{5}$

21. $\dfrac{2}{3} + \dfrac{1}{4} = ?$

    (A) $\dfrac{11}{12}$ OR (B) $\dfrac{3}{7}$

22. $\dfrac{x+3}{3} = ?$

    (A) x OR (B) $\dfrac{x}{3} + 1$

23. $x^3 x^4 = ?$

    (A) x^7 OR (B) x^{12}

24. $(x^2)^5 = ?$

    (A) x^7 OR (B) x^{10}

25. If $x > 0$, $\dfrac{\sqrt[3]{x^2}}{\sqrt[6]{x}} = ?$

    (A) $\sqrt[3]{x}$ OR (B) $\sqrt{x}$

TIP

Even if you answered these questions correctly, carefully check out the "Concept Review" column in the answers on the next page to make sure you have memorized all of these concepts.

Solutions	Concept Review
1. **(B)** $P = 2L + 2W$ Perimeter is the sum of the lengths of the sides in the figure. As you can see in the figure below, the rectangle has two sides of width W and two sides of length L. The sum of all these sides is $L + L + W + W = 2L + 2W$. 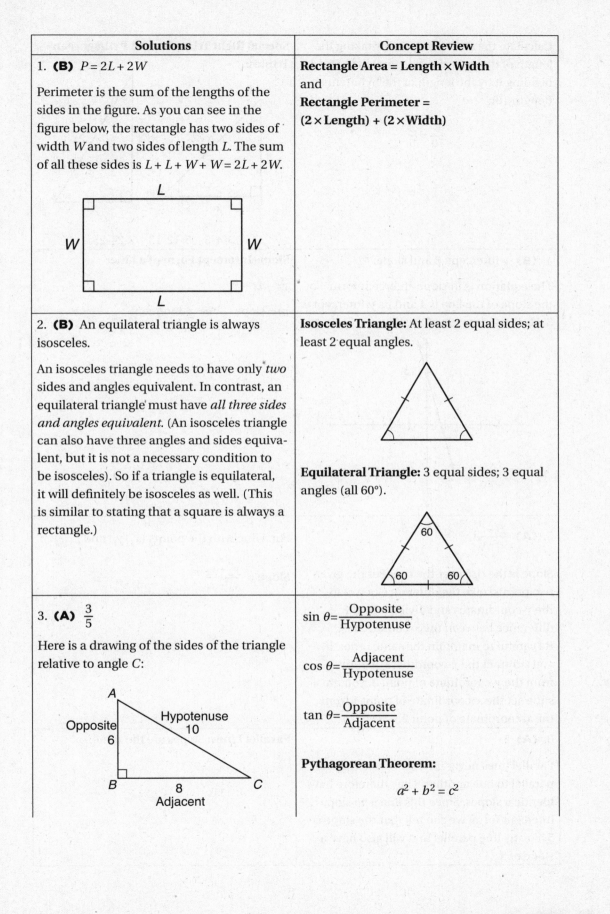	**Rectangle Area = Length × Width** and **Rectangle Perimeter =** **(2 × Length) + (2 × Width)**
2. **(B)** An equilateral triangle is always isosceles. An isosceles triangle needs to have only *two* sides and angles equivalent. In contrast, an equilateral triangle must have *all three sides and angles equivalent*. (An isosceles triangle can also have three angles and sides equivalent, but it is not a necessary condition to be isosceles). So if a triangle is equilateral, it will definitely be isosceles as well. (This is similar to stating that a square is always a rectangle.)	**Isosceles Triangle:** At least 2 equal sides; at least 2 equal angles. **Equilateral Triangle:** 3 equal sides; 3 equal angles (all 60°).
3. **(A)** $\frac{3}{5}$ Here is a drawing of the sides of the triangle relative to angle C:	$\sin \theta = \dfrac{\text{Opposite}}{\text{Hypotenuse}}$ $\cos \theta = \dfrac{\text{Adjacent}}{\text{Hypotenuse}}$ $\tan \theta = \dfrac{\text{Opposite}}{\text{Adjacent}}$ **Pythagorean Theorem:** $$a^2 + b^2 = c^2$$

Calculate the sine of angle C by taking the length of the opposite side (length 6) and dividing it by the length of the hypotenuse (length 10):

$$\frac{6}{10} = \frac{3}{5}$$

Special Right Triangles and Pythagorean Triples:

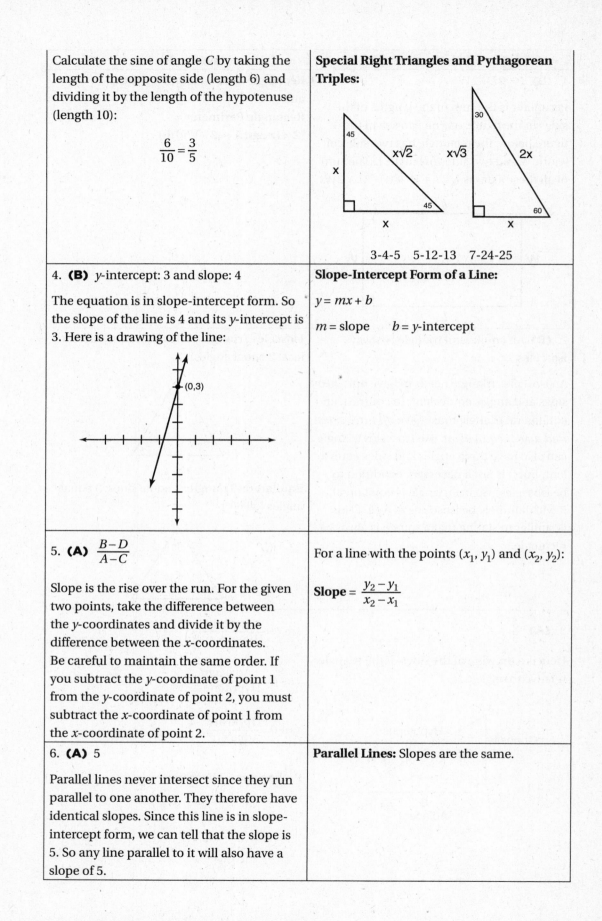

3-4-5   5-12-13   7-24-25

---

4. **(B)** y-intercept: 3 and slope: 4

The equation is in slope-intercept form. So the slope of the line is 4 and its y-intercept is 3. Here is a drawing of the line:

Slope-Intercept Form of a Line:

$y = mx + b$

$m = $ slope $b = y$-intercept

---

5. **(A)** $\dfrac{B-D}{A-C}$

Slope is the rise over the run. For the given two points, take the difference between the y-coordinates and divide it by the difference between the x-coordinates. Be careful to maintain the same order. If you subtract the y-coordinate of point 1 from the y-coordinate of point 2, you must subtract the x-coordinate of point 1 from the x-coordinate of point 2.

For a line with the points (x_1, y_1) and (x_2, y_2):

Slope $= \dfrac{y_2 - y_1}{x_2 - x_1}$

---

6. **(A)** 5

Parallel lines never intersect since they run parallel to one another. They therefore have identical slopes. Since this line is in slope-intercept form, we can tell that the slope is 5. So any line parallel to it will also have a slope of 5.

Parallel Lines: Slopes are the same.

7. (B) 5

Perpendicular lines intersect at a 90-degree angle and have slopes that are negative reciprocals of each other. The slope of the line in the equation is $-\frac{1}{5}$. To find the negative reciprocal, first find the reciprocal and then multiply that result by –1. To find the reciprocal of $-\frac{1}{5}$, determine what number you would multiply $-\frac{1}{5}$ by to get 1.

$$-\frac{1}{5} \times (-5) = 1$$

So the reciprocal is –5. To get the negative reciprocal, multiply this by –1, giving $(-1)(-5) = 5$. Thus, the slope of the line perpendicular to the given line is 5.

A shortcut to finding the slope of a line perpendicular to another is simply to invert the fraction and flip the sign.

Perpendicular Lines: Slopes are *negative reciprocals of each other* (e.g., 3 and $-\frac{1}{3}$).

8. (A) $a^2 - b^2$

If you don't remember this pattern, you can use FOIL (first, outer, inner, last) with this expression:

$(a+b)(a-b) \rightarrow$
$a^2 - ab + ab - b^2 \rightarrow$
$a^2 - b^2$

Common Factoring Patterns:

$(a+b)(a+b) = a^2 + 2ab + b^2$
Example:
$(x+4)(x+4) = x^2 + 8x + 16$

$(a+b)(a-b) = a^2 - b^2$
Example:
$(m+2)(m-2) = m^2 - 4$

9. (A) $16x^2 - 24x + 9$

FOIL the expression:

$(4x-3)^2 \rightarrow$
$(4x-3)(4x-3) \rightarrow$
$16x^2 - 12x - 12x + 9 \rightarrow$
$16x^2 - 24x + 9$

$(a-b)(a-b) = a^2 - 2ab + b^2$
Example:
$(5-y)(5-y) = 25 - 10y + y^2$

Sum of Cubes
$(a+b)(a^2 - ab + b^2) = a^3 + b^3$
Example:
$(2+x)(4 - 2x + x^2) = 8 + x^3$

Difference of Cubes
$(a-b)(a^2 + ab + b^2) = a^3 - b^3$
Example:
$(y-4)(y^2 + 4y + 16) = y^3 - 4^3 = y^3 - 64$

10. **(B)** $\lvert 3 \rvert = \lvert -3 \rvert$ Treat the absolute value sign like parentheses with the order of operations. Just like parentheses come first in the order of operations, you should calculate the absolute value expressions first before dealing with the negatives outside the absolute values. In option A, the left-hand side equals 3 since −3 is 3 units away from 0. However, on the right-hand side, the negative sign on the outside of the absolute value makes the expression negative: $$-\lvert 3 \rvert = -3.$$	**Absolute Value:** Distance along the number line from zero. Examples: $\lvert 8 \rvert = 8$ and $\lvert -8 \rvert = 8$ Remark: Taking the absolute value of something should always give a nonnegative result since absolute value represents a distance.
11. **(A)** $x = 0.4y$ To find the percent, turn 40% into a fraction by dividing 40 by 100: $$\frac{40}{100} = 0.4$$ Write an equation to show that x equals 40% of y: $$x = 0.4y$$	**General Percent Formula:** $$\frac{\text{Part}}{\text{Whole}} \times 100 = \text{Percent}$$
12. **(A)** $\dfrac{1}{2}$ Estimate the coordinates of a couple of points in the graph. Then calculate the slope. We can use $(0, 0)$ and $(6, 3)$. Plug these into the slope formula to solve: $$\frac{y_2 - y_1}{x_2 - x_1} = \frac{3-0}{6-0} = \frac{3}{6} = \frac{1}{2}$$	**Best-Fit Lines:** Look for general trend in the data (if it exists), and draw a line to model the trend.
13. **(B)** $\dfrac{2+3+5+7+11}{5}$ The mean is the simple average. Add the individual values $(2 + 3 + 5 + 7 + 11)$, and divide by the total number of values (5).	$\text{Mean} = \dfrac{\text{Sum of Items}}{\text{Number of Items}}$ **Median:** The middle term of a set of numbers when lined up small to large. Note that when the number of terms is even and the two terms in the middle are not equal, take the mean of the two middle terms to find the median. **Mode:** The most frequent term in a set of numbers. Note that if in a set of numbers, each number appears only once, there is no mode. If a set of numbers has 2 or more numbers tied for appearing the most times, the set has multiple modes.

14. (B) Range The mode is 1 for this set of numbers since 1 appears more frequently than any other number. The range is $71 - 1 = 70$, since that is the difference between the smallest and largest terms in the set. Therefore, the range is greater than the mode.	**Range:** The difference between the smallest and largest values in a set of data.
15. (A) 0.5 When the coin is flipped, it can land on either heads or tails. So there is a 1 out of 2 chance it will land on heads. In other words, 1 outcome results in success (heads) out of 2 possible outcomes (heads or tails). So the probability is $\frac{1}{2} = 0.5$.	**Probability:** The likelihood that a given event will happen, expressed as a fraction or decimal between 0 and 1 inclusive. Note that a probability of 0 means an event has no chance of occurring. A probability of 0.5 means there is a 50% chance it will occur. A probability of 1 means the event is certain to occur. In general, we can find the probability by taking the number of successes divided by the number of possible outcomes.
16. (B) $x \le 3$ The line underneath the > or < sign signifies equivalence.	< means less than when the number in question is on the left. > means greater than. ≤ means less than or equal to. ≥ means greater than or equal to.
17. (A) 10 First, calculate the value of $g(2)$: $g(x) = x + 3$ $g(2) = 2 + 3 = 5$ Then plug 5 into $f(x)$: $f(x) = 2x$ $f(5) = 2 \times 5 = 10$	**Composite Functions:** Calculate the value of the *inside* function first. Then calculate the value of the *outside* function, just as in the example problem.
18. (A) $\dfrac{-b \pm \sqrt{b^2 - 4ac}}{2a}$ This is a formula you absolutely must memorize.	**Quadratic Formula:** $x = \dfrac{-b \pm \sqrt{b^2 - 4ac}}{2a}$ An equation with the variable x and constants a, b, and c written in the form $ax^2 + bx + c = 0$ can be solved with the quadratic formula.

19. (B)
$$y = 2x + 1$$
$$3y = 6x + 3$$

These two equations have infinitely many solutions because the second equation is 3 times the first equation, making them different expressions of the same equation. Thus, any solution to one equation is a solution to the other as well. Since there are infinitely many solutions to the equations (both equations are linear and a line has infinitely many points), the system itself must have infinitely many solutions.

A system of equations will have **infinite solutions** if the equations are simple multiples of each other. The graphs of the equations are exactly the same.

A system of equations will have **no solutions** if no points are solutions to all equations in the system. Graphically, the graphs of the equations never intersect. In other words, the graphs are parallel.

A function is **undefined** at a point if inputting that value into the function produces an undefined number, such as $\frac{5}{0}$.

20. (A) $x = 3$

If $x = 3$, the denominator (bottom) of the equation equals zero since $3 - 3 = 0$. If you divide a number by zero, the result is undefined. You cannot divide a number into zero parts.

21. (A) $\frac{11}{12}$

$$\frac{2}{3} + \frac{1}{4} \rightarrow \frac{8}{12} + \frac{3}{12} \rightarrow \frac{11}{12}$$

Add fractions by (1) finding the least common denominator, (2) changing each fraction to have the same denominator, and (3) adding the numerators together.

22. (B) $\frac{x}{3} + 1$

$$\frac{x+3}{3} = \frac{x}{3} + \frac{3}{3} = \frac{x}{3} + 1$$

In general,

$$\frac{xy}{x} = \frac{\cancel{x}y}{\cancel{x}} = y \text{ and}$$

$$\frac{x+y}{y} = \frac{x}{y} + \frac{y}{y} = \frac{x}{y} + 1$$

23. (A) x^7

$$x^3 x^4 = x^{3+4} = x^7$$

24. (B) x^{10}

$$(x^2)^5 = x^{2 \times 5} = x^{10}$$

25. (B) $\sqrt{x}$

For $x > 0$,

$$\frac{\sqrt[3]{x^2}}{\sqrt[6]{x}} = \frac{x^{\frac{2}{3}}}{x^{\frac{1}{6}}} = x^{\frac{2}{3} - \frac{1}{6}} = x^{\frac{4}{6} - \frac{1}{6}} = x^{\frac{3}{6}} = x^{\frac{1}{2}} = \sqrt{x}$$

Exponent Rules:

$$a^x a^y = a^{x+y}$$

$$\frac{a^x}{a^y} = a^{x-y}$$

$$(a^x)^y = a^{xy}$$

$$a^{-x} = \frac{1}{a^x}$$

$$a^{\frac{x}{y}} = \sqrt[y]{a^x}$$

ADVANCED MATH REVIEW

These are concepts that most advanced students should brush up on before taking the PSAT.

Concept	Explanation
Polynomial Long Division	In addition to using factoring and canceling to divide polynomials, you can use long division. Here is an example of how you would divide $2x^2 - 5x + 7$ by $x + 1$: $$\begin{array}{r} 2x-7 \\ x+1{\overline{\smash{\big)}\,2x^2-5x+7}} \\ \underline{-(2x^2+2x)} \\ -7x+7 \\ \underline{-(-7x-7)} \\ 14 \end{array}$$ So the answer is $2x - 7$ with a remainder of $\dfrac{14}{x+1}$.
Synthetic Division	An alternative to polynomial long division, and the way many students learn how to divide polynomials, is synthetic division. Here is how the previous example, $2x^2 - 5x + 7$, would be divided by $x + 1$ using synthetic division: Set up the synthetic division by taking the coefficients of the terms of the polynomial and placing the numerical term of the divisor (multiplied by –1) to the left of them as follows: $$\begin{array}{c|ccc} -1 & 2 & -5 & 7 \\ & & & \\ \hline & & & \end{array}$$ Then, bring down each of the coefficients, multiplying the columns one-by-one by the –1, and create sums to see what the divided polynomial and remainder would be: $$\begin{array}{c|ccc} -1 & 2 & -5 & 7 \\ & & -2 & 7 \\ \hline & 2 & -7 & 14 \end{array}$$ So the answer would also be $2x - 7$ with a remainder of $\dfrac{14}{x+1}$.
Key Parabola Equations	**Vertex Form of a Parabola:** $y = a(x - h)^2 + k$ ■ The vertex is (h, k). ■ The x-coordinate of the vertex provides the *axis of symmetry* for the parabola. Example: A parabola with the equation $y = 3(x - 2)^2 - 4$ has a vertex of $(2, -4)$. The equation for the axis of symmetry for the parabola is $x = 2$.

Zeros	The **zero** of a function is an x-value that produces a y-value of zero. Example: $y = (x - 3)(x + 4)$ has zeros of 3 and –4 because y will be zero at either of those values.
Extraneous Solutions	Sometimes you should test solutions to see if they work in the original expression. Example: What are the solution(s) for x in this equation? $x = \sqrt{24 - 2x}$ The logical first step to solve this equation is to square both sides: $x^2 = 24 - 2x$ Rearrange and solve: $x^2 + 2x - 24 = 0 \rightarrow (x - 4)(x + 6) = 0$ So 4 and –6 both appear to be solutions. However, only 4 works in the original expression since the square root of a real number cannot be negative. Therefore, just 4 is the answer. The number –6 is an extraneous solution. Check for extraneous solutions when you start multiplying and dividing expressions containing variables.
Imaginary Numbers	The square root of –1 is written as i. $i = \sqrt{-1}$ $i^2 = -1$ $i^3 = -i$ $i^4 = 1$
Graphical Relationships	If x and y have a **linear** relationship, their graph will have a constant slope. Example: $y = x$ If x and y have a **quadratic** relationship, the variables will have a squared relationship. Example: $y = 4x^2$ If x and y have an **exponential** relationship, their function will have extreme increases or decreases because the variable is an exponent. Examples: - $y = 2(4)^x$ has y-values that become very large and positive with relatively small increases in x. - $y = 3\left(\frac{1}{5}\right)^x$ has y-values that become very small with relatively small increases in x. There can be both *positive* and *negative* relationships between variables—positive if the variables increase together and negative if one variable increases as the other variable decreases.

PSAT 1520 MATH MINDSET

How can your strengths actually be weaknesses? What should you do differently?

"I'm a fast reader." Students who are fantastic history and literature students often find that they are able to read the long math word problems on the PSAT quickly. Despite reading through the questions efficiently, they find that they don't really grasp what to do. What is going on?

- *Fast reading does not necessarily mean fast comprehension.* Students who can breeze through a novel, effortlessly remembering all the plot details, often meet their match with the highly dense, technical prose of the PSAT Math.

- *Instead of reading the question over and over, read it ONE TIME WELL and focus on setting up everything.* Be sure that you are reading only as quickly as you are comprehending—don't go on to the next sentence of the problem until you have completely grasped the first sentence of the problem. Being a speed reader will be fantastic when you have a couple of hundred pages of reading to do in an evening while in college. Speed reading, though, will stand in your way on the PSAT Math because you will fail to grasp what is being asked.

"I am a really fast math problem solver." You are one of the first to turn in your math tests in school, and you always do really well. Math homework doesn't take you long at all. You may know several "tricks" with your calculator to pick up the pace even more. If you think like this, what should you do?

- *Use all the available time on the PSAT Math.* Unlike on school math tests, you won't be able to do anything else on the PSAT if you finish the math section early. Rushing to the end may feel good and make you look smart to your fellow test takers, who may glance at you resting on your desk and assume you are a math genius. However, there is no prize for finishing early. There is a prize—thousands of dollars in scholarship money—if you answer the questions correctly.

- *Stay in the moment—don't think ahead to the next step.* When solving a problem, a desire to finish quickly will make you jump ahead to the next step instead of working through the step you are on. Fortunately, the PSAT Math problems generally *do not require many steps to solve them.* Many of the incorrect answer choices, however, will be what many students would calculate if they skipped or rushed through a step. Channel all of your intellectual energy into rigorously solving the problem, one step at a time.

"I am able to do most calculations in my head." When your math teacher asks you to do a better job taking notes and to "show your work," you are dismissive—you can do mental math like a pro and hate being slowed down by your pencil. Why can this intellectual confidence get you into trouble on the PSAT?

- *Unlike many school math tests, the PSAT doesn't just come up with random wrong numbers for the incorrect choices.* In an effort to save time while writing tests, many math teachers will find the solutions for their test questions and then use random numbers for the incorrect answers on multiple-choice tests. The PSAT, on the other hand, presents very persuasive incorrect choices. In fact, the PSAT may use numbers at which you have mentally arrived. Caution, not overconfidence, is in order.

TIP

Plan on checking your pace at reasonable intervals, not after every question. Checking your pace each time you turn the page is usually just fine. You want to spend your time figuring out the problems, not looking at your watch.

- *You should write out as much as you like as you read through and work out the problems.* No one in a later class needs to reuse your test booklet as is often the case in math class. Do not be shy about writing out your work so that you clarify what is being asked. Writing out your work will help you avoid making careless errors.

"I have a highly analytical mind." You like to consider all the possibilities of a question—some people may accuse you of thinking too much. You are not satisfied merely scratching the surface of a problem; you prefer to dive deep. If this sounds like you, keep in mind the following.

- *Know when careful analysis is needed and when it is not.* Math is the one section of the PSAT where the questions gradually increase in difficulty as you progress. Be sure that you don't overthink the early questions, and be sure you adequately analyze the later questions.
- *Keep in mind what is being tested.* This is a test designed for millions of high school juniors to demonstrate their general academic proficiency. As such, the PSAT will not be a test of obscure math concepts. Channel your analytical skills into understanding what the problem is asking you to do instead of making the problem out to be more difficult than it is.

TIP

Keep in mind that the PSAT is for students starting their junior year. If you have taken Algebra 1, Geometry, and Algebra 2, you should have covered all the concepts you will see on test day.

"I like to double-check things and to be extremely thorough." You don't see the point in finishing a test early—why not be certain you didn't make any mistakes? Not only do you write out all your work, you allow time at the end of the test to plug answers back into the problems. Why would this be an issue?

- *The PSAT Math has few problems that will allow you to do simple plug-and-chugs.* While using your answers can be a very useful technique, as we will see later in this chapter, the PSAT Math is not a test where spending several minutes plugging your answers back into equations will be helpful. Instead, invest your time in the initial setup of the question. Answer the question correctly the first time.
- *The calculations on the PSAT Math will not be overly complex.* On the no-calculator portion of the test, this is especially true. Even on the calculator portion, you will find the calculations are not terribly long and tedious. The test is much more about your ability to think than it is about your ability to plug numbers into your calculator carefully.
- *If you are very thorough and still finish with some time remaining, go ahead and double-check.* Go back to problems that are particularly susceptible to careless errors, like ones with negative numbers, fractions, and long word problems. As you go through the test the first time, you can circle any questions you would like to come back to and double-check if time permits.

"I am extremely hard working. I like to be prepared for anything." You like to be prepared for all possible scenarios—after all, that's why you are reading this book and studying hard for the upcoming PSAT! While a great work ethic is fantastic in giving you the motivation to prepare for the PSAT, it can sometimes hurt you when you're taking the actual test. Why?

- *You need to be prepared for surprises.* Look at your preparation as primarily training you to think more effectively instead of helping you merely to memorize a variety of problem-solving approaches. This is especially true because of the relative newness of this version of the PSAT. It is not possible to work through every possible version of every possible problem the PSAT Math may have. When you come across a problem on the actual PSAT that throws you off, respond by trusting your ability to think critically instead of becoming paralyzed with fear of the unfamiliar.

- *Treat the problems like puzzles.* You would not look at a maze and beat yourself up for not "knowing" how to find your way through the maze. Instead, you would allow time to try different paths and make mistakes as you worked your way to the exit. Approach the PSAT Math in a similar way—"figure it out" instead of being intimidated. Give yourself permission not to see the solution immediately.

"I don't give up—I stay after a problem until I can figure it out." Your teachers and parents may refer to this as grit—a capacity to be strong and determined in the face of difficulty. What do you need to consider if this describes you?

- *Know when to walk away from a problem.* Working on a difficult problem is great as long as you are making steady progress and are not taking more than a couple of minutes. If you have hit a wall and can't see a path to get through, step away from the problem. Your time will be better spent trying other problems and allowing your subconscious mind to attack the problem that was giving you trouble. If you have time to revisit the problem, you will be able to give it a fresh look. You may be surprised at how much easier the problem is than it appeared at first glance.

"I like to be able to justify my answers." You would be a natural math tutor—you can explain each and every step along the way to finding the solution. You feel less anxious when you can give a solid reason as to why you picked your answer. If this applies to you, you should do the following.

- *Be open to unconventional approaches.* Many of the math problems can be solved by using intuition, trying out sample values, and using the given diagrams. These approaches are not what you would find in a math textbook, yet they often work. Why? The PSAT Math has generally more elegant problems involving pattern recognition than the more cut-and-dried problems found on typical math tests.
- *You simply need to get it right—you don't need to explain yourself.* There are many ways to solve the PSAT Math problems. As long as you have a method that arrives at the correct answer, you are doing things perfectly. Let go of the little voice in your head that tells you that if you can't explain yourself, you must not truly understand the problem. Trust your intuition.

"I am a perfectionist. I have extremely high expectations for myself, and I don't want to make mistakes." This mindset will be extraordinarily useful when you are editing your college application essay, but it might hurt your creative thinking on the PSAT. Fear of failure does not generally lead to cool and calm thinking. What should you be mindful of?

- *The PSAT will be graded on a curve, so a couple of missed questions will not keep you from your goals.* This book is subtitled "Aiming for National Merit," not "Achieving Flawless Performance." Perfection is a worthy goal. However, do not waste time and energy agonizing over a question or two. You do not need to have a perfect score to earn National Merit recognition because the PSAT is always graded on a curve.

- *Mistakes lead to success.* If the PSAT Math routinely required laborious calculations, one small mistake would have a tremendous impact on your accuracy and time management. Fortunately, the math problems have plenty of patterns and relatively clean calculations. So it is easy to redo a problem if you aren't getting anywhere. Ultimately, there is a straightforward way to solve each problem.

"I am great at finding errors and inconsistencies in a test." You are quick to find typos and vague answers on your school tests. Your classmates love you for convincing the teacher to throw out a tough question and give everyone an extra point. Does this skill have an outlet on the PSAT? Not so much.

- *Know that the PSAT is a very well written test.* The College Board took years to develop the new version of the PSAT. Although the scores from the first new PSAT in 2015 took a while to come back, there were no reports of flawed questions. Don't waste your time looking for flawed questions. Instead, focus your energy on solving the well-crafted problems you find, giving the PSAT the benefit of the doubt.

FREQUENT MISTAKES AND HOW TO AVOID THEM

> **Problem: Making too many careless mistakes.**
>
> **Solution: Carefully set up word problems by writing out everything.**

A major difference between the PSAT and school tests is the widespread use of word problems on the PSAT. Many PSAT problems will require you to translate several sentences into an algebraic expression. Here are some of the key phrases that may be used in place of mathematical notations.

Wording Examples	Translation
Is, are, was, were, will be, results in, gives, yields, equals	=
Sum, increased by, more than, together, combined, total(s), added to, older than, farther than	+
Difference, decreased by, less than, fewer than, minus, younger than, shorter than	−
Multiplied by, times, of, product of, twice	×
Divided by, per, out of, ratio of, half of, one third of, split	$\div$ or $\dfrac{x}{y}$

Here is an example of a typical PSAT problem that will be easier to solve by carefully writing it out.

Alaina rents an apartment in the spring and will rent it for the rest of the calendar year. To rent it, she must pay a $500 security deposit and a monthly rent of $750. In addition, she must pay monthly utilities of $40 for water and $50 for electricity. What expression gives the total amount of money Alaina will spend if she rents the apartment for x months that year?

(A) $840 + 500x$
(B) $500 + 840x$
(C) $500x$
(D) $750x + 500$

As you read this problem, you can underline key words and write out important information. You should use abbreviations for the sake of time. For instructional purposes, though, we will write everything here using complete words. For example:

$500 = security deposit
$750 = monthly rent
$40 + $50 = $90 for total monthly utilities

To rent the apartment for x months, Alaina will need to pay the $500 security deposit one time. Then she will need to pay $750 in rent each month plus $90 in utilities each month for a total of $840 each month.

So the correct answer is (B) because there will be a flat fee of $500 plus the $840 per month, varying with how many months she rents. Writing this out, rather than doing it in your head, makes this a much easier problem to solve.

Here is another problem where writing out your work will make a big difference.

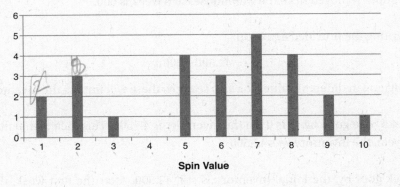

Frequency of Result

Spin Value

A board game has a circular wheel evenly divided into ten segments, each with a numerical value between 1 and 10. For the spins recorded in the above graph, what is the mean value of a spin, rounded to the nearest hundredth?

*Free-Response Question: Write Your Answer*_____

If you try to do this in your head, you will likely make a careless mistake. The formula you will

need is Mean = $\dfrac{\text{Sum of Values}}{\text{Total Number of Values}}$.

The sum of all of the responses is:

$$2(1) + 3(2) + 1(3) + 0(4) + 4(5) + 3(6) + 5(7) + 4(8) + 2(9) + 1(10) = 144$$

The total number of responses is:

$$2 + 3 + 1 + 0 + 4 + 3 + 5 + 4 + 2 + 1 = 25$$

The mean, then, is $144 \div 25 = 5.76$.

The PSAT will have questions that require you to interpret algebraic expressions. For many questions, it is helpful to look at the answer choices before solving to see where the question is headed. On questions like these, it is advisable to "look before you leap." The incorrect answers here will likely be very persuasive. So use writing to visualize what the parts of the algebraic expression signify before you evaluate the answer choices. Although this takes more time up front, it will probably save you time in the long run. Here is an example of the sort of problem to which this approach applies.

> A book warehouse has an inventory of books, I, that is modeled by the equation $I = 42{,}500 - 600w$, where w represents the number of weeks that have gone by after the beginning of the year. What do the numbers 42,500 and 600 represent in the equation?
>
> (A) The average book inventory throughout the year is 42,500. The number of books at the end of the year is 600.
> (B) The book inventory in the warehouse at the end of the year is 42,500. The number of weeks that it takes for the book inventory to be gone is 600.
> (C) The initial monetary investment in the book warehouse is 42,500. The weekly revenue from outside book sales is 600.
> (D) The warehouse book inventory at the beginning of the year is 42,500. The number of books removed from the warehouse each week is 600.

Start by rewriting the provided equation:

$$I = 42{,}500 - 600w$$

Next, try plugging in different values for w to see how these will impact the inventory, I.

When 0 weeks have gone by, w is 0. So the inventory is 42,500. This means that at the beginning of the year, the inventory was 42,500.

When 1 week goes by, the initial inventory is still 42,500. After the first week, though, 600 books have been subtracted from the inventory. After 2 weeks go by, the original inventory goes down by 1,200. So a pattern emerges—the 600 in the equation represents the amount by which the book inventory will decrease each week. The correct answer is (D).

If we had just jumped into the choices without thinking this through and making some notes, it would have been quite easy to become trapped by a persuasive answer and overthink the question.

> **Problem: Having trouble finding a "textbook" method to figuring out the question.**
>
> **Solution: Be open to using an unconventional approach when applicable, like plugging in numbers.**

TIP

Sometimes it pays to be lazy! Be open to time-saving ways of attacking these problems.

You can plug in numbers in different ways to work toward a solution. One of the most tried-and-true PSAT Math strategies is to plug the answers into an equation, starting with the middle value, like (B) or (C). Why? That way you will need to try only a maximum of two or three choices instead of potentially all four. The choices are almost certainly going to be in numerical order. So if your first value is too large, you will know which choices to try next. Here is an example of where this technique can save you time.

What is a possible value of x that satisfies the equation below?

$$-(x-3)^2 = -25$$

(A) 6
(B) 8
(C) 10
(D) 12

If you were to write all of this out, it would make for a relatively long, messy calculation. If you work backward from the choices, you will arrive at the answer with ease. Start with Choice (C), where $x = 10$, because it is a middle value among your choices:

$$-(10-3)^2 = -25 \rightarrow -49 \neq -25$$

So Choice (C) doesn't work. If you go for a larger value, like 12, the difference between the answers will be even larger. So try (B) next, where $x = 8$.

$$-(8-3)^2 = -25 \rightarrow -(5)^2 = -25$$

This is true, so our answer is (B). It is unlikely that some of the later, more challenging questions will permit this sort of backsolving. However, this method can save you time on earlier questions, giving you more time to work through the difficult questions.

Another common situation where plugging in numbers can be helpful is when the problem provides a possible range of what the variable could be. In this case, you can pick a number within the given range and plug it in to see the value of the expression. Here is an example:

Assuming that x is not equal to zero, what is the value of the following expression?

$$\frac{1}{4}\left(\frac{(2x)^3}{(3x)^3}\right)$$

Grid-In Question: Write Your Answer _____

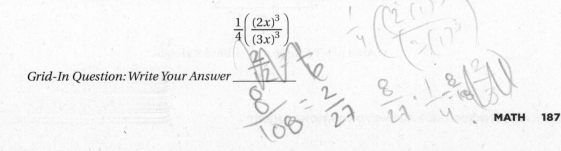

Perhaps you see that you can cancel out the x^3 from the top and bottom. If you don't make that intellectual leap, plugging in a value can make things much easier and more concrete. How about plugging in 1 for x? The answer is not equal to zero, so it is a valid input. The problem is now easy to work with since x will remain 1 when it is cubed.

$$\frac{1}{4}\left(\frac{(2x)^3}{(3x)^3}\right) \rightarrow \frac{1}{4}\left(\frac{(2\cdot1)^3}{(3\cdot1)^3}\right) \rightarrow \frac{1}{4}\left(\frac{8}{27}\right) \rightarrow \frac{8}{108} \rightarrow \frac{2}{27}$$

The answer is $\frac{2}{27}$.

Problem: You forgot an important formula, especially a geometry or trigonometry formula.

Solution: Don't forget to use the provided formulas.

Not many problems use geometry and trigonometry on the PSAT. Those that do are often toward the end of the test section. Because of this, it is easy to forget that the PSAT provides you with several extremely helpful formulas at the beginning of the test section. Although it would be best if you didn't have to look because you have the formulas memorized (as well as the formulas reviewed in this chapter in the fundamentals review quiz and advanced math review), here are the provided formulas in case you need them.

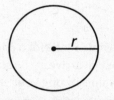

r = **Radius of the Circle**
Area of a Circle = πr^2
Circumference of a Circle = $2\pi r$

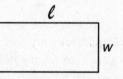

Area of a Rectangle = Length × Width

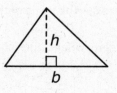

Area of a Triangle = $\frac{1}{2}$ × **Base × Height**

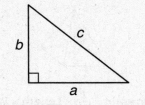

Pythagorean Theorem: $a^2 + b^2 = c^2$

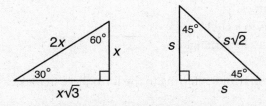

Special Right Triangles: 30-60-90 and 45-45-90

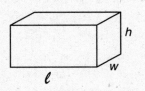
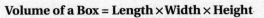
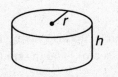

Volume of a Box = Length × Width × Height

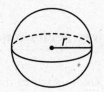

Volume of a Cylinder = $\pi r^2 h$

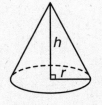

Volume of a Sphere = $\frac{4}{3} \pi r^3$

Volume of a Cone = $\frac{1}{3} \pi r^2 h$

Volume of a Pyramid = $\frac{1}{3}$ × Length × Width × Height

Key Facts:

- A circle has 360 degrees.
- There are 2π radians in a circle.
- There are 180 degrees in a triangle.

Here is the sort of problem where referring to the formulas can make a big difference.

> The area of a sector of a circle represents 20 percent of the area of the entire circle. What is the central angle that corresponds to this sector in degrees?
>
> (A) 36
> (B) 48
> (C) 54
> (D) 72

A provided fact is key to solving this problem:

A circle has 360 degrees.

If a sector is taking up 20% of the circle, it's also taking up 20% of the degrees in the center. A circle has 360 total degrees, so the sector is taking up (0.20)(360) = 72 degrees. The answer is (D).

Many students learn the process for unit conversions in chemistry or other science classes.

Problem: You get stuck on problems with currency and scientific measurements.

Solution: Be sure you know how to perform unit conversions.

Converting among different types of units—such as mass measurements, currency conversion rates, and length measurements—is a major component of the PSAT. You can do unit conversions in several ways.

First, if you are doing a relatively straightforward conversion between just a couple of units, you can set up a proportion or do simple multiplication. For example:

A cook needs to measure three and a half cups of flour for a recipe, but he has only a tablespoon available to measure the flour. Given that there are 16 tablespoons in 1 cup, how many tablespoons of flour will the cook need for the recipe?

Option 1: Set up a proportion. There are 16 tablespoons in 1 cup, and we need 3.5 cups. So set up a proportion that has the tablespoons to cup ratio on either side:

$$\frac{16 \text{ Tablespoons}}{1 \text{ Cup}} = \frac{x \text{ Tablespoons}}{3.5 \text{ Cups}}$$

Cross multiply to solve for x:

$$3.5 \times 16 \text{ Tablespoons} = 56 \text{ Tablespoons}$$

Option 2: If you are comfortable being intuitive with conversions, you could simply jump to the last step of the above calculations and multiply the 3.5 cups by 16 tablespoons to get the same result.

Option 3: If you are doing a more intricate conversion that involves three or more units, you can set it up in the same way you probably learned to do unit conversions in your science classes—it may have been called "dimensional analysis," or the "unit factor method." Here is an example:

If John traveled 20 miles in a straight line from his original destination, approximately how many meters is he from his original destination given that there are 1.609 kilometers in a mile and 1,000 meters in a kilometer?

(A) 32.18
(B) 12,430
(C) 24,154
(D) 32,180

Write this out in an organized way where you can see which units should be canceled:

$$20 \text{ miles} \times \frac{1.609 \text{ kilometers}}{1 \text{ mile}} \times \frac{1,000 \text{ meters}}{1 \text{ kilometer}} \rightarrow$$

The miles and kilometers cancel, so this equals 32,180 meters.

Don't be overly reliant on estimation, but use it when it can save you time. Here is an example.

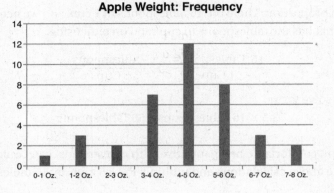

Apple Weight: Frequency

The chart above shows the distribution of individual apple weights that a customer at an apple-picking orchard placed into his bag. Which of the following could be the median weight of the 38 apples in his bag?

(A) 4.6 oz.
(B) 5.1 oz.
(C) 5.4 oz.
(D) 5.7 oz.

The median of a set of numbers is the middle value when the values are arranged from least to greatest. Although we could come up with sample values and do a laborious calculation, there is no need. The choices have only one possibility that is in the range between 4 and 5 ounces. Since the 4–5 oz. column clearly contains the median value based on a simple eyeball estimation, we can pick choice (A) and move on to the next question.

TROUBLESHOOTING

Here are some further pointers for common issues students face.

"I haven't had enough math yet."

- Most of the PSAT will be from Algebra 1 and 2. Don't worry about not having taken precalculus yet—just memorize the basic definitions of sine, cosine, and tangent.
- Review the key formulas at the beginning of the chapter. If you memorize these, you will feel much more confident.
- Keep in mind that the test primarily requires critical thinking. If you go in to the PSAT Math test ready to figure out things, you can often overcome a lack of advanced training.

"I take too long."

- Prioritize which problems you do. Don't worry about the last question or two on either PSAT Math test section. They will likely be more difficult.

- If a question is taking you more than a couple of minutes to solve, consider circling it and coming back to it. You are not writing off the problem. You will continue to think about it. If you have time to revisit the problem, it will likely seem quite a bit easier the second time around. Skip very difficult problems here and there. Then go back to them if time is available. Do not initially spend too much time on very difficult problems, because you may not have enough time to finish the test. Because the test is graded on a curve, skipping a problem isn't a big deal. However, not finishing the math section because of poor time management could be detrimental to scholarship chances if you leave enough problems incomplete. All problems are worth the same number of points. So it is better to get to the later problems and earn a few more points than just get that one tricky question but not have time for other problems you could be capable of solving. At the very least, be certain that you guess on a very difficult problem because there is no guessing penalty on the test.

- Pace yourself—take about 1.5 minutes per question on average. The earlier questions should take less time than this. The later questions should take more time. Keep yourself moving along.

"I finish too quickly."

- Consider what would be the most effective use of your extra time. For most people, it will be taking more time the first time through the questions. For some, it may be helpful to start with the most challenging questions later in the test so that you will have a couple of chances to try them—both when you start the test and when you finish. **Note:** Be sure to try this approach first on a practice test before you try it on the actual test. It is not typically an effective strategy; most students end up rushing through easier questions because they become stuck on the more difficult questions.

- Pace yourself—be sure you are taking enough time on each question, on average about 1.5 minutes a question.

"I have math anxiety."

- The confidence that comes with rigorous practice is the best bet to overcome your anxiety. If you work through the problem sets that follow, you will be ready for the PSAT.

- Realize that some anxiety is welcome—it can help you stay focused and tune out distractions. It can help push you to work through a challenging problem. Channel your nervous energy into action instead of letting it paralyze your thought process.

- Keep things in perspective. The math section represents half of the test. The PSAT, although vital for National Merit consideration, is primarily preparation for the SAT. You will have plenty of chances to take the SAT and/or ACT, the tests that colleges use for admissions decisions. All the practice you are doing for the PSAT will directly help you prepare for these later tests as well.

> **TIP**
>
> You only have so much energy to devote to thinking on test day. Focus your thinking on solving the problems, not on things like overanalyzing the questions, checking your pace too frequently, and excessively reviewing your work.

FURTHER PREPARATION

What else can you do beyond the practice drills and tests in this book to prepare for the new PSAT Math?

- Practice with the other Barron's books for the PSAT: *Barron's Strategies and Practice for the PSAT/NMSQT* and *Barron's PSAT/NMSQT.*
- Use the free practice tests and resources provided by the College Board on *KhanAcademy.org.*
- Take the most rigorous math courses offered by your school.
- Practice all of the word problems and algebra problems you can find—these are the most common types of problems you will find on the test.

> **Note:** The link to the online practice test is *http://bit.ly/barrons-PSAT-1520.* **The practice test can also be accessed on all mobile devices, including tablets and smartphones.**

Math Drills

7

This chapter consists of drills that represent the most challenging types of math questions you will encounter on the PSAT. You can practice all of these, or you can focus on the question types that give you the most difficulty. The drills as a whole are designed to give you comprehensive coverage of the variety of questions you may face on test day. The drills are arranged by topic and type of question:

19 TARGETED REVIEW DRILLS

- Heart of Algebra Drill 1 (Calculator)
- Heart of Algebra Drill 2 (Calculator)
- Heart of Algebra Drill 3 (Calculator)
- Heart of Algebra Drill 1 (No Calculator)
- Heart of Algebra Drill 2 (No Calculator)
- Problem Solving and Data Analysis Drill 1 (Calculator)
- Problem Solving and Data Analysis Drill 2 (Calculator)
- Problem Solving and Data Analysis Drill 3 (Calculator)
- Problem Solving and Data Analysis Drill (No Calculator)
- Passport to Advanced Math Drill 1 (Calculator)
- Passport to Advanced Math Drill 2 (Calculator)
- Passport to Advanced Math Drill 3 (Calculator)
- Passport to Advanced Math Drill 1 (No Calculator)
- Passport to Advanced Math Drill 2 (No Calculator)
- Additional Topics in Math Drill (Calculator)
- Calculator Problems Mixed Drill 1
- Calculator Problems Mixed Drill 2
- Free-Response Drill
- No-Calculator Problems Mixed Drill

To practice these passages under timed conditions, take about 15 minutes per drill.

Comprehensive answer explanations to all of these drills come at the end of the chapter.

Heart of Algebra Drill 1 (Calculator)

1. What is the value of x in the following equation?

$$-\frac{3}{8}x + \frac{5}{16}x - \frac{1}{2}x = \frac{18}{32}$$

(A) 1

(B) –1

(C) 3

(D) $\frac{117}{8}$

2. What is the value of a in the following equation?

$$\frac{(3a-4)}{5} = \frac{(3a-4)}{8}$$

(A) $\frac{4}{3}$

(B) 0

(C) $\frac{28}{9}$

(D) $\frac{52}{9}$

3. What is the solution with the least possible y-value that satisfies both of the following inequalities?

$$y \geq 2x + 5$$
$$\text{and}$$
$$4 - y \leq x$$

(A) $\left(\frac{1}{2}, \frac{5}{2}\right)$

(B) $\left(\frac{1}{3}, \frac{11}{3}\right)$

(C) $\left(-\frac{1}{2}, 4\right)$

(D) $\left(-\frac{1}{3}, \frac{13}{3}\right)$

4. If $|3x - 1| = 4$, what are all of the possible value(s) of x?

  I. –1

  II. $\frac{5}{3}$

  III. 1

(A) II only

(B) III only

(C) I and II only

(D) All of the above

5. What is the value of x?

$$\frac{3}{2}x - \frac{2}{3} = \frac{x}{6} - \frac{10}{27}$$

(A) $-\frac{7}{9}$

(B) $\frac{2}{9}$

(C) $\frac{17}{54}$

(D) $\frac{9}{2}$

6. The graph of each equation in the system below is a line in the xy-plane. What must be true about these two lines?

$$y = 6x - 2$$
$$-6 = 12x - 2y$$

(A) The lines are parallel.

(B) The lines are perpendicular.

(C) The lines intersect at $\left(\frac{3}{2}, 7\right)$.

(D) The lines are the same.

7. Towns A and B are 200 miles apart. Caitlin starts driving from Town A to Town B at 3 P.M. at a rate of 30 miles per hour. Hannah starts driving from Town B to Town A at 4 P.M. on the same day at a rate of 40 miles per hour. At what time will they meet (to the nearest minute)?

(A) 3:42 P.M.

(B) 5:29 P.M.

(C) 6:26 P.M.

(D) 7:32 P.M.

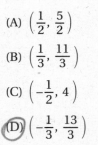

8. A person can ride a roller coaster at an amusement park if he or she is between 36 and 72 inches tall. Which of the following inequalities models all possible values of permitted heights in inches for the ride?

(A) $|x - 36| < 72$

(B) $|x - 38| < 34$

(C) $|x - 30| < 42$

(D) $|x - 54| < 18$

9. A line in the xy-plane has a slope of $\frac{3}{5}$ and passes through the origin. Which of the following is a point on the line?

(A) $(15, 10)$

(B) $(3, 5)$

(C) $\left(0, \frac{3}{5}\right)$

(D) $(10, 6)$

10. A salesperson earns a commission (C) on the number of phone plans sold (x) if the value of C is positive. (There is no penalty or cost to the salesperson for a negative value of C; simply no commission is paid.) The amount of commission in dollars is modeled by this equation:

$$C = 50x + 25(x - 100) - 2{,}000$$

What is the least number of phone plans that the salesperson must sell in order to earn a commission?

(A) 60

(B) 61

(C) 75

(D) 100

Heart of Algebra Drill 2 (Calculator)

1. If the volume of a pyramid is given by the formula $V = \frac{1}{3}lwh$, where V is the volume, l is the length, w is the width, and h is the height, what is the width of the pyramid in terms of the other variables?

(A) $\frac{V}{3lh}$

(B) $\frac{3V}{lw}$

(C) $\frac{3V}{lh}$

(D) $\frac{lh}{3V}$

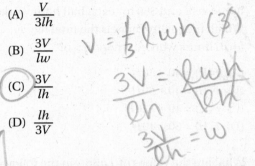

2. What is the negative solution to the following equation, rounded to one decimal place?

$$18x - \frac{21}{x} = \frac{2x}{3} + 12$$

(A) 1.5

(B) −0.8

(C) −0.6

(D) −1.5

3. An employee at a company has the following rules for days off from work:

- Employees are granted 30 flex days paid time off in a year for non-weekend and holiday days.
- Sick days with a doctor's note count as half a flex day.
- Personal days count as a full flex day.

If an employee wants to use at least half of the flex days but less than $\frac{5}{6}$ of them, what inequality would express the total number of sick days, S, and personal days, P, he or she could take in a year?

(A) $\frac{1}{2} \le \frac{1}{2}S + P < \frac{5}{6}$

(B) $15 \le \frac{1}{2}S + P < 25$

(C) $15 \le 2S + P < 25$

(D) $15 \le S + 2P < 30$

4. If $g(x) = 9x + 2$, what does $g(-4x)$ equal?

(A) $-36x - 8$
(B) $-36x + 2$
(C) $5x + 2$
(D) $-36x^2 + 2$

5. A carpenter charges a $40 initial fee for an in-home visit and $60 for each half hour worked. Which inequality models the total fee, F, for H hours worked where $H > 0$?

(A) $F(H) = 40 + 30H$
(B) $F(H) = 40 + 60H$
(C) $F(H) = 40 + 120H$
(D) $F(H) = 60 + 40H$

6. What are the values of x and y in the following equations?

$$0.75x - 0.1y = 1.2$$
$$2.6x + 3.4y = 15.4$$

(A) $x = 1$, $y = -4.5$
(B) $x = 2$, $y = 3$
(C) $x = 3$, $y = 10.5$
(D) $x = 4$, $y = 18$

7. If $\dfrac{m}{n} = -3$, what does $-2\dfrac{n}{m}$ equal?

(A) -6
(B) $\dfrac{2}{3}$
(C) $\dfrac{3}{2}$
(D) 6

8. If Equation A is defined by $y = \dfrac{2}{3}x - 4$ and if Equation B is defined by $3y = 2x + 3$, what must be done to Equation B so that the system of both Equation A and Equation B will have infinitely many solutions?

(A) Add 9 to the right side
(B) Subtract 5 from the right side
(C) Subtract 7 from the right side
(D) Subtract 15 from the right side

9. At 1:00 P.M., a blimp and a hot-air balloon are above the cities of Springfield and Washington, respectively. The two cities are 300 miles apart horizontally. The blimp is moving from Springfield to Washington at a horizontal speed of 10 miles per hour; the balloon is moving from Washington to Springfield at a horizontal speed of 200 miles per hour. The blimp starts at an altitude of 5,000 feet and is descending at a rate of 5 feet per minute; the balloon starts at an altitude of 500 feet and is ascending at a rate of 4 feet per minute. At what time will the blimp and balloon be at the same altitude, to the nearest minute?

(A) 6:20 P.M.
(B) 7:20 P.M.
(C) 8:20 P.M.
(D) 9:20 P.M.

10. Rosa's metabolism is 65 calories per hour when resting and 300 calories per hour when exercising. If Rosa wants to burn more than 2,000 calories per day, what is the range of hours, H, she should spend exercising, calculated to the nearest tenth, assuming that she is either resting or exercising at any time in a given day?

(A) $24 > H > 1.9$
(B) $24 > H > 2.4$
(C) $24 > H > 6.7$
(D) $24 > H > 22.1$

Heart of Algebra Drill 3 (Calculator)

1. Solve for x:

$$1\frac{7}{8}x + \frac{5}{32} = 3\frac{3}{4}x - 1\frac{1}{4}$$

(A) $\dfrac{3}{4}$
(B) $2\dfrac{17}{32}$
(C) $\dfrac{15}{16}$
(D) $-\dfrac{45}{76}$

2. When 2 times a number is subtracted from 14, the result is 2 greater than the number. What is the number in question?

(A) $\frac{16}{3}$

(B) 4

(C) 12

(D) 16

3. In 2015, Andre had 210 coins in his collection. If Andre adds 5 new coins a year starting in 2015 through the end of 2022 and then adds 8 coins a year starting in 2023, how many coins will he have in his collection at the end of 2045?

(A) 224

(B) 421

(C) 429

(D) 434

4. How many pairs (x, y) satisfy both $x - y > 3$ and $y - 5 > x$?

(A) 0

(B) 1

(C) 2

(D) Infinitely many

5. What is the solution (x, y) to the following set of equations?

$$4x - 3y = \frac{11}{3} \text{ and } -\frac{2}{3}x + \frac{1}{4}y = -\frac{13}{18}$$

(A) $\left(\frac{4}{3}, \frac{5}{4}\right)$

(B) $\left(\frac{5}{4}, \frac{4}{9}\right)$

(C) $\left(-\frac{37}{12}, -\frac{16}{3}\right)$

(D) $\left(\frac{7}{4}, 10\right)$

6. How many ordered pairs (x, y) satisfy the following system of equations?

$$(x - 2)(y + 5) = 0 \text{ and } 3x + y = 1$$

(A) 0

(B) 1

(C) 2

(D) Infinitely many

7. What are the solutions to the following series of equations?

$$\frac{3}{8}a + \frac{2}{3}b = 4.3 \text{ and } -12.9 + 1.125a = -2b$$

(A) $a = 0.8$ and $b = 6$

(B) $a = 16.8$ and $b = -3$

(C) No solutions

(D) Infinitely many solutions

8. Candidate M and Candidate N are the only candidates running for city mayor. If the total number of votes the two candidates receive is 50,000 and if Candidate M receives 3 times as many votes as Candidate N, what is the total number of votes Candidate N receives?

(A) 12,500

(B) 16,667

(C) 21,500

(D) 37,500

9. Jennifer's yearly salary, S, is modeled using the equation $S = 2,500Y + 40,000$, where Y represents how many years she has been working at the company. What does the number 2,500 represent in this equation?

(A) The amount Jennifer's salary increases for each year she has been working

(B) Jennifer's starting salary

(C) The amount of money Jennifer has made in year Y

(D) The number of hours Jennifer has worked in year Y

10. If Avinash reads 2 fiction articles per day and 14 nonfiction articles per week, which expression models the total number of articles he would read in w weeks?

(A) $2w + 14$

(B) $16w$

(C) $28w$

(D) $112w$

$14w + 14n$

Heart of Algebra Drill 1 (No Calculator)

1. If $\dfrac{-2x - 4}{5} > 2$, what is the range of x?

(A) $x > -7$

(B) $x < -\dfrac{11}{2}$

(C) $x < -7$

(D) $x > 7$

2. Susan is given a piggybank for her birthday that can hold a maximum of 500 quarters. The piggybank initially has 120 quarters. Each day after she receives the bank, 4 quarters are added. No coins or other objects are added to the piggybank. Which equation could be used to solve for the number of days (D) after Susan's birthday that it will take to fill the bank?

(A) $500 = 120 + 4D$

(B) $500 = 4D - 120$

(C) $120 = 4D$

(D) $500 = 4 + 120D$

3. In basketball, 1 point is awarded for a free throw, 2 points for a shot within the three-point line, and 3 points for shots outside the three-point line. If the number of points from x two-point shots is at least as great as the number of points from y three-point shots and z free throws, which expression would represent this relationship?

(A) $x \geq y + z$

(B) $x \geq 3y + z$

(C) $2x \geq 3y + z$

(D) $2x \geq y + 3z$

4. What is the value of x in this pair of equations?

$$5 - \frac{2}{3}y = x \text{ and } 4\left(10 - \frac{4}{3}y\right) = 2x + 5$$

(A) -20

(B) $\dfrac{5}{6}$

(C) $\dfrac{25}{4}$

(D) $\dfrac{75}{2}$

5. If $-2|-3| < -3|x + 5|$, what are all possible values of x?

(A) $-7 < x < -3$

(B) $-3 < x$ OR $-7 > x$

(C) $-3 < x$

(D) No solutions

6. Machine 1 can manufacture one box in A hours, and Machine 2 can manufacture an identical box in B hours. When working simultaneously, Machines A and B can produce 1 box in T hours. This relationship is given by the following formula:

$$\frac{1}{A}+\frac{1}{B}=\frac{1}{T}$$

What is the value of B in terms of the other two variables?

(A) $\dfrac{1}{\dfrac{1}{T}-\dfrac{1}{A}}$

(B) $\dfrac{1}{\dfrac{1}{A}-\dfrac{1}{T}}$

(C) $\dfrac{1}{T}-\dfrac{1}{A}$

(D) $\dfrac{AT}{T-A}$

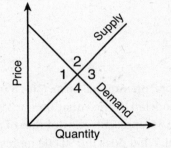

7. If the manufacturer of the XYZ machine develops new technology that makes creating the machine less expensive, in which zone(s) of the graph would the new supply curve most likely be?

(A) 1 and 2
(B) 2 and 3
(C) 3 and 4
(D) Unchanged

8. Line A has points (1, –2) and (–1, 0). Line B has point (3, 4). What would the y-value of the y-intercept of line B need to be in order for line A and line B to intersect at a 90° angle?

(A) –7
(B) –1
(C) 1
(D) 4

9. A library fines a patron who fails to return a book on time the replacement cost of the book plus an additional 10 cents each day that the fine is not paid in full. On December 1, Jane borrowed a book with a replacement cost of $30. The book was due to be returned on December 14. Which function models the total amount of dollars (A) that Jane will need to pay x days after December 14?

(A) $A(x) = 30 + 10x$
(B) $A(x) = 30 + 0.1x$
(C) $A(x) = 30 + 1.4x$
(D) $A(x) = 30 - x$

10. What is the value of a in this system of equations?

$$a = \frac{2}{3}b + 1 \text{ and } 2 + 3a = -4(2b + 1)$$

(A) $-\dfrac{9}{10}$

(B) $\dfrac{2}{5}$

(C) $\dfrac{11}{15}$

(D) $\dfrac{16}{15}$

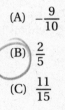

Heart of Algebra Drill 2
(No Calculator)

1. If $-(2x-4) + 3(x-5) = -4$, what is the value of x?

   (A) -3
   (B) 5
   (C) 7
   (D) 15

2. If $g(x+2) = 5x - 4$, what is the value of $g(7)$?

   (A) 21
   (B) 29
   (C) 31
   (D) 41

3. John is having an undetermined number of people over for dinner. He needs to have 6 serving utensils (used by everyone collectively) plus a knife, fork, and spoon for each diner. Which of the following equations correctly models the total number of utensils, U, John will need for x number of diners, himself included?

   (A) $U = 3x$
   (B) $U = 9x$
   (C) $U = 3x + 6$
   (D) $U = 6x + 3$

4. If $f(x) = 4x + 7$ and if $g(x) = -3x + 2$, what is the value of $f(g(3))$?

   (A) -27
   (B) -21
   (C) -7
   (D) 19

5. Under a new state law, a massage therapist will be required to charge sales tax on her services. If the sales tax rate is 7%, by what ratio would she need to multiply the current price of her services to determine the new total amount customers will pay under the new law?

   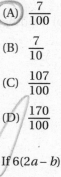

   (A) $\dfrac{7}{100}$
   (B) $\dfrac{7}{10}$
   (C) $\dfrac{107}{100}$
   (D) $\dfrac{170}{100}$

6. If $6(2a - b) = 4b$, what is the ratio of b to a?

   (A) $\dfrac{2}{3}$
   (B) $\dfrac{5}{6}$
   (C) $\dfrac{6}{5}$
   (D) $\dfrac{12}{5}$

7. The total operational costs C for a restaurant are modeled by the equation $C = 2M + 50{,}000$, where M represents the number of meals served. What does the 50,000 represent in the equation?

   (A) The total operational costs
   (B) The fixed operational costs
   (C) The cost per meal
   (D) The minimum number of meals served

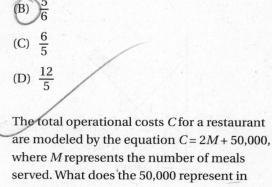

8. The total costs, C, to operate a factory are represented by the function $C(n) = an + b$, where n is the number of days the factory is operational. If the daily operations costs were to increase beyond the given rate and if the initial startup costs were to decrease beyond the given rate, how would this affect the constants a and b?

(A) a would increase, and b would increase.
(B) a would increase, and b would decrease.
(C) a would decrease, and b would increase.
(D) a and b would remain the same.

9. How will the function $f(x) = 4x - 5$ be affected by the translation

$$g(x) = f(x - 1) + 2?$$

(A) It will be shifted up 2 units and 1 unit to the left.
(B) It will be shifted down 1 unit and 2 units to the left.
(C) It will be shifted up 2 units and 1 unit to the right.
(D) It will be shifted down 1 unit and 2 units to the right.

10. A company is conducting an online campaign to increase its social media followers. The number of social media followers, N, is estimated by the equation $N = 30W + 250$, where W represents the number of weeks of the campaign (and $W > 0$). What does the number 250 represent in the equation?

(A) The number of weeks of the campaign
(B) The number of new social media followers each week
(C) The number of social media followers at the start of the campaign
(D) The number of social media followers at the end of W weeks

Problem Solving and Data Analysis Drill 1 (Calculator)

1. In an animal shelter consisting of only dogs and cats, the ratio of dogs to cats is 3 to 1. If there are 360 animals in the shelter, how many dogs must be present?

(A) 90
(B) 120
(C) 270
(D) 300

2. A reporter finds that on average, a particular politician receives 14 seconds of applause out of every minute of a speech. If the politician were to give a speech for exactly two hours, how many minutes of the speech would be devoted to applause?

(A) 14
(B) 28
(C) 37
(D) 1,680

3. Whole milk has 3.5% fat content. If you used equal amounts of 1% and 2% milk, how many total gallons of the combined milk would you use to equal the fat content in exactly 1 gallon of whole milk?

(A) $\dfrac{1}{200}$

(B) $\dfrac{1}{2}$

(C) $1\dfrac{1}{6}$

(D) $2\dfrac{1}{3}$

4. Katie is interested in running a marathon, which is 26.2 miles long. She just finished a 5-kilometer race, and she wants to see how many 5K races she would have to complete in order to equal a full marathon. Given that there are approximately 0.62 miles in 1 kilometer, how many complete 5K races would Katie have to finish to go at least the distance of a marathon?

(A) 6
(B) 8
(C) 9
(D) 10

5. At the beginning of the year, 1 U.S. dollar can be exchanged for 0.9 euros, and 1 Canadian dollar can be exchanged for 0.7 U.S. dollars. If someone wants to convert 100 Canadian dollars to euros at these exchange rates and assuming that there are no transaction fees, how many euros would the person have after the conversion?

(A) 63
(B) 78
(C) 129
(D) 158

Spread of a Computer Virus

Day	Number of Computers Infected
1	101
2	110
3	200
4	1,100
5	10,100

6. The table above gives the number of computers infected with a virus. Which of the following functions models the number of computers infected, $C(d)$, after d days?

(A) $C(d) = 10^{2d} + 10(d-1) + 1$
(B) $C(d) = 100 + 10^d$
(C) $C(d) = 100 + 10(d-1) + 1$
(D) $C(d) = 100 + 10^{(d-1)}$

7. Light travels at approximately 3.00×10^8 meters per second. When the planet Jupiter is at its closest point to Earth, it is 588 million kilometers away. When Earth and Jupiter are this close, approximately how many minutes does light reflected off of Jupiter take to reach Earth?

(A) 3 minutes
(B) 33 minutes
(C) 58 minutes
(D) 18 minutes

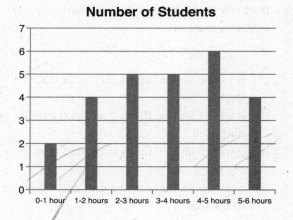

Number of Students

8. A group of 26 teenagers was asked about their daily smartphone usage. What was the median range of hours that this group used smartphones each day?

(A) Between 1 and 2
(B) Between 2 and 3
(C) Between 3 and 4
(D) Between 4 and 5

Questions 9–10 are about the following table.

	Finished Summer Reading	Did Not Complete Summer Reading	
Mrs. Smith's Class	21	8	29
Mr. Walker's Class	14	17	31
	35	25	

9. Given that the average of Mrs. Smith's and Mr. Walker's classes together represents the average enrollment in each English class at the school and that there are a total of 14 English classes, how many total students are enrolled in English classes at the school, assuming that students are enrolled in exactly one English class?

(A) 280
(B) 420
(C) 560
(D) 840

10. The high school principal wants to evaluate the effectiveness of the teachers in getting their students to complete the summer reading assignments. The principal assigns 5 points to each student who completes the assignment and gives 0 points to each student who fails to complete the assignment. What is the difference between the mean and the median of the point values given to students in Mr. Walker's class?

(A) 1.38
(B) 1.60
(C) 2.26
(D) 2.74

Problem Solving and Data Analysis Drill 2 (Calculator)

1. A student writes a double-spaced typed paper using Times New Roman 12-point font. He finds that each page contains an average of 240 words. If the student changes to Comic Sans 12-point font, each page contains an average of only 170 words. If the student is required to write a 10-page double-spaced report, how many fewer words would he be required to write if the teacher accepts Comic Sans 12-point font instead of Times New Roman 12-point font?

(A) 70
(B) 170
(C) 700
(D) 1,700

2. On a map of a rectangular fenced-in area, the drawing of the enclosed area has a surface area of 20 square inches. If one side of the fenced-in area drawing is 4 inches long and the key of the map indicates that for every 1 inch drawn on the map there are 6 feet in actual distance, what is the perimeter of the actual fence, assuming there are no gaps or gates?

(A) 18 ft
(B) 108 ft
(C) 120 ft
(D) 720 ft

3. John's performance on his first test was only 60%. His performance increased by 20% on the next test, and it increased an additional 25% on the third test. What did John earn on the third test, to the nearest whole percent?

(A) 72%
(B) 75%
(C) 90%
(D) 105%

4. Linda's 15-gallon car tank has only 2 gallons left when she pulls into a gas station. She wants to purchase only the gas she will need to drive 240 miles and still have 1 gallon remaining. Her car gets 28 miles to the gallon. How many gallons should Linda purchase, to the nearest tenth of a gallon?

(A) 6.6 gallons
(B) 7.6 gallons
(C) 8.6 gallons
(D) 9.6 gallons

Questions 5–6 use the following graph.

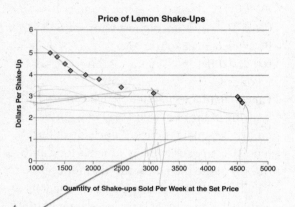

Price of Lemon Shake-Ups

5. If you were to graph dollars per shake-up along the x-axis and quantity of shake-ups sold per week at the set price on the y-axis, which of the following would be a property of the function between the values of 3 and 5 dollars?

(A) It would be a decreasing exponential function.
(B) It would be an increasing exponential function.
(C) It would be a decreasing linear function.
(D) It would be an increasing linear function.

6. At which of the following prices of a lemon shake-up would the total revenue be maximized?

(A) $2.50
(B) $3.00
(C) $3.50
(D) $5.00

Questions 7–8 use the following graph and information.

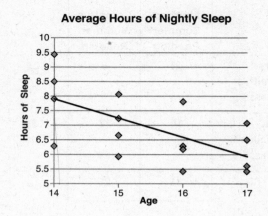

Average Hours of Nightly Sleep

A scientist surveys 16 randomly selected teenage students, recording their ages and their average number of hours of nightly sleep.

7. If x represents the age and y represents the average hours of sleep, which of the following gives the equation of the best-fit line for the survey results?

(A) $y = -0.6x + 7.8$
(B) $y = 0.8x + 7.8$
(C) $y = -0.6x + 16.2$
(D) $y = -1.9x + 16.2$

8. Which of the following would most likely cause the greatest obstacle to the accuracy of the sleep survey results?

(A) If the student survey responses are self-reported
(B) Whether the survey was conducted during the school year or during summer break
(C) If not all of the 16 teenagers respond
(D) If the scientist misreads the number of hours of one responder and records one more hour of sleep on average than what was reported

Questions 9–10 use the following graph.

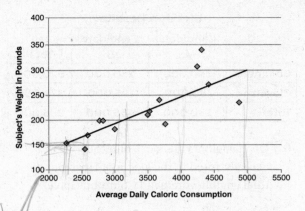

Average Daily Caloric Consumption

9. What choice most closely approximates the slope of the best-fit line of the graph above?

   (A) $-\dfrac{1}{10}$

   (B) $\dfrac{3}{50}$

   (C) $\dfrac{1}{5}$

   (D) $\dfrac{50}{3}$

10. What is the most logical explanation as to why the *x*- and *y*-axes begin as they do, as opposed to at zero values?

   (A) The researcher is not interested in the relationship between weight and caloric intake for a subject less than 100 pounds who eats under 2,000 calories per day.
   (B) No person weighs less than 100 pounds.
   (C) No person eats under 2,000 calories in a day.
   (D) A person cannot weigh zero pounds, and a person cannot consistently eat zero calories each day.

Problem Solving and Data Analysis Drill 3 (Calculator)

1. If there are 4 cars for every 5 trucks in the parking lot (with no other types of vehicles), what is the ratio of cars to the total number of vehicles in the parking lot?

   (A) 1 to 5
   (B) 4 to 9
   (C) 5 to 9
   (D) 4 to 5

2. On Monday, the highest temperature reached was 70 degrees Fahrenheit. On Tuesday, the highest temperature increased by 20%. On Wednesday, the highest temperature decreased by 25% from the previous day. What was the difference between Monday's and Wednesday's highest temperatures in degrees Fahrenheit?

   (A) 5
   (B) 7
   (C) 14
   (D) 21

3. A recipe calls for 3 cups of sugar. There are 16 tablespoons in a cup and 3 teaspoons in a tablespoon. If a cook has 1.5 cups of sugar available in the pantry, how many teaspoons of sugar must the cook obtain from other sources to follow the recipe?

   (A) 72
   (B) 104
   (C) 144
   (D) 216

Price per Gallon of Milk	Number of Gallons Sold
$1.50	650
$0.90	780
$1.95	530
$2.80	330
$3.40	190

4. Which of these functions best models the relationship between the number of gallons of milk sold, $N(g)$, and the price per gallon of milk, g?

(A) $N(g) = 530 + 590(g - 1.95)^2$
(B) $N(g) = 1000 - 240g$
(C) $N(g) = 1000 + 240g$
(D) $N(g) = 780 - 360(g - 0.9)^2$

	Employed	Unemployed
Population X	890	112
Population Y	748	205

5. What is the difference between the unemployment percentage in Population Y and the unemployment percentage in Populations X and Y combined, calculated to the nearest tenth?

(A) 5.0 percent
(B) 5.3 percent
(C) 5.8 percent
(D) 6.2 percent

Questions 6–7 use the following table.

Election Results

	Candidate A	Candidate B	Total
Columbus	350,000	270,000	620,000
Cleveland	180,000	195,000	375,000
Total	530,000	465,000	995,000

6. Of all eligible voters in Columbus, 40% actually voted in the election. How many total eligible voters did Columbus have?

(A) 248,000
(B) 875,000
(C) 1,550,000
(D) 2,487,500

7. Suppose that a survey of 200 randomly selected voters from both cities accurately predicted the results of the election. How many of the people surveyed would have been supporters of Candidate A from Columbus?

(A) 50
(B) 70
(C) 113
(D) 132

Questions 8–9 use the following table.

Grade	Test 1	Project 1	Test 2	Project 2	Total
A	5	8	9	7	29
B	7	6	5	10	28
C	6	7	4	5	22
D	4	1	3	2	10
F	1	1	3	0	5
Total	23	23	24	24	94

8. The median letter grade for assignments in the class is:

    (A) A
    (B) B
    (C) C
    (D) D

9. For which assignment is the standard deviation of the grade results the least?

    (A) Test 1
    (B) Project 1
    (C) Test 2
    (D) Project 2

_____

10. An online shopping site allows customers to post 1-star, 2-star, 3-star, 4-star, and 5-star reviews for products. If an item currently has an average star rating of 2.3 based on a total of 10 reviews, what is the minimum number of reviews that could bring up the overall average rating to at least a 3.0?

    (A) 2
    (B) 3
    (C) 4
    (D) 5

Problem Solving and Data Analysis Drill (No Calculator)

1. For every 8 units of x, there are consistently 12 units of y. If the relationship between x and y is given as an equation of the form $y = kx$, where k is a constant, what is the value of k?

    (A) $\dfrac{1}{4}$
    (B) $\dfrac{2}{3}$
    (C) $\dfrac{3}{2}$
    (D) 4

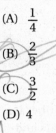

2. In a science class, for every two people who are failing, there are three people who have C's and D's. For every one person who has C's and D's, there are two people who have A's and B's. What is the ratio of those who are failing the class to those who have A's and B's?

    (A) 1 to 1
    (B) 1 to 3
    (C) 2 to 3
    (D) 1 to 6

3. A restaurant charges a $5 standard delivery fee plus a 15% tip on the amount of the bill before the delivery fee. Which of these expressions would model the total cost to have x dollars worth of food delivered?

    (A) $0.15x + 5$
    (B) $1.15x + 5$
    (C) $5x + 15$
    (D) $15x + 5$

Questions 4–5 use the following graph.

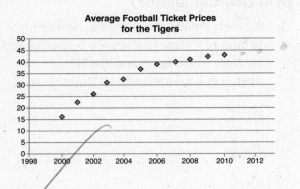

Average Football Ticket Prices for the Tigers

4. Which of the following best describes the general relationship between years and average football ticket price?

   (A) As the years go by, the average football ticket price increases.
   (B) As the years go by, the average football ticket price decreases.
   (C) As the years go by, the average football ticket price stays the same.
   (D) There is no general relationship between years and average football ticket price.

5. Assuming that the trend represented in the graph continues over the next decade (which is not portrayed in the graph), the average price of a football ticket in the year 2014 would most likely be:

   (A) $41
   (B) $47
   (C) $56
   (D) $62

Year	Exchange Rate of Currency X to Currency Y
2000	2.30
2001	15.35
2002	55.42
2003	121.56
2004	237.83

6. Which of these statements accurately represents the data in the table above?

   (A) As time goes by, Currency X is becoming relatively more valuable than Currency Y.
   (B) As time goes by, Currency Y is becoming relatively more valuable than Currency X.
   (C) As time goes by, Currency X is approaching the same value as Currency Y.
   (D) No relationship can be determined between Currency X and Currency Y.

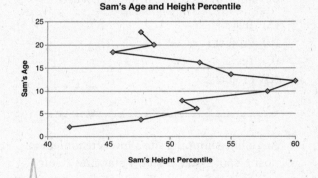

Sam's Age and Height Percentile

7. Which of the following is a logical conclusion about the data about Sam's age and height percentile?

   I. Sam's height grew exponentially quickly between ages 12 and 18.
   II. Sam's height relative to that of other men was lower when he was less than 5 years old than when he was between 10 and 15 years old.
   III. Sam continued to experience changes in his height between the ages of 18 and 22.

   (A) I only
   (B) II only
   (C) II and III only
   (D) I, II, and III

8. An amusement park researcher compiles data about the average height of ten-year-old children in a certain town to determine whether this age group will meet the minimum height requirements for a new attraction. The researcher selects 100 ten-year-old children at random from the town and finds that the average height has a 95% confidence interval between 42 and 48 inches. Which of the following conclusions could the researcher most reasonably make?

(A) There is a 5% chance that the average ten-year-old child in the town will have a height between 42 and 48 inches.

(B) It is very likely that the average ten-year-old child in the town will be less than 42 inches tall.

(C) It is very likely that the average ten-year-old child in the town will have a height between 42 and 48 inches.

(D) It is very likely that the average ten-year-old child in the town will not have a height between 42 and 48 inches.

9. If a store has a sale in which all prices are discounted by two-thirds and also distributes coupons that take an additional 20 percent off the price, what is the fraction of the original price that a customer using a coupon would pay during the store's sale?

(A) $\frac{1}{15}$

(B) $\frac{2}{15}$

(C) $\frac{4}{15}$

(D) $\frac{8}{15}$

10. A pollster wishes to project the winner for an upcoming election in her small city. Which of the following approaches to selecting a sample size would give the most accurate polling results?

(A) Interviewing randomly selected shoppers at the grocery store

(B) Contacting residents who live within half a mile of polling locations

(C) Contacting a random selection of registered voters

(D) Inviting voters to submit results to an online survey

Passport to Advanced Math Drill 1 (Calculator)

1. A cubic function would be most appropriate when modeling which of the following mathematical relationships?

(A) A sphere's volume and its radius

(B) A circle's circumference and its diameter

(C) A triangle's area and its height

(D) A cube's edge length and its total surface area

2. $\dfrac{a^3 - b^3 + 2a^2b - 2ab^2 + ab^2 - ba^2}{a^2 - b^2}$ equals which of the following, given that $a \neq \pm b$?

(A) $a + b$

(B) $a - b$

(C) $a^2b - ab^2$

(D) $a^2 + b^2$

3. If $-5m^5 + 3m^3 = 2m^7$, what is the sum of all possible values of m^2?

(A) -2.5

(B) 0

(C) 0.5

(D) 2.5

4. Solve for x: $\frac{1}{2}x^2 + \frac{1}{4}x - \frac{1}{8} = 0$

(A) $\frac{1}{2}(-1\pm\sqrt{3})$

(B) $\frac{1}{2}(-1\pm\sqrt{5})$

(C) $\frac{1}{4}(-1\pm\sqrt{3})$

(D) $\frac{1}{4}(-1\pm\sqrt{5})$

5. What is/are the solution(s) to the following equation?

$$a + 4 = \sqrt{a^2 - 2}$$

(A) $-\frac{9}{4}$

(B) $\frac{9}{4}$

(C) $\frac{-7}{4}$ and $\frac{9}{4}$

(D) No solutions

6. How many zeros does the function $f(x) = (x-3)(x+7)(x-3)$ have?

(A) 0
(B) 1
(C) 2
(D) 3

7. Consider the function $f(x) = x^2 + 2$. What operation could be performed on the right-hand side of the equation to expand the range to include negative values?

(A) Add 5
(B) Add –2
(C) Subtract 3
(D) Subtract 1

8. What is the vertex of the parabola $(y-4)^2 = 17(x+2)$?

(A) (–2, 4)
(B) (2, –4)
(C) (–4, 2)
(D) (4, –2)

9. The root mean squared speed of a molecule, v_{rms}, is calculated using the formula $v_{rms} = \sqrt{\frac{3RT}{M}}$, where R is a gas constant, T is the temperature, and M is the molecular mass. The molecular mass of substance A is most likely to be less than the molecular mass of substance B if the temperature and v_{rms} of substance A compare in which ways to those of substance B?

(A) Greater v_{rms} and lower temperature
(B) Lower v_{rms} and greater temperature
(C) Lower v_{rms} and equal temperature
(D) Cannot be determined

10. Two different stock portfolios, A and B, have had no new deposits or withdrawals over a ten-year period and had the same initial amount in the account. If stock portfolio A has grown at an annual rate of $x\%$, if stock portfolio B has grown at an annual rate of $y\%$, and if $x > y$, what would represent the ratio of the value of portfolio A over that of portfolio B at the end of the ten-year period?

(A) $\left(\dfrac{1+\frac{x}{100}}{1+\frac{y}{100}}\right)^{10}$

(B) $\left(\dfrac{x}{y}\right)^{10}$

(C) $10\left(\dfrac{x}{y}\right)$

(D) $\left(\dfrac{1-\frac{x}{100}}{1-\frac{y}{100}}\right)^{10}$

Passport to Advanced Math Drill 2 (Calculator)

1. A car and a truck are initially 180 miles apart and are driving toward each other on a straight road when an observer measures their respective speeds. The car is driving at a constant speed of x miles per hour, and the truck is going twice this speed. If the car and the truck meet each other after three hours of driving, what is the speed of the truck?

   (A) 20 mph
   (B) 30 mph
   (C) 40 mph
   (D) 60 mph

2. The formula for the area of a trapezoid is $\frac{B_1 + B_2}{2} \times H$, where B_1 and B_2 are the bases of the trapezoid and H is its height. If the mean of the bases of the trapezoid is twice the height and if the area of the trapezoid is 72 square inches, what is the trapezoid's height in inches?

   (A) 6
   (B) $6\sqrt{2}$
   (C) 24
   (D) 36

3. $2m^{-2} - 4m^{-3}$ is equivalent to which of the following?

   (A) $\frac{2m-1}{4m^3}$
   (B) $\frac{-2}{m^5}$
   (C) $\frac{2m-4}{m^3}$
   (D) $-2m^2 + 4m^3$

4. $(2y^4 + 3x^6) + (5x^6 + 3y^4)$ is equivalent to which of the following?

   (A) $5y^4 + 8x^6$
   (B) $7y^4 + 6x^6$
   (C) $13y^4x^6$
   (D) $5y^8 + 8x^{12}$

5. Which of the following is equivalent to the expression $\frac{2x^2 - 12x + 18}{3(x-3)^3}$?

   (A) $\frac{x^2+9}{x-3}$
   (B) $\frac{2(x+3)}{3(x-3)^2}$
   (C) $\frac{2(x-6)}{(x-3)}$
   (D) $\frac{2}{3(x-3)}$

6. What are the solutions to $21x^2 = 15x + 18$?

   (A) $\frac{5 \pm \sqrt{193}}{14}$
   (B) $\frac{15 \pm \sqrt{1527}}{14}$
   (C) $\frac{5 \pm \sqrt{67}}{14}$
   (D) No real solutions

7. The supply for a given item at a varying price p (in dollars) is given by the equation $s(p) = 3p + 6p^2$. The demand for the same item at a varying price p is given by the equation $d(p) = 156 - 12p$. At what price are the supply and the demand for the item equivalent?

   (A) $3.50
   (B) $4
   (C) $6.50
   (D) $12

8. If x and y are variables and if c is a nonzero constant, which of the following choices would not necessarily have a y-intercept when graphed?

   I. $x = c$
  II. $y = -c$
 III. $y = cx$

(A) I only
(B) I and II only
(C) II and III only
(D) None of the above

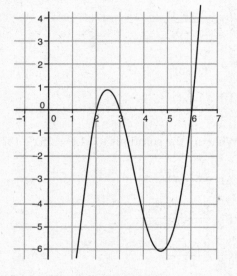

9. Which of the following equations represents the function graphed above?

(A) $x^3 + 11x^2 + 36x + 36$
(B) $x^3 - 11x^2 + 36x - 36$
(C) $x^3 + x^2 - 24x + 36$
(D) $x^2 - 5x + 6$

10. The formula for annual compounded interest is $A = P\left(1 + \dfrac{r}{n}\right)^{nt}$, where P is the initial amount invested, A is the future value of the initial amount, r is the annual interest rate expressed as a decimal, n is the number of times the investment is compounded each year, and t is the number of years the amount is invested. If an initial investment, P, is compounded once every 12 months, which expression is equivalent to the future value of the investment if its interest rate is 5% and if the money is invested for exactly 1 year?

(A) $0.05P$
(B) $0.5P$
(C) $1.05P$
(D) $1.50P$

Passport to Advanced Math Drill 3 (Calculator)

1. An element's half-life is the amount of time that it takes for the element to decay by half. If there is x amount of element Z initially, which of the following represents the amount, A, of Z that would remain after n whole half-lives of Z had passed?

(A) $A = \dfrac{x}{2n}$

(B) $A = \dfrac{x}{2^n}$

(C) $A = \dfrac{n}{2x}$

(D) $A = \dfrac{x}{2^{n-1}}$

2. $\sqrt[5]{32x^8y^{11}}$ is equivalent to which of the following?

(A) $2xy^2 \sqrt[5]{x^3y}$

(B) $2x^5y^{10} \sqrt[5]{x^3y}$

(C) $2x^3y^6 \sqrt[5]{xy}$

(D) $2xy^2 \sqrt[5]{2x^3y^2}$

3. If $x > 0$, then $\dfrac{1}{2x} + \dfrac{1}{3x}$ is equivalent to which of the following?

(A) $\left(\dfrac{25}{6x^2} \right)^{\frac{1}{2}}$

(B) $\left(\dfrac{4}{25x^2} \right)^{\frac{1}{2}}$

(C) $\left(\dfrac{5}{6x} \right)^{2}$

(D) $\left(\dfrac{25}{36x^2} \right)^{\frac{1}{2}}$

4. If $x^2 + ax = b$, where a and b are constants, what are the solutions for x?

(A) $x = -\dfrac{a}{2} \pm \sqrt{2b + \dfrac{a^2}{2}}$

(B) $x = -\dfrac{a}{2} \pm \sqrt{b + \dfrac{a^2}{4}}$

(C) $x = -\dfrac{b}{2} \pm \sqrt{\dfrac{a^2}{2} - 2b}$

(D) $x = -\dfrac{a}{2} \pm \sqrt{b^2 + \dfrac{a^2}{4}}$

5. $6x^2 + 15xy + 6y^2 = ?$

(A) $3(2x + y)^2$
(B) $(3x + y)(x + 3y)$
(C) $(3x + 3y)(2x + 2y)$
(D) $3(x + 2y)(2x + y)$

6. What are the solution(s) for x in the equation below?

$$x - 6 = \sqrt{75 - 2x}$$

(A) 13
(B) 13 and –3
(C) –3 and 3
(D) No solution

7. At what points will $f(x) = 8x^2 - 22x + 15$ intersect the x-axis?

(A) 15

(B) $\dfrac{3}{2}$ and $\dfrac{5}{4}$

(C) $-\dfrac{5}{4}$ and $-\dfrac{3}{2}$

(D) $\dfrac{5}{4}$ and $\dfrac{15}{2}$

8. Which value of n will cause the value of $f(x) = x^n$ to be consistently positive and increase the most rapidly, given that x is greater than 1 and that n is an even integer?

(A) –2
(B) –1
(C) 1
(D) 2

9. To see if two sets of data are correlated, one can calculate the correlation coefficient between two populations, r_{xy}, using the formula $r_{xy} = \dfrac{s_{xy}}{s_x s_y}$, where s_{xy} is the covariance of the population, s_x is the standard deviation of population x, and s_y is the standard deviation of population y. If the dispersion of population x and the dispersion of population y both increase while the covariance between the populations remains the same, what would happen to the correlation coefficient of the two populations?

(A) It would decrease.
(B) It would increase.
(C) It would stay the same.
(D) Cannot be determined

10. If the function $f(x) = x^n + 3x^m$ has 5 zeros and if $f(x)$ is multiplied by -1, how many zeros will the resulting function have?

(A) -5
(B) 4
(C) 5
(D) 6

Passport to Advanced Math Drill 1 (No Calculator)

1. A square piece of paper is folded in half n times. If L is the length of an edge, what is the area of the piece of paper after it is folded in half n times?

(A) $\dfrac{L^2}{2^{n-1}}$

(B) $\dfrac{L^2}{2^n}$

(C) $\dfrac{L^2}{n}$

(D) $\dfrac{L^2}{2n}$

2. $\left(81^{-\frac{1}{4}}\right)\left(64^{\frac{1}{3}}\right)$ equals

(A) -12

(B) $-\dfrac{4}{3}$

(C) $\dfrac{1}{12}$

(D) $\dfrac{4}{3}$

3. Which of the following is equivalent to $\dfrac{3x^3 + 2x^2 - 5x + 6}{x+2}$ for x not equal to -2?

(A) $3x^2 - 4x + 3$
(B) $3x^2 + 8x + 11$
(C) $x^2 - 3x + 3$
(D) $3x^2 + 4x + 12$

4. What relationship must exist between the constants a, b, and c for the equation $ax^2 + bx + c = 0$ to have only real solutions?

(A) $b^2 \le 4ac$
(B) $b^2 \ge 4ac$
(C) $2a > -b$
(D) Cannot be determined

5. $(3x^3 - 2x^2 + 5x + 7) - (x^4 + x(x+2)) = ?$

(A) $2x^3 - x^2 + 7x + 9$
(B) $-x^4 + 3x^3 - x^2 + 7x + 7$
(C) $2x^4 - 3x^2 + 5x + 5$
(D) $-x^4 + 3x^3 - 3x^2 + 3x + 7$

6. How many solutions does the following equation have?
$$a - \sqrt{a} = 6$$

(A) 0
(B) 1
(C) 2
(D) 4

7. Out of all possible solutions (x, y) to the pair of equations below, what is the greatest possible product xy that can be obtained?
$$x(y+2) - 3x - 4(y+2) = -12$$
$$\text{and}$$
$$3x - 6 = 3y$$

(A) 3
(B) 4
(C) 6
(D) 8

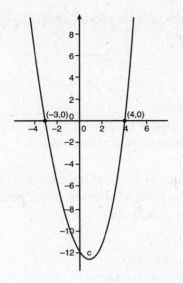

(−3,0)

(4,0)

c

8. Based on the graph of $f(x)$ above, $f(x)$ is divisible by which of the following expressions?

I. $x - 4$
II. $x + 1$
III. $x + 3$

(A) I and II only
(B) I and III only
(C) All of the above
(D) None of the above

9. What happens to the vertex (h, k) of $y = x^2 + 3$ if the 3 is replaced by a 6 and if x is changed to $(x - 5)$?

(A) h decreases by 5, k increases by 6
(B) h increases by 5, k increases by 3
(C) h increases by 5, k increases by 6
(D) h remains the same, k increases by 31

10. If $f(x) = g(x) + 4$ and if $g(x) = x - \dfrac{5}{x}$, what is the value of $f(10)$?

(A) 9.5
(B) 10
(C) 13.5
(D) 14

Passport to Advanced Math Drill 2 (No Calculator)

1. A particular savings account provides no interest in the first year of a deposit and 3% annual compounded interest on a deposit for each year thereafter. If x dollars are deposited initially, which of the following equations expresses the total amount of money $A(n)$ in the account n years later, where n is an integer greater than 2?

(A) $A(n) = x\left[(0.03)^n\right]$
(B) $A(n) = x\left[(0.97)^n\right]$
(C) $A(n) = x\left[(0.03)^{n-1}\right]$
(D) $A(n) = x\left[(1.03)^{n-1}\right]$

2. What is the value of x in the following equation?
$$x^2 + 9 = -6x$$

(A) −3
(B) 0
(C) 3
(D) No solution

3. For $y < 0$, which of the following is equivalent to $\dfrac{3}{x^2 y}$?

(A) $\dfrac{3x^{-2}}{\sqrt[4]{y^2}}$

(B) $\dfrac{3x^{-2}}{-\sqrt[4]{y^4}}$

(C) $\dfrac{3x^{\frac{1}{2}}}{\sqrt[4]{y^4}}$

(D) $\dfrac{3x^{-2}}{\sqrt[4]{y^4}}$

4. For positive x and y, $x^{-\frac{3}{4}} y^{\frac{4}{3}}$ is equivalent to

(A) $-\dfrac{x^3 y^4}{x^4 y^3}$

(B) $\dfrac{\sqrt[4]{y^3}}{\sqrt[3]{x^4}}$

(C) $\dfrac{y\sqrt[3]{y}}{\sqrt[4]{x^3}}$

(D) $\dfrac{y^4 \sqrt[3]{y}}{x^3 \sqrt[4]{x}}$

5. What are the possible values of x in the following equation?

$$3x^2 + 12x + 6 = 0$$

(A) $-12 \pm \sqrt{3}$

(B) $-2 \pm \sqrt{2}$

(C) $-2 \pm \sqrt{3}$

(D) $2 \pm \sqrt{2}$

6. If $x^2 + x - 12 = 0$ and if $x < 0$, what is the value of x?

(A) -6

(B) -4

(C) -3

(D) 3

7. $64x^6 - 16y^8$ is equivalent to which of the following expressions?

(A) $16(4x^3 + y^4)(x^3 - y^4)$

(B) $16(4x^3 - y^4)(x^3 - y^4)$

(C) $16(2x^3 + y^4)(2x^3 - y^4)$

(D) $16(2x^6 - y^8)(2x - y)$

8. Solve the following equation for all possible x-values.

$$x = \sqrt{11x - 24}$$

(A) 3

(B) 3 and 8

(C) -3 and -8

(D) Infinitely many solutions

9. The graph of $x - 4 = y^4$ has a minimal x-value that compares in what way to the minimal x-value of the graph $x = y^4$?

(A) It is 4 less.

(B) It is 4 greater.

(C) They are the same.

(D) The answer cannot be determined.

10. Which of the following functions represents the reflection across the x-axis of $y = 3(x - 5)^2 + 4$?

(A) $y = -3(x + 5)^2 - 4$

(B) $y = -3(x - 5)^2 - 4$

(C) $y = 3(-x - 5)^2 + 4$

(D) $y = 3(-x + 5)^2 + 4$

Additional Topics in Math Drill (Calculator)

1. A right circular cylinder has a volume of $30x$ cubic feet, and a cube has a volume of $21x$ cubic feet. What is the sum of the volumes of a cone with the same height and radius as the cylinder and of a pyramid with the same length, width, and height of the cube?

(A) $7x$ cubic feet

(B) $10x$ cubic feet

(C) $17x$ cubic feet

(D) $51x$ cubic feet

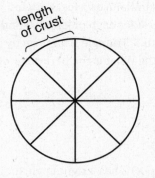

2. Andrew rides his bike 20 miles directly north and then 15 miles directly to the east. How many miles would he travel if he could fly directly from his starting point to his ending point?

   (A) 25
   (B) 31
   (C) 35
   (D) 625

3. In a right triangle with legs of length a and b, what is the value of the hypotenuse of the triangle?

   (A) $\sqrt{a+b}$
   (B) $\sqrt{a^2-b^2}$
   (C) $\sqrt{a^2+b^2}$
   (D) a^2+b^2

4. If $i = \sqrt{-1}$, $2i^2(3i)^4 = ?$

   (A) -162
   (B) -6
   (C) $162i$
   (D) 162

5. What would be the measure, in radians, of an arc on a circle if the measure of the arc in degrees was 270?

   (A) $\dfrac{2\pi}{3}$
   (B) $\dfrac{3\pi}{2}$
   (C) 270π
   (D) $\dfrac{48,600}{\pi}$

6. A circular pizza has a radius of 8 inches. If the pizza is cut into 8 equal sectors as shown in the drawing above, what is the length of the crust on the edge of each piece, rounded to two decimal places?

   (A) 0.13 inches
   (B) 0.79 inches
   (C) 3.74 inches
   (D) 6.28 inches

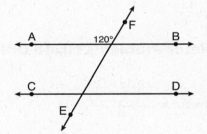

7. In the above drawing, lines AB and CD are parallel, and line EF is a transversal. How many angles made from the given lines measure 60 degrees?

   (A) 1
   (B) 2
   (C) 4
   (D) 6

8. $\dfrac{i^3+9i-6}{3+i} = ?$

   (A) $2i-3$
   (B) $3i-1$
   (C) $3-i$
   (D) $2+3i$

9. In two similar isosceles triangles, triangle A has two sides each of length 5 and one side of length 7. Triangle B has exactly one side of length 28. What is the perimeter of triangle B?

(A) 17

(B) 20

(C) 38

(D) 68

10. Triangle XYZ has a right angle for angle Y and has side lengths of 24 for XY and 26 for XZ. For a triangle that is similar to XYZ, what would be the value of the tangent of its smallest angle?

(A) $\dfrac{5}{12}$

(B) $\dfrac{5}{13}$

(C) $\dfrac{12}{13}$

(D) $\dfrac{12}{5}$

Calculator Problems Mixed Drill 1

1. Solve for x: $\dfrac{12\left(\dfrac{5x-2x}{2}\right)}{6} = 18$

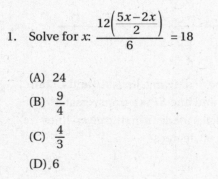

(A) 24

(B) $\dfrac{9}{4}$

(C) $\dfrac{4}{3}$

(D) 6

2. A rock is made up by volume of 32% coal, which has a specific gravity (expressed in grams per cubic centimeter) of 1.20. The rock contains 29% granite with a specific gravity of 2.60. The rock also contains 39% of an unknown mineral. If the specific gravity of the entire rock is 1.4, the unknown material has what approximate specific gravity?

(A) 0.43

(B) 0.54

(C) 0.67

(D) 0.81

3. A train is traveling for 5 hours at a constant rate of x miles per hour and then travels an additional $\dfrac{x}{10}$ hours at a speed of $\dfrac{x}{2}$ miles per hour. If the train travels a total of 300 miles during these two segments, which equation could be used to solve for x?

(A) $x^2 + 100x - 6,000 = 0$

(B) $x^2 + 100x - 300 = 0$

(C) $x^2 + 5x - 300 = 0$

(D) $3x^2 + 150x - 6,000 = 0$

4. $(6a^3)^3 - (2b)^4 + c^{-2} = ?$

(A) $6a^9 - 2b^4 + \dfrac{1}{c^2}$

(B) $18a^9 - 8b^4 + \dfrac{1}{c^2}$

(C) $21a^6 - 16b^4 + \dfrac{1}{c^2}$

(D) $216a^9 - 16b^4 + \dfrac{1}{c^2}$

Questions 5–7 use the following graph.

Company X Stock Price per Share

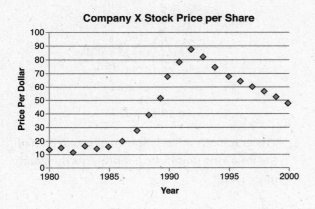

5. The relationship between year and stock price is most exponential during what range of years?

(A) 1980–1983
(B) 1984–1991
(C) 1992–1996
(D) 1997–2000

6. Between which two-year period does the Company X stock price undergo the greatest percentage increase?

(A) Between 1983–1984
(B) Between 1986–1987
(C) Between 1988–1989
(D) Between 1989–1990

7. A stockbroker sold $1,000 in shares of Company X stock. Approximately how many more shares would she have sold if the stock price is taken at the minimal value in the graph versus at the maximum value in the graph?

(A) 8
(B) 20
(C) 40
(D) 80

8. If $f(a) = a^2 - 12$, what is $f(b - a)$?

(A) $a^2 + b^2 - 12$
(B) $a^3 - b - 12$
(C) $a^2 - 2ab - b^2 - 12$
(D) $a^2 - 2ab + b^2 - 12$

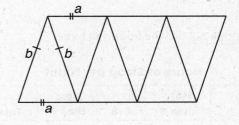

9. Six identical isosceles triangles are arranged as shown in the figure above. If one side of each triangle has length a and if the other two sides each have length b, what is the outside perimeter of the figure above in terms of a and b?

(A) $4a + 4b$
(B) $6a + 2b$
(C) $6a + 7b$
(D) $6a + 12b$

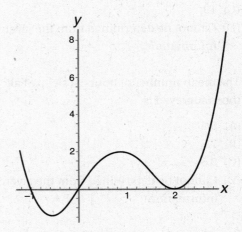

10. Which of the following could be an equation for the function graphed in the xy-plane above?

(A) $x(x - 2)(x + 1)$
(B) $x(x - 2)^2(x + 1)$
(C) $x(x + 2)^2(x - 1)$
(D) $x(x + 2)(x - 1)$

Calculator Problems Mixed Drill 2

1. Which of the following lines is perpendicular to $5y - 2.5x = -10$?

   (A) $y = -2x + 8$
   (B) $y = 0.5x + 2$
   (C) $y = 2x - 7$
   (D) $y = 0.4x + 10$

Questions 2–4 use the following table.

Hours of Sleep per Night

	More than 8	6–8	Less than 6	Total
Under Age 13	15	8	1	24
Ages 13–18	13	17	14	44
Ages 19–22	18	12	20	50
Total	46	37	35	118

2. The least possible median age of those surveyed would be which of the following?

   (A) 13
   (B) 15
   (C) 19
   (D) Cannot be determined from the given information

3. The mean number of hours of sleep of all those surveyed is

   (A) 6.5
   (B) 7.5
   (C) 8.5
   (D) Cannot be determined from the given information

4. For values of a not equal to zero, $\left(\dfrac{2}{\sqrt[3]{a}}\right)^6$ equals

   (A) $2a^{-2}$
   (B) $12a^{-2}$
   (C) $64a^{\frac{1}{2}}$
   (D) $64a^{-2}$

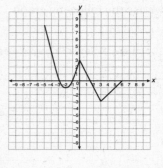

5. The graph of $y = f(x)$ is shown above. Which of the following graphs best represents the graph of $y = |f(x)|$?

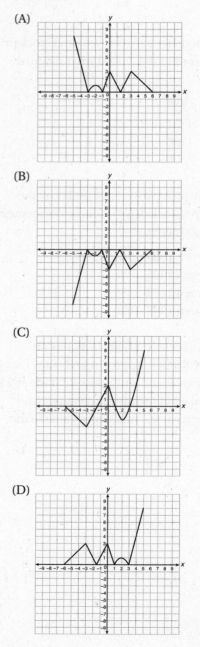

(A)

(B)

(C)

(D)

6. Which of the following is equivalent to $(6x^3 + 3x^2 - 1) + (4x^3 - 4x^2 + 2x + 3)$?

   (A) $11x^6 + 2$
   (B) $10x^3 - 7x^2 + 2x + 2$
   (C) $10x^3 - x^2 + x + 3$
   (D) $10x^3 - x^2 + 2x + 2$

7. Peter makes $15 per hour when he works 40 hours a week. For each hour exceeding 40, he is paid 50% more than his usual hourly rate. Assuming that Peter has worked at least 40 hours in a particular week, which inequality properly expresses the range of hours, h, he must work to make over $800 in that week?

   (A) $800 < 600 + 22.5 \times (h - 40)$
   (B) $800 < 600 + 22.5h$
   (C) $800 < 600 + 7.5 \times (h - 40)$
   (D) $800 < 40 + 15h$

8. In the xy-plane below, ABC is an equilateral triangle with sides of length 2. If point A has coordinates $(-2, 0)$, what are the coordinates of point B?

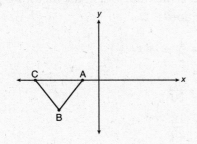

   (A) $\left(-\sqrt{3}, -3\right)$

   (B) $\left(-2, -\sqrt{3}\right)$

   (C) $\left(-3, \sqrt{2}\right)$

   (D) $\left(-3, -\sqrt{3}\right)$

9. In a pet store with 30 customers, 60 percent of the customers like dogs and 11 customers like cats. What is the minimum number of customers who like both cats and dogs?

   (A) 0
   (B) 1
   (C) 4
   (D) 7

10. The function f is defined below. If $f(n)$ and n are both integers, what is the largest value that n can be?

$$f(n) = \frac{2}{\sqrt[4]{n - 300}}$$

   (A) 0
   (B) 301
   (C) 316
   (D) 426

Free-Response Drill

NO CALCULATOR

1. A circle has the equation $x^2 + y^2 = 36$. What is the shortest distance in units from the origin to a point on the circle?

2. Jamie can run $\frac{3}{2} k$ miles in the time that Matt takes to run k miles. If Jamie and Matt run for the same amount of time and their combined mileage is 10 miles, how many miles did Jamie run?

3. What is the product of all solutions to $(x + 2)^2 = (2x - 3)^2$?

4. If $a^4 - 2a^3 + 2a^2 + ma + 2$ has $(a + 1)$ as a factor, what is the value of the constant m?

5. What will be the new slope of the line $y = 2x + 3$ after it is translated 3 units to the right and 2 units down?

CALCULATOR

1. At a particular store, customers can purchase children's outfits for $20 and adults' outfits for $45. If a family purchased 22 outfits for a total of $765, how many children's outfits did the family purchase?

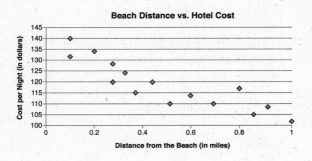

2. The scatter plot above shows the price of a room per night at 15 different hotels versus the distance the hotels are from the beach. If Hotel M is the hotel at the median distance to the beach, how many hotel rooms must be booked for the hotel to make $2,280 in one night?

3. One face of a triangular building is portrayed in a photograph in which 1 inch in the photograph corresponds to 10 feet in the actual building. If the face of the actual building has an area of 960 square feet and a base of 48 feet, what is the building's height (in inches) in the photograph?

Questions 4–5 are about the following table.

Gender	Major at ABC University			Total
	Humanities	Math/Science	Engineering	
Male	450	125	140	715
Female	520	100	155	775
Total	970	225	295	1490

4. What is the total percentage of STEM majors (math, science, engineering) out of all the students at ABC University, rounded to the nearest percent? (Ignore the percent symbol when entering your answer. For example, if your answer is 10%, enter 10 as your answer.)

5. What is the probability that a randomly selected student at ABC University will be both a female and a humanities major (calculated to the nearest hundredth)?

No-Calculator Problems Mixed Drill

1. What is the value of x in the following equation?

$$15x + \frac{1}{2} = -5\left(x - \frac{5}{2}\right)$$

(A) $-\frac{3}{20}$

(B) $-\frac{13}{20}$

(C) $\frac{3}{5}$

(D) $\frac{3}{10}$

2. If $i = \sqrt{-1}$, what is the value of $(3 - i)(4 + i)$?

(A) $11 - i$

(B) $12 + 7i$

(C) $13 - i$

(D) $13 + i$

3. What is the value of the constant c in the equation below?

$$(x-6)(x-10) = (x-8)^2 + c$$

(A) −4
(B) 0
(C) 4
(D) 16

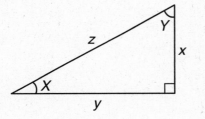

4. Which trigonometric expression would give the value of angle X?

(A) $\sin^{-1}\left(\dfrac{x}{z}\right)$

(B) $\cos^{-1}\left(\dfrac{x}{z}\right)$

(C) $\sin\left(\dfrac{x}{z}\right)$

(D) $\sin^{-1}\left(\dfrac{y}{z}\right)$

5. The ideal gas equation is $PV = nRT$, where P is the pressure, V is the volume, n is the number of moles, R is the gas constant, and T is the temperature. According to the equation, the volume of a gas is inversely related to

(A) the number of moles.
(B) gas constant.
(C) temperature.
(D) none of the above.

6. In physics, the mirror equation is

$$\frac{1}{f} = \frac{1}{d_o} + \frac{1}{d_i},$$ where f represents the mirror's focal length, d_o is the distance of an object from the mirror, and d_i is the distance of the image from the mirror. Which expression gives d_o in terms of focal length and image distance?

(A) $\dfrac{1}{\dfrac{1}{f} + \dfrac{1}{d_i}}$

(B) $\dfrac{1}{f} - \dfrac{1}{d_i}$

(C) $\dfrac{1}{\dfrac{1}{d_i} - \dfrac{1}{f}}$

(D) $\dfrac{1}{\dfrac{1}{f} - \dfrac{1}{d_i}}$

7. If the following equation is true for every value of x and if a is a constant, what is the value of a?

$$(x+4)(x^2 + ax + 2) = x^3 + x^2 - 10x + 8$$

(A) −10
(B) −3
(C) −2
(D) 1

8. $\left(6y^3 + \dfrac{1}{2}y - \dfrac{2}{3}\right) - \left(4y^3 - y^2 + \dfrac{1}{2}y + \dfrac{1}{6}\right) = ?$

(A) $2y^3 + y^2 + y + \dfrac{5}{6}$

(B) $2y^3 - y^2 + y - \dfrac{1}{2}$

(C) $2y^3 - \dfrac{1}{2}y - \dfrac{1}{2}$

(D) $2y^3 + y^2 - \dfrac{5}{6}$

9. If the slope of line A is $-\dfrac{x}{y}$, where x and y are positive numbers, what is the slope of a line that is perpendicular to A?

(A) $-\dfrac{x}{y}$

(B) $-\dfrac{y}{x}$

(C) $\dfrac{x}{y}$

(D) $\dfrac{y}{x}$

10. The formula for the surface area of a sphere is $A = 4\pi r^2$. If the volume of sphere A is 8 times the volume of sphere B, what is the ratio of the surface area of sphere A to that of sphere B?

(A) 1:2
(B) 2:1
(C) 4:1
(D) 8:1

ANSWERS EXPLAINED

Heart of Algebra Drill 1 (Calculator)

1. **(B)** To add all of these fractions, you need a common denominator. The least common denominator for the three fractions is 16. However, because the other side has a denominator of 32, let's use 32 for ease. To convert $-\frac{3}{8}x$ to a fraction with a denominator of 32, multiply both the numerator and the denominator by 4. Thus, $-\frac{3}{8}x$ becomes $-\frac{12}{32}x$.

   Similarly, $\frac{5}{16}x$ becomes $\frac{10}{32}x$ after multiplying both the numerator and denominator by 2. Finally, $-\frac{1}{2}x$ becomes $-\frac{16}{32}x$ after multiplying both the numerator and denominator by 16.

   Therefore, we're left with:

   $$-\frac{12}{32}x + \frac{10}{32}x - \frac{16}{32}x = \frac{18}{32}$$

   Combining like terms gives:

   $$-\frac{18}{32}x = \frac{18}{32}$$

   To isolate x, divide both sides by $-\frac{18}{32}$. Dividing by a fraction is the same as multiplying by its reciprocal, so you're left with:

   $$x = \left(\frac{18}{32}\right) \times \left(\frac{-32}{18}\right) = -1$$

   So $x = -1$, or Choice (B).

2. **(A)** Let's cross multiply here:

   $$8(3a - 4) = 5(3a - 4)$$

   Next we need to distribute both the 8 and the 5:

   $$24a - 32 = 15a - 20$$

   Combine both a terms by subtracting $15a$ from both sides:

   $$9a - 32 = -20$$

   Combine the constants by adding 32 to both sides:

   $$9a = 12$$

   Finally, solve for a by dividing both sides by 9:

   So $a = \frac{12}{9} = \frac{4}{3}$, Choice (A).

   Alternatively, realize that $3a - 4 = 0$ because if we plug in x for $3a - 4$, $\frac{x}{5} = \frac{x}{8}$, meaning $8x = 5x$. Therefore, x must be zero.

3. **(D)** First, get the second inequality in the same form as the first. To do this, subtract 4 from both sides of the second inequality:

   $$-y \le x - 4$$

   Then divide by –1, remembering to flip the inequality since you're dividing by a negative:

   $$y \ge -x + 4$$

If you graph these two inequalities, you'll see that the point where the lines intersect is the solution that they share that has the lowest y-value.

We can use this knowledge to set both inequalities equal to one another and solve:

$$2x + 5 = -x + 4$$

To solve for x, add an x to both sides to get all of the x-terms on the left. Subtract 5 from both sides to get all constants on the right:

$$3x = -1$$

Dividing by 3 tells us that $x = -\dfrac{1}{3}$. That's enough to narrow it down to Choice (D).

However, if we wanted to know the y-value, we could plug the x-value into the equation for either of the two lines:

$$y = -x + 4 = -\left(-\frac{1}{3}\right) + 4 = \frac{1}{3} + \frac{12}{3} = \frac{13}{3}$$

This also agrees with Choice (D).

Alternatively, you can plug in the values of the answers and see which set works for both equations.

4. **(C)** Recall that absolute value can be thought of as the distance of something from the origin. So if the absolute value of something is 4, it is 4 units away from the origin in either direction. This means that it can be either 4 or –4. Therefore, to solve for the values of x, we can set what's inside the absolute value equal to both 4 and –4 and solve. Setting it equal to 4 gives:

$$3x - 1 = 4$$

Adding 1 to both sides results in:

$$3x = 5$$

Dividing both sides by 3 gives us our first solution:

$$x = \frac{5}{3}$$

Next, set the inside of the absolute value sign equal to –4:

$$3x - 1 = -4$$

Adding 1 to both sides gives:

$$3x = -3$$

Dividing by 3 gives us our second solution:

$$x = -1$$

Therefore, there are two solutions, I and II, Choice (C).

5. **(B)** To combine the x-terms, you need a common denominator, 6. To combine the constant terms, you also need a common denominator, 27:

$$\frac{9}{6}x - \frac{18}{27} = \frac{1}{6}x - \frac{10}{27}$$

To get all x-terms on the left, subtract $\dfrac{1}{6}x$ from both sides:

$$\frac{8}{6}x - \frac{18}{27} = -\frac{10}{27}$$

Next, add $\frac{18}{27}$ to both sides to get all constants on the right:

$$\frac{8}{6}x = \frac{8}{27}$$

Finally, divide both sides by $\frac{8}{6}$ (which is the same thing as multiplying both sides by $\frac{6}{8}$) to solve for x:

$$x = \frac{8(6)}{27(8)} = \frac{48}{216} = \frac{2}{9}$$

This matches Choice (B).

6. **(A)** Let's get the second equation in $y = mx + b$ form. First, let's get the y-terms on the left by adding $2y$ to both sides:

$$2y - 6 = 12x$$

Next we need to bring the constant to the right side by adding 6 to both sides:

$$2y = 12x + 6$$

Finally, divide both sides by 2:

$$y = 6x + 3$$

Comparing the two lines shows they have the same slope but different y-intercepts. Therefore, they are parallel lines, Choice (A).

If their slopes had been negative reciprocals of one another, they would have been perpendicular lines.

If the lines had had different slopes, they would have intersected at exactly one point.

If they had had the same slope and the same y-intercept, then they would have been the same line.

7. **(C)** The women will meet when their positions are equal, so we need to come up with equations to model each of their positions. First, notice that Caitlin leaves a full hour before Hannah. In that first hour, she'll travel 30 miles since she's traveling at 30 mph. Therefore, the women start out 170 miles apart at 4:00 P.M.

Let's say that Caitlin starts at position 0, while Hannah starts at position 170. Caitlin is moving toward 170, so she's moving in the positive direction at 30 mph. Keeping in mind that distance = rate $\times$ time, Caitlin's position, s, can then be described as:

$$s = 0 + 30t = 30t$$

On the other hand, Hannah is traveling from position 170 toward position 0, so she's traveling in the negative direction. Therefore, her position can be described as:

$$s = 170 - 40t$$

In order to solve for t, we must set the women's positions equal to one another:

$$30t = 170 - 40t$$

Adding $40t$ to both sides results in:

$$70t = 170$$

Dividing by 70 tells us:

$$t = 2.429$$

Because our rates were in miles per hour, this time is in hours. Therefore, it takes the women two full hours and a fraction of a third hour, so they meet sometime between 6 and 7. This is enough information to narrow down the solution to Choice (C).

To find the exact time, we can figure out how many minutes 0.429 hours is by multiplying 0.429 hours by 60 minutes/hour.

0.429(60) = 25.74 minutes. Therefore, Caitlin and Hannah meet 2 hours and 26 minutes after the time Hannah started traveling, 4:00 P.M. So the women arrive at the same place at 6:26 P.M.

8. **(D)** Recognize that those who are allowed to ride are the ones who aren't too far in either direction from the mean of the permitted heights. If you take the mean height of the constraints, you get:

$$\frac{36+72}{2} = 54$$

72 – 54 = 18 and 36 – 54 = –18. Therefore, anyone who is less than 18 units away from 54 is allowed to ride, which is what Choice (D) says.

If you didn't recognize this, you could use the process of elimination. You could pick heights that aren't allowed to ride. If you plug in a height that isn't allowed to ride but the inequality is still true, then you'd know that you could eliminate the choice. For instance:

Choice (A): |35 – 36| = 1. Since 1 is less than 72, we can rule out this answer choice.

Choice (B): |35 – 38| = 3. Since 3 is less than 34, we can rule out this answer choice as well.

Choice (C): |35 – 30| = 5. Since 5 is less than 42, we're left with Choice (D).

9. **(D)** The answer choices are all positive, so let's come up with some of the positive points on the line. The line has a slope of $\frac{3}{5}$ and passes through the origin (thus has a y-intercept of 0). So the equation for the line is:

$$y = \frac{3}{5}x$$

The line starts at the origin and goes up 3 units and to the right 5 units. So (5, 3) is a point. From there, the line goes up 3 more units and to the right 5 more units, so (10, 6) is also a point, which is Choice (D).

Alternatively, you could have used the process of elimination by plugging in the x-coordinates of the answer choices to get the y-coordinate at that value of x.

10. **(B)** In order for the commission to be positive, change the expression to an inequality where the commission will be positive and solve for x:

$$C = 50x + 25(x - 100) - 2,000 \;\boxed{?}$$
$$0 < 50x + 25(x - 100) - 2,000 \;\boxed{?}$$
$$0 < 50x + 25x - 2,500 - 2,000 \;\boxed{?}$$
$$0 < 75x - 4,500 \;\boxed{?}$$
$$4,500 < 75x \;\boxed{?}$$
$$60 < x$$

Since the salesperson cannot sell a partial phone plan, the least number of phone plans must be the first integer greater than 60, which is 61.

Heart of Algebra Drill 2 (Calculator)

1. **(C)** This problem is simply asking you to isolate the w variable. To begin, let's move the constant to the left side of the equation by dividing both sides by $\frac{1}{3}$.

   Dividing by $\frac{1}{3}$ is the same as multiplying by 3. (Remember that dividing by a fraction is the same as multiplying by its reciprocal.) So we're left with:

   $$3V = lwh$$

   Next, let's divide both sides by l:

   $$\frac{3V}{l} = wh$$

   The final step is to divide both sides by h, giving us our final answer:

   $$\frac{3V}{lh} = w$$

   This is Choice (C).

2. **(B)** First, we need to get the x out of the denominator by multiplying both sides of the equation by x:

   $$18x^2 - 21 = \frac{2x^2}{3} + 12x$$

   We have two x^2-terms to combine. So we need a common denominator, which is 3:

   $$\frac{54x^2}{3} - 21 = \frac{2x^2}{3} + 12x$$

   This is a quadratic equation since the highest degree of the terms is 2. We bring all terms to the same side so that we can eventually use the quadratic formula:

   $$\frac{52x^2}{3} - 12x - 21 = 0$$

   Recall the quadratic formula for a quadratic equation of the form $ax^2 + bx + c$:

   $$x = \frac{-b \pm \sqrt{b^2 - 4ac}}{2a}$$

   Filling in our values for a, b, and c gives:

   $$x = \frac{12 \pm \sqrt{(-12)^2 - 4\left(\frac{52}{3}\right)(-21)}}{2\left(\frac{52}{3}\right)}$$

   $$x = \frac{12 \pm \sqrt{1600}}{\left(\frac{104}{3}\right)} = \frac{12 \pm 40}{\left(\frac{104}{3}\right)}$$

   So $x = \frac{3}{2}$ or $x = -\frac{21}{26}$.

We're looking only for the negative value of x, so we only care about the second value. This second value can also be expressed as -0.8077. Rounded to one decimal place, we get Choice (B).

3. **(B)** First, figure out what $\frac{1}{2}$ and $\frac{5}{6}$ of 30 are so that you know what range of flex days an employee wants to take:

$$\frac{1}{2}(30) = 15 \text{ and } \frac{5}{6}(30) = 25$$

So the employee wants to take at least 15 days but fewer than 25 days. If we consider F to be the number of flex days taken, this can be expressed as:

$$15 \le F < 25$$

Now we need an expression for flex days using sick days, S, and personal days, P.

A sick day counts as half of a flex day, and a personal day counts as a total flex day. So the number of flex days used will be represented by:

$$\frac{1}{2}S + P = F$$

We can plug in this expression for F in our previous inequality:

$$15 \le \frac{1}{2}S + P < 25$$

This is Choice (B).

4. **(B)** For this question, we simply plug in $-4x$ for every x in the original function:

$$g(-4x) = 9(-4x) + 2 = -36x + 2$$

This answer matches Choice (B).

5. **(C)** The carpenter charges a flat fee of \$40, so our equation will have a constant of 40. The carpenter also charges \$60 for each half hour worked. Therefore, the carpenter charges \$120 for each hour, H, worked. Therefore, the carpenter's total fee for working H hours is:

$$F(H) = 40 + 120H$$

This is answer (C).

6. **(B)** Let's use elimination to get rid of the y-terms. Start by multiplying the first equation by 34: $34(0.75x - 0.1y = 1.2)$.

This results in:

$$25.5x - 3.4y = 40.8$$

Now we can add this new equation to the second equation to eliminate the y-terms:

$$
\begin{array}{r}
25.5x - 3.4y = 40.8 \\
+\ \underline{2.6x + 3.4y = 15.4} \\
28.1x = 56.2
\end{array}
$$

Dividing by 28.1 tells us that $x = 2$. This is enough to narrow the answer down to Choice (B). However, let's solve for y just for practice:

$$2.6(2) + 3.4y = 15.4$$
$$5.2 + 3.4y = 15.4$$

Subtract 5.2 from both sides and then divide by 3.4 to learn that $y = 3$.

7. **(B)** If $\dfrac{m}{n} = -\dfrac{3}{1}$, then $\dfrac{n}{m} = -\dfrac{1}{3}$. Therefore, $-2\left(\dfrac{n}{m}\right) = -2\left(-\dfrac{1}{3}\right) = \dfrac{2}{3}$, which is Choice (B).

8. **(D)** First, you must consider how two lines could have infinitely many solutions. The answer is that they need to have the same slope and the same y-intercept. In other words, they are the same line when graphed.

Let's start by rewriting Equation B in slope-intercept form by dividing both sides by 3:

$$y = \frac{2}{3}x + 1$$

The equations already have the same slope. However, they also need to have the same y-intercept: –4.

Let's subtract 5 from the right side of Equation B so that it matches Equation A:

$$y = \frac{2}{3}x - 4$$

However, we want to know what we need to change about the *original* Equation B. Therefore, we want to get Equation B back in its original form to see what changed. We can do this by multiplying both sides by 3:

$$3\left(y = \frac{2}{3}x - 4\right) \text{ becomes } 3y = 2x - 12.$$

Now we can see that from Equation B to this final equation, we subtracted 15 from the right side to change the y-intercept from +3 to –12. This matches Choice (D).

9. **(D)** Don't get confused by all of the unnecessary information here! We want to know when the hot-air balloon and the blimp will be at the same altitude. Since altitude deals with only vertical movement, we only care about their vertical movements. The balloon and blimp will be at the same altitude when their vertical positions are equal.

Start with some notation. Let's say that traveling up is in the positive direction. So the balloon is traveling in the positive direction. Let's also say that traveling down is in the negative direction. So the blimp is traveling in the negative direction.

Remember that distance = rate × time.

The blimp's position can be defined as $s = 5,000 - 5t$.

The balloon's position can be described as $s = 500 + 4t$.

The blimp and balloon will be at the same altitude when their positions are equal. So we can set the two expressions equal to one another:

$$5,000 - 5t = 500 + 4t$$

Add $5t$ to both sides while subtracting 500 from both sides:

$$4,500 = 9t$$

Dividing by 9 tells us that $t = 500$.

Because our rates were in feet/minute, our time is in minutes. Let's divide by 60 to convert this to hours:

$$\frac{500}{60} = 8.333$$

So it takes 8 hours and $\dfrac{1}{3}$ of the 9th hour. One-third of an hour is 20 minutes since $\dfrac{1}{3}(60) = 20$. So it takes 8 hours and 20 minutes. Since the balloon and blimp started moving toward one another at 1:00 P.M., they'll meet at 9:20 P.M., which is Choice (D).

10. **(A)** Let's first set up an inequality that models this situation. Rosa wants to burn more than 2,000 calories, so we can represent this as 2,000 < calories.

Next, we need to come up with an expression that represents the number of calories Rosa burns.

Rosa is either burning 65 calories per hour by resting or burning 300 calories per hour while exercising. Let's call H the number of hours she spends exercising. Since there are 24 hours in a day and she's not exercising for the rest of the hours outside of H, the hours spent resting will be $24 - H$.

Therefore, the number of calories Rosa burns can be expressed as:

$$2{,}000 < 300H + 65(24 - H)$$

Now we solve for H. First, distribute the 65:

$$2{,}000 < 300H + 1560 - 65H$$

Combine like terms:

$$2{,}000 < 235H + 1560$$

Subtract 1,560 from both sides:

$$440 < 235H$$

Divide both sides by 235:

$$1.87 < H$$

This means that Rosa has to work out for at least 1.9 hours. She can't work out more than 24 hours per day since there are only 24 hours in a day. So the correct answer is (A).

Heart of Algebra Drill 3 (Calculator)

1. **(A)** To make solving this problem a bit easier, let's convert all of our mixed numbers into improper fractions:

$$\frac{15}{8}x + \frac{5}{32} = \frac{15}{4}x - \frac{5}{4}$$

We eventually want to combine our x-terms and combine our constant terms. So our x-terms need a common denominator (8), and our constant terms need a common denominator (32). Thus, let's rewrite our fractions with these common denominators. Our full equation is now:

$$\frac{15}{8}x + \frac{5}{32} = \frac{30}{8}x - \frac{40}{32}$$

To avoid dealing with negatives, let's bring the constants to the left by adding $\frac{40}{32}$ to both sides:

$$\frac{15}{8}x + \frac{45}{32} = \frac{30}{8}x$$

We then want to get all x-terms on the right by subtracting $\frac{15}{8}x$ from both sides:

$$\frac{45}{32} = \frac{15}{8}x$$

To solve for x, divide both sides by $\frac{15}{8}$ (in other words, multiply both sides by $\frac{8}{15}$):

$$\frac{45(8)}{32(15)} = x \text{ so } \frac{360}{480} = x$$

This reduces to $\frac{3}{4} = x$, which is Choice (A).

2. **(B)** Let x be the number we are trying to find.

"2 times a number is subtracted from 14" can be written as $14 - 2x$. (We are subtracting 2 times a number, or $2x$, from the 14.)

"The result is" means an equals sign.

"2 greater than the number" can be written as $x + 2$. Thus, the whole sentence can be written as:

$$14 - 2x = x + 2$$

Add $2x$ to both sides to get all x-terms on the right. Then subtract 2 from both sides to get all constants on the left:

$$12 = 3x$$

Dividing by 3 tells us that $x = 4$, which is answer (B).

3. **(D)** Between 2015 and 2022, Andre adds 5 coins 8 times:

2015, 2016, 2017, 2018, 2019, 2020, 2021, and 2022.

Adding 5 coins 8 times means he added a total of $5(8) = 40$ coins in those years.

Between 2023 and 2045, he added 8 coins 23 times:

2023, 2024, 2025, 2026, 2027, 2028, 2029, 2030, 2031, 2032, 2033, 2034, 2035, 2036, 2037, 2038, 2039, 2040, 2041, 2042, 2043, 2044, and 2045.

Thus, from 2023 to 2045, he added a total of $8(23) = 184$ coins.

Andre started with 210 coins. So the sum of the coins in his collection will be the original 210 plus the number of coins he added:

$$210 + 40 + 184 = 434$$

This is Choice (D).

4. **(A)** Since we have two inequalities, we can use elimination to get rid of one variable. Let's add both equations together:

$$\begin{array}{r} x - y > 3 \\ + \underline{\quad y - 5 > x} \\ x - 5 > 3 + x \end{array}$$

Subtracting x from both sides and adding 5 to both sides leaves you with $0 > 8$. Because we know that under no circumstances is 0 greater than 8, there are no solutions.

5. **(B)** In a system of two equations, we can either use substitution or elimination to solve.

If we multiply the second equation by 12 and add the equations together, our y-terms will cancel out. Start by multiplying the second equation by 12:

$$12\left(-\frac{2}{3}x + \frac{1}{4}y = -\frac{13}{18}\right) = -8x + 3y = -\frac{26}{3}$$

Now we can add this equation to the first equation:

$$4x - 3y = \frac{11}{3}$$
$$+ {-8x} + 3y = -\frac{26}{3}$$
$$-4x = -\frac{15}{3}$$

To solve for x, divide by -4:

$$x = \frac{15}{12} = \frac{5}{4}$$

This is enough to narrow down the answer to Choice (B). However, you could plug this x-value into one of your functions to solve for y if you wanted.

Alternatively, you could have used substitution by solving for x in the first equation and then plugging that equation back into the second equation.

To solve for x, first add $3y$ to both sides:

$$4x = 3y + \frac{11}{3}$$

Then divide both sides by 4 to isolate x:

$$x = \frac{3y}{4} + \frac{11}{12}$$

Now you can plug this expression into the second equation for x:

$$-\frac{2}{3}\left(\frac{3y}{4} + \frac{11}{12}\right) + \frac{1}{4}y = -\frac{13}{18}$$

Next, distribute the $-\frac{2}{3}$:

$$-\frac{6}{12}y - \frac{22}{36} + \frac{1}{4}y = -\frac{13}{18}$$

Some of these fractions can be reduced. For our purposes, though, it doesn't really matter. Next, we need to combine our y-terms, but first we need a common denominator. Let's convert $\frac{1}{4}y$ to $\frac{3}{12}y$:

$$-\frac{6}{12}y - \frac{22}{36} + \frac{3}{12}y = -\frac{13}{18}$$

Now combine like terms:

$$-\frac{1}{4}y - \frac{22}{36} = -\frac{13}{18}$$

To add $\frac{22}{36}$ to both sides, we need to first convert $-\frac{13}{18}$ to $-\frac{26}{36}$ so that our constants have a common denominator:

$$-\frac{1}{4}y - \frac{22}{36} = -\frac{26}{36}$$

$$-\frac{1}{4}y = -\frac{1}{9}$$

To solve for y, divide both sides by $-\frac{1}{4}$ (multiply both sides by -4):

$$y = \frac{4}{9}$$

This is enough to narrow it down to Choice (B). However, we can solve for x by plugging the y-value into our equation for x:

$$x = \frac{3}{4}y + \frac{11}{12} = \frac{3}{4}\left(\frac{4}{9}\right) + \frac{11}{12} = \frac{12}{36} + \frac{11}{12} = \frac{12}{36} + \frac{33}{36} = \frac{45}{36} = \frac{5}{4}$$

Finally, we could have solved this problem by plugging each answer choice into the two equations to see which set of points work. If using this method, be careful to check that the points satisfy BOTH equations. For instance, Choice (C) works when plugged into the first equation but not the second.

6. **(B)** In the first equation, one of those factors must equal 0 for the whole equation to equal 0. Therefore, we will find the possible solutions by setting each factor equal to 0:

$$x - 2 = 0$$

Adding 2 to both sides tells us that $x = 2$ is a possible solution:

$$y + 5 = 0$$

Subtracting 5 from both sides tells us that $y = -5$ is another possible solution.

Plugging these values into the second equation will tell us the solutions to it:

$$3(2) + y = 1$$

So $6 + y = 1$.

Subtracting 6 from both sides tells us that $y = -5$, which is the original y-value we got from the first equation.

Let's try the y-value that we already determined:

$$3x + -5 = 1$$

So $3x = 6$. Dividing by 3 tells us that $x = 2$. However, this is the x-solution that we already tried. Therefore, there is only one solution:

$$(2, -5)$$

This is Choice (B).

7. **(D)** Let's use substitution. Solve for b in the 2nd equation by dividing both sides by -2:

$$6.45 - 0.5625a = b$$

Let's now plug the left side of this equation into the first equation for b:

$$\frac{3}{8}a + \frac{2}{3}(6.45 - 0.5625a) = 4.3$$

Distributing the $\frac{2}{3}$ leaves us with:

$$\frac{3}{8}a + 4.3 - 0.375a = 4.3$$

Let's get that $\frac{3}{8}a$ into decimal form so that we can easily combine our like terms:

$$0.375a + 4.3 - 0.375a = 4.3$$

Combining both a terms results in:

$$4.3 = 4.3$$

We know that this is always true, meaning we have an infinite number of solutions. Alternatively, you may have noticed that if you multiply the second equation by $-\frac{1}{3}$ and convert any fractions in the two equations into decimals, the two equations are exactly the same. Since they are the same line, there are infinitely many solutions.

8. **(A)** Let's turn what we know into equations. Let m equal the number of votes that Candidate M receives and let n equal the number of votes that Candidate N receives.

First, we know that the sum of the votes that the two candidates receive is 50,000. In other words:

$$m + n = 50{,}000$$

Additionally, we know that the number of votes Candidate M receives is 3 times the number of votes that Candidate N receives. This can be expressed by the equation

$$m = 3n$$

Now we can plug in $3n$ for m in the first equation:

$$3n + n = 50{,}000$$

Combining like terms results in:

$$4n = 50{,}000$$

We can solve for n by dividing both sides by 4:

$$n = 12{,}500$$

This is answer (A).

9. **(A)** We're told that Y is the number of years Jennifer has worked at the company. We can see that each time Y increases by 1, her salary goes up \$2,500. For instance, when $Y = 0$, Jennifer's salary is \$40,000. When $Y = 1$, her salary is \$42,500. When $Y = 2$, her salary is \$45,000. Therefore, Choice (A) is correct.

Choice (B) is incorrect because it can be shown that Jennifer's starting salary (when $Y = 0$) is \$40,000.

Choice (C) is incorrect because the amount of money made is given by the variable S.

Choice (D) is incorrect because the equation tells us nothing about the number of hours Jennifer worked.

10. **(C)** We want to know how many articles Avinash reads in w weeks. So we first need to figure out how many articles he reads per week. We can then multiply this number by w to give the number of articles he reads in w weeks.

Avinash reads 2 fiction articles per day. Since there are 7 days in a week, he reads $2(7) = 14$ fiction articles per week. He also reads 14 nonfiction articles per week. So Avinash reads $14 + 14 = 28$ fiction and nonfiction articles per week.

Therefore, the number of articles Avinash reads in w weeks is given by the expression $28w$, which is Choice (C).

Heart of Algebra Drill 1 (No Calculator)

1. **(C)** Inequalities can be solved just like equations. The only difference is you must remember to flip the inequality sign if you multiply or divide by a negative number.

The first step is to get rid of the denominator by multiplying both sides by 5:

$$-2x - 4 > 10$$

Add 4 to both sides:

$$-2x > 14$$

Divide both sides by -2 to solve for x. Since we are dividing by a negative number, we need to flip the inequality as follows:

$$x < -7$$

The answer is Choice (C).

2. **(A)** When the piggybank is full, it will have 500 quarters in it. Let's write an expression for how many quarters the piggybank contains on any given day, D, after Susan's birthday.

Susan starts with 120 quarters on day 0 (her birthday), so 120 is a constant. Every day, 4 quarters are added to the bank. Thus, on day 1, 4 quarters have been added. On day 2, Susan adds an additional 4 quarters to the bank so that $4(2) = 8$ quarters total have been added since her birthday. On day 3, $4(3) = 12$ quarters total have been added, and so on. This part of the expression can be written as $4D$.

Adding in the original 120 quarters she started with gives an expression for the total number of quarters in the bank D days after Susan's birthday:

$$120 + 4D$$

We know the bank is full when it contains 500 quarters. So we can set our expression equal to 500 and solve for D to determine how many days after Susan's birthday the piggybank will be filled. Thus Choice (A), $500 = 120 + 4D$, is correct.

3. **(C)** The number of points from x two-point shots will be $2x$. Similarly, making y three-point shots and z free throws corresponds to $3y$ points and z points, respectively. So the number of points earned from y three-point shots combined with z free throws will be $3y + z$. If the number of points from the two-point shots has to be at least as much (implying at least as much if not more) than the combined points from three-pointers and free throws, it follows that:

$$2x \geq 3y + z$$

This is Choice (C).

Choice (A) doesn't work because it doesn't take into account the different values of each shot.

Choice (B) doesn't account for each two-point shot giving 2 points.

Choice (D) implies that three-point shots score only 1 point and that free throws score 3 points.

4. **(B)** First, let's distribute the 4 in the second equation:

$$40 - \frac{16}{3}y = 2x + 5$$

Next, notice that if you multiplied the first equation by 8, the y-terms (and in fact the entire left-hand side of both equations) would be the same:

$$8\left(5 - \frac{2}{3}y = x\right) = 40 - \frac{16}{3}y = 8x$$

You could subtract the second equation from the first to cancel the y-terms:

$$40 - \frac{16}{3}y = 8x$$

$$-\left(40 - \frac{16}{3}y = 2x + 5\right)$$

$$0 = 6x - 5$$

Add 5 to both sides:

$$5 = 6x$$

Now divide by 6 to solve for x:

$$\frac{5}{6} = x$$

This is Choice (B).

5. **(A)** Let's start with the left side of the inequality. The absolute value of -3 is 3, so:

$$-2|-3| = -2(3) = -6$$

$$-6 < -3|x + 5|$$

We want to isolate our absolute value. So let's divide by -3, flipping the inequality since we are dividing by a negative number:

$$2 > |x + 5|$$

Because 2 has to be greater than the absolute value, the expression inside of the absolute value symbol can be anything between $(-2, 2)$. In other words, $x - 5$ needs to be greater than -2 but less than 2. To find the x-values such that $x - 5$ is less than 2, simply take away the absolute value signs and solve for x:

$$2 > x + 5$$

Subtracting 5 from both sides gives:

$$-3 > x$$

Next, we want to find the values of x such that $x - 5$ is greater than -2. In other words, we want to solve for x in the inequality $-2 < x + 5$. Subtracting 5 tells us:

$$-7 < x$$

We have found that $-3 > x$ and that $-7 < x$. In other words, $-7 < x < -3$, which is Choice (A).

6. **(A)** First, we'll solve for $\frac{1}{B}$. To do this, subtract $\frac{1}{A}$ from both sides:

$$\frac{1}{B} = \frac{1}{T} - \frac{1}{A}$$

Don't be tempted to pick Choice (C)! We've solved for $\frac{1}{B}$, not for B as asked in the question. To solve for B, we must take the reciprocal of what we have:

$$B = \frac{1}{\dfrac{1}{T} - \dfrac{1}{A}}$$

This matches answer (A).

7. **(C)** If creating the machine is now less expensive, the manufacturer can afford to make more machines for a given price. Therefore for each price, the quantity will be higher. Thus, the supply curve should shift to the right, shifting it into zones 3 and 4, which is Choice (C).

8. **(C)** Let's first find the slope of line A. The formula for slope is Change in y/Change in x:

$$\frac{0-(-2)}{-1-1} = \frac{2}{-2} = -1$$

If the lines are to intersect at a 90° angle, they must be perpendicular. Any line perpendicular to this one would have a slope of 1, since 1 is the negative reciprocal of -1.

We can now use the one given point of line B and the slope in the point-slope formula in order to get the equation of line B.

The point-slope formula is given by the equation $y - y_1 = m(x - x_1)$:

$$y - 4 = 1(x - 3)$$

Distributing the 1 gives:

$$y - 4 = x - 3$$

To get the line into slope-intercept form, add 4 to both sides:

$$y = x + 1$$

Therefore, line B has a y-intercept of 1, which is answer (C).

Alternatively, once it is known that the slope of the new line is 1, the equation must be $y = x + b$. Plug in the point (3, 4) to the line to solve for b:

$$4 = 3 + b \rightarrow b = 1$$

9. **(B)** The book will have a fixed replacement cost of $30, so +30 will be a constant term in the function. For each day that the book goes unreturned past December 14, Jane owes another 10 cents. Thus on day 1 after the return date, she owes a $30 replacement fee and 10 more cents, for a total of $30.10. On the second day, she owes the $30 replacement fee and 2 days' worth of late fees, $(2)(10) = 20$ cents, for a total of $30.20. By continuing in this manner, on day x, Jane will owe the $30 replacement fee and x days' worth of late fees, which is $(x)(10) = 10x$ cents or $0.1x$ dollars. The total cost is shown by $A(x) = 30 + 0.1x$.

This relationship is best described in Choice (B).

Choice (A) is tempting, but you must remember that 10 cents is expressed in dollars as $0.10. Choice (A) instead indicates that Jane pays an additional $10 of fees every day plus the $30 replacement fee.

10. **(B)** Since a is already solved for in the first equation, let's plug the right side of that equation into the second equation wherever there is an a:

$$2 + 3\left(\frac{2}{3}b + 1\right) = -4(2b + 1)$$

Next, distribute the 3 and the -4:

$$2 + 2b + 3 = -8b - 4$$

You can combine the constants on the left side of the equation:

$$2b + 5 = -8b - 4$$

Now add $8b$ to both sides and subtract 5 from both sides:

$$10b = -9$$

Dividing by 10 gives you

$$b = -\frac{9}{10}$$

However, the question asks us for the value of a. So let's plug the b-value into the first equation:

$$a = \frac{2}{3}b + 1 = \frac{2}{3}\left(-\frac{9}{10}\right) + 1 = -\frac{18}{30} + 1 = -\frac{3}{5} + \frac{5}{5} = \frac{2}{5}$$

This is Choice (B).

This can be solved in other ways, such as by trying elimination instead of substitution.

Heart of Algebra Drill 2 (No Calculator)

1. **(C)** First, we need to distribute. Don't forget to distribute the negative sign to the $(2x - 4)$ term. Distributing gives us:

$$-2x + 4 + 3x - 15 = -4$$

Combining like terms on the left side gives:

$$x - 11 = -4$$

Adding 11 to both sides tells us that $x = 7$, which is Choice (C).

Note that you could also plug each answer choice into the equation to see which one gives the correct equality, but doing this could be more time consuming.

2. **(A)** First, we must determine what number we should plug in for x. Our original function is $g(x + 2)$, and we're looking for $g(7)$. That means that we want x such that $x + 2 = 7$. Subtracting 2 from both sides gives $x = 5$. So to find $g(7)$, we simply plug in 5 for x in the original function:

$$g(5 + 2) = 5(5) - 4 = 25 - 4 = 21$$

The correct answer is Choice (A).

3. **(C)** John needs 6 utensils no matter how many people come, so +6 will be a constant. He also needs 3 utensils per person, which can be represented as $3x$. Thus, he needs $3x + 6$ utensils, Choice (C).

Choice (A) is incorrect because although it correctly depicts the 3 utensils needed for each person, it neglects the 6 serving utensils.

Choice (B) is incorrect because it states that each person needs 9 utensils.

Choice (D) is incorrect because it states that there are 3 utensils needed no matter how many people come, rather than the 6 utensils actually needed.

Alternatively, you could have imagined a scenario in which John invited 1 other person over, making a total of 2 people at dinner. They need 6 serving utensils, plus each one of them needs a knife, spoon, and fork. This makes a total of 2 knives, 2 spoons, and 2 forks, or 6 more utensils. The total number of utensils needed in this case is $6 + 6 = 12$.

You could have then plugged in 12 for U, plugged in 2 for x, and chosen the answer choice that worked, which is Choice (C):

$$12 = 3(2) + 6$$

4. **(B)** First, we have to find the value of $g(3)$ by plugging in 3 wherever there's an x in $g(x)$:

$$g(3) = -3(3) + 2 = -9 + 2 = -7$$

Now we have to find $f(-7)$ by plugging in -7 in wherever there is an x in $f(x)$:

$$f(-7) = 4(-7) + 7 = -28 + 7 = -21$$

The answer is Choice (B).

5. **(C)** Let's imagine that a massage therapist currently charges $100 for a massage. If the tax rate is 7%, or 0.07, tax on that service will be:

$$0.07(\$100) = \$7$$

Therefore, the price of the massage including the sales tax will be:

$$\$100 + \$7 = \$107$$

The ratio of the new price to the old price is:

$$\frac{107}{100}$$

The massage therapist can find the new prices for all of her services by multiplying the old prices by this ratio.

6. **(C)** First, distribute the 6:

$$12a - 6b = 4b$$

Bring the b-terms to the right side by adding $6b$ to both sides:

$$12a = 10b$$

To find the ratio of b to a, we want to solve for $\frac{b}{a}$. First, divide both sides by a:

$$12 = 10\frac{b}{a}$$

To isolate $\frac{b}{a}$, we need to divide both sides by 10:

$$\frac{b}{a} = \frac{12}{10} = \frac{6}{5}$$

The correct ratio is Choice (C).

7. **(B)** This $50,000 is some sort of cost that stays the same whether the restaurant serves 0 meals or serves 1,000 meals. Because the $50,000 doesn't vary with the variable meals, it's a fixed cost, which is Choice (B).

Choice (A) is incorrect because C represents the total costs and C varies with the number of meals served.

Choice (C) is incorrect because 2 is the cost per meal, as shown by the $2M$ in the equation.

Choice (D) is incorrect because the minimum number of meals served could be any positive integer.

8. **(B)** Total cost is found by adding together the variable costs and the fixed costs. In this problem, the variable cost is an since this value depends on n, the number of days the factory is operational. Since an is a cost and since n is a number of days, it follows that

the daily operational cost is given by a. Therefore, if the daily operational cost increases, a will increase.

The initial startup costs, or fixed costs, are given by variable b because b is a constant that isn't affected by the variable n. Therefore, if the startup costs decrease, b will decrease.

The correct scenario is depicted in Choice (B).

9. **(C)** In general, if $f(x)$ is our original function and if c is a constant, then:

- $f(x - c)$ shifts $f(x)$ to the right by c units.
- $f(x + c)$ shifts $f(x)$ to the left by c units.
- $f(x) + c$ shifts $f(x)$ up by c units.
- $f(x) - c$ shifts $f(x)$ down by c units.

In this particular problem, $g(x) = f(x - 1) + 2$. Using the above properties, $f(x - 1)$ tells us that $f(x)$ is shifted to the right by 1 unit. The +2 in the expression tells us that $f(x)$ is shifted up by 2 units. This corresponds to Choice (C).

10. **(C)** The number 250 is in the equation regardless of the value of W. Therefore, it makes sense that 250 would be the initial number of followers the campaign had. We can see this by plugging 0 in for W in the equation. This gives us the initial number of followers before the company starts campaigning:

$$N = 30(0) + 250 = 0 + 250 = 250$$

So we can see that when $W = 0$, $N = 250$.

Problem Solving and Data Analysis Drill 1 (Calculator)

1. **(C)** Let's use the variable d to represent the number of dogs in the shelter and the variable c to represent the number of cats. If the ratio of dogs to cats is 3:1, then there are 3 times as many dogs as cats:

$$d = 3c$$

If there are 360 animals in the shelter:

$$d + c = 360$$

We want to know the number of dogs present. So let's solve the first equation for c in terms of d and plug this into the second equation. Dividing by 3 tells us:

$$\frac{1}{3}d = c$$

Plugging this into the second equation results in:

$$d + \frac{1}{3}d = 360$$

Combining like terms gives:

$$\frac{4}{3}d = 360$$

We can divide both sides by $\frac{4}{3}$ (in other words, multiply both sides by $\frac{3}{4}$) to learn that $d = 270$, which is answer Choice (C).

Alternatively, you can solve this as a ratio problem:

$$\frac{d}{c} = \frac{3}{1}$$

As a fraction of the whole, the number of dogs can be expressed as $d = \frac{3}{(3+1)} = \frac{3}{4}$ of the

total. Then take $\frac{3}{4}$ of the total number of animals to find the number of dogs:

$$\frac{3}{4} \times 360 = 270$$

2. **(B)** Let's set up a proportion for this problem. The politician receives 14 seconds of applause for every minute of a speech. We want our units to be the same, so let's call that minute 60 seconds. We can model this part of our proportion as $\frac{14}{60}$.

We want to know how many minutes of applause he'll get for 2 hours of speech. Since we want our answer in minutes, let's call 2 hours 120 minutes. We want applause on top again. Therefore, this side of the proportion can be modeled by $\frac{x}{120}$, where x represents the number of minutes of applause the politician will receive in 120 minutes.

You can then set both sides of the proportion equal to one another:

$$\frac{14}{60} = \frac{x}{120}$$

Next, cross multiply:

$$14(120) = 60x$$
$$1{,}680 = 60x$$

Dividing by 60 gives us $x = 28$, Choice (B).

3. **(D)** A gallon of whole milk would have 3.5% of a gallon of fat, or 0.035 gallons. If we mix 1% milk and 2% milk in equal parts, we will essentially have 1.5% milk since the fat content will be the average of the two fat contents.

Therefore, the whole milk has $\frac{0.035}{0.015} = 2.333$ times the amount of fat of the 1% and 2% mixture. You would need 2.333 times the amount of milk of the mixture to have the same quantity of fat as in 1 gallon of whole milk. Because 0.333 can be represented as $\frac{1}{3}$, the answer is Choice (D).

Alternatively, take the combined average of the lower-fat milks:

$$\frac{1+2}{2} = 1.5$$

Then using x as the number of gallons needed of the combined milks, you can set up this equation:

$$1.5x = 3.5$$

Then solve for x to get $2\frac{1}{3}$.

4. **(C)** Let's first convert the marathon distance to kilometers:

$$26.2 \text{ miles} \times \frac{1 \text{ kilometer}}{0.62 \text{ miles}} = 42.26 \text{ kilometers}$$

If Katie has to run 42.26 km and if she's doing it 5 km at a time, she would need to run:

$$\frac{42.26}{5} = 8.45 \text{ races}$$

Therefore, she would need to run a minimum of 9 whole races to run the distance of a marathon.

Alternatively, you could have done dimensional analysis for the last step, canceling out units that you don't want and leaving only the units that you do want. Katie wants to go 42.26 km, and she's running 5 km/race. Cancel out kilometers, so that we're left with number of races:

$$42.26 \text{ kilometers} \times \frac{1 \text{ race}}{5 \text{ kilometers}} = 8.45 \text{ races}$$

We again need to round up to 9 so that Katie runs the full marathon distance.

5. **(A)** Let's use dimensional analysis, canceling out the units that we don't want and leaving the units that we do want (euros). In the dimensional analysis, let CAD mean Canadian dollars, let USD mean U.S. dollars, and let EUR mean euros:

$$100 \text{ CAD} \times \frac{0.7 \text{ USD}}{1 \text{ CAD}} \times \frac{0.9 \text{ EUR}}{1 \text{ USD}} = 63 \text{ EUR}$$

The correct answer is Choice (A).

6. **(D)** The easiest way to approach a problem like this is to test some points with each equation to see which equation works.

- Choice (A):

$$C(1) = 10^{2(1)} + 10(1-1) + 1 = 100 + 1 = 101$$

So the equation works for day 1. Let's see if it works with day 2:

$$C(2) = 10^{2(2)} + 10(2-1) + 1 = 10,000 + 10 + 1 = 10,011$$

This doesn't match the number for day 2, so we can rule out Choice (A).

- Choice (B):

$$C(1) = 100 + 10^1 = 100 + 10 = 110$$

This isn't the right number for day 1, so we can rule out Choice (B).

- Choice (C):

$$C(1) = 100 + 10(1-1) + 1 = 100 + 1 = 101$$

This works, so let's try $C(2)$:

$$C(2) = 100 + 10(2-1) + 1 = 100 + 10 + 1 = 111$$

This doesn't work, so we can rule out Choice (C).

- Choice (D):

$$C(1) = 100 + 10^{1-1} = 100 + 1 = 101$$
$$C(2) = 100 + 10^{2-1} = 100 + 10 = 110$$
$$C(3) = 100 + 10^{3-1} = 100 + 100 = 200$$
$$C(4) = 100 + 10^{4-1} = 100 + 1,000 = 1,100$$
$$C(5) = 100 + 10^{5-1} = 100 + 10,000 = 10,100$$

Obviously, Choice (D) is the correct answer.

7. **(B)** Let's first convert 588 million kilometers to meters:

$$588{,}000{,}000 \text{ kilometers} \times \frac{1{,}000 \text{ meters}}{\text{kilometer}} = 588{,}000{,}000{,}000 \text{ meters}$$

Because distance = rate × time, it follows that $t = \dfrac{d}{r}$. Therefore, the t in seconds is given by the following expression:

$$t = \frac{588{,}000{,}000{,}000}{3.00 \times 10^8} = 1{,}960 \text{ seconds}$$

Because there are 60 seconds in every minute,

$$1{,}960 \text{ sec} \times \frac{1 \text{ min}}{60 \text{ sec}} = 32.67 \text{ min}$$

This answer rounds to 33 minutes, which is Choice (B).

8. **(C)** Since the total number of responses was 26, the median response will be the mean of the 13th and 14th terms.

Terms 1–2 were 0–1 hours.

Terms 3–6 were 1–2 hours.

Terms 7–11 were 2–3 hours.

Terms 12–16 were 3–4 hours.

Therefore, the 13th and 14th terms were both 3–4 hours, which is Choice (C).

9. **(B)** Every student in each class either did or did not complete summer reading. So the total number of students enrolled in Mrs. Smith's class is 29, and the total number enrolled in Mr. Walker's class is 31. The average number of students enrolled in the two classes is:

$$\frac{29 + 31}{2} = 30$$

We can assume that each of the 14 English classes has, on average, 30 people. Therefore, the total number enrolled in English classes would be:

$$14(30) = 420$$

The correct answer is Choice (B).

10. **(C)** In Mr. Walker's class, 14 students completed summer reading and earned 5 points, accounting for $14(5) = 70$ points. The remaining 17 students received 0 points. So the total points for the class were 70. There are 31 students in the class, so the mean is:

$$70 \div 31 = 2.26$$

To find the median, list the students' point values from smallest to largest. There are 17 students who earned 0 followed by 14 students who each earned 5. The median term in a 31-term series is the 16th term. (There are 15 terms on the left of the 16th term and 15 terms on the right of the 16th term.)

The 16th value is 0, so the median is 0. The difference between the mean and the median, therefore, is:

$$2.26 - 0 = 2.26$$

Choice (C) is correct.

Problem Solving and Data Analysis Drill 2 (Calculator)

1. **(C)** First, figure out the number of words that each report would have. We know the number of words per page. So if we multiply this by the number of pages, the pages unit will cancel from the top and bottom. This will leave us with the number of words. If the student uses Times New Roman, he will write:

$$240(10) = 2,400 \text{ words}$$

However, if he uses Comic Sans, he will write only:

$$170(10) = 1,700 \text{ words}$$

We want to know how many fewer words he will write in the second situation.

$$2,400 - 1,700 = 700 \text{ words}$$

So Choice (C) is correct.

2. **(B)** The area of a rectangle is given by the formula $A = lw$, where l is length and w is width. If the length of the drawing is 4 inches, we know from dividing both sides of our area equation by the length that:

$$w = \frac{A}{l} = \frac{20}{4} = 5 \text{ inches}$$

The key tells us that each inch on the map represents 6 feet. We can multiply 4 inches by 6 feet/inch to tell us that the length is 24 feet. Similarly, we can multiply the 5-inch width by 6 feet/inch to tell us that the width is 30 feet.

Alternatively, you could have solved for actual distance by setting up a proportion. For the length, the proportion might look something like:

$$\frac{1''}{6'} = \frac{4''}{x'}$$

Cross multiplying gives you:

$$1x = (4)(6)$$

So $x = 24$.

The question wants to know the perimeter of the fence. Perimeter of a rectangle is given by the formula $P = 2l + 2w$. Plugging our dimensions into the formula tells us:

$$P = 2(24) + 2(30) = 48 + 60 = 108$$

The correct answer is Choice (B).

3. **(C)** If John's performance increased by 20%, then he performed at 120% of his original performance. 120% can be expressed in decimal form as 1.2, and we can find 120% of his original score of 60 by multiplying the two:

$$1.2(60) = 72$$

So John got a 72% on his second test. His performance then increased another 25%, so his third test performance was 125%, or 1.25, of test 2. Therefore, John's third score was:

$$1.25(72) = 90\%$$

The answer is Choice (C).

Alternatively, you could have found John's second score by finding 20% of 60 and adding that to 60:

$$\text{Test 2} = 60 + (0.2)(60) = 60 + 12 = 72$$

Then you could have found the third score by finding 25% of 72 and adding that to 72:

$$\text{Test 3} = 72 + (0.25)(72) = 72 + 18 = 90$$

4. **(B)** If you were told that you had to travel 50 miles and that your car got 10 miles/gallon, you may intuitively see that you need 5 gallons of gas. You get that by dividing 50/10. Following this logic, we can get the number of gallons of gas Linda needs to travel 240 miles by dividing 240 by 28:

$$240 \div 28 = 8.57 \text{ gallons}$$

If this doesn't quite make sense, you could also do dimensional analysis to cancel out the units you don't want. You want to cancel out miles and end up with gallons:

$$240 \text{ miles} \times \frac{1 \text{ gallon}}{28 \text{ miles}} = 8.57 \text{ gallons}$$

Linda also wants to have 1 gallon left, so she'll want to have 9.57 gallons in her tank when she starts out.

Linda already has 2 gallons in her tank, so she needs to buy $9.57 - 2 = 7.57$ gallons, or 7.6 rounded to the nearest tenth. This matches Choice (B).

5. **(A)** We can see from the negative slope that as the quantity of shake-ups increases, price decreases. Therefore, we know that the function will be decreasing, eliminating Choices (B) and (D).

We can also see that the slope isn't constant. Therefore, it can't be linear, as in Choice (C). The graph starts off fairly steep and then it becomes less steep, consistent with exponential decay, as in Choice (A).

6. **(B)** Revenue means money made. The amount of money made at any price will be that price times the number of shake-ups sold. Find the approximate revenue at all of the given prices:

Choice (A): $2.50(4,700) = $11,750

Choice (B): $3.00(4,600) = $13,800

Choice (C): $3.50(2,600) = $9,100

Choice (D): $5.00(1,300) = $6,500

Therefore, the largest revenue occurs with Choice (B).

7. **(C)** An equation of a line is given by $y = mx + b$, where m is the slope and b is the y-intercept. The formula for slope is calculated by finding the rise over the run, which is illustrated by this formula:

$$m = \frac{\Delta y}{\Delta x} = \frac{y_2 - y_1}{x_2 - x_1}$$

Plug in values for the endpoints:

$$m = \frac{5.9 - 7.8}{17 - 14} = \frac{-1.9}{3} = -0.633$$

Thus, the slope is approximately –0.6, so we can rule out Choices (B) and (D).

Next, we need to determine the y-intercept b. To do this, we can plug a particular point on the line into the equation and solve for b. For instance, (14, 7.8) appears to be a point on the line. Plugging these values into the equation gives:

$$7.8 = -0.6(14) + b$$

So $7.8 = -8.4 + b$

Adding 8.4 to both sides gives $16.2 = b$. Therefore, Choice (C) must be correct.

With this graph, you cannot find the y-intercept, b, just by looking at the where the line crosses the y-axis. On this graph, the y-axis crosses the x-axis at 14, not at 0. However, the y-intercept is, by definition, the value of y when the value of x equals 0.

8. **(A)** Students may be entirely unaware of how many hours they're sleeping. Alternatively, they may modify their answers for a variety of reasons, possibly to give the answers they suspect the researchers want to hear. This makes self-reporting a fairly inaccurate technique, as in Choice (A).

Choice (B) isn't correct because although students may get a different number of hours of sleep during the school year versus the summer, the study asks for the average number of hours. This should take into account variations due to time of year.

Choice (C) isn't correct because the researchers could simply ask more teenagers.

Choice (D) isn't correct because changing one response by a small margin shouldn't have a large result on the accuracy of the entire study.

9. **(B)** We can rule out Choice (A) because the slope is clearly positive. Use the slope formula:

$$m = \frac{\Delta y}{\Delta x} = \frac{y_2 - y_1}{x_2 - x_1}$$

Plug in the values for the approximate endpoints of the line of best fit to get:

$$m = \frac{300 - 150}{5,000 - 2,500} = \frac{150}{2,500} = \frac{3}{50}$$

The answer is Choice (B).

10. **(D)** There's no need to start the y-axis at 0 pounds, because it's impossible to weigh 0 pounds. There's no reason to start the x-axis at 0 calories, because it's not possible to average 0 calories daily. This situation matches Choice (D).

Problem Solving and Data Analysis Drill 3 (Calculator)

1. **(B)** Let's imagine the simplest version of this ratio: there are only 4 cars and 5 trucks in the parking lot. So how many total vehicles are there?

$$4 \text{ cars} + 5 \text{ trucks} = 9 \text{ vehicles}$$

So the ratio of cars to vehicles is 4 cars to 9 vehicles, Choice (B).

2. **(B)** If the highest temperature on Tuesday increased 20% from the highest temperature on Monday, then the highest temperature on Tuesday was 120%, or 1.2, of Monday's temperature. Find 120% of 70 degrees:

$$1.2(70) = 84$$

So Tuesday's high temperature was 84 degrees Fahrenheit. Wednesday's high was 25% lower than Tuesday's temperature, so it was only 75%, or 0.75, of Tuesday's temperature. Find 75% of 84 degrees:

$$0.75(84) = 63$$

The highest temperature on Wednesday was 63 degrees Fahrenheit. We want to know the difference between Monday's high temperature and Wednesday's high. The difference is given by 70 − 63 = 7, which is Choice (B).

3. **(A)** If a cook has 1.5 cups of sugar in the pantry but needs 3 cups, he needs 3 − 1.5 = 1.5 more cups from other sources. We want to convert this to teaspoons:

$$1.5 \text{ cups} \times \frac{16 \text{ tablespoons}}{\text{cup}} \times \frac{3 \text{ teaspoons}}{\text{tablespoon}} = 72 \text{ teaspoons}$$

The answer is Choice (A).

4. **(B)** Test the answer choices.

Choice (A):

$$N(1.50) = 530 + 590(1.50 - 1.95)^2 = 649.48$$

This is a fairly good estimate, so let's try another value:

$$N(0.90) = 530 + 590(0.90 - 1.95)^2 = 1,180.48$$

We can rule out Choice (A).

Choice (B):

$$N(1.50) = 1000 - 240(1.50) = 640$$

This is also a fairly good estimate, so let's try the other values:

$$N(0.90) = 1000 - 240(0.90) = 784$$
$$N(1.95) = 1000 - 240(1.95) = 532$$
$$N(2.80) = 1000 - 240(2.80) = 328$$
$$N(3.40) = 1000 - 240(3.40) = 184$$

All of these values are pretty close to the actual values, so this answer choice may be correct. However, the question asks for the best model, so we need to make sure that there are no better models.

Choice (C):

$$N(1.50) = 1,000 + 240(1.50) = 1,360$$

We can rule out Choice (C).

Choice (D):

$$N(1.50) = 780 - 360(1.50 - 0.9)^2 = 650.4$$
$$N(0.90) = 780 - 360(0.90 - 0.9)^2 = 780$$
$$N(1.95) = 780 - 360(1.95 - 0.9)^2 = 383.1$$

We can rule out Choice (D).

Choice (B) is the best model of the relationship.

5. **(B)** In Population Y, 205 of the 748 + 205 = 953 people are unemployed. Therefore, the unemployment percentage is:

$$\frac{205}{953} \times 100\% = 21.51\%$$

In both populations combined, there are a total of 112 + 205 = 317 unemployed people, and a total population of 890 + 112 + 748 + 205 = 1,955. Therefore, the unemployment rate is:

$$\frac{317}{1,955} \times 100\% = 16.21\%$$

The difference between the two unemployment rates is 21.51% − 16.21% = 5.3% , which is Choice (B).

6. **(C)** The number of people who voted in Columbus was 620,000. If this number represents only 40% of eligible voters, you can set up a proportion to solve for 100% of the number of eligible voters:

$$\frac{620,000}{40} = \frac{x}{100}$$

In the proportion, x represents the number of eligible voters in Columbus. Cross multiply to get:

$$620,000(100) = 40x$$

$$62,000,000 = 40x$$

Dividing by 40 tells you that $x = 1,550,000$, which is Choice (C).

Another way we can solve this problem is as follows. We know that 620,000 is 40% of the eligible voters, x, in Columbus. In other words, $620,000 = 0.4x$. Dividing by 0.4 gives 1,550,000, which is Choice (C).

7. **(B)** Since there are 350,000 Columbus voters who support Candidate A and 995,000 voters in the two cities combined, we know that $\frac{350,000}{995,000} = 0.352$ of the voters in the table were supporters of Candidate A from Columbus. We would expect the same proportion of the 200 randomly surveyed voters to be supporters of Candidate A from Columbus. This can be found by taking 0.352(200) = 70.4. Thus, we could expect about 70 of the randomly surveyed to fall into this category. So the correct answer is Choice (B).

8. **(B)** There are 94 total grades. To find the median term in a series with an even number of terms, you have to take the mean of the two middle terms. To find these two middle terms, first divide the total number of terms by 2. This will tell you the number of the 1st term you'll use in your average. Then add 1 to that number to find the number of the 2nd term you'll use in your average.

If we listed all 94 grades starting with the lowest grades, the F's, and ending with the highest grades, the A's, the median terms would be the average of the $\frac{94}{2} = 47$th term and the $\frac{94}{2} + 1 = 48$th term.

F's take us through the first 5 terms.

D's take us through 10 more, to the 15th term.

C's take us through another 22, to the 15 + 22 = 37th term.

B's take us through another 28 to the 37 + 28 = 65th term. The 47th and 48th terms will then both be B's, so the median grade is a B, which is Choice (B).

9. **(D)** Standard deviation is lowest when range is lowest because it means that more values are centered near the mean. Because no one received an F on project 2, the range was only between an A and a D, with only two people receiving D's. Because this project

has a rather small range, it will have a rather small standard deviation. In all of the other assignments, at least one student earned an A and at least one earned an F, so the ranges will be higher for all other answer choices. Thus, Choice (D) is the best choice.

Note: Standard deviation may or may not be a topic tested on the PSAT. It is definitely something that could be on the SAT. So this problem was included to prepare you.

10. **(C)** An average (in other words, a mean) is given by the following expression:

$$\text{Mean} = \frac{\text{Sum}}{n}$$

In the expression, "sum" is the total of the terms you're averaging and n is the number of terms you're averaging. In order to calculate the minimum number of reviews needed to raise the mean to a 3.0, we'll need to know the sum of the current ratings. Plugging the numbers into the equation gives:

$$2.3 = \frac{\text{Sum}}{10}$$

Therefore, the sum of the current ratings is 2.3(10) = 23.

In order to raise the average with the minimum number of reviews, the reviews need to all be as high as possible, so they must all be 5-star reviews.

Let's test our answer choices. When plugging in answer choices, start with one of the middle answers since answers tend to be arranged from smallest to largest or from largest to smallest.

Choice (B):

If the product gets 3 new 5-star reviews, this will add 3(5) = 15 to our current sum. This will also add 3 to our current n:

$$\text{Mean} = \frac{23+15}{10+3} = \frac{38}{13} = 2.92$$

The mean is not high enough yet, so we need more reviews.

Choice (C):

If the product gets 4 new 5 star reviews, this will add 4(5) = 20 to our current sum and 4 to our current n:

$$\text{Mean} = \frac{23+20}{10+4} = \frac{43}{14} = 3.07$$

This mean is higher than our desired mean, so 4 is the minimum number of reviews needed, Choice (C).

Alternatively, you could have solved this algebraically. Adding x more 5-star reviews will add $5x$ to the sum and x to n, the total number of reviews. Therefore, the mean can be represented with the following equation:

$$\text{Mean} = \frac{23+5x}{10+x}$$

Since we know we want the mean to be 3.0, we can set the right side of our equation equal to 3.0:

$$3.0 = \frac{23+5x}{10+x}$$

Let's get rid of the denominator by multiplying both sides by $(10 + x)$:

$$30 + 3.0x = 23 + 5x$$

Combine like terms by subtracting $3.0x$ and 23 from both sides:

$$7 = 2.0x$$

Dividing both sides by 2.0 tells you that the minimum number of new reviews needed is 3.5. Recall that we want the minimum number of reviews needed to raise the average to a 3.0. Since 3 reviews would not be enough and a person can't give 0.5 of a review, we must round up to the nearest integer, 4. Therefore, to raise the average to a 3.0, you need 4 new reviews.

Problem Solving and Data Analysis Drill (No Calculator)

1. **(C)** When $x = 8$, $y = 12$. We want to know the proportionality constant. We can do this by plugging the values of x and y into the equation and solving for k:

$$12 = 8k$$

Dividing by 8 tells us that $k = \dfrac{12}{8}$. Reducing this fraction gives Choice (C) as the answer, $k = \dfrac{3}{2}$.

2. **(B)** Let's imagine the simplest version of this and say that there are two people failing. Since for every two failing, three have C's and D's, that means that three in this class do have C's and D's. We also know that for every one person who has a C or a D, two people have A's and B's. Since three have C's and D's, $3(2) = 6$ have A's and B's.

   Therefore, the ratio of those failing to those with A's and B's is 2 to 6, or 1 to 3, which is Choice (B).

3. **(B)** Think of this as 3 separate charges. Let's call x the cost of the food. That's the first charge. Then there's a tip charge that is 15% of the cost of food. The 15% tip charge can be expressed as $0.15x$ since x is the cost of food. Finally, there's a $5 flat fee delivery charge that doesn't depend on the cost of the food. Therefore, the cost can be represented by:

$$C = x + 0.15x + 5$$

Combining like terms gives:

$$C = 1.15x + 5$$

Choice (B) is the correct answer.

4. **(A)** The graph has a positive slope everywhere, so the variables are positively correlated. You can tell that as the year increases from 2000 to 2010, the price increases from about $16 to about $43. Choice (A) is the correct answer.

5. **(B)** As you can see from the graph, the trend is a slight decrease in slope each year (while remaining positive). Thus, we would expect ticket prices to rise again but only slightly. You can use the slope from the previous year to get an idea of an approximate increase in the next few years. It looks like from 2009 to 2010, the price increased from $42 to $43, so the price increased by $1. If it continues to increase about $1 for the next 4 years until 2014, the price will go up a total of $4, from $43 to $47, which is Choice (B).

6. **(B)** As time goes by, the exchange rate increases drastically. In 2000, every unit of Currency Y was equal to 2.3 units of Currency X. However in 2004, 1 unit of Currency Y was equal to 237.83 units of Currency X. That means that Currency Y is becoming more

valuable with respect to Currency X because Currency Y is becoming worth more than Currency X. This matches Choice (B).

7. **(B)** Go through each possibility.

Option I: Sam's height percentile actually decreased between ages 12 and 18, so it's extremely unlikely that he experienced exponential growth. By ruling this out, we can eliminate Choices (A) and (D).

Option II: When Sam was less than 5 years old, his height percentile ranged between about the 42nd percentile and the 50th percentile. Between the ages of 10 and 15, he ranged between the 54th and 60th percentile. Therefore, he was taller than more men during these later years, making this statement true.

Option III: We can't say for sure that Sam's height changed between these years, although it's probable. Percentiles measure only your status compared to others. We know only that Sam's height compared to others changed, not that his absolute height changed.

Therefore, the answer is Choice (B).

8. **(C)** A 95% confidence interval means that if the study is done at random many times, the average height statistically should fall between these two heights 95% of the time. In other words, Choice (C) is correct. It is very likely that an average child will fall between these two heights.

9. **(C)** If prices are discounted by $\frac{2}{3}$, that means you're still paying $\frac{1}{3}$ of the original price. If you also have a coupon that discounts 20%, you're still paying 80% of that price. Since the sale price is $\frac{1}{3}$ of the original price, the price with the coupon is 80% of $\frac{1}{3}$ of the original price. The fraction $\frac{4}{5}$ (or $\frac{8}{10}$ if that makes more sense to you) can represent 80%. So we can find 80% of $\frac{1}{3}$:

$$\left(\frac{4}{5}\right)\left(\frac{1}{3}\right) = \frac{4}{15}$$

Choice (C) is the answer.

10. **(C)** A random sample is useful if it is truly random and if it is truly representative of the people being studied.

Choice (C) is correct because it polls a randomly selected group and takes into account only registered voters, which is what you would want to sample if you wanted to predict the results of an election.

Choice (A) is incorrect because it polls only people who go to that grocery store and likely excludes voters who shop elsewhere, are too elderly to shop, or don't have money to spend. It also likely samples a significant number of nonregistered voters who won't be counted in the election.

Choice (B) is incorrect because it polls only people in certain geographical locations and therefore likely people of only certain socioeconomic statuses as well.

Choice (D) is incorrect because it polls only those who have access to the Internet and actually take the time to complete the survey.

Passport to Advanced Math Drill 1 (Calculator)

1. **(A)** A cubic function has a variable raised to the third degree or, in terms of geometry, has 3 dimensions. Therefore, we need a shape that is 3-dimensional. This rules out Choices (B) and (C).

   Choice (D) may be tempting because a cube is 3-dimensional. However, surface area is actually only 2 dimensions, so this wouldn't be a cubic function.

   Choice (A) is correct because volume of a sphere varies proportionally to the cube of its radius. Volume is always in 3 dimensions, hence, the reason its units are always in cubic units.

   Alternatively, you could have written out all of the relationships depicted in the answer choices.

   The volume of a sphere is given by the formula $V = \frac{4}{3}\pi r^3$, which is a cubic function since the radius variable has degree 3. So Choice (A) is correct.

   The formula for a circle's circumference is $C = 2\pi r = \pi d$, where d represents diameter. This is a linear relationship between d and C, making Choice (B) incorrect.

   A triangle's area is $A = \frac{1}{2}bh$. This isn't a cubic function, so Choice (C) can't be correct.

   A cube's surface area is given by the formula $SA = 6x^2$, where x represents the length of each side of the cube. Again, this isn't a cubic function since the degree of x is only 2, so Choice (D) is incorrect.

2. **(A)** From all of the answer choices, we can see that the whole denominator cancels out somehow. Let's use polynomial long division to figure out an equivalent expression for our original fraction. Before we use long division, let's first combine like terms in the numerator so that the long division isn't as complicated:

$$a^3 - b^3 + 2a^2b - 2ab^2 + ab^2 - ba^2 = a^3 - b^3 + a^2b - ab^2$$

Now do polynomial long division:

$$
\begin{array}{r}
a+b \\
a^2-b^2 \overline{\smash{\big)}\, a^3 - b^3 + a^2b - ab^2} \\
-\underline{\left(a^3 \qquad -ab^2 \right)} \\
-b^3 + a^2b \\
-\underline{\left(-b^3 + a^2b \right)} \\
0
\end{array}
$$

Thus, our original fraction is equal to $a + b$, which is Choice (A).

Alternatively, you could have simplified directly by factoring. Since $a^3 - b^3 = (a - b)(a^2 + ab + b^2)$, we can rewrite the numerator:

$$a^3 - b^3 + 2a^2b - 2ab^2 + ab^2 - ba^2 = a^3 - b^3 + a^2b - ab^2 = (a - b)(a^2 + ab + b^2) + a^2b - ab^2$$

Notice that $a^2b - ab^2 = ab(a - b)$, so our numerator becomes:

$$(a - b)(a^2 + ab + b^2) + a^2b - ab^2 = (a - b)(a^2 + ab + b^2) + ab(a - b) =$$
$$(a - b)(a^2 + ab + b^2 + ab) = (a - b)(a^2 + 2ab + b^2) = (a - b)(a + b)^2$$

Thus, our original fraction can be rewritten as $\frac{(a-b)(a+b)^2}{a^2-b^2}$. Since our denominator is a difference of squares, it can be rewritten as $a^2 - b^2 = (a+b)(a-b)$.

Thus, our entire expression becomes:

$$\frac{(a-b)(a+b)^2}{a^2-b^2} = \frac{(a-b)(a+b)^2}{(a-b)(a+b)} = a+b$$

Choice (A) is correct.

3. **(C)** We can solve for all possible values of m^2 by subtracting $2m^7$ from both sides, factoring the left side, and setting the left side equal to 0:

$$-5m^5 + 3m^3 - 2m^7 = 0$$

First, factor out $-m^3$:

$$-m^3(5m^2 - 3 + 2m^4) = 0$$

Rearrange the polynomial inside the parentheses so that the terms are decreasing in degree for easier factoring:

$$-m^3(2m^4 + 5m^2 - 3) = 0.$$

Next factor the inside:

$$-m^3(2m^4 + 5m^2 - 3) = -m^3(m^2 + 3)(2m^2 - 1) = 0$$

Now set each factor equal to 0 to solve for possible values of m^2:

$$-m^3 = 0$$

Dividing both sides by $-m$ tells you that $m^2 = 0$, so this is one possible value.

$$m^2 + 3 = 0$$

Subtracting 3 from both sides gives $m^2 = -3$. However, you can't square a number and get a negative, so this solution is extraneous.

$$2m^2 - 1 = 0$$

Add 1 to both sides and divide by 2:

$$m^2 = \frac{1}{2}$$

This is another possible value. Therefore, the two possible values of m^2 are 0 and 0.5. Thus, their sum is 0.5, which is Choice (C).

4. **(D)** First, multiply by 8 to avoid dealing with fractions:

$$4x^2 + 2x - 1 = 0$$

Next, use the quadratic formula:

$$x = \frac{-b \pm \sqrt{b^2 - 4ac}}{2a} = \frac{-2 \pm \sqrt{2^2 - 4(4)(-1)}}{2(4)} = \frac{-2 \pm \sqrt{4+16}}{8} = \frac{-2 \pm \sqrt{20}}{8} = -\frac{2}{8} \pm \frac{2\sqrt{5}}{8} = -\frac{1}{4} \pm \frac{\sqrt{5}}{4}$$

This still doesn't match any of the answer choices. All of the answer choices have a fraction factored out of them. We can factor $\frac{1}{4}$ out of our expression to get the answer:

$$\frac{1}{4}\left(-1 \pm \sqrt{5}\right)$$

Choice (D) is correct.

5. **(A)** Get rid of the square root by squaring both sides. Squaring the right side simply gets rid of the square root, but be careful to FOIL the left side:

$$a^2 + 8a + 16 = a^2 - 2$$

Subtract a^2 from both sides:

$$8a + 16 = -2$$

Next, subtract 16 from both sides:

$$8a = -18$$

Solve for a by dividing by 8:

$$a = -\frac{18}{8} = -\frac{9}{4}$$

This is Choice (A).

Note that squaring equations can lead to extraneous answers. In this case, we don't get any extraneous solutions. However, you should get in the habit of checking your solutions by plugging them back into the original equation to ensure that your solution is truly a solution to the original.

6. **(C)** The zeros of a factored polynomial can be found by setting each distinct factor equal to 0 and solving for x. Here there are only 2 distinct factors, $(x-3)$ and $(x+7)$. So there will only be 2, Choice (C).

$$x - 3 = 0$$
$$x = 3$$
$$x + 7 = 0$$
$$x = -7$$

Note: Although $x - 3$ occurs twice as a factor, this still corresponds to only one zero. We say that 3 is a zero of multiplicity 2 since its corresponding factor occurs twice.

7. **(C)** This function is a parabola. It opens upward because the coefficient in front of x^2 is positive. (In this case, the coefficient of x^2 is 1.) The function has a y-intercept of 2. Therefore, the range is $[2, \infty)$. In order for the range to include negative numbers, the new function either needs to open downward or have a negative y-intercept. In order for it to open downward, you would multiply the right side by a negative number, but this isn't a choice.

The only choice that works is subtracting 3, which would make the y-intercept negative. The y-intercept of the new function would be -1 because $2 - 3 = -1$. The range of the new function would be expanded to $[-1, \infty)$.

8. **(A)** This equation is probably a bit different from the equations of the parabolas that you're used to seeing. To get it into standard form, we need to solve for x instead of the y as we usually do:

$$\frac{1}{17}(y-4)^2 - 2 = x$$

This is a parabola rotated 90 degrees clockwise. The standard form can be represented by the equation:

$$x = a(y - k)^2 + h$$

Therefore, in this problem, $k = 4$ and $h = -2$. So (h, k) is $(-2, 4)$, as shown in Choice (A). Parabola problems like this may not be on the PSAT, but it is included here so that you will be as prepared as possible.

9. **(A)** The relationship is easiest to see if you solve for M first. First, square both sides:

$$\left(v_{rms}\right)^2 = \frac{3RT}{M}$$

Multiply both sides by M to get M out of the denominator:

$$M(v_{rms})^2 = 3RT$$

Now isolate M:

$$M = \frac{3RT}{\left(v_{rms}\right)^2}$$

We can now consider how we can lower M. First, M is directly proportional to T. So decreasing T will decrease M.

Further, M is inversely proportional to the square of v_{rms}. So increasing v_{rms} will decrease M because you will be dividing by a larger number. Therefore, Choice (A) is correct.

10. **(A)** None of the answer choices has a percentage in it, so convert the percentage to a decimal by dividing by 100:

$$x\% = \frac{x}{100} \text{ and } y\% = \frac{y}{100}$$

Suppose P is the initial amount deposited into each portfolio. If portfolio A grows at a rate of $x\%$ yearly, the value after 1 year will be given by the expression:

$$P + \frac{x}{100}P = \left(1 + \frac{x}{100}\right)P.$$

The following year, the amount of money in portfolio A again increases by $x\%$. Therefore, the value after the second year will be given by the following expression:

$$\left(1 + \frac{x}{100}\right)\left[\left(1 + \frac{x}{100}\right)P\right] = \left(1 + \frac{x}{100}\right)\left(1 + \frac{x}{100}\right)P \text{ or } \left(1 + \frac{x}{100}\right)^2 P$$

The third year, the interest will be compounded on the previous value. Therefore, the value will be:

$$\left(1 + \frac{x}{100}\right)^2\left(1 + \frac{x}{100}\right)P \text{ or } \left(1 + \frac{x}{100}\right)^3 P$$

The value after n years is given by:

$$\left(1 + \frac{x}{100}\right)^n P$$

So after 10 years, the value of portfolio A will be $\left(1 + \frac{x}{100}\right)^{10} P$.

Repeat the thought process for portfolio B to arrive at the conclusion that the value of portfolio B after 10 years will be

$$\left(1 + \frac{y}{100}\right)^{10} P$$

since both portfolio A and B start out with the same amount initially, P. Therefore, the ratio of the value of portfolio A to the value of portfolio B is:

$$\frac{\left(1+\frac{x}{100}\right)^{10}P}{\left(1+\frac{y}{100}\right)^{10}P} \text{ or } \left(\frac{1+\frac{x}{100}}{1+\frac{y}{100}}\right)^{10}$$

This matches Choice (A).

Passport to Advanced Math Drill 2 (Calculator)

1. **(C)** We will use the formula $d = rt$, where d is distance, r is rate, and t is time. Let's define the car's initial position, s, as $s = 0$ and the truck's initial position as $s = 180$.

   The car's position at time t will be its initial position (0) plus the distance it has traveled in that time. We are told that the car's rate r is x, so the distance the car travels in time t is xt. Since the car starts at an initial position of 0, its position at time t will be expressed as $s = xt + 0 = xt$.

   The truck starts at position $s = 180$ and travels toward the 0 position. So the truck's position at time t will be expressed as 180 minus the distance it has traveled in time t. Its speed is twice the speed of the car, or $2x$. So the truck's position at time t will be expressed as $s = 180 - 2xt$.

   They meet where their positions are equal. So set the two equations equal to one another to solve for x:

   $$xt = 180 - 2xt$$

   We know that the vehicles meet after 3 hours, so we can plug in 3 for t:

   $$3x = 180 - 6x$$

   Adding $6x$ to both sides gives:

   $$9x = 180$$

   Dividing both sides by 9 tells results in $x = 20$.

   However, before selecting Choice (A), make sure to finish the problem.

   The question asks you what speed the truck is going. The truck has a speed of $2x$. So its speed is $2(20) = 40$, which is Choice (C).

2. **(A)** This problem mentions the "mean of the bases." Notice that $\frac{B_1 + B_2}{2}$, the first part of the area formula, is another way of saying the mean of the bases. Since the mean of the bases is twice the height, we can replace this part of the formula with $2H$:

   $$A = \frac{B_1 + B_2}{2} H = 2H \times H = 2H^2$$

   The area is 72, so plug this in for A and solve for H:

   $$72 = 2H^2$$

   Divide by 2:

   $$36 = H^2$$

   Take the square root of both sides to arrive at the answer $6 = H$, which is Choice (A).

3. **(C)** If the negative exponent is in the numerator, it can send whatever is being raised to that exponent to the denominator, but be careful here. In both terms, only the m is being raised to the negative exponents, so the constants stay in the numerator:

$$2m^{-2} - 4m^{-3} = \frac{2}{m^2} - \frac{4}{m^3}$$

However, this doesn't match an answer choice. Based on the answer choices, it looks like we may need to add the two fractions together to get just one fraction overall. To add the two fractions, we need a common denominator. If you multiplied the first fraction by $\frac{m}{m}$, both terms would have a denominator of m^3:

$$\frac{2}{m^2} - \frac{4}{m^3} = \frac{2m}{m^3} - \frac{4}{m^3}$$

Now that they have a common denominator, you can add the two fractions together:

$$\frac{2m}{m^3} - \frac{4}{m^3} = \frac{2m-4}{m^3}$$

Choice (C) is correct.

4. **(A)** Since there's nothing to distribute, you can just drop the parentheses and combine like terms:

$$2y^4 + 3x^6 + 5x^6 + 3y^4 = 5y^4 + 8x^6$$

The correct answer is Choice (A).

5. **(D)** Look at the answer choices. All of the choices indicate that at least one $(x-3)$ factor cancels out, so divide the numerator by $(x-3)$:

$$
\begin{array}{r}
2x-6 \\
x-3 \overline{\smash{\big)}\, 2x^2 - 12x + 18} \\
\underline{-\left(2x^2 - 6x\right)} \\
-6x + 18 \\
\underline{-(-6x + 18)} \\
0
\end{array}
$$

So the expression can be rewritten as:

$$\frac{(x-3)(2x-6)}{3(x-3)^3}$$

You can cancel an $(x-3)$ term from the top and bottom:

$$\frac{(2x-6)}{3(x-3)^2}$$

The number 2 can be factored out of the numerator:

$$\frac{2(x-3)}{3(x-3)^2}$$

Another $(x-3)$ term cancels:

$$\frac{2}{3(x-3)}$$

This is Choice (D).

Alternatively, you could have factored the numerator directly:

$$2x^2 - 12x + 18 = 2(x^2 - 6x + 9) = 2(x-3)^2$$

Then you could have canceled out the $(x-3)^2$ term from the denominator.

6. **(A)** To find the solutions, subtract $15x$ and 18 from both sides to get everything on the left side:

$$21x^2 - 15x - 18 = 0$$

Next, factor out a 3 to make the quadratic equation a bit simpler:

$$3(7x^2 - 5x - 6) = 0$$

Divide both sides by 3:

$$7x^2 - 5x - 6 = 0$$

Notice that the answer choices look similar in structure to the quadratic formula $x = \dfrac{-b \pm \sqrt{b^2 - 4ac}}{2a}$. This suggests that we try to factor our quadratic equation using the quadratic formula. Letting $a = 7$, $b = -5$, and $c = -6$ in the quadratic formula above, we get Choice (A).

7. **(B)** Find where the supply and demand are equivalent by setting the two equations equal to one another and solving for p:

$$3p + 6p^2 = 156 - 12p$$

Subtract 156 and add $12p$ to both sides:

$$15p + 6p^2 - 156 = 0$$

Rearrange the equation to get it in $ax^2 + bx + c$ form while simultaneously factoring out a 3:

$$3(2p^2 + 5p - 52) = 0$$

Divide both sides by 3:

$$2p^2 + 5p - 52 = 0$$

Factor to get:

$$(2p + 13)(p - 4) = 0$$

Set each factor equal to 0 and solve for p to get the two possible values of p:

$$2p + 13 = 0 \text{ so } p = -\frac{13}{2}$$

$$p - 4 = 0 \text{ so } p = 4$$

In this situation, p must be positive since it represents the price of the item, which can't be negative. Therefore, p equals only 4, Choice (B).

Alternatively, if you didn't recognize that the quadratic equation could be factored, you could have used the quadratic formula:

$$x = \frac{-5 \pm \sqrt{5^2 - 4(2)(-52)}}{2(2)} = \frac{-5 \pm \sqrt{441}}{4} = \frac{-5 \pm 21}{4}$$

$$x = 4 \text{ or } x = -\frac{13}{2}$$

8. **(A)** Look at each option to see whether it is an answer.

Option I: $x = c$ is a vertical line at c. The line will cross the y-axis only if $c = 0$. Since we are told that c is a nonzero constant, this equation does not have a y-intercept.

Option II: $y = -c$ is a horizontal line at the $-c$ value. The line will cross the y-axis at $-c$. This option, therefore, must have a y-intercept.

Option III: $y = cx$ is a line with slope c. Note that when $x = 0$, $y = c(0) = 0$. So the line has a y-intercept at 0.

Thus, only option I is true, which is Choice (A).

9. **(B)** The function has zeros at 2, 3, and 6. We can use this to find the factors of the function.

If $x = 2$, $x - 2 = 0$. So $(x - 2)$ is a factor.

If $x = 3$, $x - 3 = 0$. So $(x - 3)$ is a factor.

If $x = 6$, $x - 6 = 0$. So $(x - 6)$ is a factor.

Therefore, the function can be rewritten as $y = (x - 2)(x - 3)(x - 6)$. All of the answer choices are in their unfactored forms, so use FOIL. Start by using FOIL with the first two factors:

$$y = (x^2 - 5x + 6)(x - 6)$$

Then multiply the remaining factors:

$$y = x^3 - 11x^2 + 36x - 36$$

This matches Choice (B).

10. **(C)** First, let's identify all of the givens.

Since we're not provided a value for P, we will leave it as is in the formula.

We're also given that the interest is compounded once every 12 months. In other words, it's compounded once every year. Since n is the number of times the investment is compounded yearly, $n = 1$.

We're also told that the investment rate is 5%. Because r is the interest rate expressed as a decimal, $r = \frac{5}{100} = 0.05$.

We want to know A after 1 year, so $t = 1$.

Now plug everything into the equation:

$$A = P\left(1 + \frac{0.05}{1}\right)^{(1)(1)} = P(1.05) = 1.05P$$

Choice (C) is the answer.

Passport to Advanced Math Drill 3 (Calculator)

1. **(B)** The amount after one half-life is $\frac{1}{2}x$. After the second half-life, half of this new amount decays, and we're left with:

$$\frac{1}{2}\left(\frac{1}{2}x\right) = \frac{1}{4}x = \left(\frac{1}{2^2}\right)x$$

After the third half-life, half of that amount left decays. We now have left:

$$\frac{1}{2}\left(\frac{1}{4}x\right) = \frac{1}{8}x = \left(\frac{1}{2^3}\right)x$$

We can start to see a pattern: each time a half-life passes, we multiply the amount we previously had by $\frac{1}{2}$. So after n half-lives, $A = \left(\frac{1}{2^n}\right)x$ remains, or $A = \frac{x}{2^n}$. This matches Choice (B).

2. **(A)** $\sqrt[5]{32} = 2$

So go ahead and bring a 2 outside of the radical before dealing with the variables:

$$\sqrt[5]{32x^8y^{11}} = 2\sqrt[5]{x^8y^{11}}$$

Let's deal with the x-term under the root next. Notice the following:

$$\sqrt[5]{x^8} = \sqrt[5]{x^5x^3} = \sqrt[5]{x^5}\sqrt[5]{x^3} = x\sqrt[5]{x^3}$$

Similarly, we can rewrite the y-term under the root as follows:

$$\sqrt[5]{y^{11}} = \sqrt[5]{y^5y^5y} = \sqrt[5]{y^5}\sqrt[5]{y^5}\sqrt[5]{y} = y \cdot y\sqrt[5]{y} = y^2\sqrt[5]{y}$$

Thus, the entire expression can be rewritten as:

$$\sqrt[5]{32x^8y^{11}} = 2\sqrt[5]{x^8y^{11}} = 2\sqrt[5]{x^8}\sqrt[5]{y^{11}} = 2xy^2\sqrt[5]{x^3y}$$

This is Choice (A).

3. **(D)** All of the answer choices are a single fraction. So first find a common denominator and add the two fractions. The least common denominator is $6x$. Multiply the first fraction by $\frac{3}{3}$ and the second by $\frac{2}{2}$:

$$\frac{3}{6x} + \frac{2}{6x} = \frac{5}{6x}$$

We can rule Choice (C) out because it's our answer squared, so it will not equal our answer.

The rest of the answers are being raised to the $\frac{1}{2}$ power, which is equivalent to taking the square root. In order to find out what should be inside the parentheses, we must work backward by doing the opposite to our function. Because the answer choices take the square root of an expression, we must square our expression to find what should go inside the parentheses:

$$\left(\frac{5}{6x}\right)^2 = \frac{5^2}{(6x)^2} = \frac{25}{36x^2}$$

Therefore, the answer is Choice (D).

Alternatively, we could have taken the square root of Choices (A), (B), and (D) to see which one is equivalent to $\frac{5}{6x}$:

$$\left(\frac{25}{6x^2}\right)^{\frac{1}{2}} = \frac{\sqrt{25}}{\sqrt{6x^2}} = \frac{5}{\sqrt{6}x}$$

So Choice (A) is incorrect.

$$\left(\frac{4}{25x^2}\right)^{\frac{1}{2}} = \frac{\sqrt{4}}{\sqrt{25x^2}} = \frac{2}{5x}$$

So Choice (B) is wrong.

$$\left(\frac{25}{36x^2}\right)^{\frac{1}{2}} = \frac{\sqrt{25}}{\sqrt{36x^2}} = \frac{5}{6x}$$

This matches the expression we obtained, so Choice (D) is correct.

4. **(B)** In their structure, the answer choices all look like the quadratic formula. So subtract b from both sides:

$$x^2 + ax - b = 0$$

Now you can use the quadratic formula:

$$x = \frac{-b \pm \sqrt{b^2 - 4ac}}{2a}$$

We have to be careful, though. Our equation has a and b coefficients, but they don't match up exactly with the a and b given in the quadratic formula. In the quadratic formula, a is the coefficient in front of the x^2-term, b corresponds to the coefficient in front of the x-term, and c represents the constant. In our case, however, the coefficient in front of the x^2-term is 1, the coefficient of the x-term is a, and the constant is b. Keep this in mind while using the quadratic formula to get:

$$x = \frac{-a \pm \sqrt{a^2 - 4(1)(-b)}}{2(1)} = \frac{-a \pm \sqrt{a^2 + 4b}}{2}$$

This doesn't match any of the answer choices, so we need to simplify further. All of the answer choices have the leading term over 2, so let's divide this into two fractions:

$$\frac{-a \pm \sqrt{a^2 + 4b}}{2} = -\frac{a}{2} \pm \frac{\sqrt{a^2 + 4b}}{2}$$

From the leading term, you can narrow it down to Choices (A), (B), and (D). It looks like the answer choices have pulled the denominator of the second term into the square root. Because 2 equals $\sqrt{4}$, we can change the denominator to $\sqrt{4}$:

$$-\frac{a}{2} \pm \frac{\sqrt{a^2 + 4b}}{2} = -\frac{a}{2} \pm \frac{\sqrt{a^2 + 4b}}{\sqrt{4}} = -\frac{a}{2} \pm \sqrt{\frac{a^2 + 4b}{4}}$$

In all of the answer choices, the fraction inside the square root appears to be broken up, so do that:

$$-\frac{a}{2} \pm \sqrt{\frac{a^2 + 4b}{4}} = -\frac{a}{2} \pm \sqrt{\frac{a^2}{4} + \frac{4b}{4}} = -\frac{a}{2} \pm \sqrt{\frac{a^2}{4} + b}$$

Reordering what's inside the root gives you Choice (B).

5. **(D)** One easy way to solve this problem is to use FOIL on the answer choices and see which matches the original:

Choice (A):

$$3(2x + y)^2 = 3[(2x + y)(2x + y)] = 3(4x^2 + 4xy + y^2) = 12x^2 + 12xy + 3y^2$$

This does not match our expression, so we can rule out this choice.

Choice (B):

$$(3x + y)(x + 3y) = 3x^2 + 10xy + 3y^2$$

This does not match the original.

Choice (C):

$$(3x + 3y)(2x + 2y) = 6x^2 + 12xy + 6y^2$$

This does not quite match the original.

Choice (D):

$$3(x + 2y)(2x + y) = 3(2x^2 + 5xy + 2y^2) = 6x^2 + 15xy + 6y^2$$

This matches the original expression, so the answer is Choice (D).

Another way to solve the problem is to factor. Since each term is divisible by 3, we can factor out a 3 to get:

$$3(2x^2 + 5xy + 2y^2)$$

Next we factor the expression inside the parenthesis as follows:

$$3(2x + y)(x + 2y)$$

This matches Choice (D).

6. **(A)** Look at the answer choices. There are only three possible x-values in the answer choices (13, 3, and −3), so it's probably easiest to just plug in these three values for x in our original equation to see which ones work:

$$13 - 6 = \sqrt{75 - 2(13)}$$

$$7 = \sqrt{49}$$

The square root of 49 is 7, so 13 works.

$$-3 - 6 = \sqrt{75 - 2(-3)}$$

$$-9 = \sqrt{81}$$

Square roots always give nonnegative answers, so this one doesn't work.

$$3 - 6 = \sqrt{75 - 2(3)}$$

$$-3 = \sqrt{69}$$

Only 13 works, so the answer is Choice (A).

You could also solve this directly by squaring both sides of the equation:

$$(x - 6)^2 = \left(\sqrt{75 - 2x}\right)^2$$

Squaring gives:

$$x^2 - 12x + 36 = 75 - 2x$$

This is a quadratic equation. So we move everything over to one side, combine like terms, and factor:

$$x^2 - 10x - 39 = 0$$

Factoring gives:

$$(x - 13)(x + 3) = 0$$

So $x = 13$ or $x = -3$. Since we initially squared our equation, we have to check our answers since this procedure can lead to extraneous answers. Indeed, only $x = 13$ works. So 13 is the only solution to the equation.

7. **(B)** Functions intersect the x-axis at their zeros. Zeros can be found by setting the function equal to 0 and either factoring or using the quadratic formula to solve for possible values of x.

The polynomial can be factored to $(4x-5)(2x-3) = 0$. Set each factor equal to 0 and solve for x:

$$4x-5 = 0$$

Adding 5 to both sides and then dividing by 4 gives you $x = \dfrac{5}{4}$.

$$2x-3 = 0$$

Adding 3 to both sides then dividing by 2 gives you $x = \dfrac{3}{2}$.

Choice (B) is the answer.

Alternatively, you could have used the quadratic formula:

$$x = \frac{-b \pm \sqrt{b^2 - 4ac}}{2a} = \frac{22 \pm \sqrt{(-22)^2 - 4(8)(15)}}{2(8)} = \frac{22 \pm \sqrt{4}}{16} = \frac{22 \pm 2}{16}$$

$$x = \frac{24}{16} = \frac{3}{2} \ \text{ or } \ x = \frac{20}{16} = \frac{5}{4}$$

8. **(D)** We are told that x is greater than 1, so the function will always be positive regardless of n. We are also told that n is an even integer, so this narrows down the answer to 2 or -2. In order for the function to increase most rapidly, you want the exponent n to be the largest even number possible, which is Choice (D).

9. **(A)** If the dispersion of population x increases, the standard deviation of x increases. If the dispersion of population y increases, the standard deviation of y increases. Therefore, you'd be holding the numerator constant while increasing the denominator. Therefore, the correlation coefficient would decrease, which is Choice (A).

10. **(C)** Multiplying a function by -1 will flip it about the x-axis. The new function will still cross the x-axis the same number of times at the same values of x as the original function. So the zeros will not change. If $f(x)$ has 5 zeros, $-f(x)$ will also have 5 zeros.

Consider this simpler function to see how multiplying it by -1 would affect its graph.

The graph of $y = x^2 - 5$ is shown:

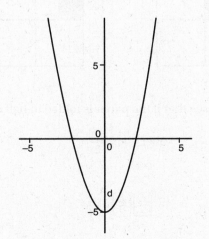

If the function is multiplied by –1 on the right-hand side, it will give the function $y = -x^2 + 5$, which is shown:

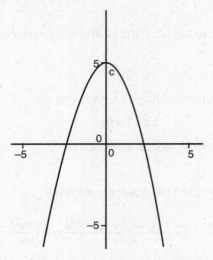

So the functions have the same zeros even though they are mirror images of one another.

Passport to Advanced Math Drill 1 (No Calculator)

1. **(B)**

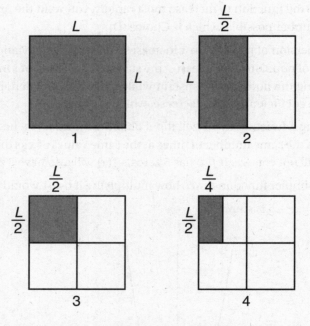

From the drawings, we can see that if the paper is folded in half once, the area is:

$$A = L\left(\frac{L}{2}\right) = \frac{L^2}{2}$$

After the second fold:

$$A = \left(\frac{L}{2}\right)\left(\frac{L}{2}\right) = \frac{L^2}{4}$$

After the third fold:

$$A = \left(\frac{L}{4}\right)\left(\frac{L}{2}\right) = \frac{L^2}{8}$$

We can see that each time, the numerator stays the same while the denominator is multiplied by 2. Therefore, the numerator will always be L^2, while the denominator will be 2^n. Therefore, area can be represented by:

$$A = \frac{L^2}{2^n}$$

Choice (B) is the correct answer.

Alternatively, you could have plugged the values for the areas for each fold into the answer choices to see that only Choice (B) works.

2. **(D)** Numbers with negative exponents in the numerator can be rewritten with a positive exponent by moving that number to the denominator (i.e., $a^{-k} = \frac{1}{a^k}$). Fractional exponents are the same as roots. So the entire expression can be rewritten as:

$$\frac{\sqrt[3]{64}}{\sqrt[4]{81}} = \frac{4}{3}$$

The answer is Choice (D).

3. **(A)** Let's use polynomial long division to divide the numerator by the denominator:

$$
\begin{array}{r}
3x^2 - 4x + 3 \\
x+2 \overline{)3x^3 + 2x^2 - 5x + 6} \\
-\left(3x^3 + 6x^2\right) \\
\hline
-4x^2 - 5x + 6 \\
-\left(-4x^2 - 8x\right) \\
\hline
3x + 6 \\
-(3x + 6) \\
\hline
0
\end{array}
$$

Therefore, $(3x^3 + 2x^2 - 5x + 6) \div (x + 2) = 3x^2 - 4x + 3$, which is Choice (A).

You could also use synthetic division to solve this problem. Alternatively, if you were unsure of how to divide polynomials, you could have multiplied the answer choices by $x + 2$ to see which choice equaled the numerator.

4. **(B)** Recall that the quadratic formula tells us that solutions to the quadratic equation $ax^2 + bx + c = 0$ are $x = \frac{-b \pm \sqrt{b^2 - 4ac}}{2a}$. Thus, for a quadratic function to only have real solutions, we need $\frac{-b \pm \sqrt{b^2 - 4ac}}{2a}$ to be real numbers. This means that the expression under the square root, $b^2 - 4ac$, must be positive or 0. (If the value underneath the square root sign is negative, the solutions will be imaginary since the square roots of negative numbers are imaginary.)

In other words:

$$b^2 - 4ac \geq 0$$

If we add 4*ac* to both sides:

$$b^2 \geq 4ac$$

The answer is Choice (B).

5. **(D)** First, distribute the x in the second part of the expression:

$$x^4 + x(x + 2) = x^4 + x^2 + 2x$$

Next, distribute the negative sign:

$$(3x^3 - 2x^2 + 5x + 7) - (x^4 + x^2 + 2x) = 3x^3 - 2x^2 + 5x + 7 - x^4 - x^2 - 2x$$

Next, combine like terms:

$$3x^3 - 2x^2 + 5x + 7 - x^4 - x^2 - 2x = 3x^3 - 3x^2 + 3x + 7 - x^4$$

Rearrange the terms in descending order:

$$-x^4 + 3x^3 - 3x^2 + 3x + 7$$

So Choice (D) is correct.

6. **(B)** Add $\sqrt{a}$ to both sides while subtracting 6 from both sides:

$$a - 6 = \sqrt{a}$$

If we square both sides, we can get rid of the square root:

$$a^2 - 12a + 36 = a$$

Subtract a from both sides to set the expression equal to 0:

$$a^2 - 13a + 36 = 0$$

Factoring tells us:

$$(a - 9)(a - 4) = 0$$

So a should equal 9 or 4. However, we have to be careful when square roots are involved. Although squaring both sides was useful when solving for a, this method can produce extraneous solutions. So we have to go back and check our answers to make sure that they are actually solutions to our original equation. Plug both numbers back in to the original equation to make sure that they work:

$$9 - \sqrt{9} = 6$$
$$9 - 3 = 6$$

So 9 does work and is a solution to the original equation.

$$4 - \sqrt{4} = 6$$
$$4 - 2 \neq 6$$

So 4 is an extraneous solution. Therefore, there is only one solution, Choice (B).

7. **(D)** The second equation is simpler, so solve for y and then plug your expression for y back into the first equation:

$$3x - 6 = 3y$$

Divide by 3 to solve for y:

$$y = \frac{3x-6}{3} = \frac{3x}{3} - \frac{6}{3} = x - 2$$

Now you can plug $x - 2$ in for y in the first equality:

$$x[(x-2)+2] - 3x - 4[(x-2)+2] = -12$$

Combine like terms within the parentheses:

$$x(x) - 3x - 4(x) = -12$$

Combine like terms and bring the 12 to the left side:

$$x^2 - 7x + 12 = 0$$

Factor this, or use the quadratic equation if you're not great at factoring:

$$(x-3)(x-4) = 0$$

Set each factor equal to 0 to solve for the possible values of x:

$$x - 3 = 0$$

$$x = 3$$

$$x - 4 = 0$$

$$x = 4$$

Next, plug these values into either of the two equations to solve for y. It'll be easiest to plug them into the equation that you already solved for y:

$$y = x - 2 = 3 - 2 = 1$$
$$y = x - 2 = 4 - 2 = 2$$

So x can equal 3 or 4, and y can equal 1 or 2. Therefore, the greatest product xy will be:

$$4 \times 2 = 8$$

Choice (D) is the answer.

8. **(B)** From the graph, the function has zeros at $x = -3$ and at $x = 4$.

Starting with the $x = -3$, add 3 to both sides:

$$x + 3 = 0$$

Therefore, $x + 3$ is a factor. This means that the function must be divisible by $x + 3$.

Similarly, $x = 4$, so:

$$x - 4 = 0$$

Therefore, $x - 4$ is a factor of the function, meaning the function is divisible by $x - 4$. These are the only two zeros. So the function has only two distinct factors, which we have already found. Therefore, Options I and III are correct, which is Choice (B).

9. **(B)** The vertex form of a parabola is $y = (x - h)^2 + k$, where (h, k) are the coordinates of the vertex. Our original equation can be written in this form as $y = (x - 0)^2 + 3$. So $h = 0$ and $k = 3$.

The second parabola would be written as $y = (x - 5)^2 + 6$. So $h = 5$ and $k = 6$.

Therefore, h increases by 5 and k increases by 3, which is Choice (B).

10. **(C)** First, you must plug the expression for $g(x)$ into $f(x)$ where it's indicated:

$$f(x) = g(x) + 4 = x - \frac{5}{x} + 4$$

Next, plug 10 in for x in $f(x)$:

$$f(10) = 10 - \frac{5}{10} + 4 = 14 - \frac{1}{2} = 13\frac{1}{2} = 13.5$$

Choice (C) is the correct answer.

Passport to Advanced Math Drill 2 (No Calculator)

1. **(D)** If 3% is added annually after the first year is complete, after the second year, 3% will have been added. Thus, after 2 years, the total amount of money in the account can be represented as:

$$x + 0.03x$$

By combining like terms, it can also be expressed as:

$$1.03x = x(1.03)^1$$

After three years, another 3% is added to the new amount:

$$1.03x + 0.03(1.03x) = 1.03(x + 0.03x) = 1.03(1.03x) = x(1.03)^2$$

Continue in this manner. So after the fourth year, the amount of money in the account is $x(1.03)^3$.

Keeping this pattern in mind, the money in the account after n years is $x(1.03)^{n-1}$, which is Choice (D).

Note that raising 1.03 to the $n-1$ power means that you're multiplying x by 1.03 one time less than the number of years that have passed. This is because no interest is added in the first year.

2. **(A)** Add the $6x$ to both sides so that the polynomial is equal to 0:

$$x^2 + 6x + 9 = 0$$

You can either factor this or use the quadratic formula. This is easily factorable:

$$(x + 3)(x + 3) = 0$$

You can set each factor equal to 0 to solve for the possible values of x. However, since they're the same factor, you need to do it only once:

$$x + 3 = 0$$

Subtracting 3 from both sides tells you that $x = -3$, which is Choice (A).

3. **(B)** The key here is to notice that in the problem, $y < 0$. In the original expression, x is squared. So regardless of its sign, x^2 will be positive. Therefore, $\frac{3}{x^2 y}$ will be negative when y is negative. Thus, the new expression must also be negative.

Simplify the answer choices to see which matches the original expression.

Choice (A):

Negative exponents get sent to the denominator:

$$\frac{3x^{-2}}{\sqrt[4]{y^2}} = \frac{3}{x^2\sqrt[4]{y^2}}$$

Roots can be expressed as fractional exponents:

$$\frac{3}{x^2\sqrt[4]{y^2}} = \frac{3}{x^2 y^{\frac{2}{4}}}$$

However, $y^{\frac{2}{4}} \neq y$. So this is different than our original expression. We can rule out Choice (A).

Choice (B):

Following the same process as the previous answer choice, we can rewrite this answer as:

$$\frac{3x^{-2}}{-\sqrt[4]{y^4}} = -\frac{3}{x^2\sqrt[4]{y^4}}$$

Now consider $\sqrt[4]{y^4}$. It is tempting to say that this just equals $y^{\frac{4}{4}} = y$, but we have to be careful not to ignore a subtle point. When we take the fourth root of something, or in general the even root of something, we necessarily get a result that is nonnegative. In particular, $\sqrt[4]{y^4}$ must be nonnegative. However, y is negative, so the expression can't equal y. The expression actually equals $-y$, which is positive since y is negative.

(Convince yourself of this. For example, let $y = -2$ and consider $\sqrt[4]{y^4} = \sqrt[4]{(-2)^4}$. This expression is equal to $\sqrt[4]{16} = 2 = -(-2) = -y$ since $y = -2$.)

Thus, plugging in $-y$ for $\sqrt[4]{y^4}$ in our expression gives the following after canceling out the negative signs:

$$\frac{3x^{-2}}{-\sqrt[4]{y^4}} = -\frac{3}{x^2\sqrt[4]{y^4}} = -\frac{3}{x^2(-y)} = \frac{3}{x^2 y}$$

This is our original expression, so Choice (B) must be the correct answer.

If you wanted to explore the other answer choices, you could.

Choice (C):

By the same logic as before, this simplifies to:

$$\frac{3x^{\frac{1}{2}}}{\sqrt[4]{y^4}} = \frac{3\sqrt{x}}{-y} = -\frac{3\sqrt{x}}{y}$$

This clearly doesn't match the original expression, so it can be eliminated.

Choice (D):

Simplifying gives:

$$\frac{3x^{-2}}{\sqrt[4]{y^4}} = \frac{3}{x^2(-y)} = -\frac{3}{x^2 y}$$

This is close to our original expression but has a negative sign in front, so we can eliminate this choice.

4. **(C)** Remember that negative exponents can be made positive by moving whatever is being raised to that exponent to the denominator:

$$x^{-\frac{3}{4}} y^{\frac{4}{3}} = \frac{y^{\frac{4}{3}}}{x^{\frac{3}{4}}}$$

Fractional exponents are the same as roots:

$$\frac{y^{\frac{4}{3}}}{x^{\frac{3}{4}}} = \frac{\sqrt[3]{y^4}}{\sqrt[4]{x^3}}$$

This doesn't match any answer choices, so we need to simplify further. The y is being raised to a power higher than its root, so we should be able to pull something out of the root.

Since y is positive:

$$\sqrt[3]{y^4} = \sqrt[3]{y^3 y} = \sqrt[3]{y^3}\,\sqrt[3]{y} = y\sqrt[3]{y}$$

Therefore, our whole expression can be rewritten as:

$$\frac{y\sqrt[3]{y}}{\sqrt[4]{x^3}}$$

Choice (C) is the correct answer.

5. **(B)** Factor out a 3:

$$3(x^2 + 4x + 2) = 0$$

Divide both sides by 3:

$$x^2 + 4x + 2 = 0$$

This isn't easily factorable, so use the quadratic formula:

$$x = \frac{-b \pm \sqrt{b^2 - 4ac}}{2a} = \frac{-4 \pm \sqrt{4^2 - 4(1)(2)}}{2(1)} = \frac{-4 \pm \sqrt{8}}{2} = \frac{-4 \pm 2\sqrt{2}}{2} = -2 \pm \sqrt{2}$$

Choice (B) is the answer.

6. **(B)** We need to find all solutions less than 0. This equation is easily factorable:

$$x^2 + x - 12 = (x + 4)(x - 3) = 0$$

If $x + 4$ or $x - 3$ equaled 0, the whole expression would equal 0. Therefore, setting both factors equal to 0 will tell us the two potential values of x:

$$x + 4 = 0 \text{ so } x = -4$$

$$x - 3 = 0 \text{ so } x = 3$$

The question asks for only the value of x that's less than 0, so the answer is $x = -4$, which is Choice (B).

7. **(C)** All of the answers have a 16 factored out, so do that first:

$$64x^6 - 16y^8 = 16(4x^6 - y^8)$$

When anything is in the form $(a^2 - b^2)$, it can be factored using the difference of squares formula: $(a + b)(a - b)$. The trick to this problem is figuring out what a and b are. Set $4x^6$ equal to a^2 to find a:

$$4x^6 = a^2$$
$$a = \sqrt{4x^6}$$

Take the square root of both 4 and the x-term:

$$a = 2x^{\frac{6}{2}} = 2x^3$$

Next, set y^8 equal to b^2 to solve for b:

$$y^8 = b^2$$
$$b = \sqrt{y^8} = y^{\frac{8}{2}} = y^4$$

Therefore, if you wanted to express $(4x^6 - y^8)$ in the form of $(a + b)(a - b)$, it would be:

$$(2x^3 + y^4)(2x^3 - y^4)$$

Putting the 16 in front gives you Choice (C).

8. **(B)** Get rid of the square root by squaring both sides:

$$x^2 = 11x - 24$$

To find the possible values of x, subtract $11x$ and add 24 to both sides, setting the left side equal to 0. Then factor or use the quadratic formula to solve:

$$x^2 - 11x + 24 = 0$$

This equation factors as:

$$(x - 3)(x - 8) = 0$$

This statement would hold true if $x - 3 = 0$ or if $x - 8 = 0$. In other words, the statement would hold true if $x = 3$ or if $x = 8$, which is Choice (B).

Be careful, though. When we squared both sides of the equation, we were no longer guaranteed to get the same exact solutions as our original equation. In other words, because we square both sides, it is possible that we get extraneous solutions. So we should get in the habit of checking that both of our solutions are indeed solutions. We can do this by plugging both answer choices into our original equation:

$$x = 3$$
$$\sqrt{11(3) - 24} = \sqrt{9} = 3 = x$$

This solution checks out.

$$x = 8$$
$$\sqrt{11(8) - 24} = \sqrt{64} = 8 = x$$

This solution checks out as well.

In this problem both solutions check out. However, you should be cautious in general when squaring equations.

9. **(B)** The first function can be expressed as $y = \sqrt[4]{x-4}$. It's an even root. This means that the value within the root must be greater than or equal to 0 since we can find only the even root of a nonnegative number:

$$x - 4 \geq 0$$

$$x \geq 4$$

Therefore, the domain of the function is $[4, \infty)$.

The second function can be expressed as $y = \sqrt[4]{x}$. Again, it's an even root. So what's within the root must be greater than or equal to 0:

$$x \geq 0$$

The domain of this function then is $[0, \infty)$.

Therefore, the minimal x-value of the first function is 4 more than the minimal x-value of the second function. Choice (B) is the answer.

10. **(B)** To reflect something across the x-axis, multiply the entire equation by -1:

$$-y = -[3(x-5)^2 + 4] = -3(x-5)^2 - 4$$

Alternatively, notice that our original function gives the equation of a parabola; think about what this parabola looks like. Recall that the vertex form of a parabola is $y = a(x-h)^2 + k$. Our original parabola will open upward since $a = 3$ is positive. This parabola will also have a vertex at $(h, k) = (5, 4)$. If you want to reflect this across the x-axis, it would need to open downward and have a vertex at $(5, -4)$. Therefore, the vertex form of this new parabola would be:

$$y = -3(x-5)^2 - 4$$

The answer is Choice (B).

Additional Topics in Math Drill (Calculator)

1. **(C)** Let's do this one in two parts. First, we have a right cylinder with a volume of $30x$. We form a cone with the same height and radius as that cylinder. The formula for the volume of a cylinder is $V = \pi r^2 h$, while the formula for the volume of a cone is $V = \frac{1}{3}\pi r^2 h$.

Notice that the volume of a cone is just $\frac{1}{3}$ the volume of a cylinder with the same dimensions. Thus, if the volume of the cylinder is $30x$, the volume of a cone with the same dimensions is $\frac{1}{3}(30x)$ or $10x$.

For the second part of this problem, there's a cube with a volume of $21x$. We have a pyramid with the same length, width, and height as the cube. The formula for the volume of a cube is $V = LWH = L^3$ because the length, width, and height are all the same. The formula for the volume of a pyramid is $V = \frac{1}{3}LWH$.

In this case, the pyramid has the same length, width, and height as the cube, so the volume for the pyramid can be expressed as $V = \frac{1}{3}L^3$.

Notice that in this case, the volume of the pyramid is just $\frac{1}{3}$ of the volume of the cube.

The volume of the cube is $21x$, so the volume of the pyramid is $\frac{1}{3}(21x) = 7x$.

The question asked us the sum of the volume of the cone and the pyramid, which can be expressed by:

$$V = V_{\text{cone}} + V_{\text{pyramid}} = 10x + 7x = 17x$$

Choice (C) is correct.

2. **(A)** The length Andrew would fly would simply be the hypotenuse of a right triangle with side lengths of 20 miles and 15 miles. So we can use the Pythagorean theorem, which states that $a^2 + b^2 = c^2$, where a and b represent the sides and c represents the hypotenuse:

$$(20)^2 + (15)^2 = c^2$$

$$400 + 225 = c^2$$

$$c = \sqrt{625} = 25$$

Choice (A) is correct.

Alternatively, you could have saved a bit of time by noticing that this is just a variation of a 3-4-5 triangle:

$$15 = 3(5) \text{ and } 20 = 4(5)$$

Thus, the hypotenuse will be 5(5) or 25.

3. **(C)** In a right triangle, we can use the Pythagorean theorem to solve for an unknown hypotenuse.

$a^2 + b^2 = c^2$ where a and b are the 2 shorter legs and c is the hypotenuse. To solve for c, you take the square root of both sides:

$$c = \sqrt{a^2 + b^2}$$

This matches Choice (C).

4. **(A)** Remember the cycle of how i^n repeats as we increase the integer n by 1 each time:

$$i = \sqrt{-1}$$

$$i^2 = -1$$

$$i^3 = -i$$

$$i^4 = 1$$

Therefore, $2i^2 = 2(-1) = -2$.

For $(3i)^4$, we have to remember to raise both the 3 and the i to the fourth power:

$$3^4 = 81$$

$$i^4 = 1$$

$$(3i)^4 = (81)(1) = 81$$

Multiply the two terms together:

$$2i^2(3i)^4 = (-2)(81) = -162$$

The answer is Choice (A).

5. **(B)** To convert degrees to radians, simply multiply the number of degrees by $\frac{\pi}{180}$:

$$270\left(\frac{\pi}{180}\right) = \frac{3\pi}{2}$$

Choice (B) is the answer.

Alternatively, you could have realized that 270 degrees is $\frac{3}{4}$ of a circle. A circle is 2π radians, so 270 degrees corresponds to:

$$\frac{3}{4}(2\pi) = \frac{6\pi}{4} = \frac{3\pi}{2} \text{ radians}$$

Note: Radians may or may not be a topic tested on the PSAT. It is definitely something that could be on the SAT. So this problem was included here to prepare you.

6. **(D)** To find the length of the crust, we want to find $\frac{1}{8}$ of the total crust measure. The total crust measure is the circumference of a circle with radius 8. So the crust of one piece is $\frac{1}{8}C$. Because $C = 2\pi r$, the measure we're looking for is:

$$\frac{1}{8}2\pi r = \frac{\pi r}{4} = \frac{8\pi}{4} = 2\pi$$

Note that $2(3.14) = 6.28$, or Choice (D).

7. **(C)** The angle next to the 120-degree angle on line AB is 60 degrees because two angles on a given line (supplementary angles) must add up to 180 degrees.

The angle directly opposite that first 60 degree angle must also be 60 degrees, because angles opposite one another (called vertical angles) are equal. Furthermore, that vertical angle is along line EF with the 120-degree angle. So the sum of these supplementary angles must also be 180 degrees, making the vertical angle 60 degrees.

Because lines AB and CD are parallel and line EF is a transversal, opposite interior angles are also congruent. Therefore, the acute angle along line CD is also 60 degrees.

Because that angle is 60 degrees, the acute angle across from it (also along line CD) is also 60 degrees since angles opposite one another (vertical angles) must be congruent.

8. **(B)** For this problem, we can employ a little trick so that we have an i^2 term and can factor out an i in the numerator. We can use the knowledge that $i^2 = -1$ to change -6 to $6(-1)$ or $6i^2$. Thus, we can rewrite the original numerator as:

$$i^3 + 6i^2 + 9i$$

An i can be factored out, leaving us with the following in the numerator:

$$i(i^2 + 6i + 9)$$

The part inside the parentheses can be factored as:

$$(i + 3)^2$$

Therefore, our whole expression can be rewritten as:

$$\frac{i(i+3)^2}{3+i}$$

Since $i + 3$ is the same as $3 + i$, we can cancel one of the $i + 3$ terms from the numerator with the $3 + i$ term in the denominator. This leaves:

$$i(i + 3) \text{ or } i^2 + 3i$$

Because we know that $i^2 = -1$, we can rewrite this as $-1 + 3i$, which is the same as Choice (B).

Alternatively, we can first simplify the numerator since $i^3 = -i$:

$$i^3 + 9i - 6 = -i + 9i - 6 = 8i - 6$$

Now notice that none of the answer choices are fractions, so we want to get rid of the denominator. We can get rid of the i-term in the denominator by multiplying by its complex conjugate. This is found by changing the sign of all terms with an i in them and leaving the signs of all real numbers the same. So in our case, the complex conjugate of the denominator $3 + i$ is $3 - i$. We multiply both the numerator and denominator by this conjugate:

$$\frac{8i-6}{3+i} \cdot \frac{3-i}{3-i} = \frac{(8i-6)(3-i)}{(3+i)(3-i)}$$

By using FOIL and simplifying, we have:

$$\frac{(8i-6)(3-i)}{(3+i)(3-i)} = \frac{24i-8i^2-18+6i}{9-3i+3i-i^2} = \frac{30i-8(-1)-18}{9-(-1)} = \frac{30i-10}{10}$$

Factoring out a 10 from the numerator gives:

$$\frac{10(3i-1)}{10} = 3i-1$$

Choice (B) is the answer.

9. **(D)** Similar triangles have similar side lengths, meaning that the side lengths vary in fixed proportions. We know that triangle B has exactly one side length of 28. Since exactly one side of triangle A has length 7, this is $28 \div 7 = 4$ times the side length of the unique side in triangle A. Thus, the two shorter sides in triangle B will also be 4 times the side length of the shorter sides in triangle A. Since the two other sides of triangle A have length 5, triangle B has two sides of length $4(5) = 20$ and one side of length of 28.

This could have also been determined using a proportion:

$$\frac{28}{7} = \frac{x}{5}$$

Cross multiplication yields:

$$(28)(5) = 7x$$

$$140 = 7x$$

Dividing both sides by 7 tells us that $20 = x$.

Here we need to be careful. Notice that Choice (B) is 20, so you may be tempted to pick Choice (B). However, the question is asking us for the perimeter of the triangle rather than for the unknown side length.

The perimeter is $20 + 20 + 28 = 68$, Choice (D).

An alternative approach would have been to recognize that the perimeters of similar triangles will vary in the same proportion as the side lengths. We know that triangle B has sides 4 times longer than those of triangle A, so triangle B will also have a perimeter 4 times that of triangle A.

Triangle A has a perimeter of $5 + 5 + 7 = 17$.

Triangle B therefore has a perimeter of $4(17) = 68$.

10. **(A)** We can solve for the unknown side using the Pythagorean theorem:

$$a^2 + b^2 = c^2$$

It follows that:

$$b = \sqrt{c^2 - a^2} = \sqrt{26^2 - 24^2} = \sqrt{676 - 576} = \sqrt{100} = 10$$

Similar triangles have the same trigonometric ratios because the similar sides simplify to their lowest multiples.

The smallest angle in this triangle is angle X, as it is across from the shortest side length.

Therefore, a similar triangle will have a tangent of $\frac{\text{opposite}}{\text{adjacent}} = \frac{10}{24}$, which simplifies to $\frac{5}{12}$, Choice (A).

Alternatively, you could have saved yourself some time by noticing that this is just a multiple of a 5-12-13 Pythagorean triple. The two known sides are 2(12) = 24 and 2(13) = 26. The only side length we were missing was the 5 side, which has a measure of:

$$2(5) = 10$$

Calculator Problems Mixed Drill 1

1. **(D)** We want to isolate what's inside the parentheses with the goal of eventually isolating x. Let's first get that 6 out of the denominator by multiplying both sides by 6:

$$12\left(\frac{5x - 2x}{2}\right) = 108$$

To isolate what's inside the parentheses, we have to divide both sides by 12:

$$\left(\frac{5x - 2x}{2}\right) = 9$$

Now we can get rid of the parentheses:

$$\frac{5x - 2x}{2} = 9$$

To isolate our x-terms, multiply both sides by 2:

$$5x - 2x = 18$$

Combine the like x-terms:

$$5x - 2x = 3x = 18$$

Because $3x = 18$, it follows that $x = 6$.

2. **(C)** Let's imagine the total volume of this rock to be 1 cubic centimeter. Therefore, 0.32 cubic centimeters are coal, 0.29 cubic centimeters are granite, and 1 − 0.32 − 0.29 = 0.39 cubic centimeters are an unknown mineral. Using the specific gravities, we can calculate the mass of each species.

For coal:

$$0.32 \text{ cm}^3 \times \frac{1.20 \text{ grams}}{\text{cm}^3} = 0.384 \text{ grams}$$

For granite:

$$0.29 \text{ cm}^3 \times \frac{2.60 \text{ grams}}{\text{cm}^3} = 0.754 \text{ grams}$$

For the unknown:

$$0.39 \text{ cm}^3 \times \frac{x \text{ grams}}{\text{cm}^3} = 0.39x \text{ grams}$$

We know that the specific gravity of the whole thing is 1.4 grams/centimeter cubed, so its mass is:

$$1 \text{ cm}^3 \times \frac{1.4 \text{ grams}}{\text{cm}^3} = 1.4 \text{ grams}$$

Because all of the masses together must equal 1.4, it follows that:

$$0.384 + 0.754 + 0.39x = 1.4$$

Subtract the first 2 terms from both sides:

$$0.39x = 0.262$$

Divide both sides by 0.39:

$$x = 0.67$$

3. **(A)** Remember that $d = rt$, where d is distance, r is rate, and t is time. We have two different rates and two different times. We can multiply the coinciding rates and times together and then can add them to obtain the total distance traveled, 300 miles:

$$5x + \left(\frac{x}{10}\right)\left(\frac{x}{2}\right) = 300$$

Multiplying the two fractions together leaves:

$$5x + \frac{x^2}{20} = 300$$

None of the answer choices has a denominator, so let's multiply both sides by 20 to get rid of the denominator:

$$100x + x^2 = 6,000$$

Subtracting 6,000 from both sides and rearranging the terms gives:

$$x^2 + 100x - 6,000 = 0$$

This matches Choice (A).

4. **(D)** Take each term one at a time. When you cube $6a^3$, you're cubing both the 6 and the a^3. When you raise an exponent to another exponent, multiply the exponents. Therefore:

$$(6a^3)^3 - (2b)^4 + c^{-2} = 216a^9 - (2b)^4 + c^{-2}$$

Next, raise $2b$ to the fourth power by raising 2 to the fourth power and raising b to the fourth power:

$$216a^9 - (2b)^4 + c^{-2} = 216a^9 - 16b^4 + c^{-2}$$

Lastly, deal with the negative exponent. Something with a negative exponent can be rewritten by moving that something to the denominator and making the corresponding exponent positive:

$$216a^9 - 16b^4 + c^{-2} = 216a^9 - 16b^4 + \frac{1}{c^2}$$

Choice (D) is the correct answer.

An alternative to solving this problem to completion is to realize that once there is the $216a^9$, the answer must have this term in it. Choice (D) is the only option with this term, so you can pick it without having to do the last steps as discussed above.

5. **(B)** Exponential growth has initially slow growth that later becomes fast growth. In other words, it starts with a small slope that quickly turns into a steep slope. Only Choice (B) shows this kind of growth.

6. **(B)** Percent change is given by the following equation:

$$\frac{New - Original}{Original} \times 100\%$$

We can rule out Choice (A) since stock price decreased between 1983 and 1984. Calculate the approximate percent increase for the remaining answer choices.

Choice (B):

$$\frac{29 - 20}{20} \times 100\% = 45\%$$

Choice (C):

$$\frac{52 - 39}{39} \times 100\% = 33\%$$

Choice (D):

$$\frac{68 - 52}{52} \times 100\% = 31\%$$

Therefore, Choice (B) has the greatest percent increase.

7. **(D)** The minimal stock price is about \$11/share. Since the stockbroker sold \$1,000 in shares, she must have sold:

$$1,000 \times \frac{1 \, share}{\$11} = 90.91 \, shares$$

The maximum price is about \$88/share:

$$1,000 \times \frac{1 \, share}{\$88} = 11.36 \, shares$$

She would have sold 90.91 − 11.36 = 79.55 more shares at the lower price, or about 80 as in Choice (D).

8. **(D)** Just plug in $(b - a)$ wherever there is an a in the expression for $f(a)$:

$$f(b - a) = (b - a)^2 - 12$$

Next, use FOIL for $(b - a)^2$:

$$(b - a)^2 = (b - a)(b - a) = b^2 - ab - ab + a^2 = b^2 - 2ab + a^2$$

Plug this back into $f(b - a)$:

$$f(b - a) = b^2 - 2ab + a^2 - 12$$

This can be arranged as $f(b - a) = a^2 - 2ab + b^2 - 12$, Choice (D).

9. **(B)** Notice that the top and bottom sides each have a length of $3a$, while the left and right sides will each have a length of b. Therefore, $P = 3a + b + 3a + b$. Combine like terms:

$$P = 6a + 2b$$

The answer is Choice (B).

10. **(B)** This function turns 3 times, so it's a quartic function, meaning it must have 4 factors. Right away, we can eliminate Choices (A) and (D) because these functions each have only 3 factors; they're cubics. To conceptualize, a quadratic function—a parabola—turns once. A cubic function turns twice.

The function has zeros at −1, 0, and 2. We can use this to solve for the factors.

If $x = -1$, $x + 1 = 0$. So $(x + 1)$ is a factor. From this, you can eliminate Choice (C), thus leaving Choice (B) as the correct answer. However, if you want to see where the rest of the factors come from, read on.

If $x = 0$, x must be a factor. Why? Because if $x = 0$, the whole function equals zero; so x must be a factor.

If $x = 2$, $x - 2 = 0$. So $(x - 2)$ must be a factor. This factor must actually be squared. In general, if $(x - a)^m$ is a factor of a function, then the function crosses the x-axis at a if m is odd and does not cross the x-axis at a if m is even. In our case, if we look at the graph at $x = 2$, we can see that the graph never crosses the x-axis at 2; it stays above the x-axis right before and after 2. This means that $(x - 2)$ must be raised to an even power. We know that our graph is quartic. Since we already have 2 other distinct factors, the only option is for the exponent to be 2. In other words, $(x - 2)^2$ is a factor. Notice that the graph crosses the x-axis at the other two zeros: –1 and 0. At –1, the graph goes from the positive side to the negative side of the x-axis. The graph goes from the negative side to the positive side of the x-axis at 0. So their corresponding factors must occur an odd number of times (in this case, they each occur once). This matches Choice (B).

Calculator Problems Mixed Drill 2

1. **(A)** We first need to get the given line into slope-intercept form, i.e., $y = mx + b$, so that we can easily see the slope. Begin by adding $2.5x$ to both sides:

$$5y = 2.5x - 10$$

Now divide by 5:

$$y = \frac{1}{2}x - 2$$

The slope of this line is $\frac{1}{2}$. The slope of a line perpendicular to this will have a slope that is the negative reciprocal of $\frac{1}{2}$. The negative reciprocal of $\frac{1}{2}$ is –2, and only Choice (A) has a slope of –2.

2. **(A)** There were 118 people surveyed. If you lined up the people by age, the median age would be the average of the 59th and 60th persons. (Prove this to yourself. If you have a series of four terms, the median is between your second and third term. Divide your even number by 2 to get the first term, and add 1 to get the next.)

The first 24 people are younger than 13.

People numbered 25–68 are between ages 13 and 18. Therefore, the 59th and 60th people are both within this age category. If this whole age group were 13 (or even if all but 8 of them were), then the median age would be 13. This is the least possible age in this category, so it is the least possible median age.

3. **(D)** Without knowing everyone's exact response or the average number of hours slept per group, we can't calculate the mean. There's no way to add up the responses without knowing the responses or averages of the responses.

4. **(D)** Raising a fraction to an exponent raises both the numerator and the denominator to that exponent:

$$\left(\frac{2}{\sqrt[3]{a}}\right)^6 = \frac{2^6}{\sqrt[3]{a^6}}$$

Roots can be written as fractional exponents. So the expression can be rewritten as:

$$\frac{64}{a^{\frac{6}{3}}}$$

$a^{\frac{6}{3}}$ simplifies to a^2:

$$\frac{64}{a^{\frac{6}{3}}} = \frac{64}{a^2}$$

An exponent in the denominator of a fraction can be expressed as a negative exponent in the numerator:

$$\frac{64}{a^2} = 64a^{-2}$$

Choice (D) is the answer.

5. **(A)** If the new function is the absolute value of the old function, the graphs should be the same in all of the places where y is already 0 or positive. This includes the intervals from $-5 \le x \le -3$ and from $-1 \le x \le 1.5$. For the values for when the function is below the x-axis, $-3 < x < -1$ and $1.5 < x < 6$, will simply be their positive counterparts; they will be reflected above the x-axis.

The only graph that shows this relationship is Choice (A).

6. **(D)** There's nothing to distribute, so you can just get rid of the parentheses and combine like terms:

$$6x^3 + 3x^2 - 1 + 4x^3 - 4x^2 + 2x + 3$$

It's probably easiest if you start with the highest degree of x and move downward:

There's a $6x^3$ term and a $4x^3$ term. Combine these:

$$10x^3 + 3x^2 - 1 - 4x^2 + 2x + 3$$

Next, there's $3x^2$ and $-4x^2$:

$$10x^3 - x^2 - 1 + 2x + 3$$

There's only one term with an x in it, so move on to the constant terms: -1 and 3:

$$10x^3 - x^2 + 2x + 2$$

This corresponds to Choice (D).

7. **(A)** If Peter wants to make at least $800, we can come up with an expression for the amount of money that he'll make working h number of hours and set that expression greater than 800:

$$\text{Amount of money Peter makes weekly} > 800$$

The problem states that he makes $15/hour for his first 40 hours, and we assume that he's already worked 40 hours this week. Thus, Peter will make $15(40) = $600 for those 40 hours. This is a fixed constant.

For every hour after his 40th hour, he makes 50% more than his original hourly wage, for a total of 150% of his hourly wage. Thus, every hour Peter works after his 40th hour, he makes 1.5($15) = $22.50.

However, we can't just express this as 22.5h, because that would imply that Peter makes $22.50 for every single hour that he works rather than for just the hours past 40. Thus, it must be expressed as 22.5(h – 40).

To see that this is true, we can plug 41 in for h to see that for the 41st hour he works, Peter makes an extra:

$$22.5(41 - 40) = 22.5(1) = 22.5$$

This is what we would expect.

Our total expression for the amount of money Peter makes for working h hours, then, is:

$$600 + 22.5(h - 40)$$

Plug this into our original inequality to get:

$$600 + 22.5(h - 40) > 800$$

This is the same as Choice (A).

8. **(D)**

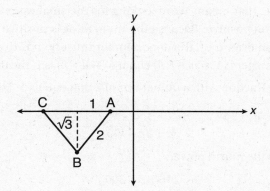

We are told that this triangle is equilateral, so each of the three angles is 60 degrees. We are also told that point A has coordinates (–2, 0). Since point C is on the x-axis and is 2 units to the left of point A, point C must have coordinates (–4, 0). By drawing a line that starts halfway between points A and C and bisects the angle at point B, as shown in the drawing, we can split this equilateral triangle into two 30-60-90 triangles. Because the equilateral triangle has side lengths of 2 and the line splits the side along the x-axis in half, the new triangles have side lengths of 1 along the x-axis.

You can see, then, that point B has an x-value 1 unit from both point A's and point C's x-values. Because points A and C have x-values of –2 and –4, respectively, point B will have an x-value of –3.

You may remember that a 30-60-90 triangle is a special right triangle that has opposite side lengths of 1, $\sqrt{3}$, and 2, respectively. Since you've already found side lengths of 1 and 2, the dotted line will have a length of $\sqrt{3}$. Because it's in the negative y-direction, it will have a y-coordinate of $-\sqrt{3}$. Therefore, the coordinates for point B are $\left(-3, -\sqrt{3}\right)$.

Alternatively, if you didn't remember the 30-60-90 triangle, you could have used the Pythagorean theorem with the two known side lengths to find the third length:

$$a^2 + b^2 = c^2$$

$$(1)^2 + b^2 = (2)^2$$

$$1 + b^2 = 4$$

Subtract 1 from both sides:

$$b^2 = 3$$

To find b, take the square root of both sides:

$$b = \sqrt{3}$$

So the third side has a length of $\sqrt{3}$.

9. **(A)** We are told that 60% of the customers like dogs. Since there are 30 customers, $0.6(30) = 18$ customers like dogs. We are also told that 11 people like cats. It is possible that 18 customers like only dogs, 11 people like only cats, and $30 - 18 - 11 = 1$ person likes neither. Thus, the minimum number of customers who necessarily like both is 0, Choice (A).

10. **(C)** If $f(n)$ needs to be an integer and we want a number in the denominator (n) to be as large as possible, that means we're looking for the smallest possible integer for $f(n)$. This integer must be positive. Because the numerator is positive and the denominator is being raised to an even root, the denominator must be positive as well. The smallest possible positive integer is 1, so set $f(n)$ equal to 1. If $f(n)$ is 1, the denominator must be 2 since $\frac{2}{2}$ is the only fraction with a numerator of 2 that equals 1. Thus, set the denominator equal to 2:

$$2 = \sqrt[4]{n - 300}$$

Raise both sides to the fourth power:

$$16 = n - 300$$

Add 300 to both sides:

$$n = 316$$

You can plug this number back into the original expression to verify.

Free-Response Drill

NO CALCULATOR

1. **(6)** A circle has the formula $(x-h)^2 + (y-k)^2 = r^2$ where (h, k) provides the coordinates for the center of the circle and r is the radius of the circle. This circle, therefore, has a center at $(0, 0)$, otherwise known as the origin. It has a radius of 6. Therefore, a line from the origin to any point on the circle has a distance of 6 units.

2. **(6)** Jamie runs $\frac{3}{2}k$ miles in the time that Matt runs k miles. Their combined distance is 10 miles, so create an equation to show this situation:

$$\frac{3}{2}k + k = 10$$

Get a common denominator so you can add like terms:

$$\frac{3}{2}k + \frac{2}{2}k = 10$$

$$\frac{5}{2}k = 10$$

To solve for k, divide both sides by $\frac{5}{2}$. This is the same as multiplying both sides by the reciprocal, $\frac{2}{5}$:

$$k = 10\left(\frac{2}{5}\right) = \frac{20}{5} = 4$$

However, the question asks how much Jamie runs, so you need to plug this value into $\frac{3}{2}k$:

$$\frac{3}{2}(4) = \frac{12}{2} = 6$$

So Jamie will run 6 miles.

3. $\left(\dfrac{5}{3}\right)$ Both sides of the equation are squared:

$$(x+2)(x+2) = (2x-3)(2x-3)$$

If you FOIL both sides:

$$x^2 + 4x + 4 = 4x^2 - 12x + 9$$

To find the solutions, you want to get everything on one side. Moving all terms on the left-hand side to the right side of the equation by subtracting gives:

$$0 = 3x^2 - 16x + 5$$

If you don't see that it can be factored as $(3x-1)(x-5)$, then use the quadratic formula:

$$x = \frac{-b \pm \sqrt{b^2 - 4ac}}{2a} = \frac{16 \pm \sqrt{(-16)^2 - 4(3)(5)}}{2(3)} = \frac{16 \pm \sqrt{196}}{6} = \frac{16 \pm 14}{6}$$

Therefore, $x = \frac{1}{3}$ or $x = 5$.

The question asks for the product of all of the solutions, so the answer is:

$$5\left(\frac{1}{3}\right) = \frac{5}{3}$$

4. **(7)** If $a + 1$ is a factor, it will divide evenly into the polynomial without a remainder. You can do polynomial long division or synthetic division. We will show the steps for long division:

$$\begin{array}{r} a^3 - 3a^2 + 5a + (m-5) \\ a+1\overline{)a^4 - 2a^3 + 2a^2 + ma + 2} \\ \underline{-\left(a^4 + a^3\right)} \\ -3a^3 + 2a^2 + ma + 2 \\ \underline{-\left(-3a^3 - 3a^2\right)} \\ 5a^2 + ma + 2 \\ \underline{-\left(5a^2 + 5a\right)} \\ (m-5)a + 2 \\ \underline{-((m-5)a + (m-5))} \\ 2 - (m-5) \end{array}$$

In order for there to be no remainder, $2 - (m - 5)$ must be equal to 0. Set it equal to 0 and solve for m:

$$2 - (m - 5) = 0$$

Distribute the negative sign:

$$2 - m + 5 = 0$$

Combine like terms on the right:

$$7 - m = 0$$

Adding m to both sides solves for m:

$$7 = m$$

5. **(2)** Translating the line will merely shift it to the right and down. It will not affect the slope. Therefore, the slope will still be 2. Picture moving a line down and to the right on a graph. Does the slope change? No, so the slope remains the same.

CALCULATOR

1. **(9)** Let's call c the number of children's outfits purchased and a the number of adults' outfits purchased. We can write two equations: one for the number of outfits purchased and one for the amount of money spent.

We know that the sum of children's outfits and adults' outfits purchased must add up to $22:

$$c + a = 22$$

We also know that each children's outfit was $20, so the amount of money spent on children's outfits was $20c$. Similarly, each adults' outfit was $45. So the amount of money spent on adults' outfits was $45a$. We are also told that the family spent a total of $765. Therefore, our second equation is:

$$20c + 45a = 765$$

We want to know how many children's outfits were purchased. Let's solve for a in the first equation so that we can substitute a out of the second equation, leaving only c-terms.

$$a = 22 - c$$

Plug this into the second equation:

$$20c + 45(22 - c) = 765$$

Distributing the 45 gives us:

$$20c + 990 - 45c = 765$$

We can now combine both c-terms on the left:

$$-25c + 990 = 765$$

Subtracting 990 from both sides leaves:

$$-25c = -225$$

Finally, dividing both sides by −25 will tell us the number of children's outfits purchased:

$$c = 9$$

2. **(19)** The hotel at the median distance in a series of 15 terms will have 7 terms on both sides. Therefore, the hotel that we are looking for is the 8th term. Count 8 points from the left. Then follow that point along to the y-axis to find its cost per night. The cost per night at Hotel M is $120.

Let x be the number of rooms the hotel books. Since the hotel wants to make $2,280 and each room costs $120, we have the following equation: $2,280 = 120x$. Divide $2,280 by $120 to tell how many rooms must be booked:

$$\$2{,}280 \div \$120 = 19$$

So 19 rooms must be booked. Alternatively, we could have used dimensional analysis in the last step to eliminate units that we didn't want:

$$2{,}280 \times \frac{1 \text{ room}}{120} = 19 \text{ rooms}$$

3. **(4)** The formula for the area of a triangle is $A = \frac{1}{2}BH$. Plug the given numbers in to solve for the building's actual height:

$$960 = \frac{1}{2}(48)H$$

Divide both sides by $\frac{1}{2}$ (in other words, multiply both sides by the reciprocal, 2):

$$1{,}920 = 48H$$

Isolate H by dividing both sides by 48:

$$H = 40 \text{ feet}$$

This is the building's actual height, but we want to know its height in the picture. Let's set up a proportion to find the height in the photograph:

$$\frac{1''}{10'} = \frac{x''}{40'}$$

If we cross multiply:

$$(1)(40) = 10x$$

Dividing both sides by 10 gives:

$$x = 4$$

4. **(35)** The number of math/science majors is 225, and the number of engineering majors is 295. So the total number of STEM majors is 225 + 295 = 520. The total number of students at the university is 1,490. Therefore, the total percentage of STEM majors at the university is:

$$\frac{520}{1,490} \times 100\% = 34.9\%$$

When rounded to the nearest percent, we get 35%.

5. **(0.35)** The probability is given by (number of successes) ÷ number of chances. The number of successes is the number of female humanities majors, which is 520. The total number of chances is the total number of students in the school, which is 1,490. Therefore, the probability is:

$$\frac{520}{1,490} = 0.349$$

When rounded to the nearest hundredth, we get 0.35.

No-Calculator Problems Mixed Drill

1. **(C)** First, distribute the –5:

$$15x + \frac{1}{2} = -5x + \frac{25}{2}$$

Now we want to get all of the x-terms on one side and all of the constant terms on the other side. Let's start by adding $5x$ to both sides:

$$20x + \frac{1}{2} = \frac{25}{2}$$

Now all of the x-terms are on the left, so we want all constant terms on the right. Let's subtract $\frac{1}{2}$ from both sides:

$$20x = \frac{24}{2} = 12$$

Dividing both sides by 20 will isolate the x:

$$x = \frac{12}{20}$$

This simplifies to $x = \frac{3}{5}$, which is Choice (C).

2. **(C)** Use FOIL for this like you would anything else. When you FOIL the expression, you get:

$$12 + 3i - 4i - i^2 = 12 - i - i^2$$

Because $i = \sqrt{-1}$, $i^2 = -1$. Thus, we can rewrite our equation as:

$$12 - i - (-1)$$

Therefore, the final answer is $13 - i$, which is Choice (C).

3. **(A)** Use FOIL on both sides to get:

$$x^2 - 16x + 60 = x^2 - 16x + 64 + c$$

The coefficients of like terms of both sides of the equation must equal one another. The coefficients of the x^2-terms and of the x-terms are already equal on both sides. However, the constant terms must equal one another as well:

$$60 = 64 + c$$

Subtract 64 from both sides:

$$-4 = c$$

Choice (A) is correct.

4. **(A)** Here we're looking for an angle measure, so we need an inverse trigonometry function. Let's go through the answer choices.

Choice (A) works because sine is the value of the opposite side over the hypotenuse. Side x is opposite of angle X, and side z is the hypotenuse. Thus, $\sin^{-1}\left(\dfrac{x}{z}\right)$ would provide the measure of angle X.

Choice (B) doesn't work because side x is opposite of angle X rather than adjacent, so we don't want to use $\cos^{-1}$.

Choice (C) won't work because we want an inverse trigonometry function rather than a trigonometry function. The output of an inverse trigonometry function is an angle. In contrast, the output of a trigonometry function is the ratio of two sides of a right triangle.

Choice (D) doesn't work because side y is adjacent to angle X, so $\sin^{-1}$ is not the appropriate inverse trigonometry function to use.

5. **(D)** Solve for V:

$$V = \frac{nRT}{P}$$

Recall that, in general, y is directly proportional to x if $y = cx$ for some constant c, and y is inversely p,roportional if $y = \dfrac{c}{x}$. In our case, we are told that R is the gas constant, so we can think of this as our constant. So V is directly proportional to n and T. If you increased either of these variables, V would also increase. V is inversely proportional only to P, which isn't an answer choice. So Choice (D) is the correct answer.

6. **(D)** First, isolate $\dfrac{1}{d_o}$ by subtracting $\dfrac{1}{d_i}$ from both sides of the equation:

$$\frac{1}{f} - \frac{1}{d_i} = \frac{1}{d_o}$$

We want to find d_o, so we need the reciprocal of $\dfrac{1}{d_o}$, which is d_o. To find the reciprocal, simply take 1 over both sides:

$$\frac{1}{\dfrac{1}{f} - \dfrac{1}{d_i}} = d_o$$

The answer is Choice (D).

7. **(B)** First, use FOIL for the left side of the equation:

$$x^3 + ax^2 + 2x + 4x^2 + 4ax + 8$$

Next, combine like terms:

$$x^3 + (a + 4)x^2 + (2 + 4a)x + 8$$

We know that this has to equal the right side of the original equation:

$$x^3 + (a+4)x^2 + (2+4a)x + 8 = x^3 + x^2 - 10x + 8$$

The coefficients of the like terms on both sides of the equation must equal one another. The coefficients on the x^3-terms are already equal and the constants are equal. So we need to worry about only the x^2-terms and the x-terms. Set the coefficients on the x^2-terms equal to one another:

$$a + 4 = 1$$

Subtracting 4 from both sides reveals that $a = -3$, which is Choice (B).

We also could have set the coefficients of the x-terms equal to each other to solve for a:

$$2 + 4a = -10$$

Subtracting 2 from both sides and then dividing by 4 gives $a = -3$ as well.

8. **(D)** Distribute the negative sign:

$$\left(6y^3 + \frac{1}{2}y - \frac{2}{3}\right) - \left(4y^3 - y^2 + \frac{1}{2}y + \frac{1}{6}\right) = 6y^3 + \frac{1}{2}y - \frac{2}{3} - 4y^3 + y^2 - \frac{1}{2}y - \frac{1}{6}$$

Next combine like terms:

$$6y^3 + \frac{1}{2}y - \frac{2}{3} - 4y^3 + y^2 - \frac{1}{2}y - \frac{1}{6} = 2y^3 + y^2 - \frac{5}{6}$$

This matches Choice (D).

9. **(D)** A line perpendicular to line A has a slope that is the negative reciprocal of $-\frac{x}{y}$.

The negative reciprocal is $-\left(-\frac{y}{x}\right)$, or $\frac{y}{x}$.

10. **(C)** We're given that $V_A = 8V_B$. From the formula for the volume of a sphere ($V = \frac{4}{3}\pi r^3$), it follows that $\frac{4}{3}\pi r_A^3 = 8\left(\frac{4}{3}\pi r_B^3\right)$. The $\frac{4}{3}\pi$ term cancels out on both sides, leaving us with $r_A^3 = 8r_B^3$. Taking the cube root of both sides gives $r_A = 2r_B$. Thus, the radius of sphere A is twice the radius of sphere B. We ultimately want to find the ratio of the surface areas, so consider the surface areas of the two spheres:

$$SA_A = 4\pi r_A^2 = 4\pi(2r_B)^2 = 4\pi(4r_B^2)$$

and

$$SA_B = 4\pi r_B^2$$

To find the ratio of the surface area of sphere A to the surface area of sphere B, we divide the surface area of sphere A by the surface area of sphere B:

$$\frac{SA_A}{SA_B} = \frac{4\pi\left(4r_B^2\right)}{4\pi r_B^2}$$

We can cancel a 4π and an r_B^2 out of both the numerator and the denominator, which leaves us with $\frac{SA_A}{SA_B} = 4$.

Thus, the ratio of the surface area of sphere A to sphere B is $\frac{4}{1}$ or 4:1, which is Choice (C).

Practice Test

ANSWER SHEET
Practice Test

Section 1: Reading Test

1. Ⓐ Ⓑ Ⓒ Ⓓ
2. Ⓐ Ⓑ Ⓒ Ⓓ
3. Ⓐ Ⓑ Ⓒ Ⓓ
4. Ⓐ Ⓑ Ⓒ Ⓓ
5. Ⓐ Ⓑ Ⓒ Ⓓ
6. Ⓐ Ⓑ Ⓒ Ⓓ
7. Ⓐ Ⓑ Ⓒ Ⓓ
8. Ⓐ Ⓑ Ⓒ Ⓓ
9. Ⓐ Ⓑ Ⓒ Ⓓ
10. Ⓐ Ⓑ Ⓒ Ⓓ
11. Ⓐ Ⓑ Ⓒ Ⓓ
12. Ⓐ Ⓑ Ⓒ Ⓓ
13. Ⓐ Ⓑ Ⓒ Ⓓ

14. Ⓐ Ⓑ Ⓒ Ⓓ
15. Ⓐ Ⓑ Ⓒ Ⓓ
16. Ⓐ Ⓑ Ⓒ Ⓓ
17. Ⓐ Ⓑ Ⓒ Ⓓ
18. Ⓐ Ⓑ Ⓒ Ⓓ
19. Ⓐ Ⓑ Ⓒ Ⓓ
20. Ⓐ Ⓑ Ⓒ Ⓓ
21. Ⓐ Ⓑ Ⓒ Ⓓ
22. Ⓐ Ⓑ Ⓒ Ⓓ
23. Ⓐ Ⓑ Ⓒ Ⓓ
24. Ⓐ Ⓑ Ⓒ Ⓓ
25. Ⓐ Ⓑ Ⓒ Ⓓ
26. Ⓐ Ⓑ Ⓒ Ⓓ

27. Ⓐ Ⓑ Ⓒ Ⓓ
28. Ⓐ Ⓑ Ⓒ Ⓓ
29. Ⓐ Ⓑ Ⓒ Ⓓ
30. Ⓐ Ⓑ Ⓒ Ⓓ
31. Ⓐ Ⓑ Ⓒ Ⓓ
32. Ⓐ Ⓑ Ⓒ Ⓓ
33. Ⓐ Ⓑ Ⓒ Ⓓ
34. Ⓐ Ⓑ Ⓒ Ⓓ
35. Ⓐ Ⓑ Ⓒ Ⓓ
36. Ⓐ Ⓑ Ⓒ Ⓓ
37. Ⓐ Ⓑ Ⓒ Ⓓ
38. Ⓐ Ⓑ Ⓒ Ⓓ
39. Ⓐ Ⓑ Ⓒ Ⓓ

40. Ⓐ Ⓑ Ⓒ Ⓓ
41. Ⓐ Ⓑ Ⓒ Ⓓ
42. Ⓐ Ⓑ Ⓒ Ⓓ
43. Ⓐ Ⓑ Ⓒ Ⓓ
44. Ⓐ Ⓑ Ⓒ Ⓓ
45. Ⓐ Ⓑ Ⓒ Ⓓ
46. Ⓐ Ⓑ Ⓒ Ⓓ
47. Ⓐ Ⓑ Ⓒ Ⓓ

Section 2: Writing and Language Test

1. Ⓐ Ⓑ Ⓒ Ⓓ
2. Ⓐ Ⓑ Ⓒ Ⓓ
3. Ⓐ Ⓑ Ⓒ Ⓓ
4. Ⓐ Ⓑ Ⓒ Ⓓ
5. Ⓐ Ⓑ Ⓒ Ⓓ
6. Ⓐ Ⓑ Ⓒ Ⓓ
7. Ⓐ Ⓑ Ⓒ Ⓓ
8. Ⓐ Ⓑ Ⓒ Ⓓ
9. Ⓐ Ⓑ Ⓒ Ⓓ
10. Ⓐ Ⓑ Ⓒ Ⓓ
11. Ⓐ Ⓑ Ⓒ Ⓓ

12. Ⓐ Ⓑ Ⓒ Ⓓ
13. Ⓐ Ⓑ Ⓒ Ⓓ
14. Ⓐ Ⓑ Ⓒ Ⓓ
15. Ⓐ Ⓑ Ⓒ Ⓓ
16. Ⓐ Ⓑ Ⓒ Ⓓ
17. Ⓐ Ⓑ Ⓒ Ⓓ
18. Ⓐ Ⓑ Ⓒ Ⓓ
19. Ⓐ Ⓑ Ⓒ Ⓓ
20. Ⓐ Ⓑ Ⓒ Ⓓ
21. Ⓐ Ⓑ Ⓒ Ⓓ
22. Ⓐ Ⓑ Ⓒ Ⓓ

23. Ⓐ Ⓑ Ⓒ Ⓓ
24. Ⓐ Ⓑ Ⓒ Ⓓ
25. Ⓐ Ⓑ Ⓒ Ⓓ
26. Ⓐ Ⓑ Ⓒ Ⓓ
27. Ⓐ Ⓑ Ⓒ Ⓓ
28. Ⓐ Ⓑ Ⓒ Ⓓ
29. Ⓐ Ⓑ Ⓒ Ⓓ
30. Ⓐ Ⓑ Ⓒ Ⓓ
31. Ⓐ Ⓑ Ⓒ Ⓓ
32. Ⓐ Ⓑ Ⓒ Ⓓ
33. Ⓐ Ⓑ Ⓒ Ⓓ

34. Ⓐ Ⓑ Ⓒ Ⓓ
35. Ⓐ Ⓑ Ⓒ Ⓓ
36. Ⓐ Ⓑ Ⓒ Ⓓ
37. Ⓐ Ⓑ Ⓒ Ⓓ
38. Ⓐ Ⓑ Ⓒ Ⓓ
39. Ⓐ Ⓑ Ⓒ Ⓓ
40. Ⓐ Ⓑ Ⓒ Ⓓ
41. Ⓐ Ⓑ Ⓒ Ⓓ
42. Ⓐ Ⓑ Ⓒ Ⓓ
43. Ⓐ Ⓑ Ⓒ Ⓓ
44. Ⓐ Ⓑ Ⓒ Ⓓ

Section 3: Math Test—No Calculator

1. Ⓐ Ⓑ Ⓒ Ⓓ   5. Ⓐ Ⓑ Ⓒ Ⓓ   9. Ⓐ Ⓑ Ⓒ Ⓓ   13. Ⓐ Ⓑ Ⓒ Ⓓ
2. Ⓐ Ⓑ Ⓒ Ⓓ   6. Ⓐ Ⓑ Ⓒ Ⓓ   10. Ⓐ Ⓑ Ⓒ Ⓓ
3. Ⓐ Ⓑ Ⓒ Ⓓ   7. Ⓐ Ⓑ Ⓒ Ⓓ   11. Ⓐ Ⓑ Ⓒ Ⓓ
4. Ⓐ Ⓑ Ⓒ Ⓓ   8. Ⓐ Ⓑ Ⓒ Ⓓ   12. Ⓐ Ⓑ Ⓒ Ⓓ

14.   15.   16.   17.

ANSWER SHEET
Practice Test

Section 4: Math Test—Calculator

1. Ⓐ Ⓑ Ⓒ Ⓓ
2. Ⓐ Ⓑ Ⓒ Ⓓ
3. Ⓐ Ⓑ Ⓒ Ⓓ
4. Ⓐ Ⓑ Ⓒ Ⓓ
5. Ⓐ Ⓑ Ⓒ Ⓓ
6. Ⓐ Ⓑ Ⓒ Ⓓ
7. Ⓐ Ⓑ Ⓒ Ⓓ
8. Ⓐ Ⓑ Ⓒ Ⓓ

9. Ⓐ Ⓑ Ⓒ Ⓓ
10. Ⓐ Ⓑ Ⓒ Ⓓ
11. Ⓐ Ⓑ Ⓒ Ⓓ
12. Ⓐ Ⓑ Ⓒ Ⓓ
13. Ⓐ Ⓑ Ⓒ Ⓓ
14. Ⓐ Ⓑ Ⓒ Ⓓ
15. Ⓐ Ⓑ Ⓒ Ⓓ
16. Ⓐ Ⓑ Ⓒ Ⓓ

17. Ⓐ Ⓑ Ⓒ Ⓓ
18. Ⓐ Ⓑ Ⓒ Ⓓ
19. Ⓐ Ⓑ Ⓒ Ⓓ
20. Ⓐ Ⓑ Ⓒ Ⓓ
21. Ⓐ Ⓑ Ⓒ Ⓓ
22. Ⓐ Ⓑ Ⓒ Ⓓ
23. Ⓐ Ⓑ Ⓒ Ⓓ
24. Ⓐ Ⓑ Ⓒ Ⓓ

25. Ⓐ Ⓑ Ⓒ Ⓓ
26. Ⓐ Ⓑ Ⓒ Ⓓ
27. Ⓐ Ⓑ Ⓒ Ⓓ

28.

29.

30.

31.

READING TEST

60 MINUTES, 47 QUESTIONS

Turn to Section 1 of your answer sheet to answer the questions in this section.

Directions: Following each of the passages (or pairs of passages) below are questions about the passage (or passages). Read each passage carefully. Then, select the best answer for each question based on what is stated in the passage (or passages) and in any graphics that may accompany the passage.

Questions 1–9 are based on the passage that follows.

Upton Sinclair's 1906 The Jungle *recounts the immigration of Jurgis Rudkus and Ona Lukoszaite from Lithuania to Chicago. The text raised social awareness of the unhealthy standards of industrial work at the turn of the century.*

Promptly at seven the next morning Jurgis reported for work. He came to the door that had been pointed out to him, and there he
Line waited for nearly two hours. The boss had
(5) meant for him to enter, but had not said this, and so it was only when on his way out to hire another man that he came upon Jurgis. He gave him a good cursing, but as Jurgis did not understand a word of it he did not object.
(10) He followed the boss, who showed him where to put his street clothes, and waited while he donned the working clothes he had bought in a secondhand shop and brought with him in a bundle; then he led him to the
(15) "killing beds." The work which Jurgis was to do here was very simple, and it took him but a few minutes to learn it. He was provided with a stiff besom, such as is used by street sweepers, and it was his place to follow down
(20) the line the man who drew out the smoking entrails from the carcass of the steer; this mass was to be swept into a trap, which was then closed, so that no one might slip into

it. As Jurgis came in, the first cattle of the
(25) morning were just making their appearance; and so, with scarcely time to look about him, and none to speak to any one, he fell to work. It was a sweltering day in July, and the place ran with steaming hot blood—one waded
(30) in it on the floor. The stench was almost overpowering, but to Jurgis it was nothing. His whole soul was dancing with joy—he was at work at last! He was at work and earning money! All day long he was figuring
(35) to himself. He was paid the fabulous sum of seventeen and a half cents an hour; and as it proved a rush day and he worked until nearly seven o'clock in the evening, he went home to the family with the tidings that he
(40) had earned more than a dollar and a half in a single day!
  At home, also, there was more good news; so much of it at once that there was quite a celebration in Aniele's hall bedroom. Jonas
(45) had been to have an interview with the special policeman to whom Szedvilas had introduced him, and had been taken to see several of the bosses, with the result that one had promised him a job the beginning
(50) of the next week. And then there was Marija Berczynskas, who, fired with jealousy by the success of Jurgis, had set out upon her own responsibility to get a place. Marija had nothing to take with her save her two
(55) brawny arms and the word "job," laboriously

GO ON TO THE NEXT PAGE

learned; but with these she had marched
about Packingtown all day, entering every
door where there were signs of activity. Out
of some she had been ordered with curses;
(60) but Marija was not afraid of man or devil,
and asked every one she saw—visitors and
strangers, or work-people like herself, and
once or twice even high and lofty office
personages, who stared at her as if they
(65) thought she was crazy. In the end, however,
she had reaped her reward. In one of the
smaller plants she had stumbled upon a
room where scores of women and girls were
sitting at long tables preparing smoked beef
(70) in cans; and wandering through room after
room, Marija came at last to the place where
the sealed cans were being painted and
labeled, and here she had the good fortune
to encounter the "forelady." Marija did not
(75) understand then, as she was destined to
understand later, what there was attractive
to a "forelady" about the combination of a
face full of boundless good nature and the
muscles of a dray horse; but the woman had
(80) told her to come the next day and she would
perhaps give her a chance to learn the trade
of painting cans. The painting of cans being
skilled piecework, and paying as much as two
dollars a day, Marija burst in upon the family
(85) with the yell of a Comanche Indian, and fell
to capering about the room so as to frighten
the baby almost into convulsions.

1. The major thematic contrast in the narrative is between
   (A) being motivated to find a job and deciding to take it easy.
   (B) strict vegetarianism and a willingness to eat meat.
   (C) becoming an immigrant and staying in one's native country.
   (D) the attitudes of the workers and the true nature of their work.

2. The two successful job seekers discussed in the passage have what general attitude upon being hired?
   (A) Optimism
   (B) Pessimism
   (C) Resignation
   (D) Peacefulness

3. It can be reasonably inferred from the passage that the supervisors in the meat-packing factories viewed employees as
   (A) skillful.
   (B) disposable.
   (C) valuable.
   (D) interesting.

4. Which option gives the best evidence for the answer to the previous question?
   (A) Lines 4–7 ("The boss . . . Jurgis")
   (B) Lines 15–17 ("The work . . . learn it")
   (C) Lines 32–35 ("His whole . . . himself")
   (D) Lines 42–44 ("At home . . . bedroom")

GO ON TO THE NEXT PAGE

5. What is the purpose of lines 15–24?

(A) To analyze a character's motivations
(B) To summarize the major point of the paragraph
(C) To describe a character's professional tasks
(D) To consider a likely objection by the reader

6. As used in line 34, "figuring" most closely means

(A) believing.
(B) calculating.
(C) assuming.
(D) doubting.

7. As used in line 67, "plants" most closely means

(A) vegetation.
(B) stations.
(C) factories.
(D) houses.

8. The passage suggests that Marija has what level of proficiency in the English language?

(A) Totally fluent
(B) Mostly fluent
(C) Somewhat proficient
(D) Very limited

9. Which option gives the best evidence for the answer to the previous question?

(A) Lines 50–53 ("And then . . . place")
(B) Lines 53–56 ("Marija . . . learned")
(C) Lines 66–74 ("In one . . . forelady")
(D) Lines 82–87 ("The painting . . . convulsions")

Questions 10–19 are based on the passage and supplementary material that follow.

"Santa's Big Helpers"—An economist discusses American overnight-delivery logistics. Written in 2015.

Each year the holiday season rolls around and most people have difficulty doing all the things to get ready for family gatherings
Line and traditions. Black Friday is either an
(5) adrenaline-laced day of chaos when bargains can be garnered, or it is an experience to avoid by sitting at a keyboard and becoming part of the e-commerce movement. Some people love the thrill of the hunt and others
(10) enjoy the peace and quiet of working down a list with a company like Amazon.com.
　　Whatever your preference, the method by which a product finds its way to you, the consumer, is logistics. Originally a term
(15) that described the flow of materiel for the military in the conflicts around the globe, it has now found its way into every element of consumerism. Major retailers have emerged that specialize in online shopping; others
(20) have outlet stores and websites where the buyer can choose a channel for procurement. Other "big box" retailers have stores in malls and large distribution centers where product is delivered from the various manufacturers
(25) and moved through an integrated supply chain to the point-of-sale retail establishment. Making sure that your size and desired color of clothing is on the hanger is no small task and large teams of employees
(30) manage the information and product flows to provide a seamless experience for the customer.

GO ON TO THE NEXT PAGE

Companies like FedEx have grown to be an integral part of the American landscape.
(35) FedEx first specialized in overnight deliveries via aircraft and then grew into a full service provider using a truck network in conjunction with air transport. *"When it absolutely, positively has to be there*
(40) *overnight"* is its mantra, and it basically provides certainty of service for a premium price that consumers are willing to bear. Product is prepared for shipment and FedEx picks it up at the factory or distribution
(45) center. If it is traveling from New York City to Los Angeles, California, it is loaded on an aircraft in the early evening and flown to Memphis, TN, arriving after midnight or before. This massive influx of aircraft must
(50) be unloaded piece by piece, sorted to a new destination, loaded on an out-going aircraft and flown out in the early morning hours. In Los Angeles, the plane is unloaded, the items are taken by truck to a dispatching center and
(55) white delivery vans will navigate the perils of rush hour traffic to make the delivery to the person who wants the package.

FedEx and UPS now provide online tracking of packages for the consumer. It
(60) is interesting to log on and see the journey that a purchase has traveled to go from source to destination. Each time an arrival and a departure are scanned, that item has to be picked up by an employee, placed on
(65) a moving belt to take to a sortation system, and then placed on another vehicle for its next leg in the sojourn. Holiday seasons put these logistics systems to a severe test each year, and companies in the business of
(70) logistics are constantly investing in new ways to handle the information and the items as they flow through the pipelines. Billions of dollars have been invested in these types of

service industries, and the activity behind
(75) the scenes is something to behold. Santa does indeed have his helpers, but instead of a red sleigh and cute little reindeer, a 747 jet aircraft and a white or brown delivery truck are the real implements in keeping people
(80) happy in their gift giving. And if the recent past is any indication, consumer spending on e-commerce will only continue to increase.

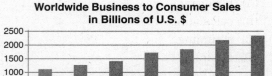

Figure 1

Figure 2

Source: Statista.com

GO ON TO THE NEXT PAGE

10. What is the purpose of the passage?

    (A) To analyze a phenomenon
    (B) To argue against conventional wisdom
    (C) To justify a decision
    (D) To describe a historical event

11. What is the purpose of lines 14–16 ("Originally . . . globe")?

    (A) To define current usage of a phrase
    (B) To address a likely reader objection
    (C) To use primary source evidence
    (D) To explain the root of a concept

12. As used in line 34, "integral" most closely means

    (A) essential.
    (B) economic.
    (C) geographic.
    (D) capitalist.

13. The author suggests that, in general, customers who use overnight delivery services are primarily concerned with

    (A) cost.
    (B) reliability.
    (C) holiday incentives.
    (D) fashion choices.

14. Which option gives the best evidence for the answer to the previous question?

    (A) Lines 4–8 ("Black Friday . . . movement")
    (B) Lines 27–32 ("Making sure . . . customer")
    (C) Lines 38–42 ("When it . . . bear")
    (D) Lines 59–62 ("It is . . . destination")

15. It is reasonable to infer that the author's attitude toward the process of logistical distribution is

    (A) skeptical.
    (B) positive.
    (C) neutral.
    (D) bellicose.

16. Which option gives the best evidence for the answer to the previous question?

    (A) Lines 8–11 ("Some people . . . Amazon.com")
    (B) Lines 18–21 ("Major . . . procurement")
    (C) Lines 62–67 ("Each time . . . sojourn")
    (D) Lines 72–75 ("Billions . . . behold")

17. Figure 1 provides the most direct support for which of the following statements in the passage?

    (A) Lines 1–4 ("Each year . . . traditions")
    (B) Lines 22–27 ("Other . . . establishment")
    (C) Lines 49–52 ("This massive . . . hours")
    (D) Lines 80–82 ("And if . . . increase")

18. Figure 2 is most helpful in explaining which action mentioned in the passage?

    (A) Lines 43–45 ("Product . . . center")
    (B) Lines 45–49 ("If it is . . . before")
    (C) Lines 62–64 ("Each time . . . employee")
    (D) Lines 69–72 ("companies . . . pipelines")

19. According to Figures 1 and 2, the relationship between the worldwide business to consumer sales and the worldwide number of digital consumers can best be described as

    (A) inversely related.
    (B) positively correlated.
    (C) exponentially related.
    (D) negatively related.

GO ON TO THE NEXT PAGE

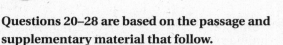

Questions 20–28 are based on the passage and supplementary material that follow.

A nurse practitioner shares information about treatments for antimicrobials. Written in 2016.

Antimicrobials, commonly known as antibiotics, have been around in different forms for thousands of years. It is believed
Line that the ancient Egyptians and Greeks were
(5) some of the first societies to use garlic and other spices for medicinal purposes to help boost the strength and endurance of their workers and soldiers. While the use of spices as antimicrobials is still a practice within
(10) Traditional Chinese Medicine, the utilization of pharmaceutical antimicrobials is more widespread in Western culture.

The past few decades have seen an explosion in antibiotic use as scientists
(15) continue to develop and release new medicines for bacterial, viral, and fungal infections. Antibiotics prescribed by doctors today are so advanced that they are able to target the action mechanisms of certain
(20) microorganisms. For example, one class of antibiotics targets cell wall synthesis of the microorganism, while another class inhibits protein synthesis. Targeting different mechanisms of action will either completely
(25) kill the microorganism or slow its growth. If the antibiotic kills the microorganism, it is classified as a bactericidal drug, while if it only slows the growth, it is considered bacteriostatic. Both categories of drugs have
(30) their advantages and disadvantages.

Bacteriostatic antibiotics are often prescribed to patients who have an intact immune system that can assist in killing the microorganism causing the infection.
(35) Allowing the innate immune system to

do some of the work decreases the length of time the patient needs to be on the antibiotic, which can help eliminate some of the unwanted side effects. Bactericidal
(40) drugs are prescribed when the patient may be immunocompromised (i.e., the natural immune system is not functioning properly) and cannot fight off the infection. Depending on the severity and type of
(45) infection, a doctor may select a narrow or broad-spectrum bactericidal drug. Narrow spectrum drugs are better for the patient as they only kill the microorganism causing the infection via a specific mechanism of
(50) action. This differs from broad-spectrum drugs as they kill the microorganism and any other cell with the same type of mechanism of action. This often causes serious and unpleasant side effects for the patient, such
(55) as superinfections and a wipeout of the body's natural flora barrier.

Both doctors and patients want to avoid complications from antibiotics, which is why doctors will often collect a sample
(60) of the microorganism from the patient in order to perform a culture and sensitivity test. This test helps to identify the specific microorganism causing the infection as well as the best antibiotic for treatment.
(65) Lab technicians are able to pinpoint the best antibiotic by measuring the "zone of inhibition" on the microorganism growth plate. The zone with the largest diameter typically signifies that it will be the best
(70) at fighting the infection. Prescribing an antibiotic that tests positive for the inhibition of growth or completely stops the growth of the microorganism will hopefully help the patient heal faster and experience
(75) fewer side effects.

GO ON TO THE NEXT PAGE

As the use of antibiotics continues to increase, there is growing concern within the healthcare community about the development of antibiotic resistant (80) microorganisms. Microorganisms that cause infections are able to gain resistance when their DNA spontaneously mutates, or when they receive DNA from another microorganism via conjugation. Once the (85) microorganism has secured the needed DNA sequence, many common antibiotics become ineffective in fighting the infection. The most common example of this is MRSA (methicillin-resistant *staphylococcus* (90) *aureus*), which has become a frequent hospital-acquired infection for many sick patients. MRSA is very difficult to fight and requires the use of very potent antibiotic treatments, such as IV vancomycin, for full (95) body infections. To help prevent these types of infections, the healthcare community is trying to better educate patients on proper use of antibiotics.

When patients receive a prescription (100) for an antibiotic from their pharmacy, they also receive instructions on how to properly complete the antibiotic regimen. Instructions include taking the entire prescription, even if the patient feels better half-way (105) through the regimen, as well as taking the correct dosage of the medication (e.g., do not double a dose). These instructions are important to follow because patients do not want to provide an optimal environment for (110) microorganisms to thrive. By following these simple instructions, patients will help to decrease antibiotic-resistant infections.

Antibiotic Tested	*E. coli* Zone of Inhibition	*S. aureus* Zone of Inhibition
Vancomycin	0 mm	20 mm
Ciprofloxacin	17 mm	16 mm
Amoxicillin	10 mm	15 mm

Zone of Inhibition measurements to determine the effectiveness of certain antibiotics against the microorganisms E. coli *and* S. aureus.

20. The passage as a whole most strongly suggests that medical professionals

(A) should push for more stringent licensure requirements for first responders.

(B) must educate patients on how to properly diagnose bacteriological infections.

(C) can improve their bedside manner if they recognize the common fears of the sick.

(D) need to consider how treatments will impact people other than the patient.

21. What is the primary function of the sentence in lines 29–30 ("Both categories . . . disadvantages")?

(A) To define a couple of major concepts

(B) To give examples in support of a claim

(C) To provide a transition to the following paragraph

(D) To state the thesis of the essay

GO ON TO THE NEXT PAGE

22. It is reasonable to infer from the passage that a bacteriostatic medicine and a bactericidal medicine would be optimally used on patients in which of the following respective situations?

(A) Relatively healthy, relatively ill
(B) Generally unhealthy, generally healthy
(C) Internally sick, externally sick
(D) Physically ill, mentally ill

23. Which of the following is a major concern of the passage's author?

(A) That doctors will lose the capacity to treat bacterial infections
(B) That patients will overdose on their antibiotic prescriptions
(C) That MRSA will lose its prominence in the medical community
(D) That Western medicine will not be open to alternative approaches

24. Which option gives the best evidence for the answer to the previous question?

(A) Lines 8–12 ("While the . . . culture")
(B) Lines 76–80 ("As the use . . . microorganisms")
(C) Lines 88–92 ("The most . . . patients")
(D) Lines 102–107 ("Instructions . . . dose")

25. As used in line 53, "serious" most closely means

(A) severe.
(B) thoughtful.
(C) genuine.
(D) quiet.

26. As used in line 82, "spontaneously" most closely means

(A) impulsively.
(B) extemporaneously.
(C) randomly.
(D) deliberately.

27. The information in the figure would most likely result from a medical practitioner doing which of the following actions mentioned in the passage?

(A) "Use garlic and other spices for medicinal purposes" (lines 5–6)
(B) "Develop and release new medicines" (lines 15–16)
(C) "Perform a culture and sensitivity test" (lines 61–62)
(D) "Better educate patients on proper use of antibiotics" (lines 97–98)

28. Based on the information in the passage and on the figure, which of these antibiotics would be most helpful in treating someone with an *E. coli* infection, assuming the patient was not allergic to any antibiotics and had no other illnesses besides the *E. coli* infection?

(A) Vancomycin
(B) Ciprofloxacin
(C) Amoxicillin
(D) Staphylococcus

GO ON TO THE NEXT PAGE

Questions 29–38 are based on the passage that follows.

Passage 1 is the beginning of Benjamin Franklin's 1771 autobiography. Passage 2 includes the opening of another autobiography published much later, in 1901, that of Booker T. Washington.

Passage 1

Dear son: I have ever had pleasure in obtaining any little anecdotes of my ancestors. You may remember the inquiries
Line I made among the remains of my relations
(5) when you were with me in England, and the journey I undertook for that purpose. Imagining it may be equally agreeable to you to know the circumstances of my life, many of which you are yet unacquainted
(10) with, and expecting the enjoyment of a week's uninterrupted leisure in my present country retirement, I sit down to write them for you. To which I have besides some other inducements. Having emerged from the
(15) poverty and obscurity in which I was born and bred, to a state of affluence and some degree of reputation in the world, and having gone so far through life with a considerable share of felicity, the conducing means I made
(20) use of, which with the blessing of God so well succeeded, my posterity may like to know, as they may find some of them suitable to their own situations, and therefore fit to be imitated.
(25) That felicity, when I reflected on it, has induced me sometimes to say, that were it offered to my choice, I should have no objection to a repetition of the same life from its beginning, only asking the advantages
(30) authors have in a second edition to correct some faults of the first. So I might, besides correcting the faults, change some sinister

accidents and events of it for others more favourable. But though this were denied,
(35) I should still accept the offer. Since such a repetition is not to be expected, the next thing most like living one's life over again seems to be a recollection of that life, and to make that recollection as durable as possible
(40) by putting it down in writing.

Passage 2

I was born a slave on a plantation in Franklin County, Virginia. I am not quite sure of the exact place or exact date of my birth, but at any rate I suspect I must have
(45) been born somewhere and at some time. As nearly as I have been able to learn, I was born near a cross-roads post-office called Hale's Ford, and the year was 1858 or 1859. I do not know the month or the day. The
(50) earliest impressions I can now recall are of the plantation and the slave quarters—the latter being the part of the plantation where the slaves had their cabins.
My life had its beginning in the midst
(55) of the most miserable, desolate, and discouraging surroundings. This was so, however, not because my owners were especially cruel, for they were not, as compared with many others. I was born in a
(60) typical log cabin, about fourteen by sixteen feet square. In this cabin I lived with my mother and a brother and sister till after the Civil War, when we were all declared free.
Of my ancestry I know almost nothing.
(65) In the slave quarters, and even later, I heard whispered conversations among the coloured people of the tortures which the slaves, including, no doubt, my ancestors on my mother's side, suffered in the middle
(70) passage of the slave ship while being conveyed from Africa to America. I have been

GO ON TO THE NEXT PAGE

PRACTICE TEST

unsuccessful in securing any information
that would throw any accurate light upon the
history of my family beyond my mother. She,
(75) I remember, had a half-brother and a half-
sister. In the days of slavery not very much
attention was given to family history and
family records—that is, black family records.
My mother, I suppose, attracted the attention
(80) of a purchaser who was afterward my owner
and hers. Her addition to the slave family
attracted about as much attention as the
purchase of a new horse or cow. Of my father
I know even less than of my mother. I do not
(85) even know his name. I have heard reports to
the effect that he was a white man who lived
on one of the near-by plantations. Whoever
he was, I never heard of his taking the least
interest in me or providing in any way for my
(90) rearing. But I do not find especial fault with
him. He was simply another unfortunate
victim of the institution which the Nation
unhappily had engrafted upon it at that time.

29. The tone of Passage 1 is best described as

   (A) abstract.
   (B) personal.
   (C) serious.
   (D) melancholy.

30. It is reasonable to conclude from Passage 1
    that Franklin's personal financial situation

   (A) was as strong later in his life as it was
       when he was young.
   (B) worsened as he advanced in years.
   (C) had a random pattern of booms and busts
       over his life.
   (D) improved greatly over his lifetime.

31. Which option gives the best evidence for the
    answer to the previous question?

   (A) Lines 7–13 ("Imagining . . . for you")
   (B) Lines 14–17 ("Having emerged . . . world")
   (C) Lines 27–31 ("I should . . . first")
   (D) Lines 35–40 ("Since . . . writing")

32. As used in line 22, "suitable" most closely
    means

   (A) historical.
   (B) memorable.
   (C) applicable.
   (D) delightful.

33. Washington's most likely purpose in lines
    41–53 is best described as

   (A) to lament his increased senility.
   (B) to express his true identity.
   (C) to critique his familial relations.
   (D) to underscore his rootlessness.

34. As used in line 72, "securing" most closely
    means

   (A) reading.
   (B) obtaining.
   (C) creating.
   (D) safeguarding.

35. The source of information Washington
    primarily draws upon for the information in
    lines 64–93 is

   (A) publications.
   (B) hearsay.
   (C) statistics.
   (D) scholarship.

GO ON TO THE NEXT PAGE

1

36. The passages suggest that something that Washington was more likely to feel than Franklin was

   (A) unhappiness with societal conditions.
   (B) disappointment in his father's conduct.
   (C) curiosity about his heritage.
   (D) an interest in recording his thoughts for posterity.

37. It is reasonable to conclude that Booker T. Washington would very much like to have had the opportunity to do which of the following things that Benjamin Franklin spoke about in Passage 1?

   (A) Obtain anecdotes about his ancestors
   (B) Take time to write a memoir
   (C) Have a relationship with his children
   (D) Relive his life

38. Which option gives the best evidence for the answer to the previous question?

   (A) Lines 49–53 ("The earliest . . . cabins")
   (B) Lines 59–63 ("I was . . . free")
   (C) Lines 71–74 ("I have . . . mother")
   (D) Lines 91–93 ("He was . . . time")

Questions 39–47 are based on the passage that follows.

The Death of Physics—a scientist presents information on recent developments in physics. Written in 2015.

At the turn of the nineteenth century, a prominent physicist stated that physics as a field of study was finished due to the belief
Line that everything about the physical world
(5) had already been discovered. Newtonian Mechanics had held sway for over two hundred years and our understanding of the atom had not advanced much beyond the concepts of the ancient Greeks. The view of
(10) a static universe was the accepted construct and humanity's ignorance was a kind of simple bliss and arrogance.

This all changed soon after the turn of the next century. A German patent clerk, Albert
(15) Einstein, turned Newtonian Mechanics on its head and developed the Theory of Relativity and the notion of space-time. In the 1920s, women studying photographic plates of various star systems took measurements that
(20) Edwin Hubble used to demonstrate that the universe is not static at all, but is expanding in all directions, no matter where you might be; this became known as Hubble's Law. Hubble's constant—the rate at which the
(25) universe is expanding—is currently estimated to be 21 km/s per one million light-years from Earth. This ushered in the notion of the Big Bang as the singular beginning of an expanding space-time and everything in it.
(30) As years went by, the precision of measuring the age of the Universe since the Big Bang kept evolving to a current estimate of 13.2 billion years. Arno Penzias and Robert Wilson provided additional evidence for this view
(35) of cosmology when an antenna they were

GO ON TO THE NEXT PAGE

adjusting in the 1960s detected a small amount of radiation from every direction in space.

Scientists also began to explore the world (40) of the very small, and the field of quantum mechanics was hatched. From a world of fundamental particles that included only protons, neutrons, and electrons, a never-ending march toward more fundamental (45) building blocks ensued, and now quarks, leptons, bosons, gravitons, etc. have become the particles that physicists use to try to make sense out of the nano-world. The recent discovery (2015) of the Higgs Boson (50) at the Large Hadron Collider in Europe created much excitement in the scientific community. This particle and the Higgs Field are responsible for giving every substance its mass and had been elusive since Peter Higgs (55) postulated their existence in 1964.

Where will this process end? Each time we cause particles to collide at ever-increasing energies, new constituents are created and investigated. It is as if we continue to peel (60) back the layers of an onion only to find more layers that invite exploration. In the modern era, the field of String Theory has been posited, theorizing that the vibrations of tiny string-like mechanisms provide the building (65) blocks of all particles. From String Theory, the idea of Multiple Universes has been proposed and evidence of this mind-blowing idea was reported in late 2015.

Now scientists insist that the "visible" (70) universe only contains about 30% of what is really out there, and the concepts of dark matter and dark energy are invoked to explain the motions of various large bodies that permeate our universe. We are 120 years (75) beyond the time when physics was declared dead to any new inquiries. Now, the steady

arrival of new and exciting perspectives and data from more precise and powerful instruments and machines launch new (80) explorations on a monthly basis. There is nothing dead about the field of physics, and I would claim it has never been more alive.

39. What is the principal claim of the passage?

(A) Dark matter and dark energy have become the primary focus for modern physicists.
(B) Rather than remaining static, physics is continuing to evolve just as it has in the past.
(C) The contributions of Peter Higgs to science exceed those of Albert Einstein.
(D) After many years of ignorant theorizing, physicists have finally uncovered the ultimate truth of the universe.

40. The author suggests that as physics has advanced, its theories are often

(A) practically applicable.
(B) ethically offensive.
(C) historically consistent.
(D) more counterintuitive.

41. Which option gives the best evidence for the answer to the previous question?

(A) Lines 5–9 ("Newtonian . . . Greeks")
(B) Lines 30–33 ("As years . . . years")
(C) Lines 48–52 ("The recent . . . community")
(D) Lines 65–68 ("From String . . . 2015")

GO ON TO THE NEXT PAGE

42. As used in line 10, "construct" most closely means

    (A) building.
    (B) observation.
    (C) theory.
    (D) astronomy.

43. As used in line 28, "singular" most closely means

    (A) odd.
    (B) unattached.
    (C) definitive.
    (D) lonely.

44. According to the passage, when did the scientific consensus most likely shift from an understanding of the universe as being static to being expansive?

    (A) Approximately 1800
    (B) The early 1900s
    (C) The late 1900s
    (D) 2015

45. Which option gives the best evidence for the answer to the previous question?

    (A) Lines 1–9 ("At the turn . . . Greeks")
    (B) Lines 13–23 ("This all . . . Law")
    (C) Lines 33–38 ("Arno . . . in space")
    (D) Lines 48–55 ("The recent . . . 1964")

46. What is the purpose of the sentence in lines 59–61 ("It is as if . . . invite exploration")?

    (A) To use an analogy to illustrate a concept
    (B) To describe the latest scientific evidence
    (C) To make connections between physics and biology
    (D) To express dismay at the state of modern science

47. It is reasonable to infer that the author's primary interest in physics is its potential to

    (A) provide practical inventions for everyday consumer use.
    (B) give a military advantage to those empowered with its findings.
    (C) advance medical science so that new cures for illness can be discovered.
    (D) help us understand the nature of the universe.

STOP

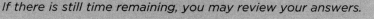
If there is still time remaining, you may review your answers.

WRITING AND LANGUAGE TEST

PRACTICE TEST

35 MINUTES, 44 QUESTIONS

Turn to Section 2 of your answer sheet to answer the questions in this section.

Directions: Questions follow each of the passages below. Some questions ask you how the passage might be changed to improve the expression of ideas. Other questions ask you how the passage might be altered to correct errors in grammar, usage, and punctuation. One or more graphics accompany some passages. You will be required to consider these graphics as you answer questions about editing the passage.

There are three types of questions. In the first type, a part of the passage is underlined. The second type is based on a certain part of the passage. The third type is based on the entire passage.

Read each passage. Then, choose the answer to each question that changes the passage so that it is consistent with the conventions of standard written English. One of the answer choices for many questions is "NO CHANGE." Choosing this answer means that you believe the best answer is to make no change in the passage.

Questions 1–11 are based on the following passage and supplementary material.

Read to Succeed

Reading is an enriching activity that is well worth making part of ❶ ones regular habits. Starting from an early age, children who read for pleasure encounter many new words and concepts that expand their minds. ❷ Although images are frequently used in society today, words, unlike images, require using one's mind to understand them, ponder their meaning, and ❸ to considering whether they are communicating something true or false. Studies have shown that reading more correlates with greater comprehension, cognitive development, and writing abilities. Those who read for fun more often have higher writing scores—in fact, those who

1. (A) NO CHANGE
   (B) one
   (C) one's
   (D) ones'

2. (A) NO CHANGE
   (B) Since
   (C) Because
   (D) In addition,

3. (A) NO CHANGE
   (B) consider
   (C) considered
   (D) considering

GO ON TO THE NEXT PAGE

Average Writing Scores by Frequency of Reading for Fun

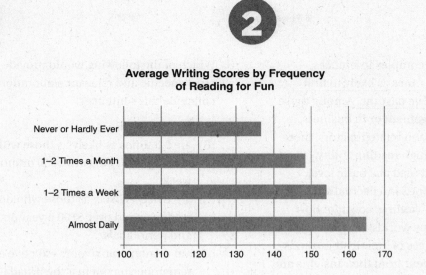

Note: Writing scores range from 0–300, and students surveyed nationwide.

Source: U.S. Department of Education, National Center for Education Statistics

read almost daily for fun outperform those who never or hardly ever read by approximately **❹** 10 points on national writing tests. This translates into higher levels of academic achievement, such as higher test scores in math, science, civics, and history.

In addition to improving one's intellectual abilities, the habit of reading has an occupational and financial payoff. **❺** Sixty-three percent of employers rate reading comprehension as being very important. There is a strong correlation between poor reading skills and unemployment, lower wages, and fewer opportunities for advancement. Those who can effectively read lengthy, complex, abstract texts, synthesize

4. Which of the following is supported by the data in the accompanying chart?

(A) NO CHANGE
(B) 30
(C) 60
(D) 120

5. The author is considering removing the underlined sentence from the passage. Should it be kept or removed?

(A) Kept, because it provides specific details in support of the previous sentence
(B) Kept, because it elaborates on salary details that result from avid reading
(C) Removed, because it repeats information already expressed in the passage
(D) Removed, because it provides far more detail than necessary to make the argument

GO ON TO THE NEXT PAGE

information, and make complex inferences ❻ are more than three times as likely to find reading to be an enjoyable pastime. Among those who have jobs in management or in business, financial, professional, and related sectors, more than 60 percent have a high reading ability, whereas only 18 percent read at a basic level.

Beyond developing one's intellectual abilities and being financially rewarding, consider how reading opens whole new worlds! It enables one to learn from the experiences of literally thousands of other people—to benefit from their insights and to avoid their mistakes. It gives access to some of the greatest minds and ideas throughout history. Reading also stimulates the ❼ imagination to identify with a hero in a story, consider what it would have been like to be at some historical event, or to form a picture of what one could accomplish in life.

Given how reading can benefit an individual, it is not surprising, then, that readers have positive effects on society. ❽ Them who read literature are more than twice as likely to volunteer or do charity work and more than three times as likely to go to museums, attend plays or concerts, and create art as those who do not. Good readers are even more likely to play sports, attend sporting events, or do outdoor activities. ❾ On the other hand, prisoners tend to have significantly worse reading skills than others.

6. Which of the following would provide the most specific and relevant elaboration to conclude this sentence?

(A) NO CHANGE
(B) are 2.5 times as likely as those with a basic reading ability to earn $850 or more per week.
(C) are twice as likely as those who do not read to spend over $100 a year on books and periodicals.
(D) are demonstrably more effective at remembering not just the broad ideas of what they read, but the finer details.

7. (A) NO CHANGE
(B) imagination: to identify with a hero in a story, to
(C) imagination; to identify with a hero in a story, to
(D) imagination, to identify with a hero in a story to

8. (A) NO CHANGE
(B) Them whom
(C) Those who
(D) Those whom

9. (A) NO CHANGE
(B) Therefore,
(C) Moreover,
(D) Thus,

GO ON TO THE NEXT PAGE

⑩ <u>More or less,</u> when one considers both the nature of the activity itself as well as the statistics, reading makes a big difference in life. ⑪ <u>Enriching one's life, and community is well worth regularly delving into great books.</u>

10. Which option best expresses that the author is confident in his point of view?

(A) NO CHANGE
(B) Dubitably,
(C) While there are merits to both sides of the issue,
(D) Clearly,

11. (A) NO CHANGE
(B) Enriching one's life and community, is well worth regularly delving into great books.
(C) Enriching one's life and community is well worth regularly delving into great books.
(D) Enriching one's life and community; is well worth regularly delving into great books.

GO ON TO THE NEXT PAGE

2

Questions 12–22 are based on the following passage.

Pluto

"My very educated mother just served us nine pizzas" is ⑫ a sentence, that may not mean much to young students anymore. However, to people of an older generation this sentence is almost universally recognized as a mnemonic device used to aid children in remembering the planets of our solar system. The sentence has changed recently, not because serving nine pizzas is against school lunch health standards, ⑬ but because the planets themselves have changed.

In 2006, ⑭ despite public outcries and complaints, scientists reclassified Pluto, effectively removing "pizzas" from the well-known memory aid. Pluto, discovered in 1930, had long been viewed as the adorable kid brother of the solar system, significantly ⑮ smallest than the older siblings and tagging along at the back of the line. That ended when several other similar sized planets were discovered in Pluto's orbit. The discovery of these smaller planets ⑯ were the beginning of Pluto's demise.

The issue with these smaller celestial objects was whether they could really be classified as planets. Many scientists wanted all of the smaller objects to be planets so that Pluto could remain one as well; ⑰ however, this proved to be impractical, as it would have resulted in objects smaller than our moon being planets. The International Astronomical Union, an organization

12. (A) NO CHANGE
(B) a sentence that may not, mean much to young students anymore.
(C) a sentence that, may not mean much, to young students anymore.
(D) a sentence that may not mean much to young students anymore.

13. (A) NO CHANGE
(B) and since
(C) for a result
(D) and

14. (A) NO CHANGE
(B) despite public outcries,
(C) even though there were complaints by members of the public,
(D) OMIT the underlined portion.

15. (A) NO CHANGE
(B) smallest then
(C) smaller than
(D) smaller then

16. (A) NO CHANGE
(B) was
(C) are
(D) is

17. (A) NO CHANGE
(B) as a result,
(C) what is more,
(D) consequently,

GO ON TO THE NEXT PAGE

that long has been in charge of classifying and naming celestial bodies, set about to solve the problem by clearly defining what a planet is. **18** Their goal was to give the criteria for what makes something a planet. Their proposal held that objects that were in orbit around the sun (but not around another planet) **19** were quite large and had a resulting large amount of gravitation, could be considered planets. Unfortunately, Pluto didn't meet these stipulations.

While Pluto is in orbit around the sun and has become nearly round, it isn't big **20** enough, and therefore doesn't have enough gravity, to clear its orbit. This is proved by the fact that many of those other small planet-like objects have been discovered in Pluto's orbit. Together, these objects now make up what has been named the Kuiper belt. They have each been classified as

18. The author is considering removing the underlined sentence. Should it be kept or removed?

   (A) Kept, because it clarifies the goal of the Astronomical Union
   (B) Kept, because it gives details on what constitutes a planet
   (C) Deleted, because it repeats the idea of the previous sentence
   (D) Deleted, because it contradicts information presented elsewhere in the passage

19. Which of the following options for the underlined portion would best elaborate on the topic of the sentence with the most specific detail?

   (A) NO CHANGE
   (B) were constituted of a great deal of mass and matter, and possessed sufficient gravitational pull to have a significant impact on their surroundings,
   (C) had enough mass to become nearly round due to pressure, and had enough gravity to clear their orbit of any other bodies,
   (D) had a tremendously large amount of mass, while enough gravity to be quite noticeable,

20. (A) NO CHANGE
   (B) enough and therefore, doesn't have enough gravity, to clear its orbit.
   (C) enough and therefore doesn't have enough gravity to clear, its orbit.
   (D) enough, and, therefore, doesn't have enough gravity, to clear its orbit.

GO ON TO THE NEXT PAGE

dwarf planets, meaning that they meet most, but not all, of the qualifications of a full-sized planet. **21** <u>Because</u> most of the world has come to accept that Pluto is no longer a planet, some people remain stubbornly attached to their older, nostalgic views of the solar system. **22** <u>It is truly a shame that people cannot give up their old-fashioned views on what constitutes a planet.</u>

21. (A) NO CHANGE
    (B) While
    (C) Since
    (D) And

22. Which of the following would provide the most effective conclusion to the passage, tying it back to the introduction?

    (A) NO CHANGE
    (B) The significance of the advances in astronomical research cannot be understated.
    (C) While Pluto may have lost its planetary recognition, Mars and Jupiter continue to be recognized as planets.
    (D) After all, saying "my very educated mother just served us nothing" doesn't have quite the same ring to it.

GO ON TO THE NEXT PAGE

Questions 23–33 are based on the following passage.

Birth Order

Siblings are something most of us take for granted. **23** We don't tend to spend a whole lot of time analyzing the people with whom we were raised—we are used to their personality quirks and we've adapted to deal with them. However, many of those traits that we take for granted in our siblings could be very different **24** based on just one thing: birth order. Birth order is a very complex theory with lots of ins and outs. But when we boil it down to the basics, we can find personality traits **25** which applies specifically to each of the positions in the family.

Firstborn children are leaders. They spend their early years getting lots of attention from their parents, and then they grow up **26** being responsible for their younger siblings. These are the people who are perfectionists. They become the best at whatever they do. Firstborn children become CEOs, lawyers, doctors, astronauts, and politicians. They excel in leadership positions. **27** In contrast, most of the presidents of the United States have been firstborn men or only

23. The author is considering inserting the following sentence at this point in the passage:

"Siblings are defined as those people to whom one is related as brothers and sisters."

Should this insertion be made?

(A) Yes, because it provides detailed examples in support of a claim.
(B) Yes, because it gives insight into the author's personal views.
(C) No, because it simply defines a widely understood term.
(D) No, because it is unrelated to the topic of the passage.

24. (A) NO CHANGE
(B) based on just one thing birth order.
(C) based, on just one thing: birth order.
(D) based on just one thing; birth order.

25. (A) NO CHANGE
(B) with apply
(C) that applies
(D) that apply

26. The author is considering removing the underlined portion of the sentence. Should it be kept or removed?

(A) Kept, because it gives statistical evidence
(B) Kept, because it provides a helpful elaboration
(C) Removed, because it is irrelevant to the topic of the sentence
(D) Removed, because it interrupts the author's line of reasoning

27. (A) NO CHANGE
(B) To object,
(C) In fact,
(D) On the other hand,

GO ON TO THE NEXT PAGE

children (only children are like firstborn children times ten). Firstborn children, though, may suffer from conditions like hypertension, as they have a hard time relaxing and letting go.

[1] A middle child can be any child born between the first and the last. [2] Middle children are very hard to pin down. [3] They often go through life feeling like they don't quite **28** fit in with their families. [4] They suffer from "middle child syndrome," which means they are overlooked or squeezed in the middle. [5] If a family is going to leave a kid at the rest stop on vacation, it is going to be the middle child. [6] This results in the middle child having a large group of friends outside the family; they are very social. [7] Many diplomats are middle children, since these people spend their childhood resolving fights within their families. **29**

This brings us to the youngest child. The youngest is often very charismatic. He or she grows up being the center of attention—fortunately, the youngest loves to entertain. **30** Entertainment is something that is quite popular with most modern-day consumers. Youngest children are free thinkers. They are artistic and creative as well. However, the youngest child doesn't have the drive that the oldest has, and can sometimes lose **31** there way in life.

28. (A) NO CHANGE
(B) fit on
(C) fits with
(D) fits in to

29. The author is considering adding the following sentence to the previous paragraph:

"Middle children are also mediators."

Where would it most logically be placed?

(A) Before sentence 1
(B) Before sentence 3
(C) Before sentence 5
(D) Before sentence 7

30. Which of the following choices provides the most relevant and detailed elaboration of the previous sentence?

(A) NO CHANGE
(B) The youngest child may be significantly younger than his or her oldest sibling, particularly if his or her parents remarried.
(C) The oldest child, to elaborate, will likely have a "take-charge" personality.
(D) Many famous comedians, actors, and musicians are the youngest in their families.

31. (A) NO CHANGE
(B) their
(C) they're
(D) his or her

GO ON TO THE NEXT PAGE

32 <u>Birth order isn't a one-size-fits-all theory, there are many loopholes and exceptions.</u> People can change, if they want to, through hard work. **33** <u>Nevertheless,</u> it can be helpful to understand the factors that influence personalities, and birth order helps a little.

32. (A) NO CHANGE
(B) Birth order isn't a one-size-fits-all theory; there are many loopholes and exceptions.
(C) Birth order, isn't a one-size-fits-all theory—there are many loopholes and exceptions.
(D) Birth order, isn't a one-size-fits-all theory, there are many loopholes and exceptions.

33. (A) NO CHANGE
(B) As a result,
(C) Due to this,
(D) Continuing,

GO ON TO THE NEXT PAGE

Questions 34–44 are based on the following passage and supplementary material.

Hermey Is Onto Something

(1)

In the 1964 Christmas classic "Rudolph, the Red-Nosed Reindeer," Hermey is a misfit elf who hopes to give up toy-making in order to practice dentistry. As a child, the only thing more appealing to me than being Santa's elf would have been to be Rudolph himself. **34** <u>A lifelong protester of bath time teeth brushing nail</u> clipping, and anything concerning strict routine hygiene, I simply could not understand the elf who would forgo the joys of Santa's workshop for a chance to play in somebody's disgusting mouth. **35** <u>On the one hand he had an amiable, loyal nature. Even though this was the case, Hermey appalled me.</u>

(2)

I recited this **36** <u>childhood memory from the early part of my life</u> to my first college roommate. Tim had just earned admission into Indiana University's School of Dentistry. After living in a single dorm room through undergraduate, I had found his apartment listed under the enticing entry "Looking for One Roommate, Cheap Rent for the Quiet and Introverted," and **37** <u>accepted</u> the adventure of graduate school and a roommate who preferred books to parties. Dental students, Tim explained, **38** <u>have many</u> reasons for pursuing the occupation.

34. (A) NO CHANGE
    (B) A lifelong protester of bath time teeth brushing, nail
    (C) A lifelong protester of bath time, teeth brushing nail
    (D) A lifelong protester of bath time, teeth brushing, nail

35. Which of the following options provides the best combined version of the two underlined sentences?

    (A) While it is truly the case that he has a nature that is loyal and amiable, he nevertheless appalled me.
    (B) Even though he had an amiable, loyal nature, I could not help but be appalled by Hermey.
    (C) Despite his amiable, loyal nature, Hermey appalled me.
    (D) Because of his amiable, loyal nature, I was appalled by Hermey.

36. (A) NO CHANGE
    (B) childhood memory
    (C) memory from my time period as a child
    (D) childhood memory and recollection

37. (A) NO CHANGE
    (B) excepted
    (C) inspected
    (D) expected

38. (A) NO CHANGE
    (B) have much
    (C) had much
    (D) has many

GO ON TO THE NEXT PAGE

(3)

Besides having great hand dexterity and steadiness, dentists also tend to be personable and interested in helping others maintain their health and self-confidence. Tim, while appropriately interested in diagnosing and treating **㊟** patients problems with their teeth and gums, demonstrated real passion for repairing teeth and aiding in cosmetic dental concerns. An accident involving stairs and a hardwood floor had left Tim missing a front tooth from the age of seven until seventeen. He understood firsthand how being ashamed of your dental health can **㊵** effect your whole demeanor. His goal, he boasted, would be to ensure no other middle school kid would go ten years without cracking a smile.

(4)

While Tim's intentions are admirable, I found, with a little research, that there are several other reasons for becoming a dentist. In 2015, average estimates of a general dentist's annual salary for dentists **㊶** with over six years experience approached $250,000. In fact, their expected

39. (A) NO CHANGE
    (B) patient's
    (C) patients'
    (D) those of patients

40. (A) NO CHANGE
    (B) effects
    (C) affects
    (D) affect

41. Which of the following statements is most consistent with the information in the supplementary graph?

    (A) NO CHANGE
    (B) with over six years experience approached $150,000.
    (C) with four to six years experience ranged between $200,000 and $250,000.
    (D) fresh out of dental school were less than $60,000.

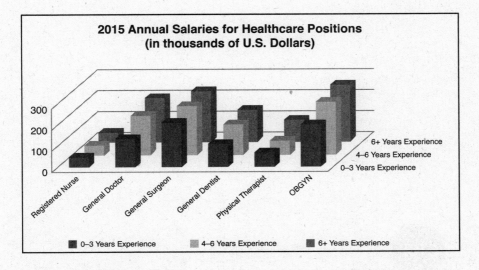

Source: onetonline.org

GO ON TO THE NEXT PAGE

salaries **42** <u>come close to those of general doctors.</u> The career prospects are equally impressive, and continuing to grow. Certainly, dentists complete a rigorous curriculum—after undergraduate, they go on to earn a doctorate in dental school, complete licensing standards, and sometimes work a 2–4 year residency—but the intense training pays off in job security and a rewarding income. **43** <u>However,</u> many dentists work in dental offices or start their own practice and enjoy normal 9 A.M. to 5 P.M., weekday hours. Even those who choose to work a more unconventional schedule find the compensation well worth their time.

(5)

Hermey, detestable as he was to my five-year-old self, might have been onto something after all. **44**

42. Which of the following properly uses information from the supplementary graph to provide logical support to the author's argument?

(A) NO CHANGE
(B) approximate those of OBGYNs.
(C) exceed those of general surgeons.
(D) roughly equal those of registered nurses.

43. (A) NO CHANGE
(B) Moreover,
(C) In contrast,
(D) Consequently,

44. The author wishes to insert the following sentence as a stand-alone paragraph in the passage.

"Anyway," he smirked, "the College of Toy-making is stingy with financial aid."

Before what paragraph would it most logically be placed?
(A) Paragraph 1
(B) Paragraph 2
(C) Paragraph 3
(D) Paragraph 5

If there is still time remaining, you may review your answers.

MATH TEST—NO CALCULATOR

25 MINUTES, 17 QUESTIONS

Turn to Section 3 of your answer sheet to answer the questions in this section.

Directions: For questions 1–13, solve each problem and choose the best answer from the given options. Fill in the corresponding circle on your answer sheet. For questions 14–17, solve each problem and enter your answer in the grid on your answer sheet.

Notes:

- Calculators are **NOT PERMITTED** in this section.
- All variables and expressions represent real numbers unless indicated otherwise.
- All figures are drawn to scale unless indicated otherwise.
- All figures are in a plane unless indicated otherwise.
- Unless indicated otherwise, the domain of a given function is the set of all real numbers x for which the function has real values.

REFERENCE INFORMATION

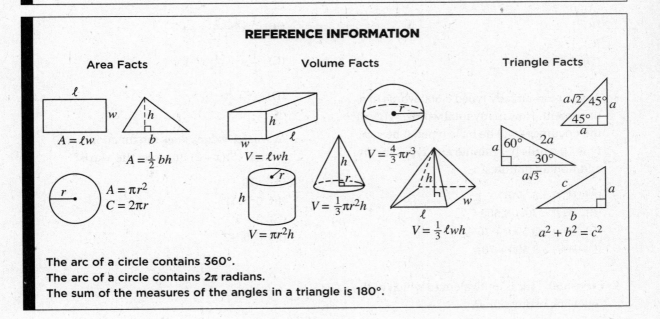

The arc of a circle contains 360°.

The arc of a circle contains 2π radians.

The sum of the measures of the angles in a triangle is 180°.

GO ON TO THE NEXT PAGE

1. What is the value of x in the following equation?

$$3x + 2 = \frac{4}{3}x$$

(A) $-\frac{6}{5}$

(B) $-\frac{2}{3}$

(C) $\frac{1}{4}$

(D) $\frac{5}{6}$

2. What are the solution(s) to the following equation?

$$5x^2 - 15x + 10 = 0$$

(A) 0

(B) 1, 2

(C) 1, 4

(D) 2, 5

3. A typist has already typed 3,500 words of a document. How many total words, $W(t)$, of the document will he have typed if he can type 70 words per minute and types for an additional t minutes?

(A) $W(t) = 3,500t$

(B) $W(t) = 70t - 3,500$

(C) $W(t) = 3,500t + 70$

(D) $W(t) = 3,500 + 70t$

4. $6a^2 + 8ab - 4ac$ is equivalent to which of the following expressions?

(A) $a(3a + 4b + 2c)$

(B) $2a(3a + 4b - 2c)$

(C) $4a(a + b - 2c)$

(D) $2a(3a - 4b + 2c)$

5. What represents the range of x-values in this inequality?

$$-3(x + 4) > 2x$$

(A) $x < -\frac{12}{5}$

(B) $x \le -\frac{1}{3}$

(C) $x > \frac{7}{8}$

(D) $x \ge 3\frac{1}{2}$

6. The expression $\left(\frac{2}{3}x + 1\right)\left(\frac{3}{4}x - 1\right) = ?$

(A) $\frac{1}{6}x^2 - \frac{1}{3}x + 1$

(B) $\frac{1}{4}x^2 + \frac{1}{12}x - 4$

(C) $\frac{1}{2}x^2 + \frac{1}{12}x - 1$

(D) $x^2 + \frac{1}{4}x - 1$

7. At what x-values does the function $y = x(x - 5)(x + 2)$ intersect the x-axis?

(A) -10

(B) 0, 3, 12

(C) 2, -5

(D) 0, 5, -2

GO ON TO THE NEXT PAGE

8. At what point in the xy-plane will the functions $y = 4x - 3$ and $y = -\dfrac{1}{2}x + 2$ intersect?

   (A) $\left(2, -\dfrac{2}{3}\right)$

   (B) $\left(-\dfrac{3}{4}, \dfrac{5}{6}\right)$

   (C) $\left(\dfrac{10}{9}, \dfrac{13}{9}\right)$

   (D) $\left(1, \dfrac{3}{7}\right)$

9. The function f is given by $f(x) = 2 - |x - 4|$. For what value of x does the function f achieve its maximum value?

   (A) 2
   (B) 4
   (C) 5
   (D) 6

10. When $x > 0$, which of these expressions is equivalent to $\dfrac{1}{\dfrac{1}{2x}} + \dfrac{3}{\dfrac{6}{4x}}$?

   (A) $4x$
   (B) $7x$
   (C) $\dfrac{1}{2}x - 4$
   (D) $x^2 - 12$

11. If $\left(x^2\right)^{\frac{1}{5}} + \sqrt[5]{32x^2} = ax^{\frac{2}{5}}$ for all values of x, what is the value of a?

   (A) 0
   (B) 3
   (C) 5
   (D) 16

12. The value of money is affected by the inflation rate—the higher the inflation rate, the less valuable money will become over time. The rate of inflation is calculated using the formula below, in which CPI represents the consumer price index, a measure of the average of a typical basket of consumer goods and services (where goods and services are weighted relative to how often they are purchased by a normal consumer):

$$\frac{\text{This Year's CPI} - \text{Last Year's CPI}}{\text{Last Year's CPI}} \times 100$$

The current rate of inflation would *definitely* be zero if the CPI a year ago equaled which of the following?

   (A) The CPI a year from now
   (B) This year's CPI
   (C) Zero
   (D) 100

13. What is the x-coordinate of the minimum of the parabola with the equation $y + 17 = 6x^2 + 12x$?

   (A) -1
   (B) 0
   (C) 2
   (D) 3

GO ON TO THE NEXT PAGE

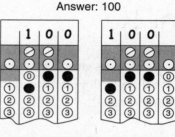

Grid-in Response Directions

In questions 14–17, first solve the problem, and then enter your answer on the grid provided on the answer sheet. The instructions for entering your answers follow.

- First, write your answer in the boxes at the top of the grid.
- Second, grid your answer in the columns below the boxes.
- Use the fraction bar in the first row or the decimal point in the second row to enter fractions and decimals.

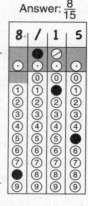

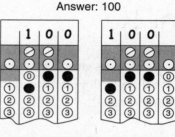

Either position is acceptable

- Grid only one space in each column.
- Entering the answer in the boxes is recommended as an aid in gridding but is not required.
- The machine scoring your exam can read only what you grid, so you **must grid-in your answers correctly to get credit**.
- If a question has more than one correct answer, grid-in only one of them.
- The grid does not have a minus sign; so no answer can be negative.
- A mixed number *must* be converted to an improper fraction or a decimal before it is gridded.

  Enter $1\frac{1}{4}$ as 5/4 or 1.25; the machine will interpret 11/4 as $\frac{11}{4}$ and mark it wrong.

- **All decimals must be entered as accurately as possible.** Here are three acceptable ways of gridding

$$\frac{3}{11} = 0.272727\ldots$$

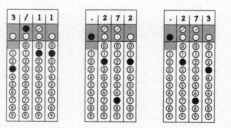

- Note that rounding to .273 is acceptable because you are using the full grid, but you would receive **no credit** for .3 or .27, because they are less accurate.

GO ON TO THE NEXT PAGE

105

14. In the isosceles trapezoid above, what is the measure of the smallest interior angle?

15. Given that (x, y) is a solution to the following system of equations, what is the sum of x and y?

$$2x - y = 3$$
$$4y = 6x$$

16. On a particular college campus, there are two men for every three women. If the total number of men and women on campus is equal to 4,000, how many more women are there on campus than men?

17. Given that $x \neq 0$, find the value of

$$\left(\frac{2x^4 + 3(2x^2)^2}{x^4} \right)^2.$$

STOP

If there is still time remaining, you may review your answers.

MATH TEST—CALCULATOR

45 MINUTES, 31 QUESTIONS

Turn to Section 4 of your answer sheet to answer the questions in this section.

Directions: For questions 1–27, solve each problem and choose the best answer from the given choices. Fill in the corresponding circle on your answer sheet. For questions 28–31, solve each problem and enter your answer in the grid on your answer sheet.

Notes:

- Calculators **ARE PERMITTED** in this section.
- All variables and expressions represent real numbers unless indicated otherwise.
- All figures are drawn to scale unless indicated otherwise.
- All figures are in a plane unless indicated otherwise.
- Unless indicated otherwise, the domain of a given function is the set of all real numbers x for which the function has real values.

REFERENCE INFORMATION

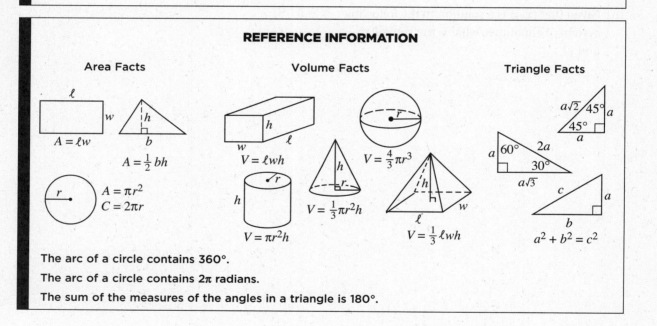

The arc of a circle contains 360°.

The arc of a circle contains 2π radians.

The sum of the measures of the angles in a triangle is 180°.

GO ON TO THE NEXT PAGE

1. A roller coaster requires riders to be at least 48 inches tall. Given that there are approximately 2.54 centimeters in an inch, how tall must a rider be to the nearest whole *centimeter* to ride the roller coaster?

   (A) 96
   (B) 122
   (C) 148
   (D) 190

2. A bus is traveling at a constant rate of 50 miles per hour. At this rate, how far will the bus travel in $3\frac{1}{4}$ hours?

   (A) 150 miles
   (B) 160 miles
   (C) 162.5 miles
   (D) 175.5 miles

3. Which of the following expressions is equivalent to $7 - 2(y - 1)$?

   (A) $9 - 2y$
   (B) $5 - 2y$
   (C) $6 - 2y$
   (D) $4 + 2y$

4. Which of the following is a solution to the equation below?

$$(x - 3)^2 - 81 = 0$$

   (A) 12
   (B) 11
   (C) 9
   (D) 8

Questions 5–7 refer to the following information and table.

The table below gives the results of a survey of a randomly selected sample of 400 individuals who are 15 and 16 years old. Each respondent selected the method of electronic communication that he or she used the most.

Primary Method of Electronic Communication

	Texting	E-mail	Video Chatting	Other	Total
15-year-olds	110	20	40	30	200
16-year-olds	85	45	30	40	200
Total	195	x	70	70	400

5. The table omits the value for x in the bottom row. Based on the structure of the table, what is the value of x?

   (A) 24
   (B) 38
   (C) 57
   (D) 65

6. The city of Springfield has 50,000 residents ages 15 and 16. Given that the sample in the table is representative of Springfield's residents, approximately how many 15- and 16-year-olds in Springfield would use video chatting as their primary method of electronic communication?

   (A) 3,100
   (B) 4,870
   (C) 8,750
   (D) 20,000

GO ON TO THE NEXT PAGE

7. What is the best estimation of the probability that a randomly selected 16-year-old from the sample would use texting as his or her primary method of electronic communication?

(A) 0.23

(B) 0.43

(C) 0.49

(D) 0.73

_____

8. If $\frac{x}{4} = \frac{1}{2}$, then $\frac{4(x-3)}{(-12)}$ equals which of the following?

(A) $\frac{1}{16}$

(B) $\frac{1}{12}$

(C) $\frac{1}{6}$

(D) $\frac{1}{3}$

9. If the sale price on a coat is $72 and the original price of the coat was $90, what is the percent discount from this sale?

(A) 14%

(B) 20%

(C) 26%

(D) 80%

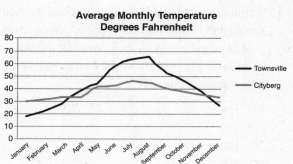

Average Monthly Temperature
Degrees Fahrenheit

Townsville
Cityberg

10. The average monthly temperatures for the cities of Townsville and Cityberg were recorded in the last calendar year. Based on the graph, which statement is true?

(A) The temperature on a randomly selected day in Townsville will be greater than the temperature on the same randomly selected day in Cityberg.

(B) The temperature on a randomly selected day in Cityberg will be greater than the temperature on the same randomly selected day in Townsville.

(C) The average monthly temperature in Townsville was greater than the average monthly temperature in Cityberg for the majority of the year.

(D) The average monthly temperature in Cityberg was greater than the average monthly temperature in Townsville for the majority of the year.

11. David has two quarters for every five dimes in his change dish, with no other coins present. If he has a total of $2 in coins in the dish, how many total coins does he have?

(A) 12

(B) 14

(C) 16

(D) 18

GO ON TO THE NEXT PAGE

12. A chef is making cookies from scratch. He requires a set period of time to gather the ingredients and to get everything set up to make the cookies. Then the chef needs a set period of time to make each individual cookie. If c represents the total number of cookies he is making and if t represents the total amount of time it takes to make c cookies, what is the meaning of the 20 in this equation: $t = 20 + 10c$?

(A) How much time it takes to make each individual cookie
(B) The fixed cost of the cookie ingredients
(C) The maximum number of cookies he can make in 10 minutes
(D) The amount of time it takes him to set things up prior to making a cookie

13. Jasmine has $100,000 in an investment portfolio, divided among only three categories: stocks, bonds, and cash. She has twice as much invested in stocks as she does in bonds. She also has three times as much invested in bonds as she has in cash. What percent of Jasmine's portfolio is invested in bonds?

(A) 22%
(B) 27%
(C) 30%
(D) 44%

Questions 14–15 refer to the following information and table.

A coffee shop recorded data on the types of beverages ordered by its patrons in a given month. Each patron visited only once during the month and purchased only one beverage. The four listed beverages are the only ones sold at this coffee shop.

	Cappuccino	Espresso	Latte	Americano	Total
Females under 18	230	125	325	170	850
Males under 18	170	185	240	220	815
Females age 18 and older	425	328	530	290	1,573
Males age 18 and older	350	429	477	313	1,569
Total	1,175	1,067	1,572	993	4,807

14. What (approximate) percentage of the drinks purchased at the coffee shop in the given month was espresso?

(A) 11%
(B) 17%
(C) 22%
(D) 36%

15. Assume that the sample in the month portrayed in the table is representative of the coffee shop's sales for an entire year. Based on these assumptions, if a female customer is selected at random, what is the approximate probability that she will purchase a latte?

(A) 0.35
(B) 0.41
(C) 0.46
(D) 0.53

GO ON TO THE NEXT PAGE

PRACTICE TEST

16. A line has the equation $y - 4x = 5$. What is the slope of a line that is perpendicular to this line?

(A) -4

(B) $-\dfrac{1}{4}$

(C) $\dfrac{5}{4}$

(D) 4

17. The formula for electric power, P, is $P = I \times V$, where I is the current and V is the voltage. The formula for voltage is $V = I \times R$, where I is also the current and R is the resistance. How will the power of a given current be affected if the resistance is doubled and the voltage is quadrupled?

(A) The power will be doubled.

(B) The power will be quadrupled.

(C) The power will be 8 times greater.

(D) The power will be 16 times greater.

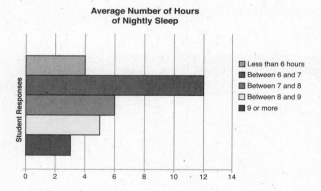

Average Number of Hours of Nightly Sleep

- Less than 6 hours
- Between 6 and 7
- Between 7 and 8
- Between 8 and 9
- 9 or more

18. In the above histogram, the distribution of the number of hours of sleep per night as self-reported by 30 students is recorded. Which of the following values would be equal for the above set of values?

(A) Mean and median

(B) Mode and mean

(C) Median and mode

(D) Mean and range

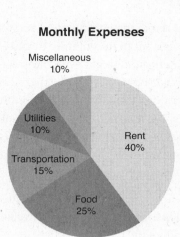

Monthly Expenses

- Miscellaneous 10%
- Utilities 10%
- Transportation 15%
- Rent 40%
- Food 25%

19. The percentages of Anita's monthly expenses are portrayed in the above chart. If Anita spent $600 on rent, what was the total of her other expenses for the month?

(A) $600

(B) $900

(C) $1,200

(D) $1,400

20. A wall's height is two-thirds that of its length. The entire wall will be painted. The paint costs $12 per gallon, and 1 gallon of paint covers 60 square feet. What expression gives the cost of the paint (assuming one can purchase partial and full gallons) to cover a wall that is L feet long?

(A) $\text{Cost} = L^2$

(B) $\text{Cost} = \dfrac{1}{5}L^2$

(C) $\text{Cost} = \dfrac{2}{15}L^2$

(D) $\text{Cost} = \dfrac{3}{64}L^2$

GO ON TO THE NEXT PAGE

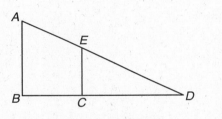

21. Consider the function $f(x) = 2x - 3$. What is the range of the absolute value of this function?

    (A) $y < -3$
    (B) $y \leq 0$
    (C) $y \geq 0$
    (D) $y > 5$

22. An animal shelter can house only cats and dogs. Each dog requires 2 cups of food and 3 treats a day, while each cat requires 1 cup of food a day and 2 treats a day. If the shelter has available a total of 400 cups of food and 500 treats a day, what expressions portray the full scope of the number of c cats and d dogs the shelter could potentially house?

    (A) $2d - c \leq 400$ and $3d + c < 500$
    (B) $2d + c \leq 400$ and $3d + 2c \leq 500$
    (C) $4d + c < 400$ and $d + c < 500$
    (D) $2d + 2c \leq 400$ and $2d + 3c \leq 500$

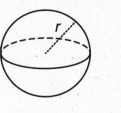

23. Which of the following expressions is equivalent to the diameter of the sphere portrayed above, with a radius of r and volume V?

    (A) $2\sqrt[3]{\dfrac{3V}{4\pi}}$

    (B) πr^3

    (C) $4\sqrt{\dfrac{2r^3}{3}}$

    (D) $\dfrac{4V^3}{3r^2}$

24. Caitlin opens a checking account that earns no interest to set aside spending money for vacations. Each month she puts the same dollar amount, $50, into the account. Unfortunately, she does not expect to be able to take a vacation at any point in the foreseeable future. Which of the following best describes the relationship between the number of months and the total amount of money in the account?

    (A) A linear relationship, with the line of the relationship having a negative slope
    (B) A linear relationship, with the line of the relationship having a positive slope
    (C) An exponentially increasing relationship
    (D) An inverse exponential relationship

Note: Figure not drawn to scale

25. In the figure above, both angles ABC and ECD are 90 degrees. If the area of triangle ECD is 20 square inches, the length of EC is 4 inches, and the length of BC is 8 inches, what is the area of triangle ABD?

    (A) 32.4 square inches
    (B) 64.8 square inches
    (C) 320 square inches
    (D) 640 square inches

GO ON TO THE NEXT PAGE

26. Which of the following is an equivalent form of $\dfrac{(7x-7)(7x+7)}{7}$?

    (A) $x^2 - 1$

    (B) $49x^2 + 7$

    (C) $7(x^2 - 1)$

    (D) $\dfrac{(x^2 - 7)}{7}$

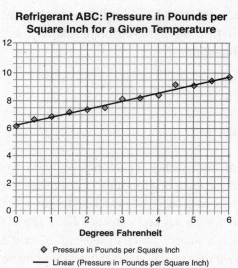

Refrigerant ABC: Pressure in Pounds per Square Inch for a Given Temperature

Degrees Fahrenheit

◇ Pressure in Pounds per Square Inch

— Linear (Pressure in Pounds per Square Inch)

27. A refrigerant manufacturer recorded the pressure associated with certain temperatures in a refrigerator using its new refrigerant, ABC. Which equation best approximates the best-fit line portrayed by the data in this graph, using P for pressure, T for temperature, and the same units as portrayed in the graph?

    (A) $P = 0.5T + 6.2$

    (B) $P = T + 6.2$

    (C) $P = 0.5T - 3$

    (D) $P = 7T + 5$

GO ON TO THE NEXT PAGE

Grid-in Response Directions

In questions 28–31, first solve the problem, and then enter your answer on the grid provided on the answer sheet. The instructions for entering your answers follow.

- First, write your answer in the boxes at the top of the grid.
- Second, grid your answer in the columns below the boxes.
- Use the fraction bar in the first row or the decimal point in the second row to enter fractions and decimals.

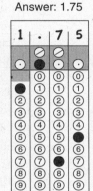

Answer: $\frac{8}{15}$ Answer: 1.75

Write your answer in the boxes

Grid in your answer

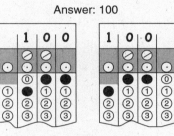

Answer: 100

Either position is acceptable

- Grid only one space in each column.
- Entering the answer in the boxes is recommended as an aid in gridding but is not required.
- The machine scoring your exam can read only what you grid, so you **must grid-in your answers correctly to get credit**.
- If a question has more than one correct answer, grid-in only one of them.
- The grid does not have a minus sign; so no answer can be negative.
- A mixed number *must* be converted to an improper fraction or a decimal before it is gridded.

  Enter $1\frac{1}{4}$ as 5/4 or 1.25; the machine will interpret 11/4 as $\frac{11}{4}$ and mark it wrong.

- **All decimals must be entered as accurately as possible.** Here are three acceptable ways of gridding:

$$\frac{3}{11} = 0.272727\ldots$$

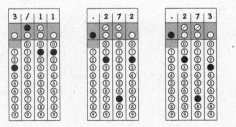

- Note that rounding to .273 is acceptable because you are using the full grid, but you would receive **no credit** for .3 or .27, because they are less accurate.

4

4

28. A certain cube has edges of length L inches, surface area of A square inches, and volume of B cubic inches. For what value of L would $A = B$?

29. If (a, b) is a solution to the system of equations below, what is the value of a?

$$2a - \frac{1}{2}b = 4$$

$$3a + b = 6$$

STOP

If there is still time remaining, you may review your answers.

Questions 30–31 refer to the following information and table.

A currency conversion store at an airport in New York City posts the following conversion rate table.

Currency Type	Currency per 1 U.S. Dollar
U.S. dollar	1.00
Euro	0.90
Indian rupee	68.01
South African rand	16.17
Japanese yen	116.36
Australian dollar	1.41

The conversion store charges 1 percent of the amount converted plus a $2 flat fee for each total transaction (including multiple-currency exchanges as long as they take place in a single visit to the store). The flat fee is assessed *in addition* to the 1 percent conversion fee.

30. Suppose a customer wanted to see the conversion rate, before doing a transaction or paying any associated fees, of U.S. dollars to Australian dollars. What is the conversion rate of U.S. dollars to 1 Australian Dollar to the nearest hundredth?

31. Andrew has come back to the United States from a trip to Asia and wishes to convert 700 Japanese yen and 900 Indian rupees. If he converts them to U.S. dollars at the airport currency store, how many U.S. dollars will he have from this conversion after the store transaction is complete to the nearest tenth of a dollar? (Ignore the dollar sign when gridding in your answer.)

ANSWER KEY
Practice Test

Section 1: Reading Test

1.	**D**	14.	**C**	27.	**C**	40.	**D**
2.	**A**	15.	**B**	28.	**B**	41.	**D**
3.	**B**	16.	**D**	29.	**B**	42.	**C**
4.	**A**	17.	**D**	30.	**D**	43.	**C**
5.	**C**	18.	**D**	31.	**B**	44.	**B**
6.	**B**	19.	**B**	32.	**C**	45.	**B**
7.	**C**	20.	**D**	33.	**D**	46.	**A**
8.	**D**	21.	**C**	34.	**B**	47.	**D**
9.	**B**	22.	**A**	35.	**B**		
10.	**A**	23.	**A**	36.	**A**		
11.	**D**	24.	**B**	37.	**A**		
12.	**A**	25.	**A**	38.	**C**		
13.	**B**	26.	**C**	39.	**B**		

Number Correct _____

Number Incorrect _____

Section 2: Writing and Language Test

1.	**C**	12.	**D**	23.	**C**	34.	**D**
2.	**A**	13.	**A**	24.	**A**	35.	**C**
3.	**B**	14.	**B**	25.	**D**	36.	**B**
4.	**B**	15.	**C**	26.	**B**	37.	**A**
5.	**A**	16.	**B**	27.	**C**	38.	**A**
6.	**B**	17.	**A**	28.	**A**	39.	**C**
7.	**B**	18.	**C**	29.	**D**	40.	**D**
8.	**C**	19.	**C**	30.	**D**	41.	**B**
9.	**A**	20.	**A**	31.	**D**	42.	**A**
10.	**D**	21.	**B**	32.	**B**	43.	**B**
11.	**C**	22.	**D**	33.	**A**	44.	**C**

Number Correct _____

Number Incorrect _____

Section 3: Math Test—No Calculator

1. **A**	5. **A**	9. **B**	13. **A**
2. **B**	6. **C**	10. **A**	
3. **D**	7. **D**	11. **B**	
4. **B**	8. **C**	12. **B**	

14. **75**   15. **15**   16. **800**   17. **196**

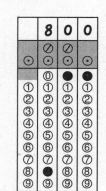

Number Correct _____

Number Incorrect _____

Section 4: Math Test—Calculator

1. **B**	7. **B**	13. **C**	19. **B**	25. **B**
2. **C**	8. **D**	14. **C**	20. **C**	26. **C**
3. **A**	9. **B**	15. **A**	21. **C**	27. **A**
4. **A**	10. **C**	16. **B**	22. **B**	
5. **D**	11. **B**	17. **C**	23. **A**	
6. **C**	12. **D**	18. **C**	24. **B**	

28. **6**   29. **2**   30. **0.71**   31. **17.1**

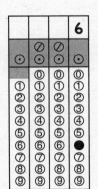

Number Correct   _____

Number Incorrect _____

SCORE ANALYSIS

Note: This table represents our <u>best estimate</u> of how many questions you will need to answer correctly to achieve a certain score on the new PSAT.

PSAT Section Score	PSAT Math— 48 Total Questions	PSAT Evidence-Based Reading and Writing 91 Total Questions	PSAT Section Score
760	48	91	760
710	45	86	710
660	43	79	660
610	38	71	610
560	34	63	560
510	28	53	510
460	24	43	460
410	18	30	410
360	13	19	360
310	8	12	310
260	4	6	260
210	2	3	210
160	0	0	160

ANSWERS EXPLAINED

Section 1: Reading Test

1. **(D)** In the passage, the workers are given menial, labor-intensive, unhygienic jobs. Nonetheless, they are thrilled to have the jobs. This is the passage's biggest contrast— that between "the attitudes of the workers and the true nature of their work." Choice (A) is flawed in that they never "take it easy." They are hard workers. Choice (B) is flawed in that the passage has nothing to do with "vegetarianism." Choice (C) is flawed in that even though the characters are immigrants, they make no mention of homesickness for their native land.

2. **(A)** The answer to this question is most apparent in lines 30–41 and 79–87. The two are absolutely thrilled about the prospect of work, and their attitude can best be described as one of "optimism." "Pessimism" and "resignation" are negative emotions that aren't applicable here. Similarly, though we might infer that this new work might bring the characters peace, there is nothing in the passage itself to suggest "peacefulness."

3. **(B)** In lines 4–7, the passage states that the boss had intended to hire another man but, upon finding Jurgis, decided that he would do instead. Really, it seems, *anyone* would do. This is most consistent with Choice (B). Workers are "disposable"—they are *easily replaceable, used until they have nothing left and then discarded in favor of someone new.* "Skillful," "valuable," and "interesting" all convey much more respect for the employees than the supervisors actually possess.

4. **(A)** See the explanation for answer 3. Lines 4–7 state, "The boss had meant for him to enter, but had not said this, and so it was only when on his way out to hire another man that he came upon Jurgis." This best exemplifies the view of the workers as replaceable. Jurgis, another man, no matter who—anyone would do given enthusiasm for the unseemly nature of the occupation.

5. **(C)** Lines 17–24 describe Jurgis's job description. These lines "describe a character's professional tasks." We see nothing of personal motivation, as in Choice (A). The major point of the paragraph is actually that Jurgis *has* a job and he is thrilled to do it, which makes Choice (B) incorrect. These lines have nothing to do with the objection of the reader, as seen in Choice (D).

6. **(B)** When handling these vocabulary questions, insert each option into the sentence to determine which is most apt in context. "All day long he was figuring to himself" means that he was *counting the money he was making*; he was "calculating" his earnings, as in Choice (B). After you insert "believing," "assuming," and "doubting" into the sentence, it will be clear that none of these three provides a logical statement.

7. **(C)** When handling these vocabulary questions, substitute each choice into the sentence to determine which option is most logical in context. As in *power plants*, "plants" sometimes has a denotation of *factories*. Such is the case in this sentence, and Choice (C) is the correct answer. "Vegetation" is the normal meaning for *plants*, but it is terribly illogical here. "Stations" and "houses" both have somewhat of a case for legitimacy in context, but "factories" is far superior given the production process occurring there.

8. **(D)** In lines 53–56, the passage mentions that Marija knew only the word "job," and even this word was very difficult for her to learn. Her English fluency, therefore, is "very limited." She has nothing of proficiency.

9. **(B)** See the explanation for question 8. Lines 53–56 state, "Marija had nothing to take with her save her two brawny arms and the word 'job,' laboriously learned; but with these, she had marched about Packingtown all day. . . ." *Laboriously* means with difficulty. If she had difficulty learning one single, simple word, clearly her English was very basic.

10. **(A)** Eliminating the incorrect choices is probably easier than finding the correct answer immediately. Choice (B) can be eliminated since the passage makes no argument at all. Choice (C) can be eliminated since no decision was made. Choice (D) can be eliminated since this passage has nothing to do with history. Choice (A) is what remains, and it is our correct answer. The passage's purpose is to analyze the phenomenon of rapid package delivery and the logistics behind that process.

11. **(D)** Lines 14–16 are used to describe what the concept of "logistics" initially meant: it was a war term used to describe the delivery of ammunition. It is thus "explaining the root of a concept," as in Choice (D). Choice (A) is flawed in that it defines *past*, not current, usage of a phrase. There is no likely reader objection, as in Choice (B). To what would the reader possibly object? There is no primary source evidence provided, as in Choice (C).

12. **(A)** When dealing with vocabulary questions, insert the options individually into the sentence to determine which is best given the context. "Essential" is the best answer, and it is the meaning normally associated with "integral." Prior knowledge of the word would have been quite helpful. These companies, the sentence is saying, have grown to be basic, fundamental parts of American society. "Economic," "geographic," and "capitalist" all fail to capture the author's desired meaning of how mainstream these companies have become.

13. **(B)** In lines 38–42, the author makes clear that customers are primarily concerned with "reliability." Customers are willing to pay "a premium price" for this "certainty," so it's reasonable to assume that reliability is most important. Choice (A) is incorrect because customers are actually paying *more* for this service. "Holiday incentives" and "fashion choices" are not mentioned in the passage.

14. **(C)** See the explanation to question 13 above. Lines 38–42 state, "*When it absolutely, positively has to be there overnight*" is the company's mantra and this idea "basically provides certainty of service for a premium price that consumers are willing to bear." If consumers are willing to pay more money for "certainty," or *reliability*, we can infer that this is something very important to them.

15. **(B)** The author mentions that logistics are "interesting" in line 60. Lines 72–75 mention that the process is "something to behold." She also speaks of how logistics keep people happy in line 80. Overall, the author's tone is therefore warm. She is appreciative and has a "positive" opinion of the concept, as seen in Choice (B). The author is not "skeptical": she does not have doubts about logistics. It is not Choice (C), as the author *does* take an opinion on the matter. "Bellicose" means warlike. Choice (D), then, is not a viable option.

16. **(D)** See the explanation to question 15. Lines 72–75 state, "Billions of dollars have been invested in these types of service industries and the activity behind the scenes is something to behold." *Something to behold* is something that is interesting, perhaps even *fascinating,* to witness. This then best aligns with a "positive" opinion of the subject matter.

17. **(D)** Lines 80–82 state, "And if the recent past is any indication, consumer spending on e-commerce will only continue to increase." Figure 1 demonstrates the validity of this statement; notice how future projections in Figure 1 increase every year. Choice (D), then, is the correct answer.

18. **(D)** Lines 69–72 state, "companies in the business of logistics are constantly investing in new ways to handle the information and the items as they flow through the pipelines." As Figure 2 demonstrates that the number of digital buyers worldwide is expanding rapidly, it stands to reason that the current infrastructure will need to be updated and optimized to handle this additional strain on the system. Choice (D) is the correct answer. Choices (A), (B), and (C) all refer to concepts that Figure 2 fails to substantiate.

19. **(B)** Both the worldwide business to consumer sales and the worldwide number of digital consumers are increasing, and the relationship between the two is linear. Therefore, the answer is Choice (B), "positively correlated." Choices (A) and (D) mean the same thing: as one variable increases, the other decreases. However, both the variables are increasing in this case. Choice (C), "exponentially related," is flawed in that the two are increasing linearly. If one variable were, for instance, the square or the cube of the other variable, then there would be an exponential relationship.

20. **(D)** The last two paragraphs analyze how improper usage of antibiotics can lead to the mutation and spread of drug-resistant infections. It stands to reason that a physician should not be overzealous in prescribing antibiotics, as there is a chance that one of these strains can mutate at any time. Physicians need not consider only the patient but, rather, society at large every time they prescribe antibiotics. The passage makes no reference at all to the topics of Choices (A) and (C). Choice (B) is flawed in that physicians still must diagnose bacteriological infections; patients are not expected to provide their own medical care.

21. **(C)** Lines 29–30 mention "both categories of drugs," and the next paragraph then goes on to describe both categories. Thus, these lines serve to "provide a transition to the following paragraph." Choice (A) is flawed in that the lines do not "define a couple of major concepts" but, rather, only *refer* to them. In Choice (B), no specific supporting examples are provided. In Choice (D), these lines, although important, do not contain the thesis (main idea) of the passage.

22. **(A)** In lines 31–34, the passage states that "bacteriostatic antibiotics are often prescribed to patients who have an intact immune system." If a person's immune system is intact, it is fair to assume that that person is "relatively healthy," as described in Choice (A). Choices (B), (C), and (D) all state that bacteriostatic antibiotics are used on people in various states of poor health, which is not the case.

23. **(A)** Lines 76–80 offer the best evidence of the author's initial reference to the risk of losing "the capacity to treat bacterial infections." In the closing lines, the author then advocates for various ways to promote proper usage of antibiotics so that infections do

not mutate into untreatable strains. There is no reference to "overdose," as in Choice (B). The passage does mention MRSA but makes no mention of it losing prominence, as stated in Choice (C). The first paragraph speaks of alternative medicine in the Far East. However, it is not a major concern of the author that the Western world will not embrace these alternatives, as stated in Choice (D).

24. **(B)** Lines 76–80 speak of "growing concern" about the "development of antibiotic resistant organisms," which would be organisms not susceptible to current medical treatments. This matches the question's requirements. Lines 8–12 speak of the use of spices, and the author makes no mention of an opinion on these. Lines 88–92 describe MRSA, which is a large problem in the medical community. However, the mention of MRSA, alone, does not constitute sufficient evidence for the question. Lines 102–107 merely mention instructions for taking antibiotics, which also doesn't entirely satisfy the question's requirement of "a major concern" for the author.

25. **(A)** In context, the use of "severe" "and unpleasant side effects" forms the most logical sentence. Side effects are never "thoughtful," "genuine," or "quiet."

26. **(C)** "Spontaneously" is used to describe actions that arise in a manner that is unplanned and without any prior indication of their occurrence. This definition is most consistent with "randomly." "Impulsively" is generally attributed to human action that occurs without prior thought. "Extemporaneously" is to speak or perform without prior planning, and "deliberately" means to do something with purpose or conviction.

27. **(C)** Lines 61–62 mention a "culture and sensitivity test," and the preceding lines define this test as one used to "identify the specific microorganism causing the infection as well as the best antibiotic for treatment." In lines 66–67, the author states that the primary determinant of these two is the "zone of inhibition." The figure shows the results of antibiotic testing on specific microorganisms and includes data on the zone of inhibition. Choice (C), then, is the best answer.

28. **(B)** Lines 68–70 state that the "zone with the largest diameter typically signifies that it will be the best at fighting infection." Under the *E. coli* column (second column), ciprofloxacin has the largest diameter at 17 mm. It would therefore be the most effective antibiotic in this particular instance, as in Choice (B). Vancomycin would be the most effective medication against *S. aureus*, not against *E. coli*. Amoxicillin is the second-most effective. Not only is there no data on *Staphylococcus*, but also it is actually a bacterial strain and not an antibiotic.

29. **(B)** Benjamin Franklin is reflecting on his own life in a candid manner. He is addressing his son, and both the nature of Franklin's reflections and the concept of writing to one's son can only be described as "personal." The tone is open, revelatory—it is Franklin at his most *personal*. It is not "abstract"; Franklin is not speaking in a roundabout, symbolic way. The passage is perhaps "serious" in that it does not trivialize the task of describing a life, but "serious" is not as apt as "personal." It is not "melancholy"; the passage is more celebration than lamentation.

30. **(D)** In lines 14–17, Franklin describes being born into poverty and then achieving affluence. He entered the world poor but obtained wealth through his endeavors. This is most consistent with Choice (D). Choices (B) and (C) imply at least some sort of financial

hardship in adulthood, which was not the case. Choice (A) is flawed in that Franklin was not born wealthy.

31. **(B)** See the explanation for question 30. Lines 14–17 mention "having emerged from the poverty . . . to a state of affluence." This is evidence that Franklin's personal situation "improved greatly over his lifetime."

32. **(C)** When handling questions of vocabulary, insert the options into the sentence to determine which is most sensible in context. "Applicable" is the most logical option since "suitable" means appropriate or apt in this instance. "Historical," "memorable," and "delightful" all create sentences with different meanings.

33. **(D)** The vocabulary of the choices is perhaps the most difficult part of this question. "To underscore his rootlessness" is another way of saying *to emphasize the uncertainty of his background*. Choice (D) is the correct answer, as Washington is emphasizing that he really has very little idea about how he came into this world. Washington is not *complaining about his dementia*, as in Choice (A), and Choice (B) is flawed in that he is uncertain of his "true identity." Choice (C) is flawed in that Washington is not critical of his family; rather, he is critical of the system of slavery that led to the instability/absence of his familial relations.

34. **(B)** With vocabulary questions, substitute the options into the sentence to determine which is most logical. Based on the context, Washington *has been unable to acquire any information about his family*. "Obtaining," as in Choice (B), is the proper word to signify *acquiring*. Choice (A) is flawed in that Washington has nothing to read; he has no information whatsoever. Choice (C) is flawed in that one does not go about "creating" a family history; the past cannot be altered, let alone *created*. "Safeguarding" means protecting, and there is nothing to protect.

35. **(B)** Washington has acquired the little knowledge he has of his family through informal conversations and speculation. This is most evident in lines 85–87, where Washington states that he has "heard reports" about his family. This type of conjecture and secondary-witness testimonial is best represented as "hearsay." There were no "publications" of his family; he mentions nothing written at all. Similarly, there were no "statistics." Washington did not learn of his family through "scholarship," or academia; there was nothing to be studied.

36. **(A)** Washington was born a slave, and he makes mention of this dismal existence in lines 54–56. Franklin, however, was wealthy. Choice (A) is the correct answer as Washington experienced societal hardship and injustice while Franklin did not. Choice (B) is flawed in that Franklin does "not find fault with [his father]," as stated in lines 90–91. Choice (C) is flawed in that both men—not only Washington—remark of genealogical curiosity. Lines 34–40 mention Franklin's desire to record his thoughts for posterity, making Choice (D) incorrect.

37. **(A)** In lines 1–3, Washington mentions "obtaining little anecdotes" about his ancestors. The consistent theme in Washington's passage is a thirst to know his roots. The ability to obtain such anecdotes would assist him in his quest for knowledge, so Choice (A) is the correct answer. Choice (B) is flawed in that Washington is already writing a memoir. Washington makes no reference to children, as in Choice (C), or to wishing to relive his life, as in Choice (D).

38. **(C)** In lines 71–74, Washington states that he has "been unsuccessful in obtaining any information that would throw any accurate light upon the history of [his] family beyond [his] mother." Thus, he has searched in the past for familial anecdotes. To his dismay, however, none could be found. Choice (C) is the correct answer.

39. **(B)** The principal claim of the passage is that the field of physics is changing, developing, revolutionizing—new and fascinating physical discoveries occur regularly (as mentioned throughout the passage), despite the unnamed physicist's claim in the first paragraph that physics was dead. Choice (B) is the best answer. As far as the incorrect choices, dark matter and dark energy are mentioned only briefly. The passage makes no comparison regarding the relative value of the contributions of Higgs and Einstein. Choice (D) has a sentiment that is close, but "ignorant" is too strong a word. Additionally, the author never takes a blatant critical stance against the physicists of the past. Moreover, the author states that physics is continuing to change all the time, so the "ultimate truth" is certainly something that is yet to be uncovered (and the passage leads one to believe that the concept of an *ultimate truth* is inconsistent with the nature of physical discoveries, as a whole).

40. **(D)** In lines 61–65, the author describes string theory, stating that the vibrations of "tiny strings" have led physicists to postulate about the nature of "multiple universes." That something tiny can lead to a hypothesis about something massive is quite paradoxical, as suggested by Choice (D)—the correct answer. The author makes no mention of practical applicability, just as he makes no mention of ethics. Choice (C), "historically consistent," is the opposite of what the author is saying.

41. **(D)** See the explanation to question 40. That "multiple universes" (in all their unfathomable enormity) can come from the vibrations of "tiny strings" is certainly something *counterintuitive*. Choices (A), (B), and (C) all refer to ideas that are not consistent with something *counterintuitive*.

42. **(C)** On vocabulary questions, if there is any uncertainty, it is best to plug the options into the passage in place of the word. "Theory," in this case, makes far more sense than "building," "observation," or "astronomy." "Construct" isn't often used as a noun rather than a verb, but when it is, its meaning is generally *an idea or a theory*.

43. **(C)** In the context of the paragraph, "singular" refers to the type of beginning that the Big Bang was, making "definitive" most appropriate. Although the other words can stand in for "singular," they are not consistent with the context of the passage.

44. **(B)** The first paragraph describes a "static universe" as the general consensus of the 19th century in lines 9–12. Lines 13–23 then transition to a discussion of a shift in that consensus, particularly as a result of Hubble's discoveries. The author prefaces the mention of this discovery with lines 13–14, "This all changed soon after the turn of the next century." Choice (B), then, is the correct answer.

45. **(B)** See the explanation to question 44. Lines 13–23 reference the shift from static to expanding universe based on discoveries by Einstein and Hubble. In the first paragraph, the passage deals with the 19th century. "After the turn of the next century" must then refer to the beginning of the 20th century.

46. **(A)** In lines 59–61, the best indication that this is an analogy is provided by the words "it is as if. . . ." *As* indicates that this is a simile, which is a type of analogy. The author

uses the image of peeling an onion to make clearer the concept of physics discoveries of late: peel a layer (discover something new) only to find that there are more layers (more discoveries yet to be found) beneath the layer just peeled. Choice (D) is incorrect in that the author is celebrating these discoveries rather than lamenting them. Choice (C) is flawed in that the onion is used metaphorically rather than literally biologically. Choice (B) is flawed in that no new evidence is being *described;* it is merely being compared metaphorically to something else.

47. **(D)** The author's primary purpose is the celebration of knowledge for knowledge's sake. He is thrilled that new physics discoveries carry us closer to understanding how the world works on a small scale and how the universe works on a larger scale. There is no mention of military application, consumer use, or medical science as described in Choices (A), (B), and (C), respectively.

Section 2: Writing and Language Test

1. **(C)** We need a possessive to illustrate the idea of the *regular habits of one*. Eliminate Choices (A) and (B) as they forget apostrophes. Choice (D) reads as *reading habits of the ones.* It is plural, whereas we need singular. Choice (C) is the correct answer.

2. **(A)** A contrasting transition is required here. Essentially, the sentence is *images are used often in society,* **but** *words require more cognitive processing.* "Although" is the only option to achieve that contrast. Choices (B) and (C) express cause and effect, while Choice (D) is acceptable when the passage is listing multiple things along the same thought process.

3. **(B)** The verb in this sentence must maintain concordance with "require using one's mind to. . . ." The *to* should signify that this must be an infinite verb. Choice (B), "consider," is infinitive. It is, therefore, the correct answer. Choice (C) is conjugated, Choice (D) is a gerund, and Choice (A) includes an incorrectly executed gerund.

4. **(B)** Analyze the chart for this question. We are comparing the writing scores of those who read for fun "almost daily" with the scores of those who read "never or hardly ever." The difference in points between these two groups is approximately 30.

5. **(A)** The underlined sentence directly builds on the claim in the previous sentence by using specific numerical evidence. Thus, it must be "kept, because it provides specific details in support of the previous sentence." Deleting the sentence sacrifices helpful information. It has nothing to do with "salary details."

6. **(B)** The previous sentence speaks of a strong connection between reading skills and career success. Our question requires a choice that is a "specific and relevant elaboration" on that previous sentence. Choice (A) refers to joy attained from reading, which is irrelevant. Choice (C) refers to consumer habits, which is irrelevant. Choice (D) refers to memory, which is irrelevant. Choice (B) is the only option that refers to career success.

7. **(B)** The independent clause is "reading also stimulates the imagination." The sentence best functions by using a colon and then listing the various ways it stimulates the imagination. Choice (B) does this perfectly. Choice (A) is a run-on sentence. Choice (C) incorrectly uses a semicolon; there must be a full sentence on both sides of the

semicolon, but there isn't a full sentence after the semicolon here. Choice (D) incorrectly attaches a list to the independent clause.

8. **(C)** It would be more appropriate to say "those are more likely" rather than "them are more likely." Eliminate Choices (A) and (B). Now rewrite the clause using *he* or *him*. It would be more appropriate to say *he reads literature*. Recall that *he* equals *who*, so Choice (C) is the correct answer.

9. **(A)** The best option here is a contrasting transition. Essentially, *good readers are active, **but** bad readers tend to end up in prison.* This is a vast generalization, but that's the structure of the sentence! "On the other hand" is the only contrasting transition. "Therefore" and "thus" are cause-and-effect transitions. "Moreover" means also.

10. **(D)** *Confidence* is the issue. "Clearly" is very confident; *it is obvious that it must be this way,* "clearly" indicates. "Dubitably" indicates strong doubt, which is the opposite of confidence. Choices (A) and (C) lack confidence in that neither really commits to an opinion; they are ambivalent and hesitant to make a judgment.

11. **(C)** Ultimately, this whole sentence is one independent clause that must not be interrupted by punctuation. There is only one subject and there is only one predicate, despite the sentence's length. Choices (A) and (B) add unnecessary commas. Choice (D) improperly employs a semicolon that requires a full sentence on both sides of the semicolon.

12. **(D)** Ultimately, unless a comma is required, avoid using one. Such is the case with this sentence, where everything reads perfectly without punctuation. Choices (A), (B), and (C) all interrupt the clause by inserting unnecessary commas.

13. **(A)** In this sentence, there is a pattern of, essentially, *not for* this *reason, **but** for* that *reason.* That "but" is necessary because it demonstrates the contrasting relationship that is apparent. "And since," "and," and "for a result" fail to capture that pattern of *not for this, but for that.*

14. **(B)** Choices (A), (B), and (C) all communicate the same message, but notice that Choice (B) does it much more concisely without sacrificing meaning. Choice (D), "omit," leads to a grammatically correct sentence, but it ultimately deletes information that is relevant and productive.

15. **(C)** "Than" is used for comparisons, while "then" is used as a sequencing term. Eliminate Choices (B) and (D) since this is a comparison. When making comparisons, it is far better to use an *-er* word, like "smaller," rather than an *-est* word, like "smallest." Choice (C) is the correct answer.

16. **(B)** Notice the other verbs in this paragraph. They are in the past tense. So stay in the past tense to preserve parallelism. Eliminate Choices (C) and (D) because they are in the present tense. The subject is "discovery," which is a singular noun that requires a singular verb. "Were" is a plural verb; eliminate it accordingly. "Was" is the best answer.

17. **(A)** Notice the relationship between the two clauses on each side of the semicolon: the second clause contrasts with the first clause. "However" is an appropriate contrasting transition. "As a result" and "consequently" both are used to express cause-and-effect relationships. "What is more" is another way of saying *additionally* or *also.*

18. **(C)** The previous sentence states, "[They] set about to solve the problem by clearly defining what a planet is." Notice that this communicates the *exact same* message as the underlined sentence. Therefore, the underlined portion should be "deleted, because it repeats the ideas of the previous sentence."

19. **(C)** The important part of this question is *specificity:* a choice is needed that provides the most relevant, logical, and "specific" information. Eliminate Choices (A) and (D) for being far too general: they lack "specific" substance. Choice (B) manages to be lengthy and yet shallow at the same time. "A great deal of mass and matter" is the best example of this wordiness. Moreover, it still doesn't provide the specificity of Choice (C), which wastes no words while still providing ample detail.

20. **(A)** The parenthetical element here was tricky to diagnose. Nonetheless, "and therefore doesn't have enough gravity" was the parenthetical element. If you remove it from the sentence, the clause still functions perfectly well. As a rule, a parenthetical element can be surrounded by two dashes or two commas to separate it from the rest of the sentence. Choice (B) uses the two commas but actually splits the parenthetical element into pieces. Choice (C) omits the first comma. Choice (D) has entirely too many commas *within* the parenthetical element, preventing continuity. Choice (A) is the best option.

21. **(B)** "While" expresses two things occurring simultaneously, which is the nature of this sentence. It also can function as a contrasting transition as it does here (but doesn't necessarily have to). Essentially, *most of the world accepts that Pluto isn't a planet,* **but, at the same time,** *some people stubbornly refuse to let Pluto go.* "Since" and "because" are cause-and-effect transitions, while "and" is a conjunction.

22. **(D)** Although all of the choices are relevant conclusions, only Choice (D) manages to tie "back to the introduction," as the question requires.

23. **(C)** When deciding whether to include or delete a portion, we must decide first if that portion is relevant. Second, we must decide if the insertion repeats information that has already been stated or if it mentions information that can be readily inferred. In this case, the issue is with the second question: the reader already knows the definition of "sibling." The answer is Choice (C).

24. **(A)** Choice (A) uses the colon perfectly as a lead-in for the term to be discussed. Choice (B) is a run-on sentence. Choice (C) places an unnecessary comma after "based." Choice (D) incorrectly employs a semicolon. Recall that a semicolon requires what would otherwise be a full sentence both before and after the semicolon. "Birth order" is not a full sentence.

25. **(D)** The subject of this clause is "personality traits," a plural noun that requires a plural verb. Eliminate Choices (A) and (C) for using singular verbs. Choice (B) uses the word "with" improperly in this context. Thus Choice (D) is the correct answer.

26. **(B)** Ultimately, if we were to delete the underlined portion, we would be removing information that is both relevant and productive. It provides a "helpful elaboration" in this sentence, and it contributes informative value to the passage. Choice (B) is the correct answer.

27. **(C)** Analyze the relationship between this sentence and the previous sentence. The first states that firstborn children "excel in leadership positions," and then the second

gives an example to illustrate this. "In fact" is an ideal transition to provide an example, and Choice (C) is the correct answer. Choices (A) and (D) both imply a contrasting relationship that is not apparent. Choice (B) speaks of an absent objection.

28. **(A)** The subject here is "they," a plural pronoun that requires a plural verb. Eliminate Choices (C) and (D) for using singular verbs. "Fit in with" means to associate with successfully, whereas "fit on" indicates something else entirely. Choice (A) is much more effective than Choice (B).

29. **(D)** The proposed insertion states that middle children are "mediators." Sentence 7 talks about mediating, which means resolving differences. Thus, it is most effective to place our insertion right before this sentence, as in Choice (D).

30. **(D)** Read the previous sentence. We need to elaborate on the claim that the youngest child is an entertainer. Eliminate Choice (A) for irrelevance. Eliminate Choice (C) because it refers to the oldest child, not the youngest. Eliminate Choice (B) for not mentioning entertaining. Choice (D), however, refers to youngest children as entertainers. It is, therefore, our best answer.

31. **(D)** This question requires a possessive pronoun to demonstrate the *youngest child's way in life*. Eliminate Choices (A) and (C) for not being possessive pronouns. Choice (B), "their," must refer to *multiple people*, whereas the "youngest child" is *one person*. "His or her" is the best set of possessive pronouns for *one person* of indeterminate gender.

32. **(B)** Choice (A) is a *comma splice*. Choices (C) and (D) place unnecessary commas after "birth order." Choice (B)'s usage of a semicolon is ideal, especially since it has two independent clauses.

33. **(A)** It really is best to read this sentence along with the previous *two* sentences. This sentence *contrasts* with the previous idea of the paragraph that "birth order isn't a one-size-fits-all theory." Essentially this sentence says: *That may be true, **but** it is still useful.* The best substitute for *but* is "nevertheless." The other three choices fail to provide the contrasting relationship that the sentence requires.

34. **(D)** This is a list and requires commas between the items being listed. Choice (A) omits commas after the first two items. Choice (B) omits a comma after the first item, while Choice (C) does not include a comma after the second item. Choice (D) includes all necessary commas.

35. **(C)** Choices (A) and (B) are simply excessively wordy versions of Choice (C), which manages concision while maintaining the initial meaning. Choice (D) changes the initial contrasting relationship to one of cause and effect.

36. **(B)** All four choices communicate the exact same sentiment. However, Choices (A), (C), and (D) are excessively wordy versions of Choice (B), which is concise without sacrificing content.

37. **(A)** The sentence requires a word that signifies *to undertake* the adventure/*to embrace* the adventure. "Inspected" the adventure and "expected" the adventure do not communicate that meaning. "Excepted" means excluded and doesn't suit our purposes. "Accepted" is the best option.

38. **(A)** The first decision is whether to use "many" or "much." The sentence mentions "reasons," which are things that are easily countable. *Many reasons* is the better usage,

so eliminate Choices (B) and (C). Recall that we use "much" to describe things we cannot count. The subject is "dental students," which is a plural noun that requires a plural verb like "have." "Has" is a singular verb. Choice (A), then, is better than Choice (D).

39. **(C)** A possessive is required that expresses the idea of *the problems of patients*, where *patients* is plural. Choice (A) isn't possessive. Choice (D) incorrectly uses both "those of" and "problems," which are illogical when combined. Choice (B) incorrectly expresses the problems of *one* patient. Choice (C) is the best answer.

40. **(D)** After the verb "can," an infinitive verb is required. Eliminate Choices (B) and (C) because they are conjugated verbs. "Effect" is rarely used as a verb, but when it is, it means to bring about. "Affect" means *to* influence. The sentence is much more logical with *influence*, so "affect" is the correct answer.

41. **(B)** Analyze the graph for this question. This is somewhat difficult to see with the added complexity of a third dimension, but general dentists with the dark gray bar (6+ years experience) have salaries that fall somewhere between 100 and 200 thousand dollars. This is consistent with Choice (B) and directly contradicts Choice (A). Choice (C)'s numbers are too large, while Choice (D)'s number is far too small.

42. **(A)** Analyze the graph. General dentists' salaries are slightly below those of general doctors, so Choice (A) is the correct answer. They are significantly less than those of OBGYNs and general surgeons, which eliminates Choices (B) and (C), respectively. They far exceed those of nurses, which eliminates Choice (D).

43. **(B)** Analyze the relationship between this sentence and the previous sentence. This sentence provides an additional reason for becoming a dentist (as referenced at the beginning of the paragraph), so "moreover" is the best choice. Choices (A) and (C) incorrectly assume a contrasting relationship, while Choice (D) improperly states a cause-and-effect relationship.

44. **(C)** This quotation should follow paragraph 2, as Choice (C) states. Essentially, this insertion is a reason to pursue dentistry rather than toy-making as offered by Tim. Tim supplies these reasons in paragraphs 3 and 4. None of the other choices offers a logical placement for the insertion.

Section 3: Math Test—No Calculator

1. **(A)** First, get all x-terms on one side by subtracting $3x$ from both sides. To combine the x-terms, we'll need a common denominator. So convert $3x$ to $\frac{9}{3}x$. After combining the x-terms, our equation becomes:

$$2 = -\frac{5}{3}x$$

Next, solve for x by dividing both sides by $-\frac{5}{3}$ (in other words, multiply both sides by $-\frac{3}{5}$):

$$-\frac{6}{5} = x$$

The answer is Choice (A).

2. **(B)** First, factor out 5:

$$5(x^2 - 3x + 2) = 0$$

Dividing both sides by 5 leaves you with:

$$x^2 - 3x + 2 = 0$$

This can be factored as:

$$(x - 2)(x - 1) = 0$$

Set each factor to 0 to solve for possible x-values:

$$x - 2 = 0 \text{ so } x = 2$$
$$x - 1 = 0 \text{ so } x = 1$$

Therefore, the answer is Choice (B). Alternatively, you could have used the quadratic formula to solve for possible x-values.

3. **(D)** The typist has already typed 3,500 words, so this will be a constant in the expression. The typist types 70 words per minute. So if he types for t minutes, he will type $70t$ more words. Therefore, the total number of words typed, $W(t)$, is given by the following expression:

$$W(t) = 3,500 + 70t$$

Choice (D) is correct.

4. **(B)** Factor out all common factors. $2a$ is a factor of all three terms, so it can be factored out:

$$2a(3a + 4b - 2c)$$

Alternatively, you could have redistributed the answer choices to eliminate Choices (A), (C), and (D), which, respectively, equal, $3a^2 + 4ab + 2ac$, $4a^2 + 4ab - 8ac$, and $6a^2 - 8ab + 4ac$.

5. **(A)** First, isolate what's inside the parentheses by dividing both sides by –3. Remember to flip the inequality sign because you are dividing by a negative:

$$x + 4 < -\frac{2}{3}x$$

Next, get a common denominator for the x-terms:

$$\frac{3}{3}x + 4 < -\frac{2}{3}x$$

Then subtract the left-side x-term from both sides of the inequality to get all x-terms on the right side:

$$4 < -\frac{5}{3}x$$

Finally, divide both sides by $-\frac{5}{3}$, which is the same as multiplying both sides by $-\frac{3}{5}$.

Again, remember to flip the inequality since we are multiplying by a negative number:

$$-\frac{12}{5} > x \text{ or } x < -\frac{12}{5}$$

The correct response is Choice (A).

6. **(C)** Use FOIL to obtain this equation:

$$\frac{6}{12}x^2 - \frac{2}{3}x + \frac{3}{4}x - 1$$

The coefficient in front of the x^2 can be reduced, giving:

$$\frac{1}{2}x^2 - \frac{2}{3}x + \frac{3}{4}x - 1$$

To combine the x-terms, they need to have a common denominator:

$$\frac{1}{2}x^2 - \frac{8}{12}x + \frac{9}{12}x - 1$$

Combining these terms gives you:

$$\frac{1}{2}x^2 + \frac{1}{12}x - 1$$

Choice (C) is the answer.

7. **(D)** A function intersects the x-axis at its roots, where $y = 0$: this will occur when any of these three factors equals 0. Set each factor equal to 0 to determine the x-values:

$$x = 0$$
$$x - 5 = 0 \text{ so } x = 5$$
$$x + 2 = 0 \text{ so } x = -2$$

Therefore, the three x-values are 0, 5, and −2, which is Choice (D).

8. **(C)** Notice that both functions give equations of lines. To find the point of intersection, we want to find the point (x, y) that is on both lines. Since (x, y) is on both lines, we can find this common x-value by setting the right sides of both equations equal to one another:

$$4x - 3 = -\frac{1}{2}x + 2$$

Combine like terms by adding $\frac{1}{2}x$ to both sides and by adding 3 to both sides:

$$\frac{9}{2}x = 5$$

Solve for x by dividing both sides by $\frac{9}{2}$ (in other words, multiply both sides by $\frac{2}{9}$):

$$x = \frac{10}{9}$$

This is enough to narrow it down to Choice (C), but you could solve for y by plugging in $\frac{10}{9}$ for x in either equation:

$$y = 4\left(\frac{10}{9}\right) - 3 = \frac{40}{9} - 3 = \frac{40}{9} - \frac{27}{9} = \frac{13}{9}$$

9. **(B)** Notice that the function is 2 minus the absolute value of something. The absolute value of something must always be greater than or equal to 0. So either $f(x) = 2 - 0 = 2$ or $f(x)$ equals 2 minus some positive number. This second case, though, will result in a value that is less than 2. (Convince yourself of this. For instance, if the absolute value is 1, then $f(x) = 2 - 1 = 1$.) Therefore, the maximum value of f is 2. To find where this maximum will occur, we need to determine which x-values give $|x - 4| = 0$. This occurs when $x - 4 = 0$. Thus, $x = 4$, which is Choice (B).

Alternatively, you could have plugged in the potential x-values to determine which gives the maximum value for $f(x)$.

10. **(A)** Dividing by a fraction is the same as multiplying by its reciprocal: $\dfrac{1}{\frac{1}{2x}} = 1 \times \dfrac{2x}{1} = 2x$

$$\frac{3}{\frac{6}{4x}} = 3 \times \frac{4x}{6} = \frac{12x}{6} = 2x$$

Therefore:

$$\frac{1}{\frac{1}{2x}} + \frac{3}{\frac{6}{4x}} = 2x + 2x = 4x$$

Choice (A) is the correct answer.

11. **(B)** Let's try to simplify the left side of the equation a bit to get it in the same form as the right side. When an exponent is raised to another exponent, you multiply those exponents:

$$\left(x^2\right)^{\frac{1}{5}} = x^{\frac{2}{5}}$$

Also, $\sqrt[5]{32x^2}$ can be broken up into $\sqrt[5]{32} \times \sqrt[5]{x^2}$. Since $\sqrt[5]{32} = 2$, the expression can be further simplified:

$$\sqrt[5]{32} \times \sqrt[5]{x^2} = 2x^{\frac{2}{5}}$$

Therefore, the left side of the equation simplifies to:

$$x^{\frac{2}{5}} + 2x^{\frac{2}{5}}$$

You can then combine like terms:

$$x^{\frac{2}{5}} + 2x^{\frac{2}{5}} = 3x^{\frac{2}{5}}$$

If $3x^{\frac{2}{5}} = ax^{\frac{2}{5}}$, then it follows from dividing both sides by $x^{\frac{2}{5}}$ that $a = 3$, which is Choice (B).

12. **(B)** In order for the inflation rate, as given by this formula, to equal 0, the numerator of the fraction must equal 0. This will happen if the current year's CPI is equal to the last year's CPI, because subtracting a number from itself equals 0. This matches Choice (B).

13. **(A)** First, get the equation in standard form by subtracting 17 from both sides:

$$y = 6x^2 + 12x - 17$$

When a parabola is in standard form, $y = ax^2 + bx + c$, the axis of symmetry is given by the equation $x = -\dfrac{b}{2a}$. Because the axis of symmetry passes through the vertex and this parabola opens up, the x-value that gives the axis of symmetry will also give the x-coordinate of the vertex. The y- and x-values of the vertex give the minimum value and its location on the parabola, respectively, so we want to know the x-value of the vertex to solve this problem.

In this case, $a = 6$ and $b = 12$, so:

$$x = -\frac{b}{2a} = -\frac{12}{2(6)} = -\frac{12}{12} = -1$$

This corresponds to Choice (A).

Alternatively, you could have converted the equation to vertex form by completing the square to get:

$$y = 6(x + 1)^2 - 23.$$

Then the vertex is $(-1, -23)$, so $x = -1$.

14. **(75)** Isosceles trapezoids have two sets of congruent angles, and their interior angles add up to 360°. Therefore, we know:

$$360 = 105 + 105 + x + x$$

Combine like terms:

$$360 = 210 + 2x$$

Subtract 210 from both sides:

$$150 = 2x$$

Dividing by 2 tells you that $x = 75$. Therefore, the smallest interior angle is 75°.

15. **(15)** Solve the second equation for y to solve this system of equations using substitution:

$$y = \frac{6}{4}x = \frac{3}{2}x$$

Next, plug in $\frac{3}{2}x$ for y in the first equation:

$$2x - \frac{3}{2}x = 3$$

In order to combine the x-terms, you need a common denominator:

$$\frac{4}{2}x - \frac{3}{2}x = \frac{1}{2}x$$

So our equation becomes $\frac{1}{2}x = 3$. Dividing both sides by $\frac{1}{2}$ tells you that $x = 6$. Next, plug in 6 for x in the equation that you already solved for y:

$$y = \frac{3}{2}x = \frac{3}{2}(6) = \frac{18}{2} = 9$$

Since $x = 6$ and $y = 9$, their sum is $6 + 9 = 15$.

16. **(800)** This is a system of equations. If there are 2 men for every 3 women, the ratio is $\frac{m}{w} = \frac{2}{3}$. If there are a total of 4,000 students, $m + w = 4,000$. To solve this system of equations, solve the first equation for m. Then plug this value into the second equation using substitution. Solving for m gives:

$$m = \frac{2}{3}w$$

So the second equation becomes:

$$\frac{2}{3}w + w = 4,000$$

Combine like terms:

$$\frac{5}{3}w = 4{,}000$$

Dividing by $\frac{5}{3}$ (the same as multiplying by $\frac{3}{5}$) tells you that $w = 2{,}400$. To figure out how many more women there are than men, you need to know also how many men there are. Plug in 2,400 for w in the equation you already solved in terms of m. Then subtract the number of men from the number of women:

$$m = \frac{2}{3}w = \frac{2}{3}(2{,}400) = 1{,}600$$

$$w - m = 2{,}400 - 1{,}600 = 800$$

So there are 800 more women than men.

17. **(196)** First, simplify the second term in the numerator:

$$3(2x^2)^2 = 3(4x^4) = 12x^4$$

So our entire expression becomes:

$$\left(\frac{2x^4 + 3(2x^2)^2}{x^4}\right)^2 = \left(\frac{2x^4 + 12x^4}{x^4}\right)^2$$

The x^4-terms of the numerator can be combined:

$$\left(\frac{2x^4 + 12x^4}{x^4}\right)^2 = \left(\frac{14x^4}{x^4}\right)^2$$

The x^4 in the numerator cancels with the x^4 in the denominator:

$$\left(\frac{14x^4}{x^4}\right)^2 = (14)^2 = 196$$

So the answer is 196.

Section 4: Math Test—Calculator

1. **(B)** You can use the conversion given in the problem (2.54 centimeters per 1 inch) to cancel out the units you don't want (inches), leaving you with only the units that you do want (centimeters):

$$48 \text{ inches} \times \frac{2.54 \text{ centimeters}}{1 \text{ inch}} = 121.92 \text{ centimeters} \approx 122 \text{ centimeters}$$

Choice (B) is the correct answer.

2. **(C)** Recognize that $d = rt$, where d is distance, r is rate, and t is time. In this problem, $r = 50$ and $t = 3\frac{1}{4} = 3.25$. Use this information to solve for distance:

$$d = rt = 50 \times 3.25 = 162.5$$

The answer is Choice (C).

Alternatively, you could have done dimensional analysis to cancel out the units you don't want, leaving you with only the units you do want (miles):

$$\frac{50 \text{ miles}}{1 \text{ hour}} \times 3.25 \text{ hours} = 162.5 \text{ miles}$$

3. **(A)** First, distribute the –2:

$$7 - 2(y - 1) = 7 - 2y + 2$$

Next, combine like terms:

$$7 - 2y + 2 = 9 - 2y$$

The answer is Choice (A).

4. **(A)** First, use FOIL for the $(x - 3)^2$ term in the equation to obtain:

$$x^2 - 6x + 9 - 81 = 0$$

Then you can combine like terms:

$$x^2 - 6x - 72 = 0$$

This factors to:

$$(x - 12)(x + 6) = 0$$

Setting each term equal to 0 tells you that x can equal either 12 or –6. Only 12 is an option, so Choice (A) is correct.

5. **(D)** Look at the bottom row. There are a total of 400 individuals. Each person selected the one type of communication that he or she prefers. So the first four numbers in the bottom row must add up to 400:

$$195 + x + 70 + 70 = 400$$

Combine like terms on the left side of the equation:

$$335 + x = 400$$

Subtract 335 from both sides to isolate x:

$$x = 65$$

The answer is Choice (D).

Alternatively, you could have added the first two terms in the e-mail column to obtain x:

$$20 + 45 = 65.$$

6. **(C)** Because we are told that the information in the table is representative of the Springfield population, we expect that the fraction of 15- and 16-year-olds in the survey that prefer video chatting will be the fraction of 15- and 16-year-olds in Springfield that prefer video chatting. The fraction in the survey that prefers video chatting is:

$$\frac{70}{400} = 0.175$$

Multiplying this decimal by the number of 15- and 16-year-olds in Springfield gives the number of 15 and 16 year olds in Springfield that we expect to prefer video chatting:

$$0.175 \times 50,000 = 8,750$$

Choice (C) is correct.

Alternatively, you could have set up a proportion, Let x denote the total number of 15- and 16-year-olds in Springfield who prefer video chatting. Since there are 50,000 15- and 16-year-old residents in Springfield, our proportion is:

$$\frac{70}{400} = \frac{x}{50,000}$$

By cross multiplying, we get:

$$3,500,000 = 400x$$

Dividing both sides by 400 gives:

$$x = 8,750$$

7. **(B)** To find any probability, divide the number of *successes* by the number of *chances*. In this case, the number of successes is the number of 16-year-olds who prefer texting, and the number of chances is the total number of 16-year-olds:

$$\frac{85}{200} = 0.425$$

This amount, 0.425, is approximately 0.43 as in Choice (B).

8. **(D)** First, solve for x by cross multiplying:

$$2x = 4$$

Dividing by 2 tells you that $x = 2$. Next, plug in 2 for x in the expression:

$$\frac{4(2-3)}{-12} = \frac{4(-1)}{-12} = \frac{-4}{-12} = \frac{1}{3}$$

The answer is Choice (D).

9. **(B)** This question is asking you what percent the discount is of 90. First, you need to know what the discount is, which you can get by subtracting the new price from the original price: $90 - 72 = 18$. Then, you can figure out what percentage 18 is of 90 by setting up a proportion, recognizing that 90 represents 100% of the quantity:

$$\frac{x}{100} = \frac{18}{90}$$

Next, cross multiply:

$$90x = 1800$$

Dividing by 90 yields $x = 20$. So $18 is 20% of $90, which is Choice (B).

As an alternative to this approach, you could plug the values from the problem into this formula for a percentage change:

$$\% \text{ Change} = 100 \times \frac{(\text{New Value} - \text{Old Value})}{(\text{Old Value})}$$

10. **(C)** From the graph, we can tell that the average monthly temperature in Townsville is greater than that in Cityberg for April, May, June, July, August, September, October, and November, or eight months. Therefore, Choice (C) is correct. Choices (A) and (B) are incorrect because the graph doesn't tell us anything about the temperature on any random day. Choice (D) is incorrect because the average temperature in Cityberg is greater only in January, February, March, and December.

11. **(B)** For this problem, you need to create a system of equations. First, having two quarters for every five dimes means that the ratio of quarters to dimes is:

$$\frac{q}{d} = \frac{2}{5}$$

Next, we need to come up with an expression that represents the value of the coins. Because quarters are worth 25 cents, the number of cents David has from q quarters will be $25q$. Similarly, the number of cents he has from d dimes will be $10d$. Because these expressions are in cents, we need the amount of money he has also to be in cents. There are 100 cents in 1 dollar, so David has 200 cents. Therefore:

$$25q + 10d = 200$$

Since $\frac{q}{d} = \frac{2}{5}$, we have:

$$q = \frac{2}{5}d$$

Next, plug this fraction in for q in the second equation:

$$25\left(\frac{2}{5}d\right) + 10d = 200$$

Combine the d-terms:

$$20d = 200 \rightarrow d = 10$$

Thus, there are 10 dimes. Plug 10 in for d in the equation that expresses q in terms of d:

$$q = \frac{2}{5}d \rightarrow q = \frac{2}{5} \times 10 = 4$$

Thus, there are four quarters and ten dimes, giving David 14 coins total, which is Choice (B).

12. **(D)** In this equation, the 20 is a constant. Therefore, this is a constant amount of time required that isn't dependent on the number of cookies the chef makes. Therefore, this is the amount of time he requires to get the ingredients and set things up, which matches Choice (D).

13. **(C)** Create a system of equations. First, you know that Jasmine has $100,000 invested among the 3 categories. So if s, b, and c represent the amount of money in stocks, bonds, and cash, respectively, then the investments can be shown as:

$$s + b + c = 100,000$$

She has invested twice as much in stocks as in bonds, so $s = 2b$.

She has invested three times as much in bonds as in cash, so $b = 3c$.

The question asks how much money is invested in bonds, so we want to get s and c in terms of b. Plug these expressions into the first equation, and solve for b. The second equation is already solved for s in terms of b, but we need to solve the third equation for c in terms of b:

$$\frac{1}{3}b = c$$

Next, plug these expressions in for s and c in the first equation:

$$s + b + c = 2b + b + \frac{1}{3}b = 100{,}000$$

You can combine like terms to get:

$$\frac{10}{3}b = 100{,}000$$

Divide both sides by $\frac{10}{3}$ to get $b = 30{,}000$. The question asks what percent is invested in bonds, so find what fraction 30,000 is of 100,000 and then multiply that number by 100%:

$$\frac{30{,}000}{100{,}000} \times 100\% = 30\%$$

Choice (C) is the answer.

Alternatively, you can figure out the ratio of the investments:

Cash : Bonds : Stocks = 1 : 3 : 6

The total of the numbers in this ratio is $1 + 3 + 6 = 10$.

Therefore, as fractions of the whole, the investments are $\frac{1}{10}$, $\frac{3}{10}$, and $\frac{6}{10}$.

The bonds are $\frac{3}{10}$, which translates to 30%.

14. **(C)** 4,807 beverages were purchased, and 1,067 of them were espresso. Therefore, the percentage of beverages that is espresso is represented by the following expression:

$$\frac{1{,}067}{4{,}807} \times 100\% = 22.2\%$$

The answer is Choice (C).

15. **(A)** If the sample is representative of the sales for a year, then we would expect the proportion of females who purchased a latte during the year to be the same as the proportion of females who purchased a latte in the sample. In the sample, there were 850 females under 18 and 1,573 females 18 and over for a total of 2,423 females. Also, 325 females under 18 and 530 females 18 and over purchased lattes, for a total of 855 lattes purchased by females in the sample. Therefore, the probability that a randomly selected female would purchase a latte is given by the following fraction:

$$\frac{855}{2{,}423} = 0.3529$$

Choice (A) is the answer.

16. **(B)** First, get this line in slope-intercept form so that you can easily identify the slope. You can do so by adding $4x$ to both sides to get:

$$y = 4x + 5$$

The slope of this line is 4. The slope of a line perpendicular to this one will have a slope that is the negative reciprocal, $-\frac{1}{4}$, which matches Choice (B).

17. **(C)** First, you need to get the power equation in terms of just resistance and voltage so that you can tell how changing these two quantities will change the power. Therefore, we need to get rid of current by solving for it in the second equation and plugging this expression into the power formula.

Since $V = IR$, then $I = \frac{V}{R}$. Now, plug this in for current in the power equation:

$$P = IV = \frac{V}{R}V = \frac{V^2}{R}$$

The problem states that resistance is doubled and voltage is quadrupled, so fill in these coefficients:

$$P = \frac{V^2}{R} = \frac{(4V)^2}{2R} = \frac{16V^2}{2R} = 8\frac{V^2}{R}$$

Therefore, you can see that power has been multiplied 8 times, which is Choice (C).

18. **(C)** In this problem, the mean can't easily be figured out because we can't sum together all of the responses without knowing the actual numerical responses. (We know only the range of hours for each student.) The mode is between 6 and 7 hours since this was the most frequent response (12 students chose this range). The median in a series of 30 terms is found by arranging the terms from smallest to largest and then taking the average of the 15th and 16th terms. In this case, the 15th and 16th terms are both between 6 and 7 hours, so the median is between 6 and 7 hours. Thus, the median and mode are the same, which is Choice (C).

19. **(B)** Anita's $600 rent represented 40% of her expenses, while 60% of her expenses were spent on everything else. We want to figure out what this 60% was, so we can set up a proportion:

$$\frac{x}{60} = \frac{600}{40}$$

Next, cross multiply:

$$40x = 36{,}000$$

Divide both sides by 40 to determine that $x = 900$. Therefore, Anita spent $900 on everything else, which is Choice (B).

20. **(C)** First, you need to come up with an expression for the area of the wall. Then recognize that paint will cost $12 for every 60 square feet (paint costs $12 per gallon and 1 gallon covers 60 square feet).

You know that $W = \frac{2}{3}L$ and $A = LW$ since the wall is a rectangle. Plugging in $\frac{2}{3}L$ for W gives $A = L\left(\frac{2}{3}L\right) = \frac{2}{3}L^2$.

Multiplying the cost/area by the area will cancel out the area and leave you with cost:

$$\left(\frac{2}{3}L^2 \text{ ft}^2\right)\left(\frac{12}{60 \text{ ft}^2}\right) = \frac{24}{180}L^2 = \frac{2}{15}L^2$$

The answer is Choice (C).

21. **(C)** This question is asking you to determine the range of the following function:

$$g(x) = |2x - 3|$$

Because the entire function is inside an absolute value symbol, $g(x)$, which is the range, cannot be negative. Therefore, the answer is Choice (C).

22. **(B)** First, let's come up with an expression to represent the amount of food consumed each day. Each dog consumes 2 cups, so d dogs consume $2d$ cups of food daily. Each cat consumes 1 cup of food per day, so c cats will consume c cups of food daily. Together, the dogs and cats consume $2d + c$ cups of food every day. The shelter has 400 cups of food, so $2d + c$ cannot exceed 400. This can be represented by the following inequality:

$$2d + c \leq 400$$

Similarly, each dog needs 3 treats daily, so d dogs eat $3d$ treats each day. Cats eat 2 treats daily, so c cats need $2c$ treats daily. The shelter has 500 treats available every day, so $3d + 2c$ cannot exceed 500:

$$3d + 2c \leq 500$$

These two equations match Choice (B).

23. **(A)** The volume of a sphere is given by the formula $V = \frac{4}{3}\pi r^3$. The diameter is twice the radius, so we can solve for the radius and multiply by 2. To solve for r, first divide both sides by $\frac{4}{3}\pi$:

$$\frac{3V}{4\pi} = r^3$$

To solve for r, take the cube root of both sides:

$$\sqrt[3]{\frac{3V}{4\pi}} = r$$

Multiply this by 2 to get an expression for the diameter:

$$d = 2\sqrt[3]{\frac{3V}{4\pi}}$$

Choice (A) is the correct answer.

24. **(B)** Each month, Caitlin adds $50, so the function will have a constant slope of 50. Because the slope is constant, the function is linear. The slope is positive 50, so the answer is Choice (B). We know that the slope will be positive because the two variables are directly proportional: as time goes on, the amount of money in the account increases.

25. **(B)** Triangle *ECD* has an area of 20 square inches and a height of 4 inches. We can plug this information into the formula for the area of a triangle ($A = \frac{1}{2}bh$) to obtain the base of the triangle, *CD*:

$$20 = \frac{1}{2}b(4) = 2b$$

Divide both sides by 2 to get that base *CD* = 10 inches. Therefore, the base of triangle *ABD*, which is side *BD*, is 8 + 10 = 18 inches. Next, we need to find the height of triangle *ABD*. We can utilize the fact that these are similar triangles to set up a proportion:

$$\frac{AB}{4} = \frac{18}{10}$$

Cross multiply:

$$10AB = 72$$

Dividing by 10 tells you that $AB = 7.2$ inches. Plug in 7.2 for the height and plug in 18 for the base in the area equation:

$$A = \frac{1}{2}(18)(7.2) = 64.8$$

The area of triangle ABD is 64.8 square inches, which is Choice (B).

26. **(C)** First, you can factor a 7 out of both factors of the numerator:

$$\frac{7(x-1) \times 7(x+1)}{7}$$

One 7 in the numerator will cancel out with the 7 in the denominator, leaving you with:

$$7(x-1)(x+1)$$

Next, use FOIL for the terms in the parentheses to get:

$$7(x^2 - 1)$$

The answer is Choice (C).

27. **(A)** The y-intercept of the function is somewhere between positive 6 and 8, so we can eliminate Choices (C) and (D). Next, find the slope. You can use any 2 points on the line of best fit, such as the endpoints:

$$m = \frac{y_2 - y_1}{x_2 - x_1} = \frac{9.6 - 6.5}{6 - 0} = \frac{3.1}{6} \approx 0.5$$

So the answer is Choice (A). The line has a slope of 0.5 and a y-intercept of 6.2.

28. **(6)** A cube has 6 sides, so its surface area is given by the formula $SA = 6L^2$. The volume of a cube is given by the formula $V = L^3$. Set these two equations equal to one another:

$$6L^2 = L^3$$

You can divide both sides by L^2 to obtain $6 = L$.

29. **(2)** Multiply the first equation by 2. Then add the two equations together to get rid of b:

$$\begin{aligned} 4a - b &= 8 \\ +(3a + b &= 6) \\ \hline 7a &= 14 \end{aligned}$$

Dividing both sides by 7 tells you that $a = 2$.

30. **(0.71)** The fees in this case are extra information that we don't even need because the customer wants to know what the conversion rate is without taking fees into account. We know the conversion rate of 1 U.S. dollar (USD) to Australian dollars (AUD):

$$1 \text{ USD} = 1.41 \text{ AUD}$$

We want to know how many U.S. dollars a person would get for 1 Australian dollar, so divide both sides by 1.41:

$$0.709 \text{ USD} = 1 \text{ AUD}$$

When rounded to the nearest hundredth, the answer is 0.71.

31. **(17.1)** First, recognize that the store takes 1%, or 0.01 of the amount converted, leaving 99%, or 0.99, of the amount you started with. Therefore, instead of converting 700 Japanese yen, you're converting 0.99(700) = 693 yen, and instead of converting 900 Indian rupees, you're converting 0.99(900) = 891 rupees.

Next, use the conversions to cancel out the units you don't want (yen and rupees) to leave you with the unit that you do want (USD):

$$693 \text{ yen} \times \frac{1 \text{ USD}}{116.36 \text{ yen}} = 5.96 \text{ USD}$$

$$891 \text{ rupees} \times \frac{1 \text{ USD}}{68.01 \text{ rupees}} = 13.10 \text{ USD}$$

Add these together to get 5.96 + 13.10 = 19.06. However, the store charges a $2 flat fee, so Andrew would end up with 19.06 − 2 = 17.06. When rounded to the nearest tenth of a dollar, we get 17.1.

Appendix:
After the PSAT

Now that you have prepared for the PSAT, what comes next in terms of the National Merit Scholarship program and your future testing?

When Should I Receive My PSAT Test Results?

PSAT results from the October test date are typically available in mid-December. Be sure to get access to your online score report so that you can review questions you missed and the correct answers. You can find your score report at *www.psat.org/myscore*.

If you forget your online access information, your guidance counselor should be able to help you figure out how to log in.

Some schools also have the hard copies of the test booklets that you used for the PSAT. If so, be sure to ask your school for these so you can use them for future practice.

How Does National Merit Recognition Work?

Each year, about 1.6 million juniors take the PSAT. Out of those 1.6 million students, these are the numbers that receive some sort of recognition:

- **COMMENDED STUDENTS:** About 34,000 top PSAT scorers (approximately the 97th–98th percentile of test takers) receive letters of commendation.

- **NATIONAL MERIT SEMIFINALISTS:** About 16,000 students (approximately the 99th percentile, or the top 1 percent of all test takers)

  - Commended students and semifinalists are notified of their status in the September after taking the PSAT.

- **NATIONAL MERIT FINALISTS:** About 15,000 of the National Merit Semifinalists are named National Merit Finalists by meeting the program requirements (including maintaining high academic standing, confirming their PSAT performance with ACT or SAT scores, and being recommended by their high school principal).

  - National Merit Finalists learn of their status in February of their senior year.

- **NATIONAL MERIT SCHOLARS:** About 7,500 of National Merit Finalists are awarded National Merit Scholarships, ranging from one-time payments of $2,500 to recurring awards depending on the scholarship. (Approximately one-half of 1 percent of PSAT test takers earn a National Merit Scholarship.)

  - National Merit Scholars learn of their status between March and June of their senior year.
  - To earn the National Merit Scholarship, students are evaluated on their test scores, academic record, school recommendation, personal essay, and other factors.[1]

What if I Was Unable to Take the PSAT Because I Was Sick or Something Unusual Happened at the Test Site That Affected the Test Administration?

You should write to the National Merit Scholarship Program and explain your situation as soon as possible. Notify them by November 15 about any testing irregularities. Notify them by April 1 about the need for an alternate entry. Mail requests to the following address:

National Merit Scholarship Corporation
Attn: Scholarship Administration
1560 Sherman Avenue, Suite 200
Evanston, IL 60201-4897

It is advisable to confirm this mailing address at *www.nationalmerit.org*.

How Can I Use My Official PSAT Score Report to Help Me?

You can access your PSAT score online at *www.psat.org/myscore*. Among the key things to check out:

- **YOUR NMSC SELECTION INDEX:** This number determines your eligibility for the National Merit Scholarship competition and is calculated by doubling your scores from the Reading, Writing/Language, and Math section scores. (Each section has a maximum score of 38, so the maximum selection index score is twice the sum of these three section scores—228.)

  - To be selected as a National Merit Semifinalist, you will typically need a National Merit selection index of around 218. National Merit Scholarships are allocated on the basis of state representation, and the cutoff scores can be different depending on the state in which you reside. If you live in Massachusetts, for example, you may need a selection index of as high as 223. If you live in Wyoming, you may only need a selection index of 212.

- **QUESTION-LEVEL FEEDBACK:** Evaluate which questions you answered correctly and which questions you missed.

  - Take advantage of the online resources that allow you to review the actual test questions and answer explanations. This is the best possible diagnostic tool you can use, since you can carefully analyze what gave you difficulty on the PSAT, which is a preview of the SAT.
  - As you review the questions you missed, look for patterns in what gave you difficulty:

[1] *www.nationalmerit.org*

- Did you have trouble with timing, either finishing too quickly and making careless errors or taking too much time and not attempting later questions?
- Should you focus your future practice on certain types of questions or material, such as grammar concepts, math concepts, or styles of reading passages?
- Did you have trouble with endurance during the test? Did your performance diminish as time went on? Do you need to do a better job getting enough rest in the days leading up to the test?

When Should I Take the SAT?

The SAT is used for college admissions purposes, and your performance on the PSAT will give you a great indication of how you will perform on the SAT. The SAT is offered several times during the year, typically during these months:

- March
- May
- June
- August
- October
- November
- December

You can register for the SAT by going to *www.collegeboard.org*. You should take the SAT at a time that works well with your schedule, and it is fine to take it at least two to three times if need be. Colleges will consider the best score you provide, and some will even "superscore"— i.e., take the best score from each section of the test.

Should I Take the ACT?

All colleges will accept either the SAT or the ACT for college admissions purposes, so you will likely want to try the ACT at least once. If you are a faster test taker and you are good at science, the ACT may be a particularly good fit for you—there is a science reasoning section on the ACT, and the ACT has more questions than the SAT to finish in the given amount of time. Fortunately, the ACT and SAT cover many of the same grammar and math concepts, so by preparing for one test, you are essentially preparing for the other.

Appendix: Vocabulary Resource

As you know, the redesigned PSAT tests contextually based words that are common in college and daily life rather than focusing on esoteric vocabulary. Most students favor this change; however, it comes with its own challenges. The words you will be tested on will be relevant and surrounded by context clues, but they will likely be ambiguous terms with multiple meanings. It will be up to you to decipher which of a particular word's many meanings best fits the context of the passage.

To prepare for the Words in Context questions, you should follow this simple but effective method.

- **COVER:** First, cover the answer choices. Since more than one of the choices will give legitimate definitions for the given word, looking at the choices can be distracting. If you look at the choices beforehand, you will likely focus on the meaning you are most familiar with and try to make it fit the passage. This is an ineffective approach that wastes time and, more often than not, confuses you.
- **CREATE:** Go back to the sentence within the passage, read it, and try to create a general synonym for the given word. This sounds tough, but it's really not. Just read the sentence with a blank where the word currently is, and replace the blank space with your own words. Don't worry about being perfect here; just have a general idea of what the passage conveys *and* how the word is used.
- **ELIMINATE:** Now go back to the answer choices and eliminate any that don't match your synonym. Don't be afraid to eliminate choices that you know are correct definitions of the given word but that don't align with your synonym. Remember, these questions are likely quizzing you on words that have multiple meanings. So don't go for the choice that is "sort of right."
- **SUBSTITUTE:** If you are down to one choice, good for you. Chances are you've found the correct answer. However, if you have two or three remaining choices, read the original sentence, substituting each answer choice for the given word. Sometimes all you need to decide between the remaining choices is to mouth the sentence and hear which word communicates the same meaning.

It might be helpful to see this method in action. For each of these questions, determine which of the choices provides the meaning closest to that of the underlined word:

1. After a long Friday afternoon meeting, the employees had failed to make progress. Although they shared several potential solutions, they couldn't come to (a/an) <u>resolution</u>. At the end of the day, they acknowledged that there would be no verdict before the weekend.

   (A) ruling
   (B) decision
   (C) purposefulness
   (D) answer

Correct Answer: **(B)**
Key in on important context clues. The employees offered solutions but couldn't come to a verdict. So you might generally say they couldn't come to an agreement or a decision. This method should allow you to eliminate Choices (A) and (C). "Ruling" has more to do with legal action, and "purposefulness" doesn't fit here. Now read the sentence with "decision" and "answer." Since multiple people are discussing possible options, "decision" fits the meaning more accurately.

2. Sheila's dogs had an allergic reaction when she first moved to Missouri. After researching online and consulting with three vets, Dr. Piper finally offered an explanation. A pollen <u>unique</u> to the Ozarks was irritating their skin.

   (A) exceptional
   (B) distinctive
   (C) uncommon
   (D) specific

Correct Answer: **(D)**
Make sure you cover the choices right away; they can be particularly distracting with a word most of us understand. Then read the sentence. You might put it in your own words by substituting *only in* or *limited*. The idea here is that the pollen is connected to a certain place. With that in mind, you can rule out Choices (A) and (C). Now you have a tough choice, so read the sentence with both remaining words. "Distinctive" sounds like special or one-of-a-kind, which is sort of right. However, "specific" captures the idea that this pollen is peculiar to this location, making it the correct choice.

3. Graduate school <u>demands</u> a great deal from its students. With classes, research, writing, and teaching, many students become overwhelmed. Yet, if you make it to graduation, the rewards seem well worth the price.

   (A) requires
   (B) commands
   (C) supplies
   (D) requests

Correct Answer: **(A)**

NOTE: Remember the method: cover and create a synonym. The sentence implies that graduate school insists on hard work and diligence; it "requires" a lot. Even if you didn't come up with that word exactly, you should have been able to eliminate Choices (B) and (C). Now decide: does graduate school *ask for* (which sounds like "requests") or *call for* (which sounds like "requires") a lot? "Requires" is the closest meaning.

THE DIFFERENT MEANINGS OF COMMON WORDS

Use this list of 160 words to become more proficient at recognizing the different meanings that common words may have.

act	1. to take action Act now before it's too late. 2. a pretense or charade He wasn't even interested; it was all an act.
affect	1. to influence The lyrics affected her on an emotional level. 2. to feign At dinner, I affected an interest in politics.
afford	1. to have financial resources to pay for Tammy could afford to vacation twice a year. 2. to supply The tenth floor affords the best views of the city.
air	1. a mixture of gases that makes up the atmosphere The air is cold today. 2. certain characteristics or the appearance of a person She has an air of mystery about her.
attribute	1. to associate one subject with another I attributed my short temper to my bad morning. 2. a characteristic His smile is one of his best attributes.
back	1. rear part of a person or an object The driver hurt his back in the car accident. 2. to support The president is backing his party's candidate.
bank	1. a slope or an elevation along which water normally runs along Down by the banks, the children are playing. 2. storage for funds and money I have to deposit money in the bank today. 3. to anticipate or expect I'm banking on his resignation.
base	1. the foundation or bottom of something I sat at the base of the steps and waited. 2. to be located at the center of operations The army is based at Fort McKinley.

bear	1. to support The roof can bear the worker's weight.
	2. to produce The apple tree bears fruit.
	3. to proceed in a direction The ship bears due south.
bend	1. to turn into a direction The tree bends in the wind.
	2. to modify The school is bending its rules this year.
bluff	1. a deception I called his bluff.
	2. plain-spoken in a good-natured way The football coach was bluff, giving constructive feedback to his players.
	3. a steep cliff Tim walked cautiously toward the edge of the bluff.
boil	1. to become agitated or upset The cyclone boiled in the sea.
	2. a painful inflammation of the skin He needs to go to the dermatologist to examine his boil.
bow	1. to give in He had to bow to defeat.
	2. to bend as a sign of respect The people bowed to their emperor.
	3. a decorative ribbon She placed the bow on top of the gift.
box	1. to group together to create one unit They box bills in Congress.
	2. to strike someone The fighter boxed his opponent.
	3. to confine In traffic, his car was boxed in.
buckle	1. to bend or give way The student buckled under the pressure.
	2. to apply oneself In order to be prepared for class, the teacher decided to buckle down with his lecture notes.
caper	1. to leap around The dancer capered during practice.
	2. a stunt or ridiculous escapade My father is too old for this type of caper.
capture	1. to apprehend or seize The tiger was captured after he escaped his exhibit.
	2. to represent accurately The song captured the essence of her thoughts.

case	1.	state of actuality, circumstance
		It is a case of low employment rates.
	2.	a lawsuit
		The judge is handling the case.
cast	1.	to throw
		When he ran out, he cast aside his glasses.
	2.	to give off
		The moon cast shadows on the lake.
catch	1.	to capture
		Catch me if you can.
	2.	to receive
		I caught the cold from my mother.
certain	1.	definite
		I am certain that he will attend.
	2.	present, yet not named
		She has a certain arrogance about her.
challenge	1.	a call to take part in a contest
		They wondered if he would accept the challenge.
	2.	an objection or dispute
		There was a challenge to the ruling.
	3.	to take issue with
		I challenged her every assumption.
change	1.	to alter in form
		The tadpole changed into a frog.
	2.	variety
		Let's try that new restaurant for a change.
channel	1.	the bed of a waterway
		He wants to navigate his boat through the channel.
	2.	to direct toward a specific route
		She channels her interests in biology.
charge	1.	to ask as a price
		That store charges $2 for a toothbrush
	2.	to attack
		The resistance charged the enemy.
	3.	to accuse formally
		The thief was charged with burglary.
clash	1.	a confrontation
		The brothers have minor clashes every now and then.
	2.	a loud bang
		The clash of the cymbals was heard down the hall.
	3.	to be incompatible
		My curtains clash with the carpet.
clear	1.	transparent
		The Gulf of Mexico has clear water.
	2.	to become unattached from something
		She was clear of her high school days.

close	1. a small range of proximity The dog was very close to the bone. 2. to shut an object Please close the door on your way out. 3. immediate All close relatives should come forward now. 4. the end of an event The meeting drew to a close around 8 P.M.
club	1. a group of people, organization The French club has a meeting after school. 2. a heavy stick or bat The giant swings a club.
common	1. prevalent Support was common among the audience. 2. vulgar She didn't ask him on another date because she found him common and uncivilized. 3. collective The roommates took turns cleaning the common area.
commune	1. a group of people coexisting I am part of the commune in Ohio. 2. to connect deeply We communed with nature.
compact	1. packed together The flowers need a compact soil mixture. 2. condense Can you compact your opening statement?
complement	1. to enhance My impressive GPA complements my test scores. 2. a capacity or total number The bank currently has a full complement of staff but will be looking to hire next year.
compound	1. to constitute The cake is compounded of many ingredients. 2. to worsen His illness was compounded by his preexisting condition.
compress	1. to shorten You need to compress this statement into 100 words. 2. an absorbent pad Alex asked the nurse for a cold compress.
compromise	1. come to an agreement We compromised on where to have dinner. 2. weaken or endanger Your immune system becomes compromised when you have an infection.

conduct	1.	behavior His conduct is gracious and helpful.
	2.	to direct The manager conducted the company.
console	1.	control unit for electrical gadget Turn on the console so we can play the game.
	2.	to soothe She consoled her friend after the dance.
construct	1.	to create a structure The workers constructed the building.
	2.	a complex idea formed by simpler facts Some consider ethics to be a social construct.
consult	1.	to seek information Please consult the handbook before further instructions.
	2.	a meeting A consult for surgery is necessary.
content	1.	satisfaction I am content with seeing that movie.
	2.	things that are included The contents of that file are confidential.
contest	1.	to question The three-point shot was contested by the player.
	2.	competition The spelling bee contest was held at the school.
contrast	1.	to show a difference. Write a paper contrasting mood and tone.
	2.	considered distinguishable from the other My personality is in direct contrast to his.
converse	1.	to talk about We are conversing about social plans.
	2.	opposite Open is the converse of closed.
convert	1.	to change I converted the water into ice.
	2.	to convince The politician converted the neutral observer to his political viewpoint.
convey	1.	to transport The wires convey the electric current.
	2.	to communicate a message Tyrone conveyed his wife's deepest apologies.
count	1.	to calculate He counted up to ten.
	2.	to consider She counted herself happy.

counter	1. to respond to The fighter countered with an uppercut. 2. a surface typically in a kitchen or restaurant Put the bowl onto the marble counter. 3. to speak in opposition She countered his argument on gun control.
credit	1. praise Our boss received all the credit. 2. to attribute or ascribe It was credited as his best work yet.
current	1. prevalent, most recent The *New York Times* just published their current issue. 2. something that flows, like a stream The current of the river is strong today.
custom	1. a habitual practice Buying presents for others is a custom during the holidays. 2. made specifically for individual customers I need to buy a custom shirt to fit my size specifically.
dash	1. to strike in a violent manner The waves dashed into the rocks. 2. a sudden movement He dashed to the finish line. 3. a small quantity Please add a dash of salt.
dear	1. cherished My dear friend is in town. 2. excessive That is a dear price to pay for that dress.
default	1. failing to meet one's obligations Because he defaulted on his loan, his credit score is going down. 2. automatic (e.g., with computers) The computer enters default mode upon restarting.
defect	1. to leave one's cause He is defecting from his military unit. 2. an imperfection The cell phone has a defect in the software.
demand	1. a request My timeline doesn't allow me to meet her demand. 2. to command I demand you come down from there. 3. to require Installation demands two persons.
digest	1. to mull over I am going to digest your plan for the future. 2. to convert food into nutrients for the body Larry's stomach doesn't digest correctly.

directly	1. frankly The teacher gave instructions simply and directly. 2. without pause Our family went directly to the airport.
discharge	1. to emit The factory discharged steam. 2. to remove The worker was discharged from the company.
dismount	1. to get off The rider dismounted his horse at the end of the race. 2. to remove Dismount the hose after you turn the knob off.
display	1. to show Shawna displayed courage in the fight. 2. an arrangement The wedding cakes were on display this weekend.
document	1. an official paper Both parties signed the document. 2. to record Tara documents all interactions between her client and the defendant.
down	1. lower The elevator goes lower as it travels from the fourth floor to the second floor. 2. a direction away from The restroom is four doors down from the kitchen. 2. depressed You seemed down today.
draft	1. a current of air in an enclosed space There is a large draft in the chimney. 2. a preliminary sketch The rough draft for the paper is due on Monday.
effect	1. operation Let's put his plan into effect. 2. a result Global warming could have many negative effects.
embrace	1. to hold affectionately Bailey embraced her mother warmly. 2. to welcome enthusiastically We embraced the new office software.
engage	1. to gain or attract attention Harold's discussion engaged the investors. 2. to participate in Our group engages in community activities.

entrance	1.	to enter a trance
		He was entranced by the bright lights.
	2.	an opening or access point
		There was a line at the entrance.
exact	1.	precise
		Be exact in your measurements.
	2.	to require
		The machine exacted immediate payment.
exploit	1.	heroic deed
		The exploits of Athena are noted in Greek mythology.
	2.	to use for one's purposes
		I exploited my friend's intelligence in the group project.
express	1.	to reveal
		The theme of love is expressed in this poem.
	2.	to force out (as juice of a fruit) by pressure
		She expressed juice from the orange.
	3.	speedy
		I paid an additional fee for express delivery.
extract	1.	to pull out
		Honey is extracted from honeycombs.
	2.	a section of a piece of writing
		Analyze the extract from his essay.
fair	1.	free from injustice
		It was a fair trial.
	2.	neither great nor terrible
		He had a fair amount of money.
fast	1.	rapid action/movement
		She was the fastest runner.
	2.	to abstain from all food
		The church was holding a fasting ceremony.
favor	1.	to prefer
		I favor the tacos over the burrito.
	2.	to resemble
		Everyone said her eyes favored her mother's.
file	3.	a collection of folders, papers
		I have a cabinet full of files.
	2.	to arrange in a line, one behind the other
		File into line!
fine	1.	exquisite
		Bring the fine linens to the party.
	2.	thin
		Use the fine point pen on the form.

firm	1. stable The roof has a firm sealant. 2. a legal partnership or association Jones and Jones is the newest firm.
flag	1. to signal or get the attention of I had to flag a taxi in New York City. 2. a piece of cloth displaying symbols The flag is a symbol of our country.
flat	1. fixed, unchanging Economic growth in the country has remained flat for the past few years. 2. without interest He bored the students by speaking in a flat voice.
force	1. strength The force of the wave knocked me backward. 2. coercion His army led by force. 3. to break open Just force the door open.
form	1. to put into shape Form that snow into a ball. 2. structure or shape The form of the essay was organized effectively. 3. manifestation His procrastination has taken the form of complete indifference.
grant	1. to give or allow I grant you permission. 2. to admit I grant that I was deceived. 3. a financial award The university awarded him a grant.
gross	1. without deduction The annual gross income is $200,000. 2. indecent, lack of manners The way he talks to women is gross.
ground	1. solid surface of the landscape They broke ground when they dug. 2. support for one's personal position, like in a debate I am on firm ground in my position on this issue.
hail	1. to greet All hail the king! 2. to call in order to get attention I tried to hail a taxi.

hatch	1. to emerge as young The baby chicks hatched this morning. 2. to mark, create The spies hatched a plan.
hold	1. to grip Hold on tightly. 2. to withstand The boat can hold up in these waters. 3. to contain My closet cannot hold any more clothes.
impact	1. collision The impact of the accident left the cars ruined. 2. influence The pastor impacted his church with his words.
implant	1. a transplant The cochlear implant was put in yesterday. 2. to establish I implanted values into the child. 3. to insert The vet implanted a microchip under the dog's skin.
import	1. a commodity brought in from another location The latest import included coffee beans and sugar cane. 2. to convey deeper meaning His speech imported peace among the public.
impound	1. to confine Dogs are impounded in the pound. 2. to seize The document was impounded this morning.
incline	1. to have a preference I am inclined to see the movie today. 2. a slant Don't park your car on that steep incline.
insert	1. to put into place You need to insert the key into the lock. 2. an extra section of a document There are so many inserts in this newspaper.
intense	1. exceptional or extreme The intense flavors quivered on my unsuspecting tongue. 2. passionate Tabitha was an intense painter and violinist.
intercept	1. to interrupt The pass was intercepted. 2. a point where lines cross (mathematics) The lines intercept at the origin.

interchange	1.	to change places The novel has been interchanged with the newer edition.
	2.	a highway intersection Get off at the I-270 interchange.
interest	1.	importance Education is of great interest to me.
	2.	share of a property The interest rates have dropped again.
intrigue	1.	to inspire curiosity The teacher was intrigued by the student's question.
	2.	trick or scheme Politicians have intrigues about their policies.
invalid	1.	someone who is sick He was an invalid after his kidney failure.
	2.	not true The answer is invalid.
invite	1.	to request someone's company Terry invited me to the party.
	2.	a request to participate or attend She sent the invite weeks ago.
	3.	to generate a reaction His rhetoric invited criticism.
jam	1.	to wedge into a space His arm was jammed between two boulders.
	2.	a difficult situation When the company went out of business, the manager was caught in a jam.
	3.	thick mixture made of fruit Virginia makes the best strawberry jam.
jar	1.	to produce harsh sounds or actions The rattle of the door jarred me awake.
	2.	a container I am going to put the cherries back into the jar.
jet	1.	a stream A jet of water gushed forth.
	2.	to move rapidly The plane jetted from the runway.
	3.	a special version of a plane We took a private jet to California.
just	1.	only You just have to finish this assignment.
	2.	right His argument is just.

key	1.	a small metal device to open locks
		The pirate searched for the key to the chest.
	2.	something that exhibits success.
		I would like to find the key to great health.
knot	1.	a piece of material tied around itself
		I learned how to make a fishing knot.
	2.	a group of people
		There is a knot of fans around the stadium.
lead	1.	to show the way
		I will lead a group of people through the mountains.
	2.	first place
		Carly became the lead in the mile race.
lean	1.	to shift one's position
		He was tired, so he leaned on the tree.
	2.	to show influence in order to gain cooperation
		The company is leaning on the public's opinion to influence delegates.
light	1.	something that increases visibility
		The light source is bright.
	2.	to brighten
		Her smile lights up the room.
litter	1.	trash
		Litter fills the hallways each day.
	2.	a number of animals born during one birth
		The litter of puppies will soon be two weeks old.
	3.	to clutter
		My locker is littered with loose papers.
lock	1.	to unite
		We locked arms as we walked in the parade.
	2.	to secure (a building, door)
		Can you lock the door when you leave?
long	1.	increased beyond a normal range
		The principal is giving a long speech again.
	2.	specified time range
		How long did she speak?
loom	1.	to rise above indistinctly
		The firefighter loomed over the little boy.
	2.	an apparatus used in weaving
		She creates quilts on the loom during the day.
low	1.	short or small
		Sit at the low table.
	2.	below average
		Cheryl raised five children with a low income.
	3.	depleted or sparse
		The selection of athletic shoes is low.

magazine	1. a room used for storing military items We have to put our weapons into the magazine. 2. a publication All of the celebrities are featured in the magazine.
manifest	1. obvious He created a manifest error. 2. to prove The data manifest the new theory. 3. to demonstrate The boy's behavior manifests signs of trauma.
maroon	1. shade of brownish red I just bought maroon pants. 2. to abandon and leave without help They marooned the captain on the island during the mutiny.
mass	1. a body of large matter There was a mass of feathers to make a coat. 2. affecting a large number of people There was a mass migration to the west.
match	1. a thin piece of wood used to light fires We ran out of matches, so we can't light the fire. 2. a person of equal value She is a match for the state champion. 3. a contest or game There is a tennis match after school.
mean	1. to intend I meant to call you yesterday. 2. malicious nature She is truly mean to me. 3. resources Many families live beyond their means. 4. the average (mathematics) The mean of all of his test scores is 85%.
might	1. physical strength Hercules had might. 2. possibility I might go to the dentist tomorrow.
mind	1. to pay attention to Mind your manners! 2. mental ability Einstein had one of the greatest minds.
minute	1. an exact moment in time Come over this minute! 2. very small This is a minute problem.

moor	1.	to secure something in place The boat was moored to the dock.
	2.	a section of land Go out to the moor.
nail	1.	to accomplish The squad nailed their cheer routine.
	2.	to secure with nails We need to nail that painting to the wall.
note	1.	a small document for reference I wrote out notes for the test tomorrow.
	2.	to notice We noted the change in rules.
novel	1.	new That seems like a novel idea.
	2.	a book Young-adult novels are common.
object	1.	the point of discussion The object of this investigation is to identify the suspect.
	2.	tangible items Can you pass that object over here?
	3.	opposition I object to your offer.
offense	1.	attack He owns a weapon of offense.
	2.	violation I have quite a few traffic offenses on my record.
	3.	resentment over perceived disrespect He took offense at my remarks.
overlook	1.	not to notice He overlooked her beauty.
	2.	to have a view of The statehouse overlooks the park.
page	1.	one side of a piece of paper This page has a poem on it.
	2.	distinct period of time or events The Great Depression was a difficult page in American history.
pale	1.	lacking color She is very pale during the winter.
	2.	lacking strength There is a pale riot dispersing outside.
patch	1.	a small piece of material to cover a gash He put a patch over his wound.
	2.	a small area of something Watch out for the patch of snow on the ground!

perfect	1. ideal I know the perfect place. 2. to finish The decor needs to be perfected.
permit	1. a license She earned her driving permit this week. 2. to allow He is permitted to use a calculator on his test.
picture	1. to imagine Be sure to picture how the buildings will be made. 2. an image The little kids love to make pictures.
pool	1. a small body of liquid My friend has practice at the pool. 2. sampling There is a random pool of survey respondents.
quarter	1. to lodge The soldiers were quartered inside the building. 2. a fourth of a whole unit We will leave in a quarter of an hour.
reason	1. motive Tasha gave several reasons for her withdrawal. 2. intellect or rationality The problem is that your emotions are not governed by reason.
recall	1. callback The lettuce products are now on recall. 2. to remember a previous notion or piece of information Do you recall what her name was?
reduce	1. to lessen I have reduced the word count. 2. to change to a basic form The fraction can be reduced to two-thirds.
refrain	1. to stop an impulse He refrained from telling her the truth. 2. a phrase repeating during intervals of a song or poem The refrain is very poetic.
repeat	1. to say again Please repeat your question. 2. a duplicate The conference will be a repeat from last year. 3. occurring more than once Will was a repeat offender.
report	1. a statement or document They wrote reports about an animal of their choice. 2. to make one's stance known I am going to report to work tomorrow.

restrain	1. to hold back Try to restrain your anger. 2. to shackle The cop restrained the suspect with handcuffs.
riot	1. chaotic public disturbance There was a riot yesterday in Atlanta. 2. someone outlandishly funny He was a riot at dinner last night.
rule	1. a regulation or law Shane disregarded the rules. 2. to govern The king rules with ultimate power. 3. a habit or an accepted method Industriousness is the rule rather than the exception within this company.
sanction	1. to approve, such as a law The president sanctioned a law. 2. to place a restriction on, especially in a disciplinary manner There is a sanction on illegal trade.
season	1. a time associated with a particular feature This season is spring. 2. period of time I am going home for the season. 3. to make more lively The professor seasons his lengthy lectures with references to popular culture.
solution	1. the act of finding the answer to a problem I found the solution to the math problem. 2. a liquid of chemical compounds Can you pass me the mixed solution?
spring	1. to rise suddenly She sprung from the bed in the morning. 2. elastic material in the shape of a helix The spring in the mattress broke.
spy	1. to keep watch He is spying on his little sister. 2. to see suddenly I spy a girl walking her dog.
stable	1. a building for livestock animals The horses have to be taken back to the stable. 2. a collection of items in an establishment The writers are part of the stable. 3. firm, resistant to change The structure of the building is stable.

state	1. a condition
	He was in a healthy mental state when he left.
	2. a political entity
	The state declared war.
	3. to express
	Jermaine stated his thoughts clearly.
stop	1. to come to the end
	The noise stopped as soon as I stood up.
	2. to refuse to go on
	I stop at controversial topics.
strong	1. powerful
	The cheetah has strong legs.
	2. well built
	The material is strong and malleable.
	3. intense or potent
	Mrs. Johnson prefers strong coffee.
suggest	1. to propose
	I suggest we take a recess.
	2. to indicate
	Her novel suggests the many social injustices oppressing her people.
trust	1. confidence
	A healthy relationship must have trust.
	2. to have confidence in
	I trust you'll do the right thing.
	3. an arrangement to hold property
	They left money to him in a trust fund.
type	1. to produce a document
	I need to type up the agreement.
	2. a particular category
	He is the fortunate type.
weak	1. lacking physical strength
	Tommy was too weak to lift his head.
	2. lacking intensity
	The diluted solution was weaker than expected.
	3. inadequate or unconvincing
	Her weak argument failed to impress her parents.
will	1. desire or intention
	Do not stay against your will.
	2. a legal document for after death
	His will outlined the plans of his estate.
	3. to wish something to happen
	Micah willed her to agree with his plan.

After reviewing these words thoroughly, you should have a good idea of what to expect on the PSAT Words in Context questions. It goes without saying, however, that while the PSAT has moved away from testing obscure vocabulary, difficult and specialized words permeate the passages. Being completely unfamiliar with several of these words can certainly decrease your understanding and negatively influence your score. It is unreasonable to think you can possibly know every word you encounter, but you absolutely can expand your knowledge and expertise by reading *a lot*. Try to start with newspapers and reputable magazines—these are excellent resources to improve your comprehension and diversify your vocabulary. In the meantime, below is a list of words that continually appear within PSAT passages.

Abase—degrade; humiliate

Abeyance—suspension; postponement

Abdicate—renounce; resign

Abject—extremely bad or unpleasant

Abstemious—self-disciplined

Admonition—a warning or reprimand

Ambiguous—having double meaning; uncertain

Ambivalent—having mixed feelings

Amicable—friendly

Anachronism—a thing belonging to another time period

Anomaly—an oddity; something that deviates from the norm

Apathetic—showing little emotion; indifferent

Autocratic—having absolute power

Autonomous—self-governing

Benediction—a blessing

Benevolent—kindly

Benign—gentle and affectionate

Cacophony—a mixture of harsh sounds

Capricious—unpredictable

Circumlocution—wordiness in an attempt to be vague

Colloquial—conversational

Condescending—conceited or snobby

Contentious—controversial

Correctitude—correctness

Cumbersome—bulky and unmanageable

Credence—believability; confidence

Cryptic—confusing or mysterious

Digress—to go off topic

Discomfiture—an embarrassment

Docile—obedient; submissive

Dogmatic—insistent; laying down opinions as truths

Eloquent—articulate

Eminent—respected; distinguished

Esoteric—obscure; specialized

Evasive—responding indirectly; ambiguous

Fallacious—incorrect or based on a mistaken belief

Genesis—creation

Hamper—to hinder progress

Ignominious—humiliating; undignified

Impecunious—poor; penniless

Impetuous—impulsive and reckless

Impudent—disrespectful; cocky

Intrinsic—essential; inborn

Irreparable—impossible to fix

Loquacious—talkative

Magnanimous—generous

Malediction—a curse

Malinger—to fake an illness

Mercurial—temperamental; unpredictable

Misogyny—a hatred of women

Novice—a beginner

Obdurate—stubborn; obstinate

Obfuscate—to make unclear; bewilder

Ostentatious—showy; attempting to impress

Perdition—hell; a state of eternal doom

Perfidy—untrustworthy

Pejorative—insulting; derogatory

Pervasive—prevalent; spreading rapidly and widely

Placate—to calm

Pretentious—attempting to impress; pompous

Prodigy—genius; a person with exceptional abilities

Sagacious—wise

Sanctify—bless; approve

Sanctimonious—acting superior to others

Sanguine—optimistic

Sullen—bad tempered; depressed

Tenacious—determined

Tandem—alongside each other; together

Tangential—diverging from a course; variable

Tenuous—insubstantial; very weak

Titular—in name only; ceremonial

Transcend—to surpass the limits of

Transient—temporary; fleeting

Transmute—to change or alter

Undulate—move in waves; swell

Unperturbed—unconcerned; undisturbed

Usurp—to take over; seize

Vagrant—a beggar; a drifter

Vehement—showing emotion and intensity

Verbose—talkative; wordy

Vindicate—to clear from blame; to justify

Visceral—associated with the gut; instinctive

Waning—to decline or shrink

Wanton—wicked; indecent

Whimsical—playful; inconsistent